犬夜叉

INUYASHA

ANI-MANGA

Vol. 1

CREATED BY
RUMIKO TAKAHASHI

INUYASHA™

ANI-MANGA™ Vol. 1

Contents

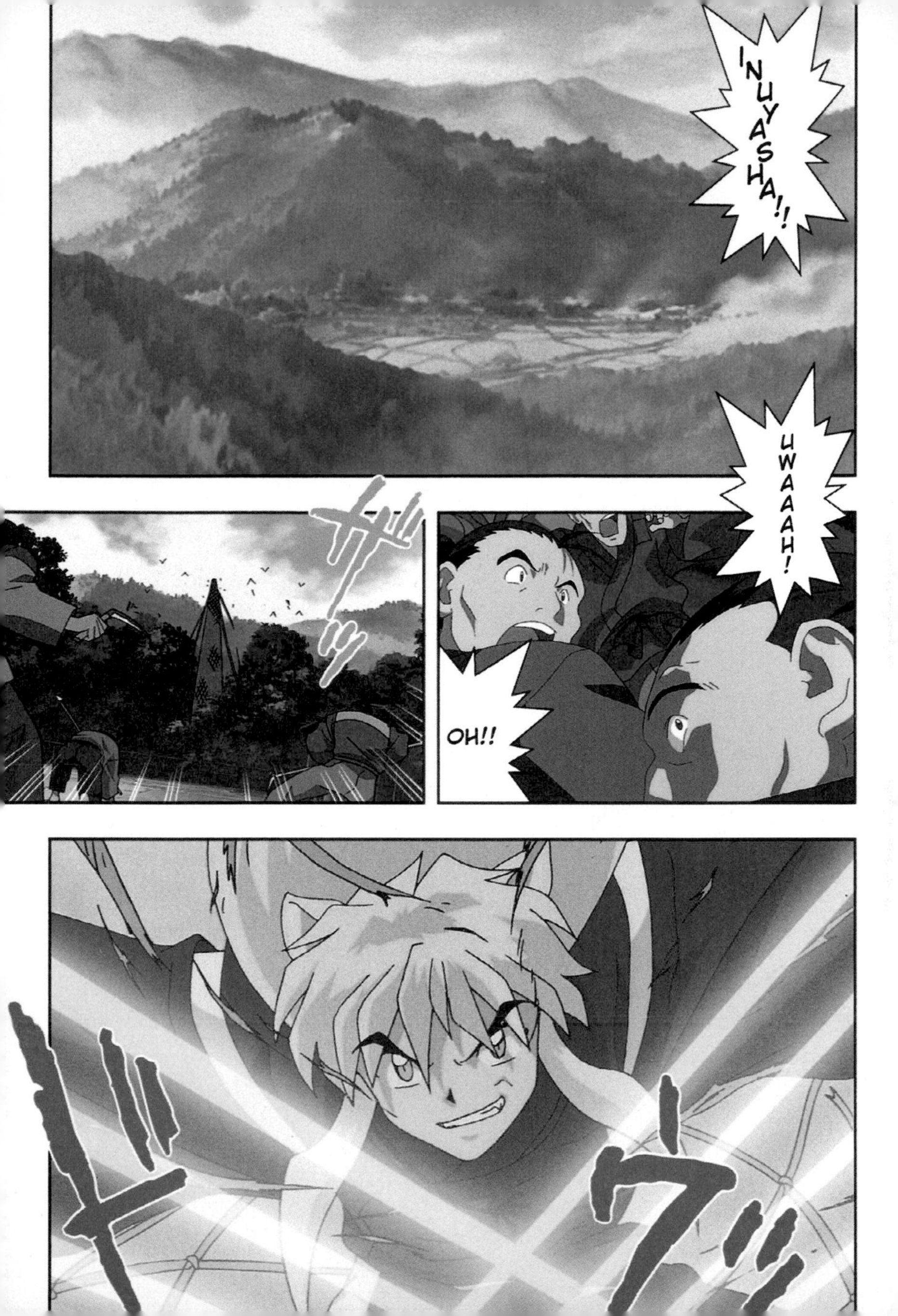
INUYASHA!!
UWAAAAH!
OH!!

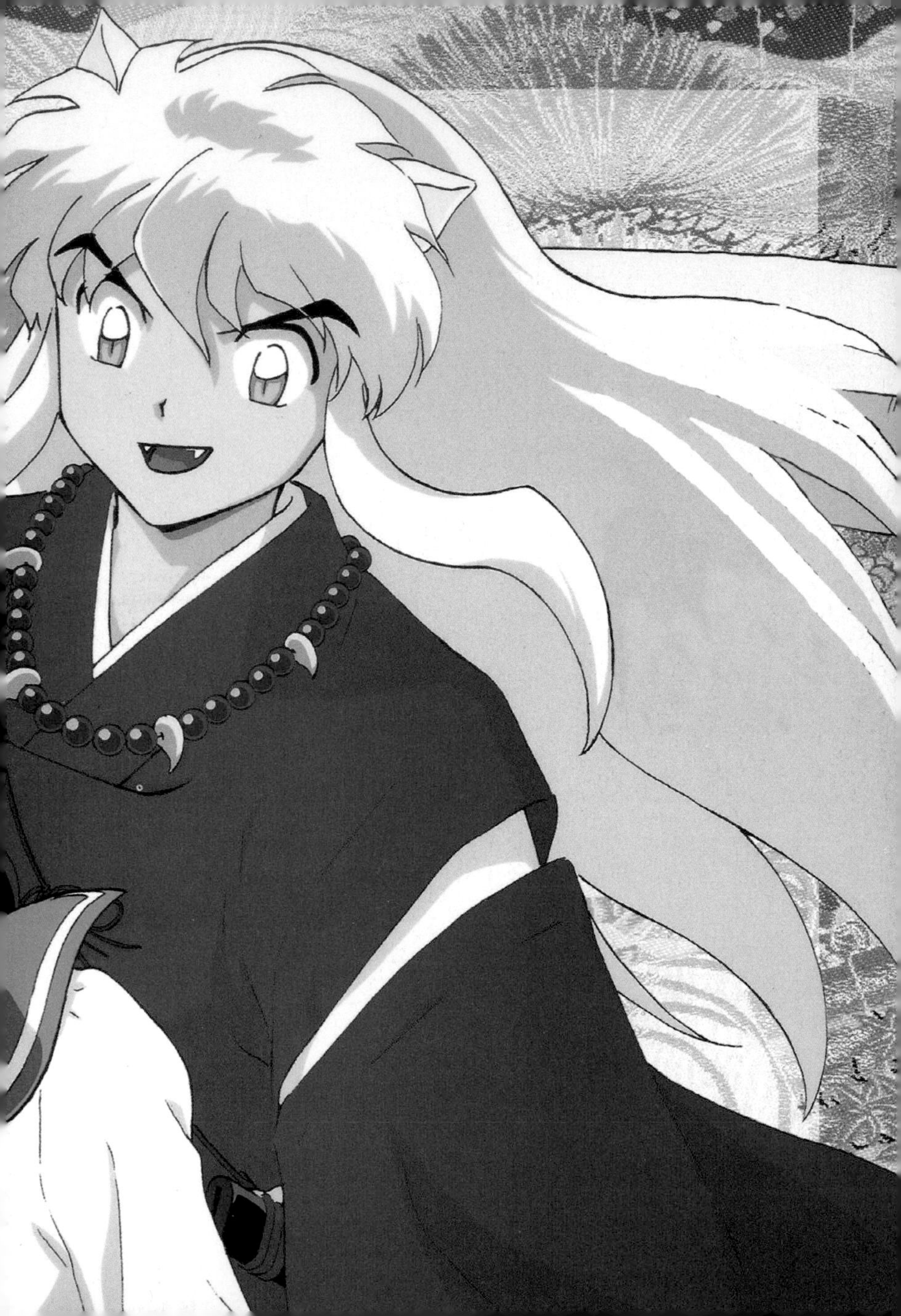

1
The Girl Who Overcame Time...and the Boy Who Was Just Overcome

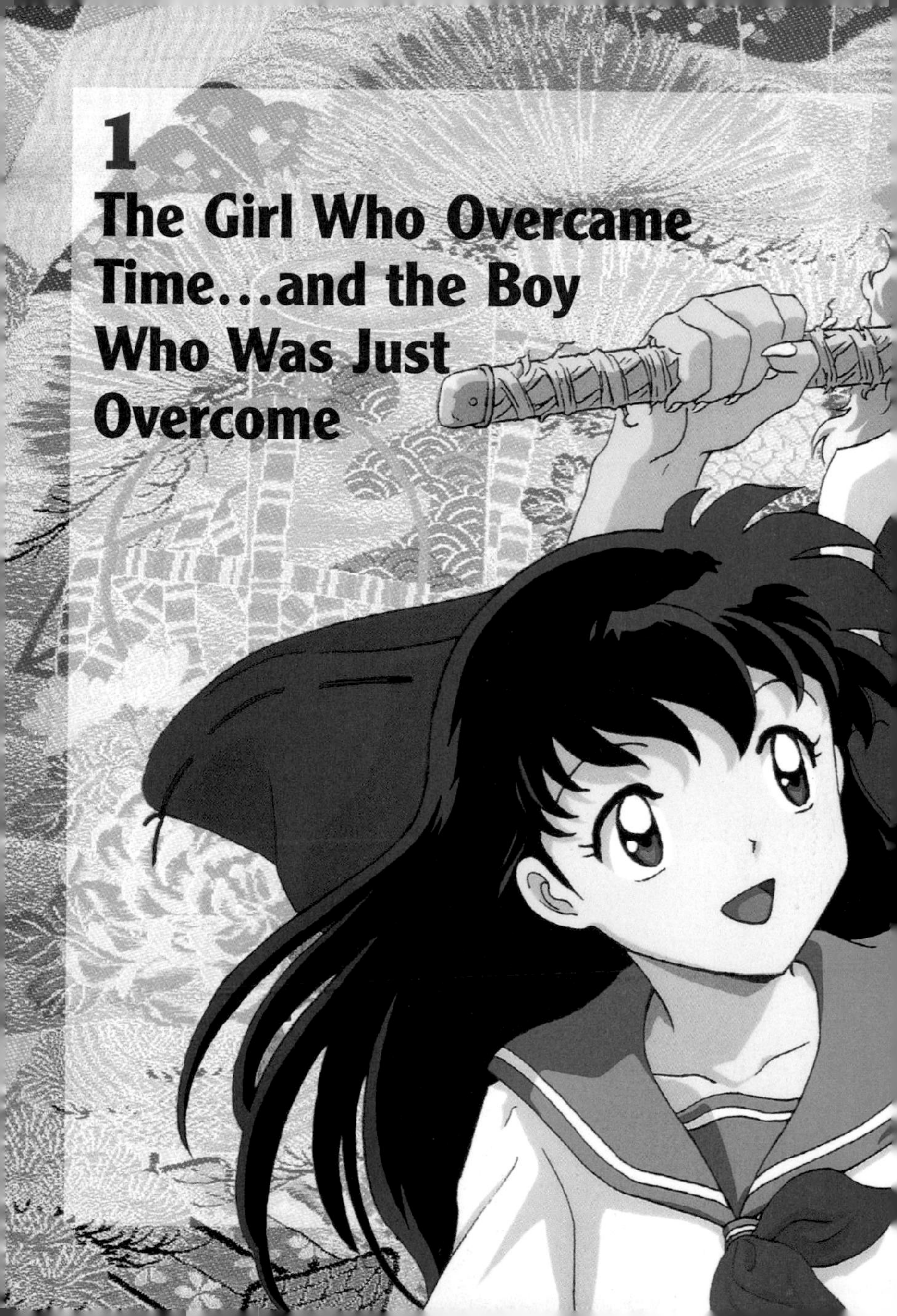

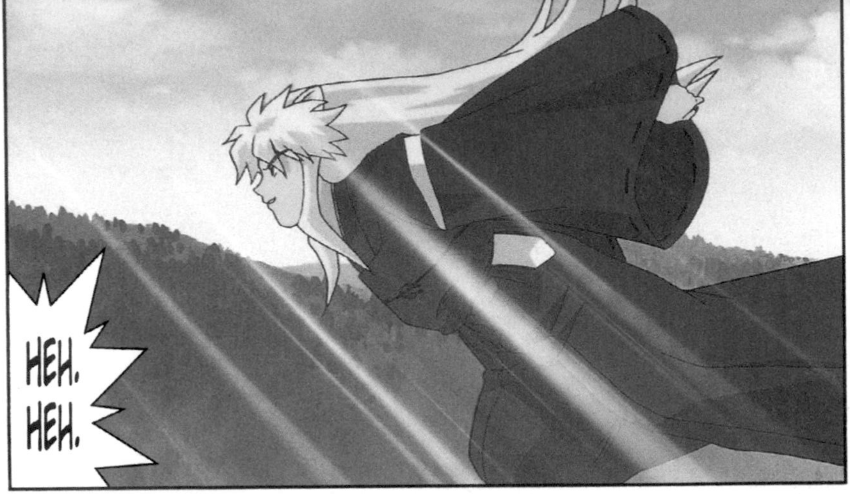
HEH.
HEH.
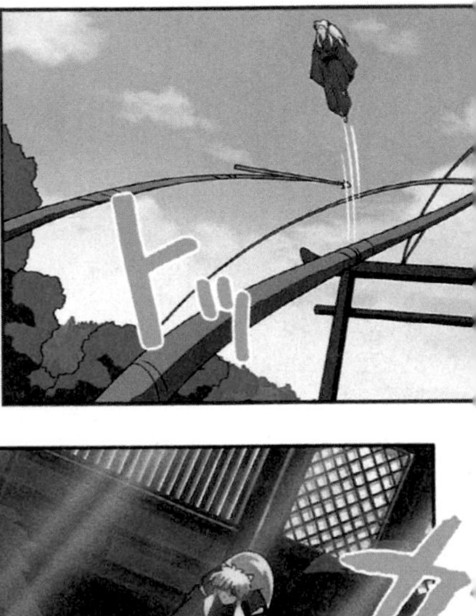
トッ
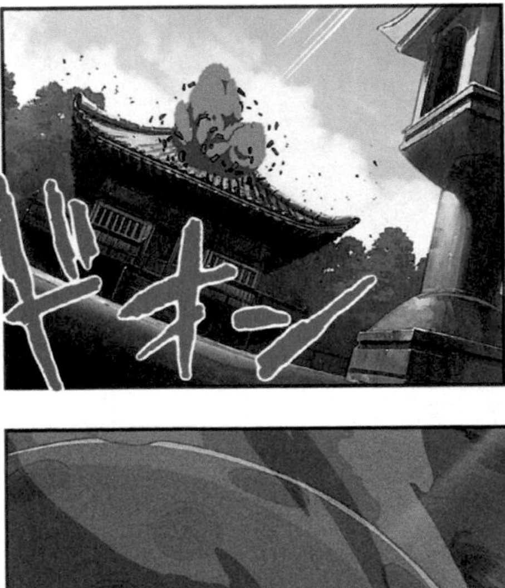
ドオーン
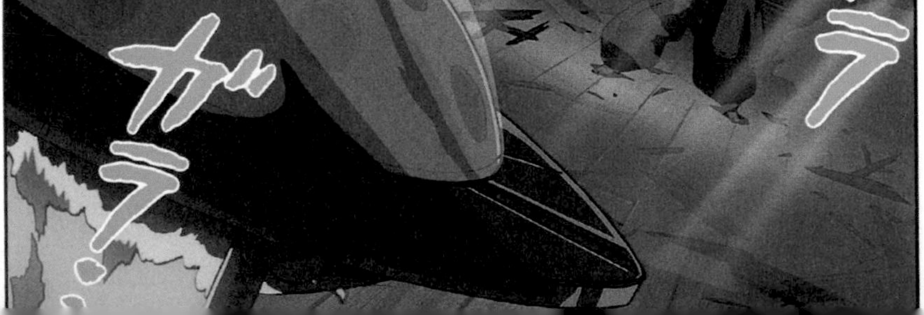
ガラ
ガラ

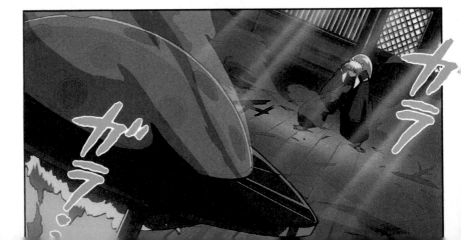

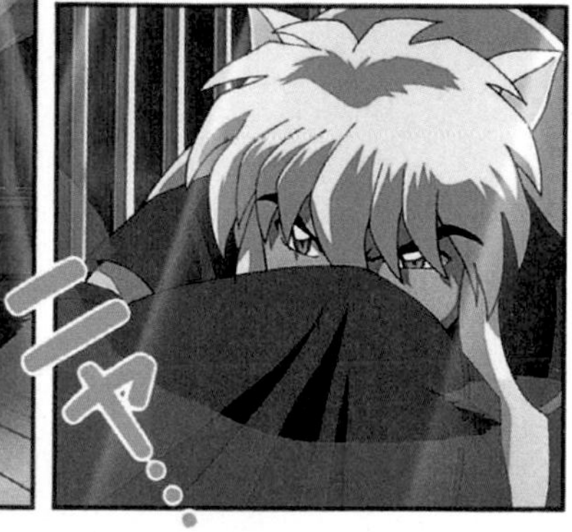
ニヤ…
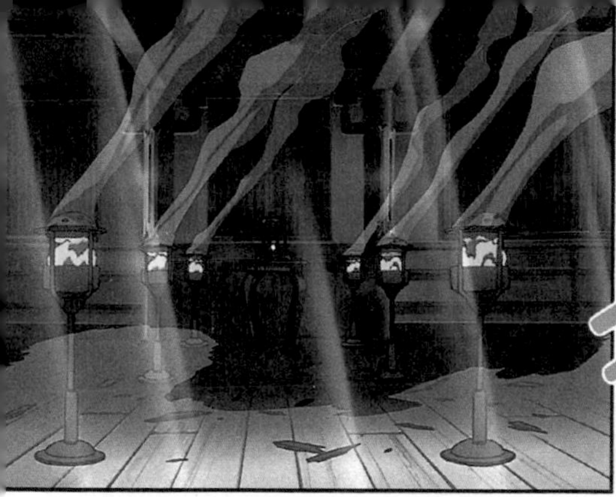
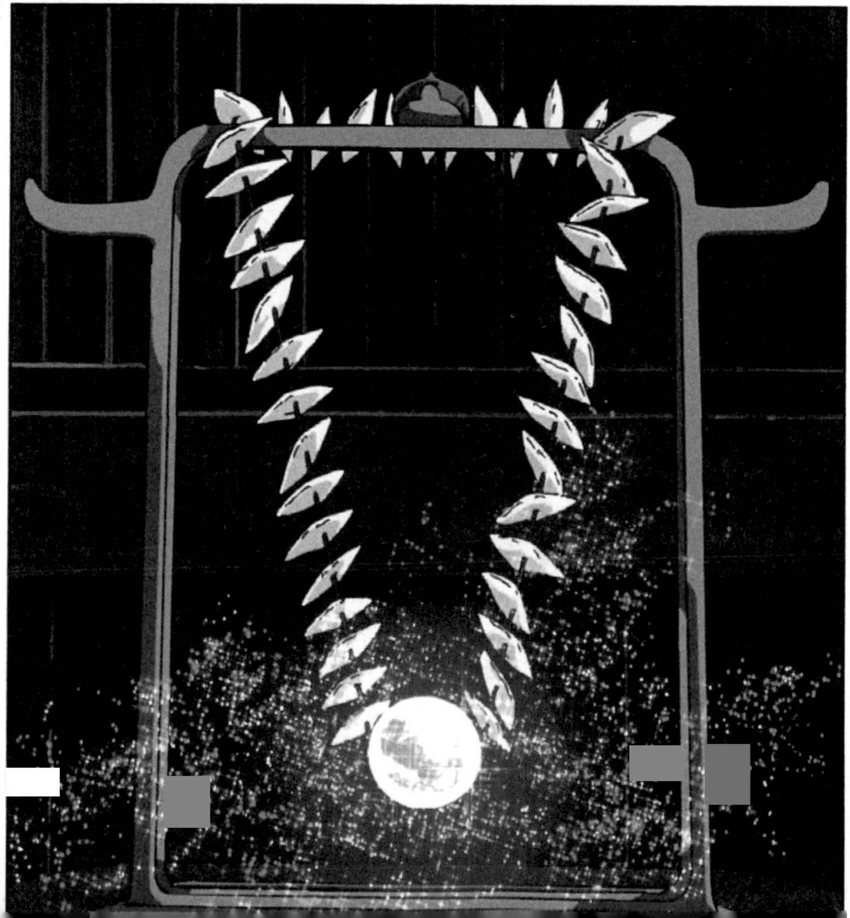

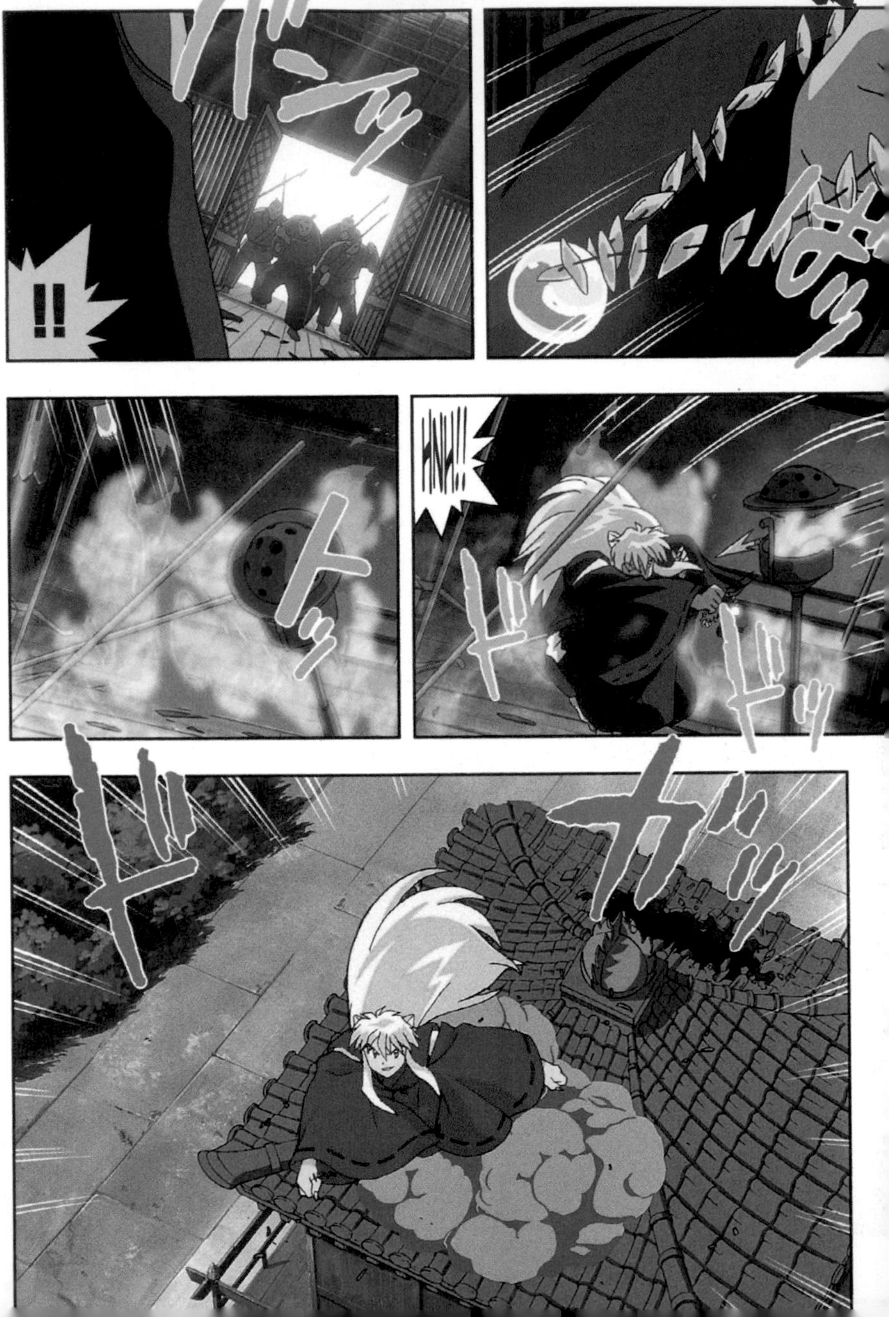
!!
HNH!!
ドッ
ドッ
ドッ
ガッ

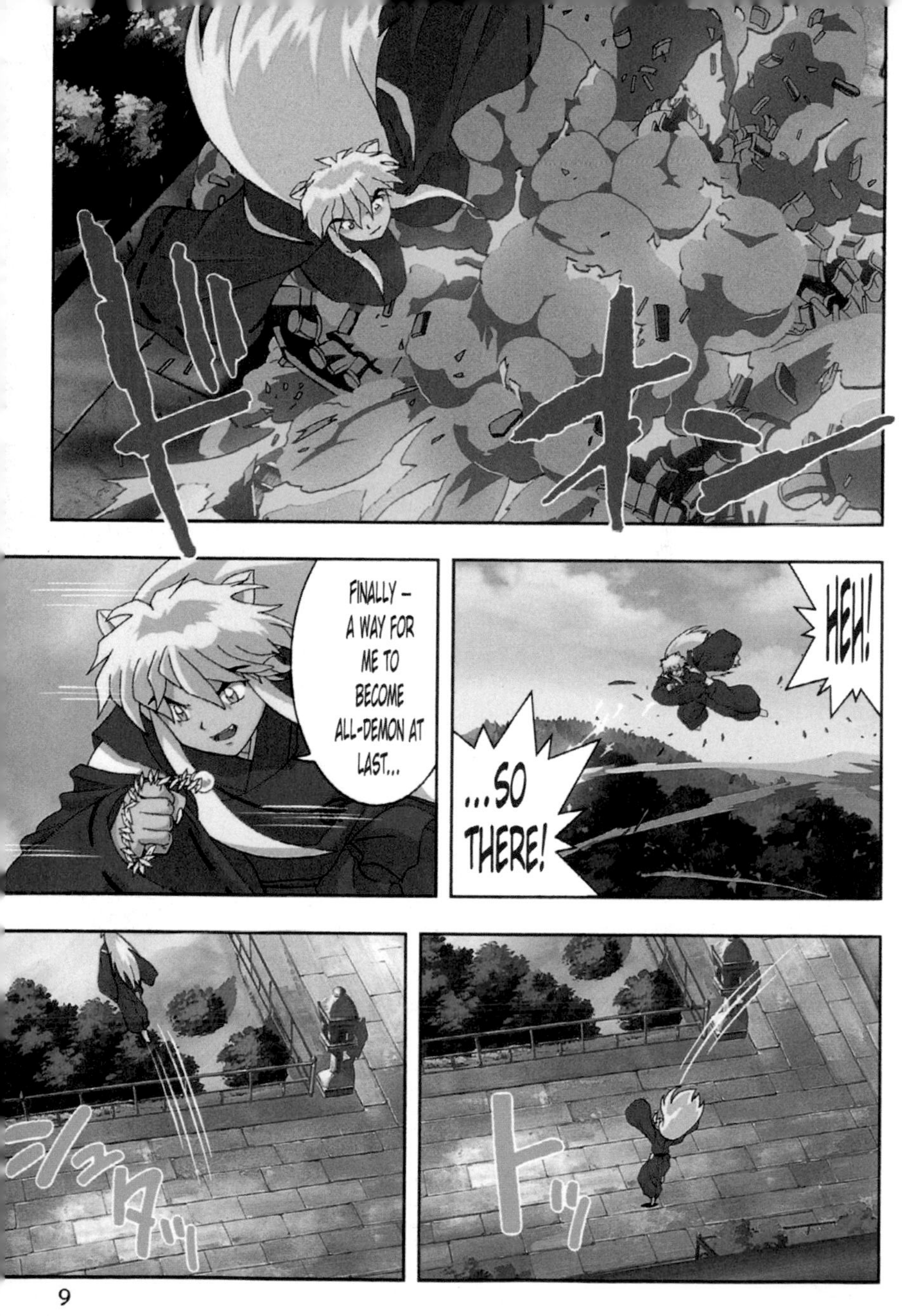
HEH!
...SO THERE!
FINALLY – A WAY FOR ME TO BECOME ALL-DEMON AT LAST...
トッ
シュタッ

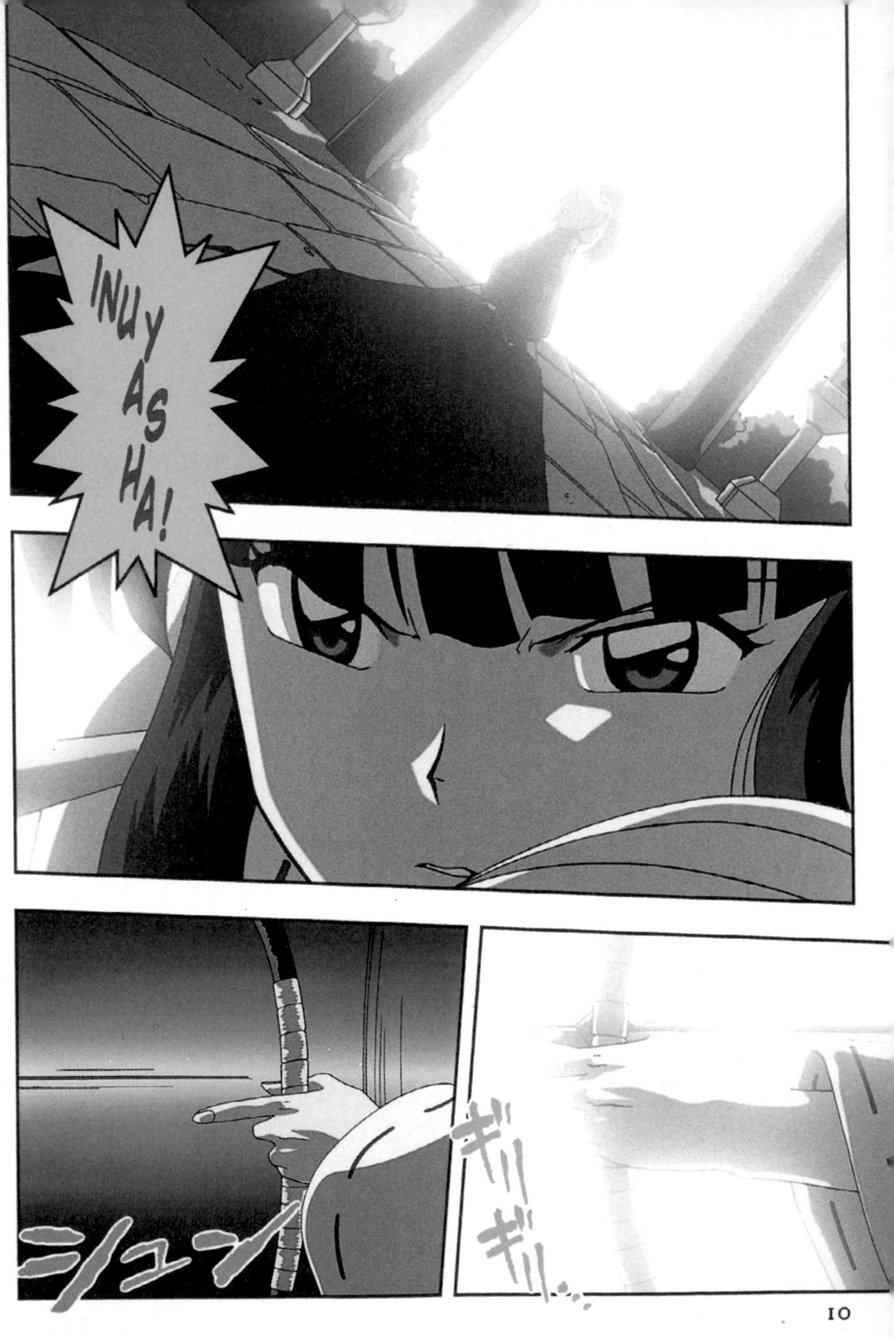
INUYASHA!
ギリギリ…
シュン

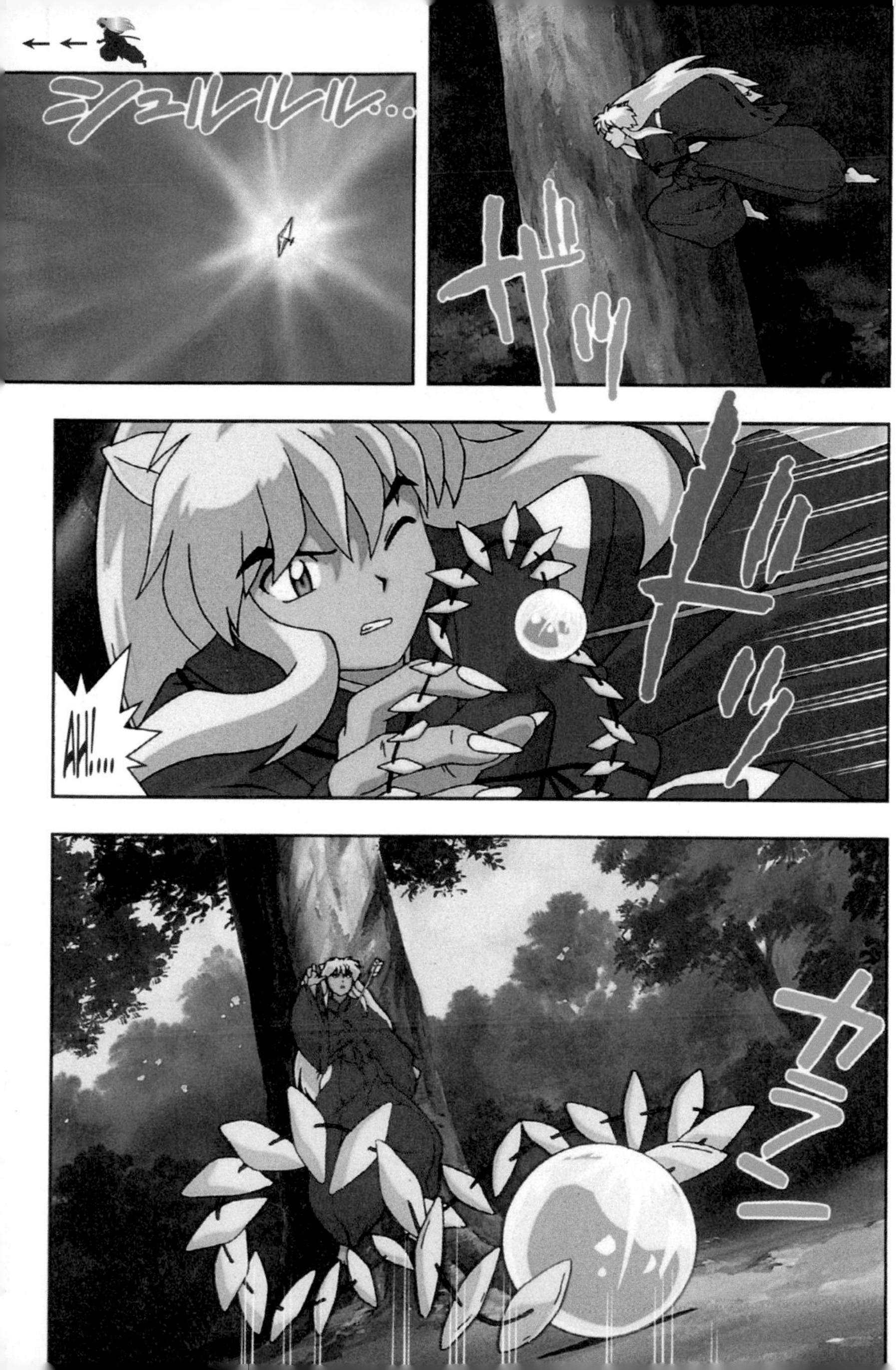
ザッ
シュルルルル..
ドッ
AH!...
カラン

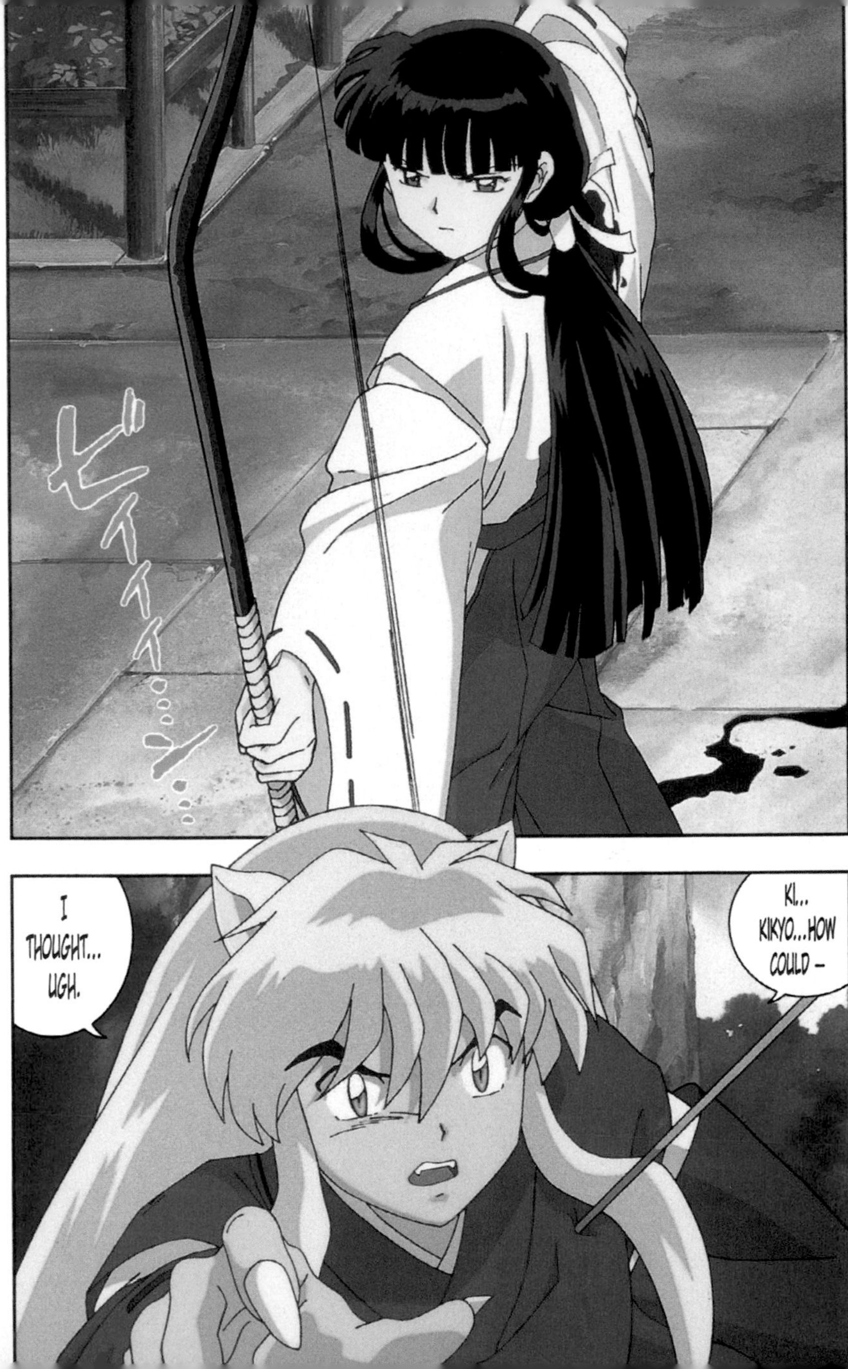
ビィイイイ…ン…
KI... KIKYO...HOW COULD –
I THOUGHT... UGH.

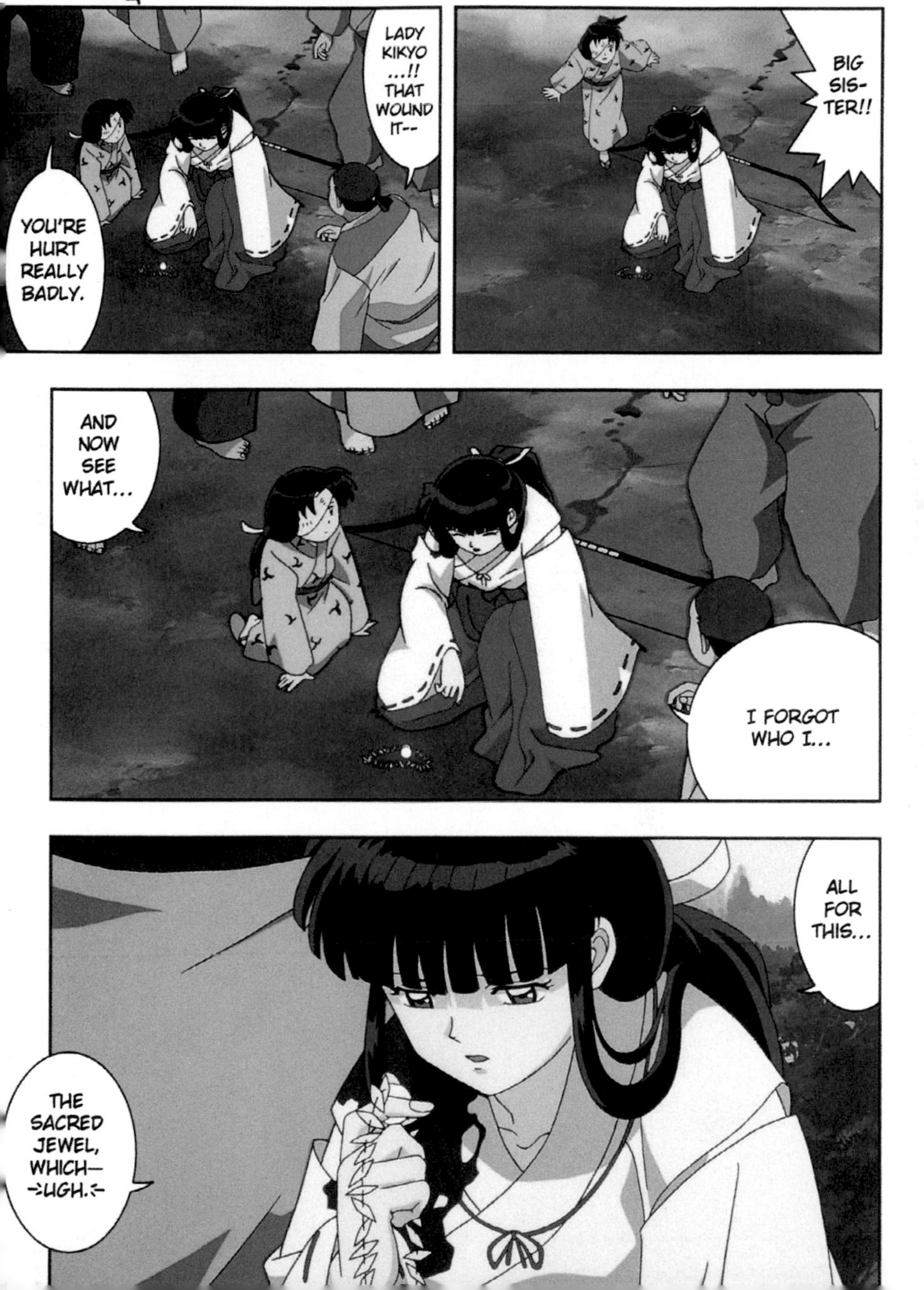
BIG SISTER!!
LADY KIKYO ...!! THAT WOUND IT--
YOU'RE HURT REALLY BADLY.
AND NOW SEE WHAT...
I FORGOT WHO I...
ALL FOR THIS...
THE SACRED JEWEL, WHICH— -:UGH.:-

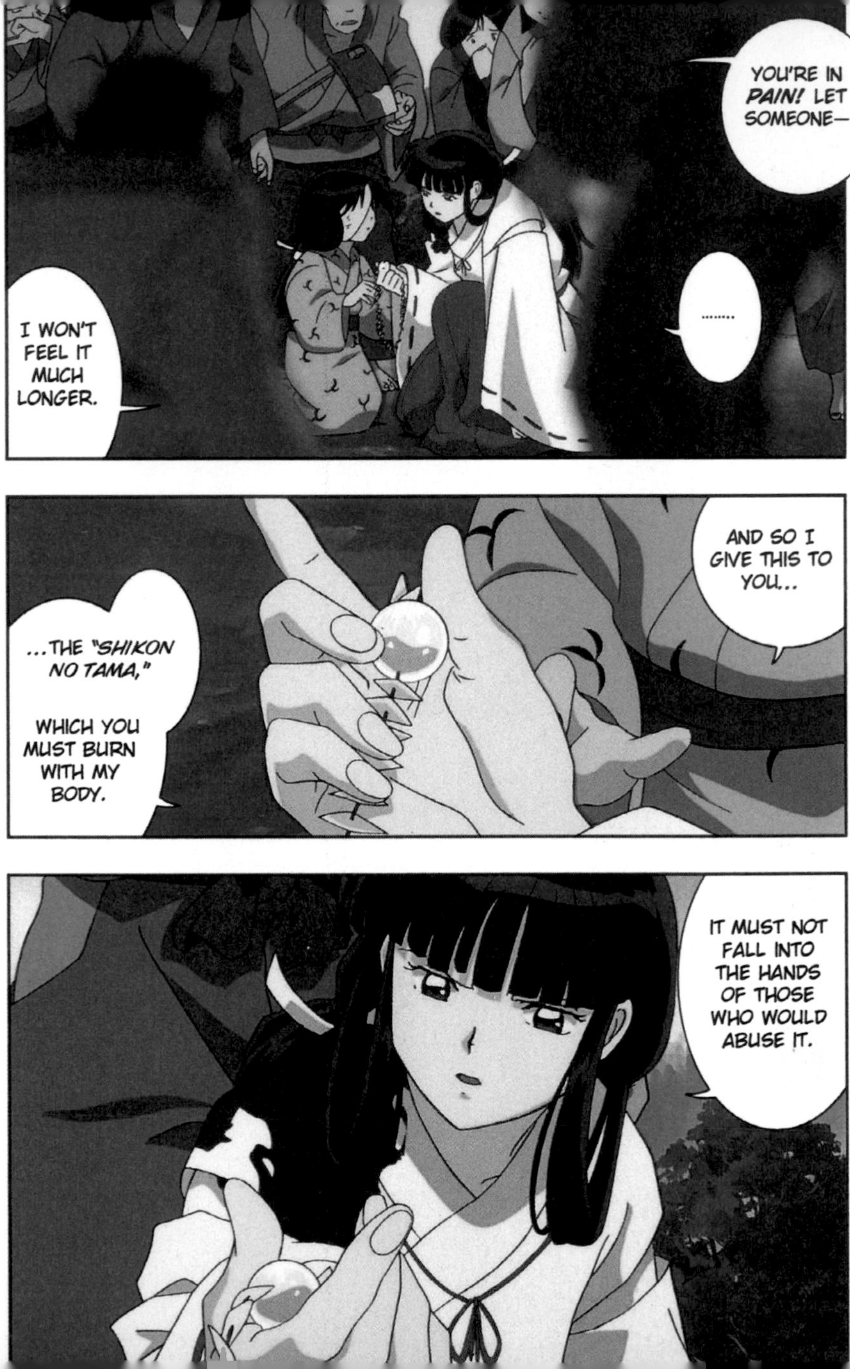
YOU'RE IN *PAIN!* LET SOMEONE—
....
I WON'T FEEL IT MUCH LONGER.
AND SO I GIVE THIS TO YOU...
...THE "*SHIKON NO TAMA,*"
WHICH YOU MUST BURN WITH MY BODY.
IT MUST NOT FALL INTO THE HANDS OF THOSE WHO WOULD ABUSE IT.

SISTER KIKYO-O-O-O-O...!!

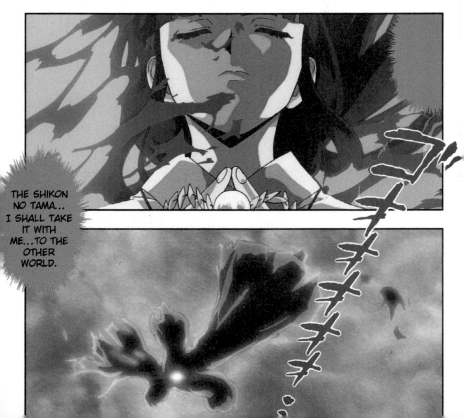

THE SHIKON NO TAMA... I SHALL TAKE IT WITH ME...TO THE OTHER WORLD.

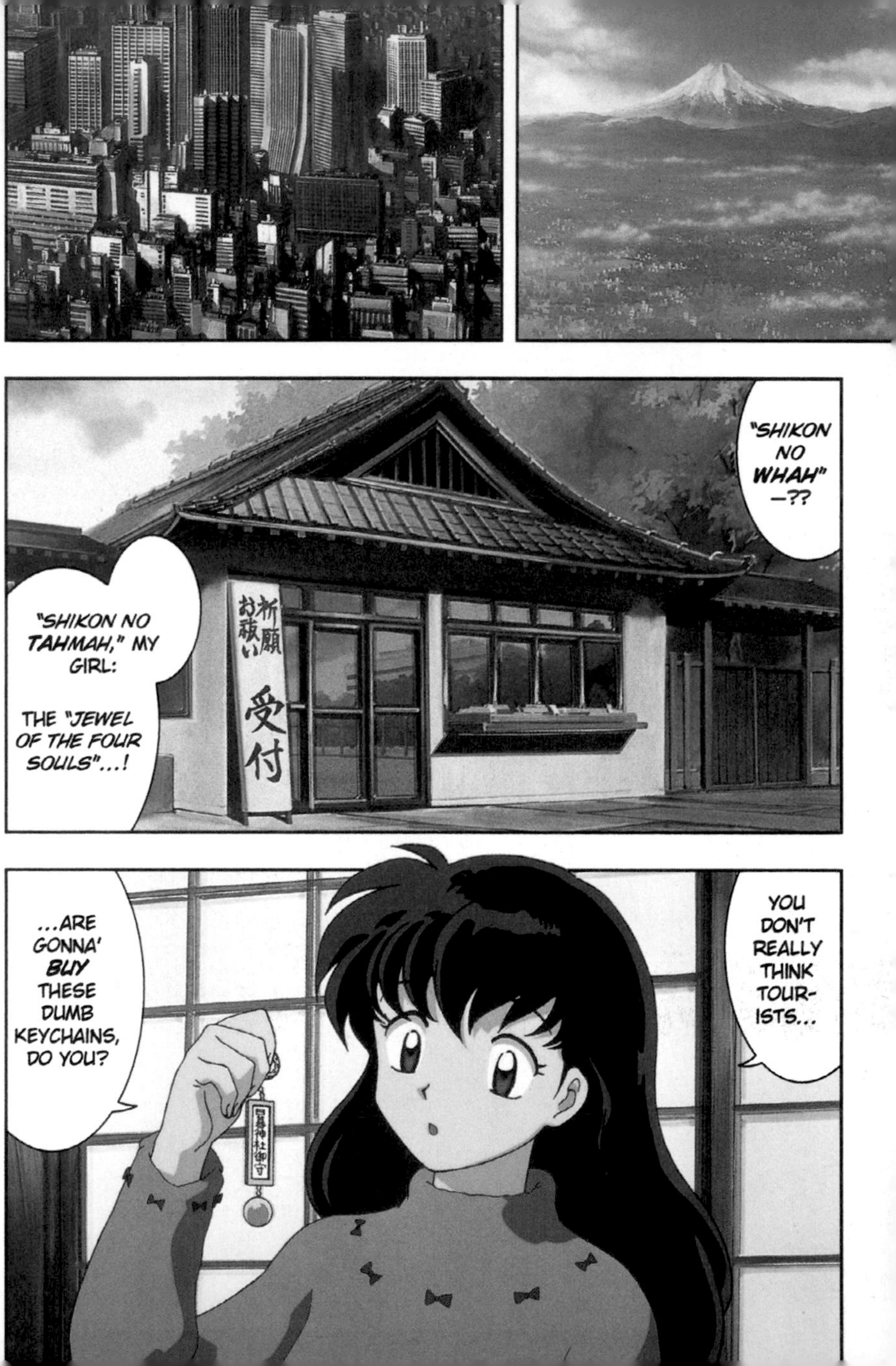
"SHIKON NO WHAH" —??
祈願
お祓い
受付
"SHIKON NO TAHMAH," MY GIRL:
THE "JEWEL OF THE FOUR SOULS"...!
YOU DON'T REALLY THINK TOUR-ISTS...
...ARE GONNA' BUY THESE DUMB KEYCHAINS, DO YOU?

THAT IS NOT "JUST A KEYCHAIN."

THAT CRYSTAL THERE AT THE END IS A REPLICA OF AN ANCIENT JEWEL WHICH...

.....?

COUGH

AS I WAS SAYING,

...HUH?

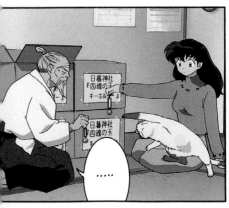

.....

THAT CRYSTAL IS A REPLICA OF AN ANCIENT JEWEL WHICH...

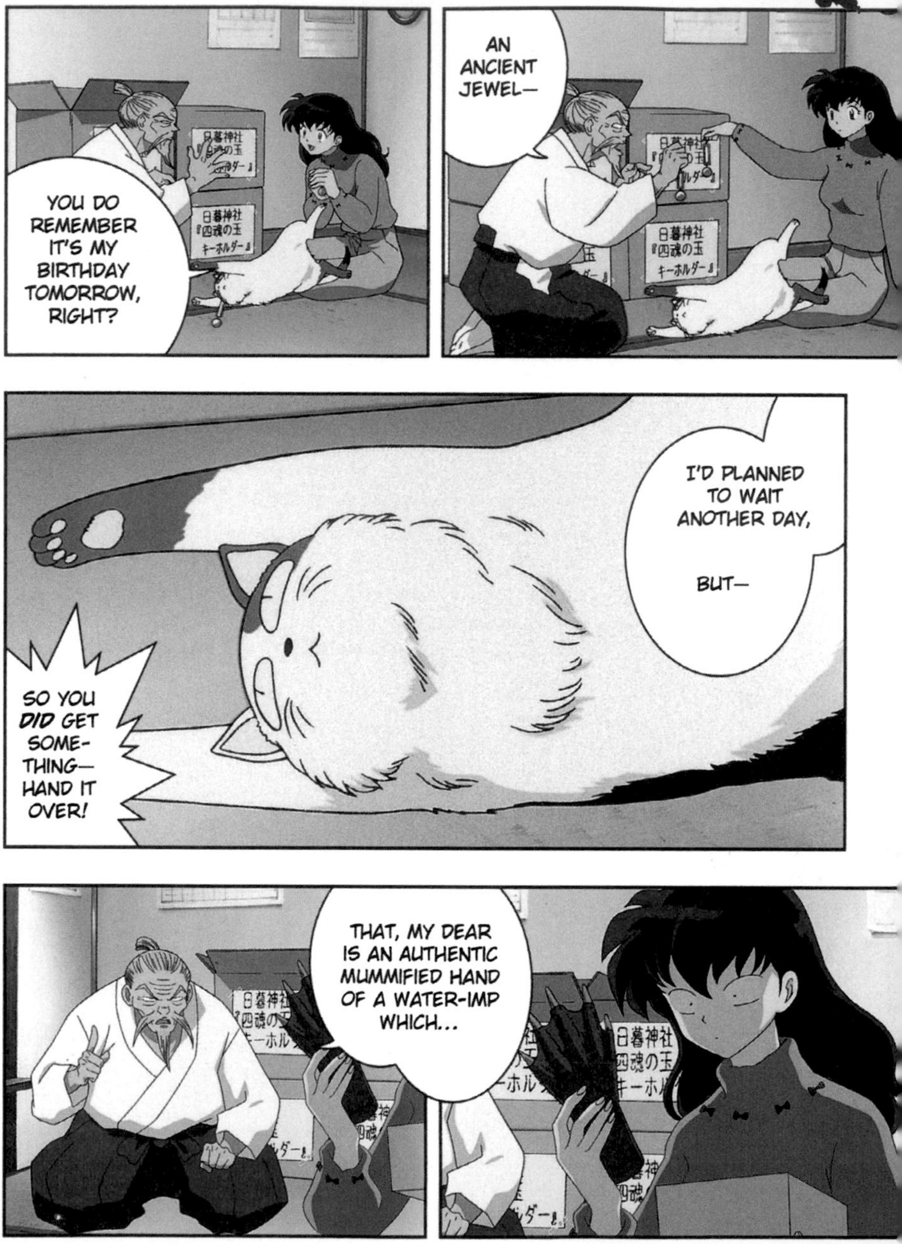
AN ANCIENT JEWEL—
YOU DO REMEMBER IT'S MY BIRTHDAY TOMORROW, RIGHT?
日暮神社
『四魂の玉
キーホルダー』
I'D PLANNED TO WAIT ANOTHER DAY,
BUT—
SO YOU *DID* GET SOME-THING— HAND IT OVER!
THAT, MY DEAR IS AN AUTHENTIC MUMMIFIED HAND OF A WATER-IMP WHICH...

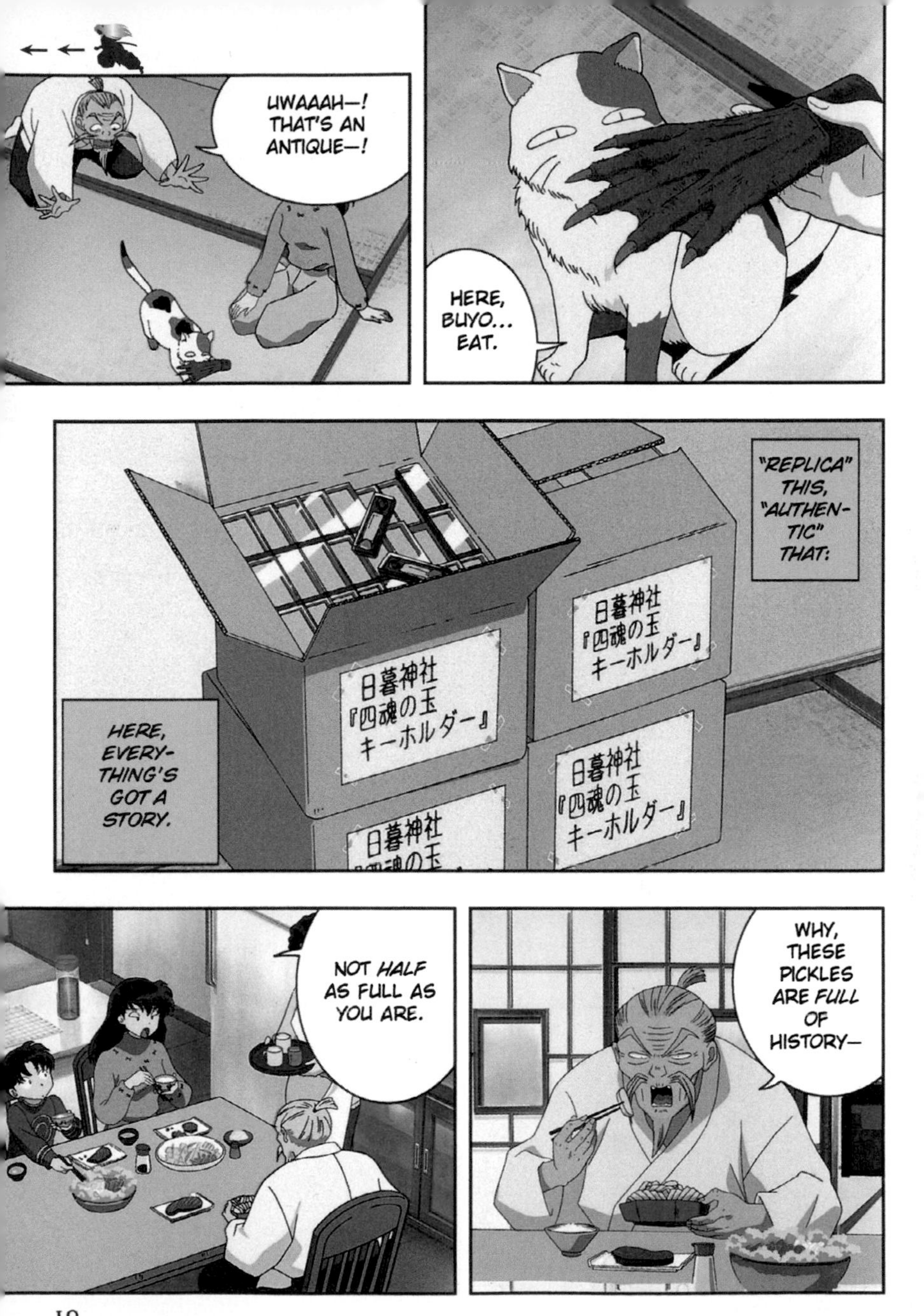
HERE, BUYO... EAT.
UWAAAH—! THAT'S AN ANTIQUE—!
"REPLICA" THIS, "AUTHEN-TIC" THAT:
日暮神社『四魂の玉キーホルダー』
日暮神社『四魂の玉キーホルダー』
日暮神社『四魂の玉キーホルダー』
日暮神社『四魂の玉
HERE, EVERY-THING'S GOT A STORY.
WHY, THESE PICKLES ARE *FULL* OF HISTORY—
NOT *HALF* AS FULL AS YOU ARE.

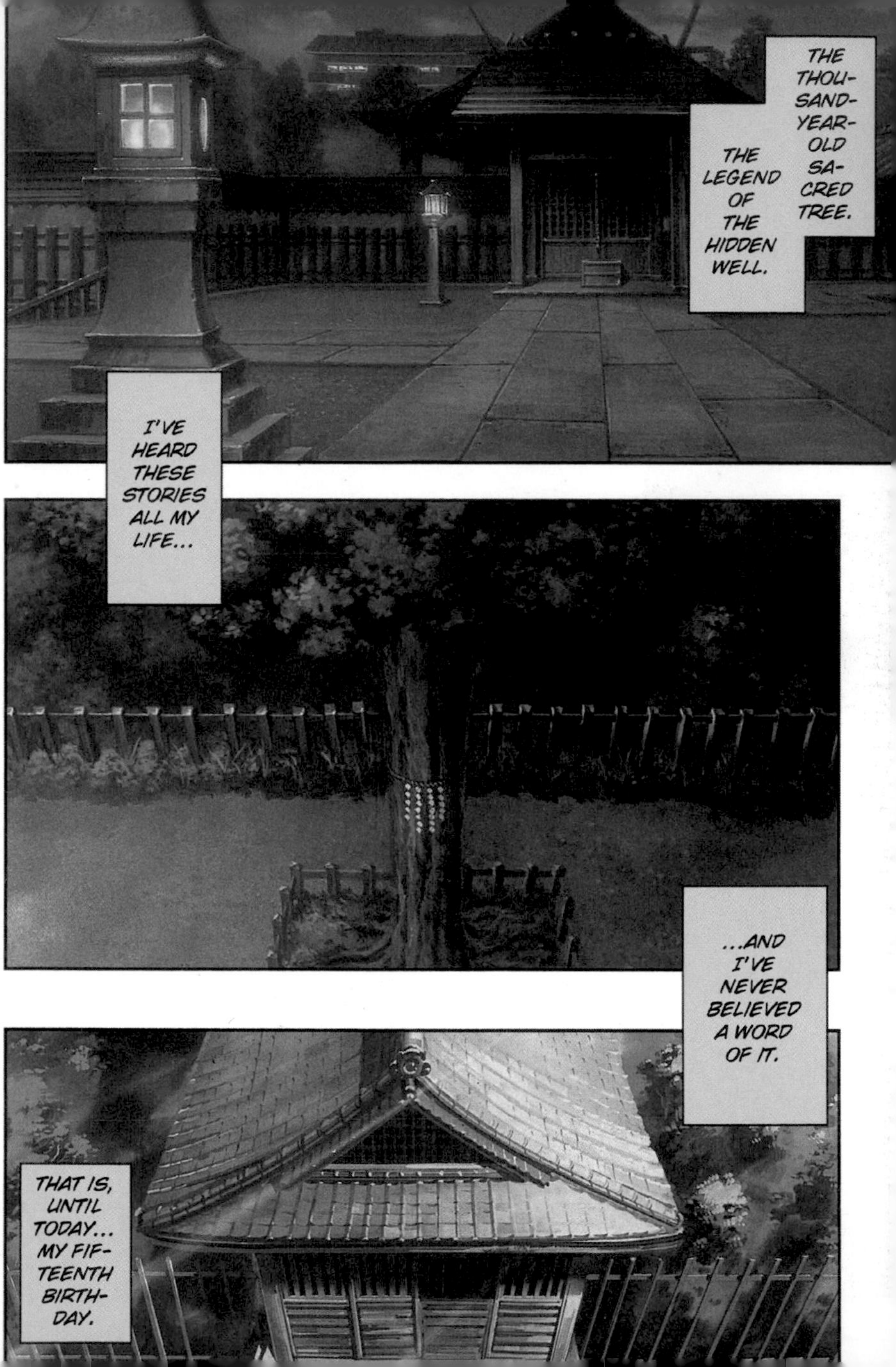
THE THOUSAND-YEAR-OLD SACRED TREE.
THE LEGEND OF THE HIDDEN WELL.
I'VE HEARD THESE STORIES ALL MY LIFE...
...AND I'VE NEVER BELIEVED A WORD OF IT.
THAT IS, UNTIL TODAY... MY FIFTEENTH BIRTHDAY.

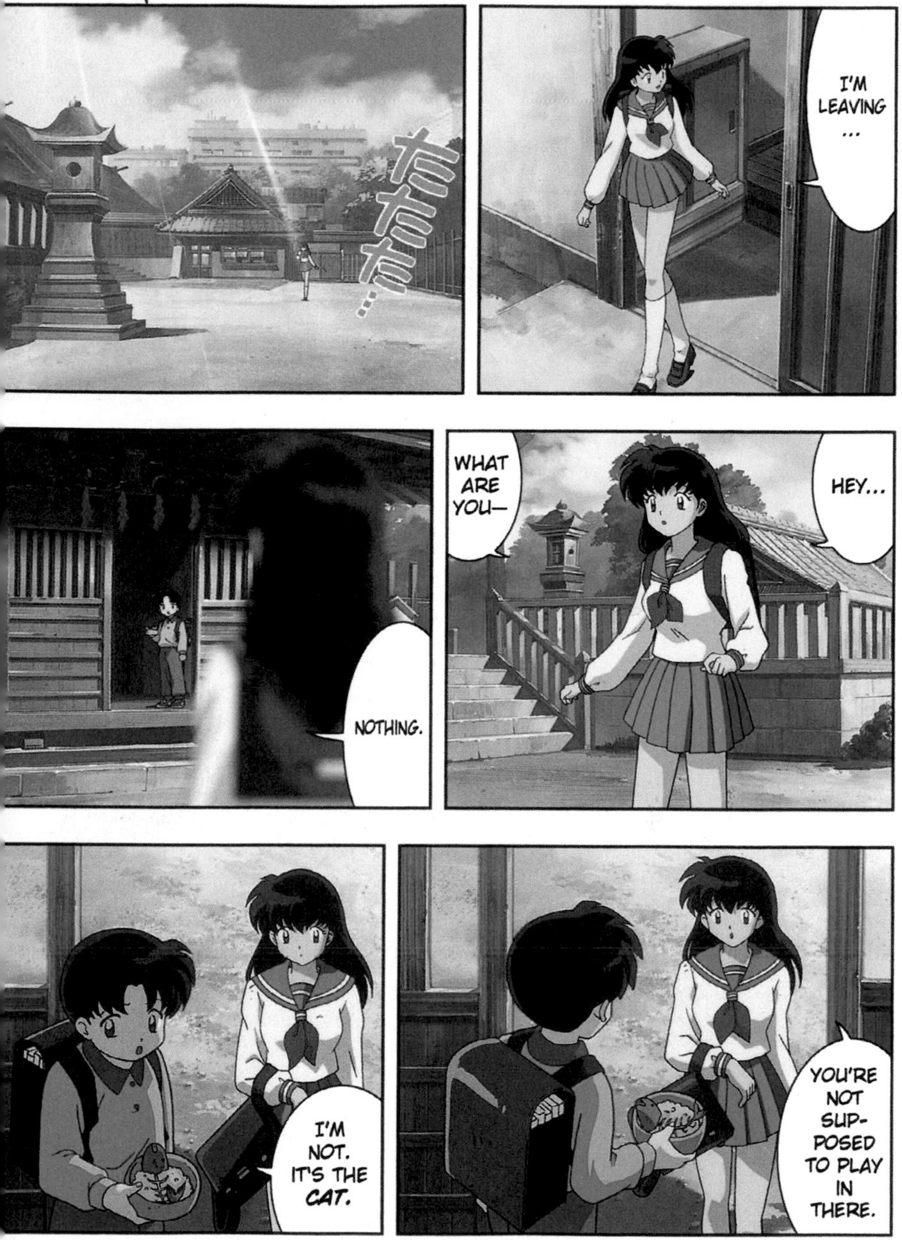
I'M LEAVING ...
たたた…
HEY...
WHAT ARE YOU—
NOTHING.
YOU'RE NOT SUP-POSED TO PLAY IN THERE.
I'M NOT. IT'S THE *CAT.*

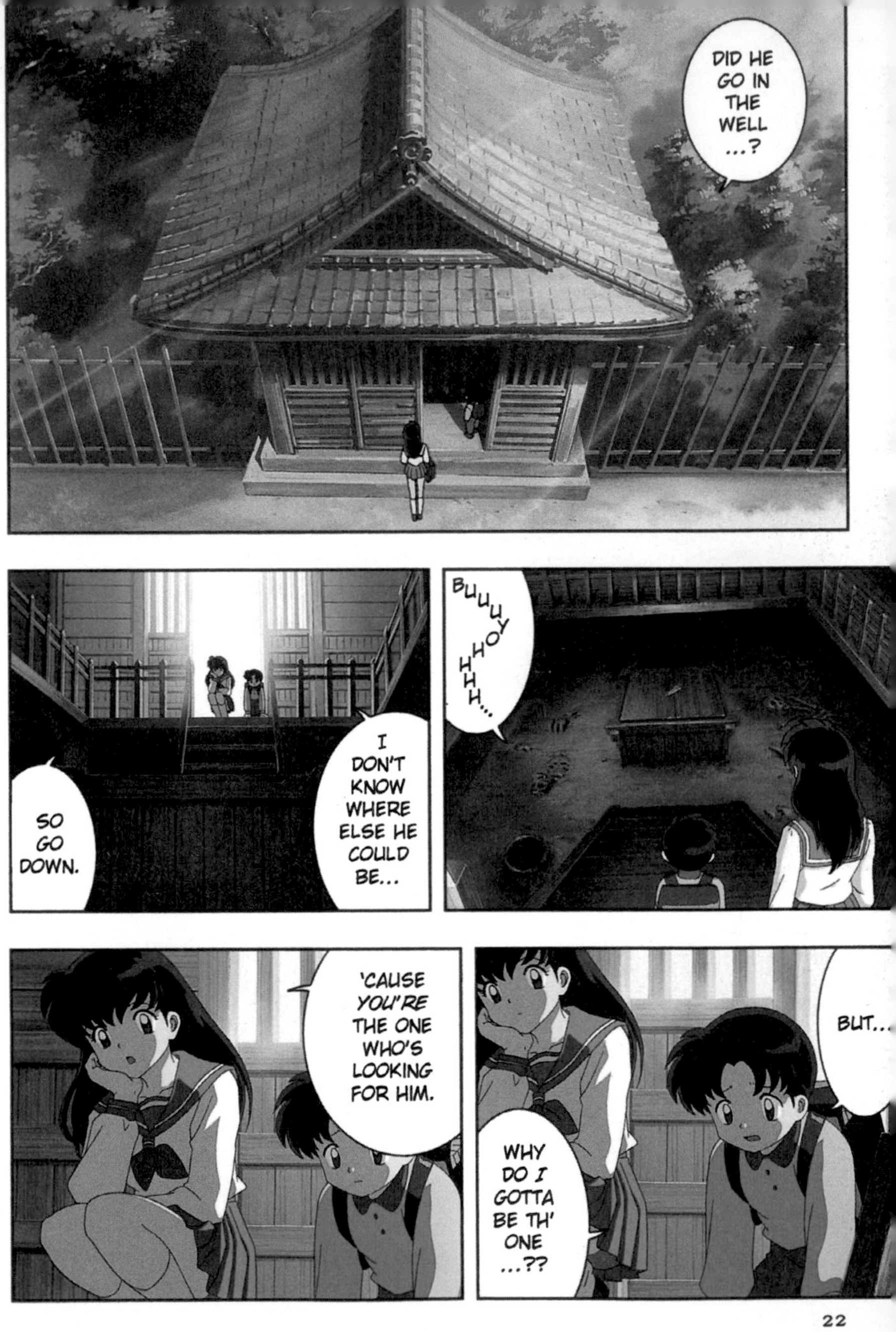
DID HE GO IN THE WELL ...?
BUUUYOHHHH...
I DON'T KNOW WHERE ELSE HE COULD BE...
SO GO DOWN.
BUT...
WHY DO *I* GOTTA BE TH' ONE ...??
'CAUSE *YOU'RE* THE ONE WHO'S LOOKING FOR HIM.

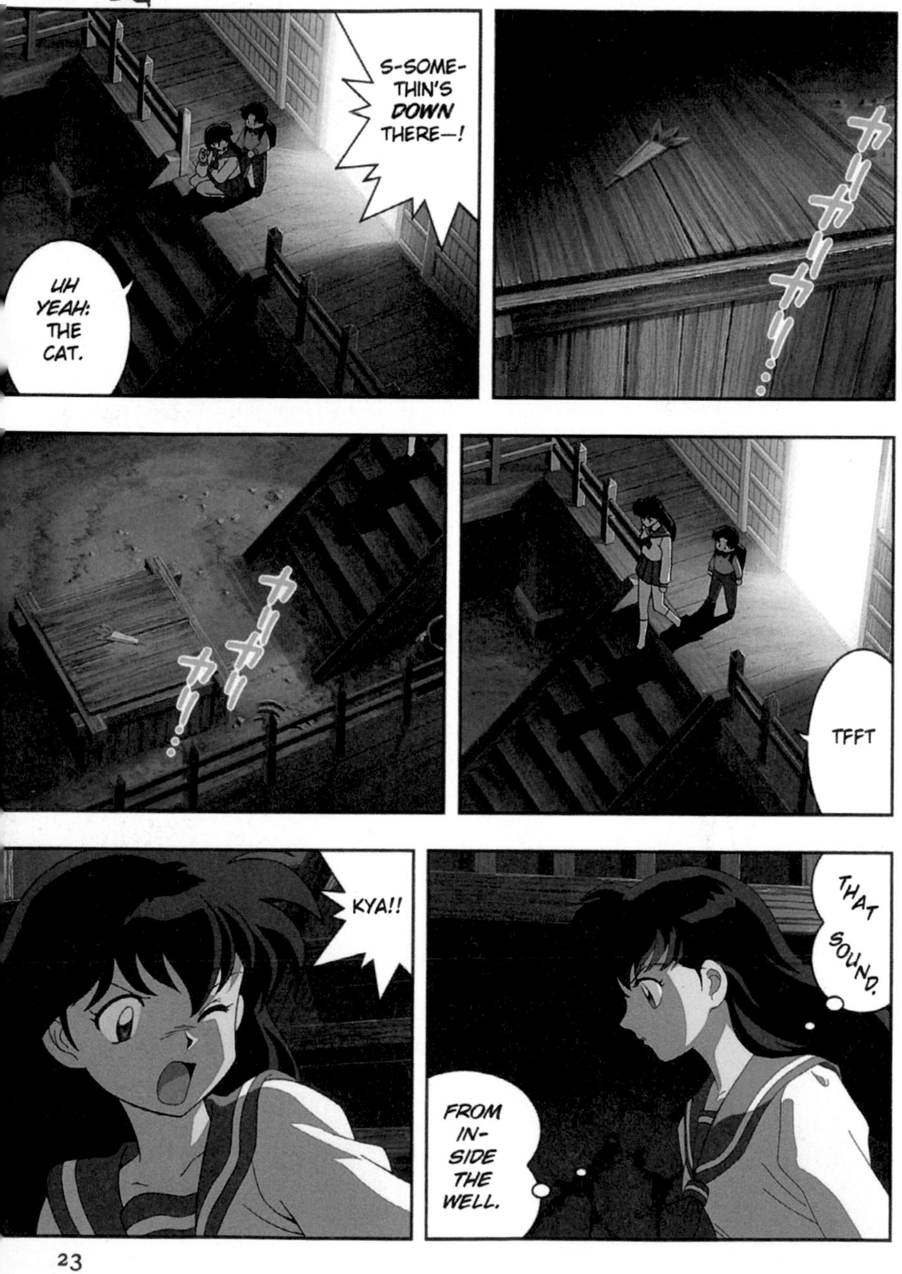

カリカリカリ…
S-SOMETHIN'S DOWN THERE—!
UH YEAH: THE CAT.
TFFT
カリカリカリ…
THAT SOUND.
FROM INSIDE THE WELL.
KYA!!

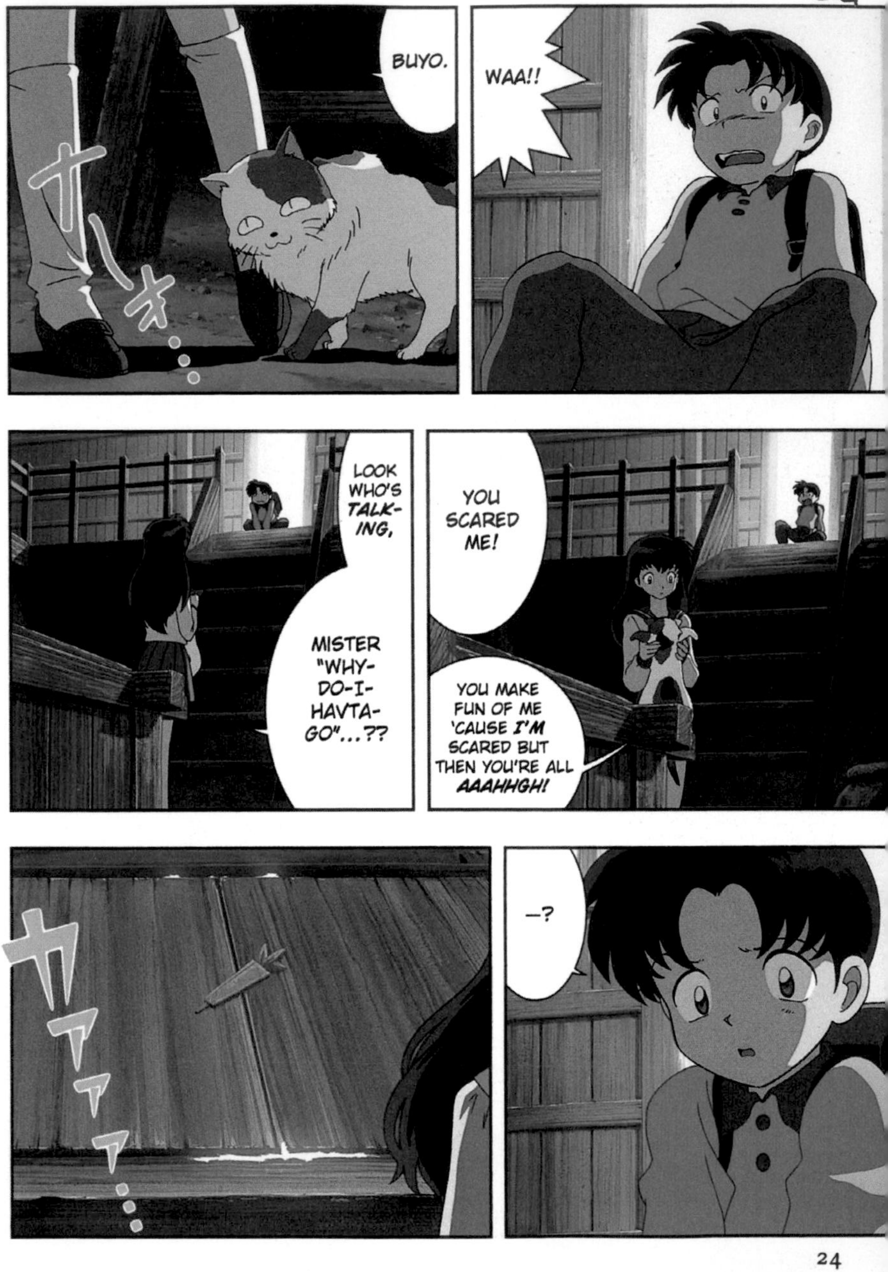
WAA!!
BUYO.
YOU SCARED ME!
YOU MAKE FUN OF ME 'CAUSE *I'M* SCARED BUT THEN YOU'RE ALL ***AAAHHGH!***
LOOK WHO'S *TALKING,*
MISTER "WHY-DO-I-HAVTA-GO"...??
—?

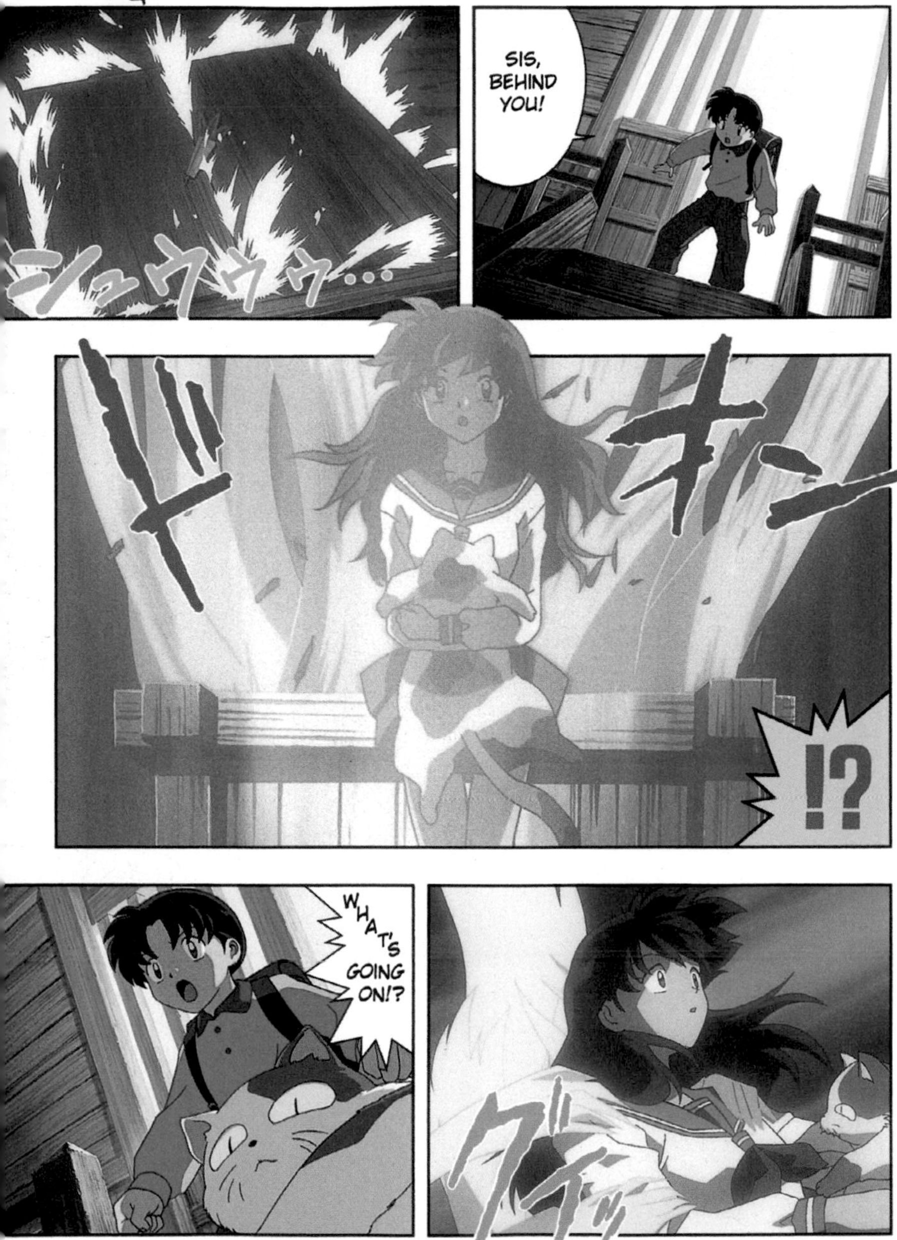
SIS, BEHIND YOU!
シュウウウ…
ドオー
!?
グイッ
WHAT'S GOING ON!?

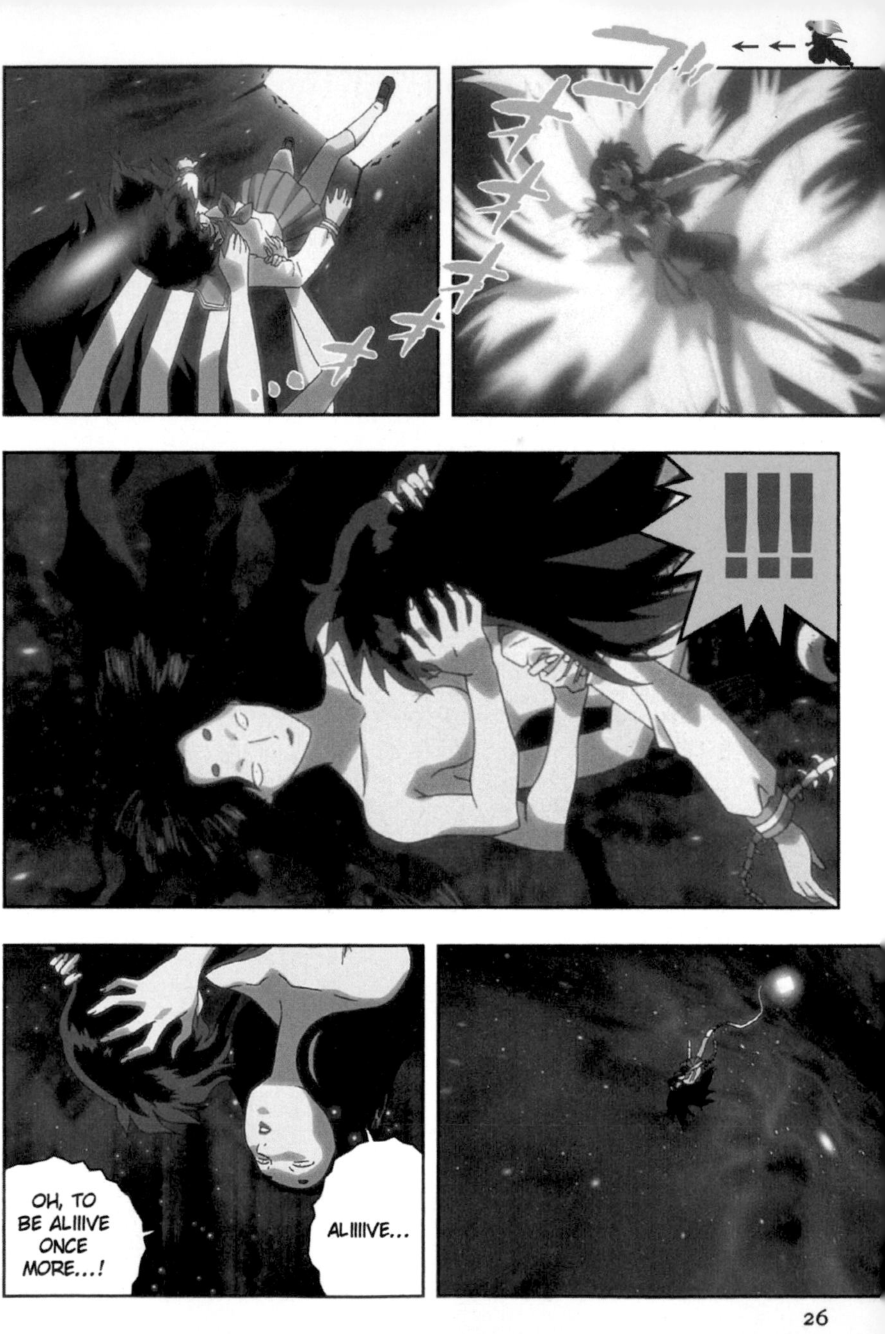
!!!!
ALIIIVE...
OH, TO BE ALIIIVE ONCE MORE...!

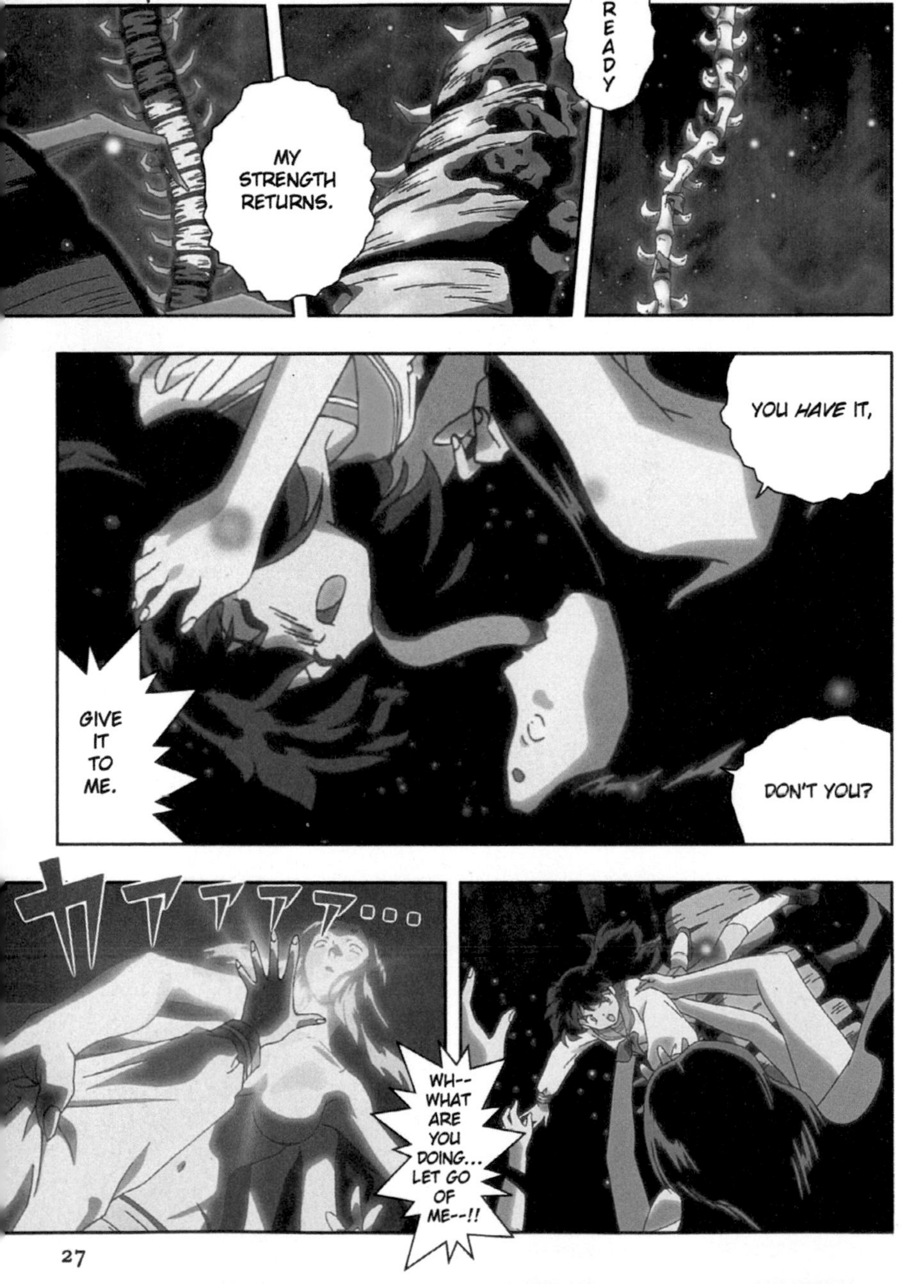
ALREADY
MY STRENGTH RETURNS.
YOU *HAVE* IT,
DON'T YOU?
GIVE IT TO ME.
WH-- WHAT ARE YOU DOING... LET GO OF ME--!!
カァァァァァ...

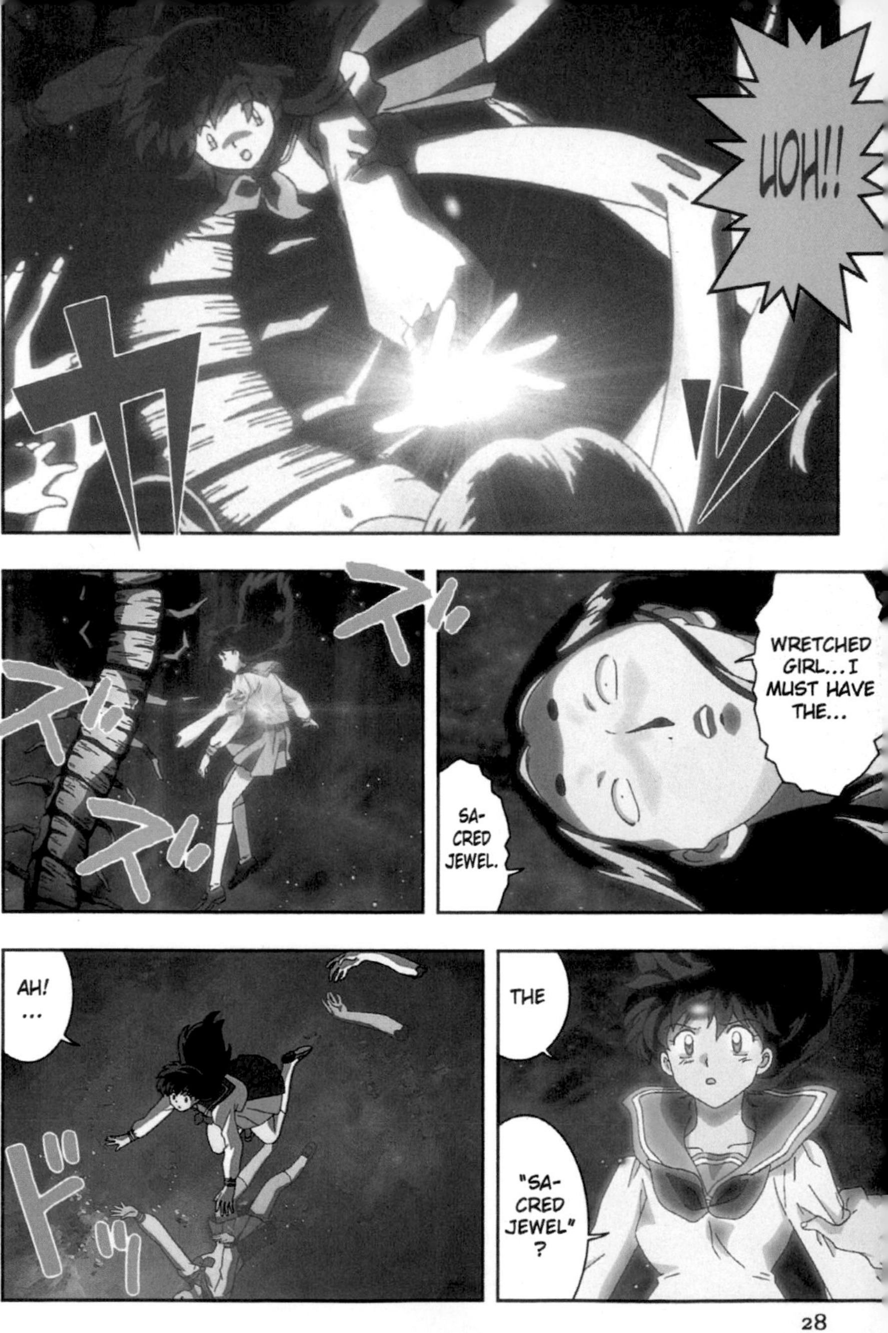
UOH!!
WRETCHED GIRL... I MUST HAVE THE...
SA-CRED JEWEL.
THE
"SA-CRED JEWEL"?
AH! ...

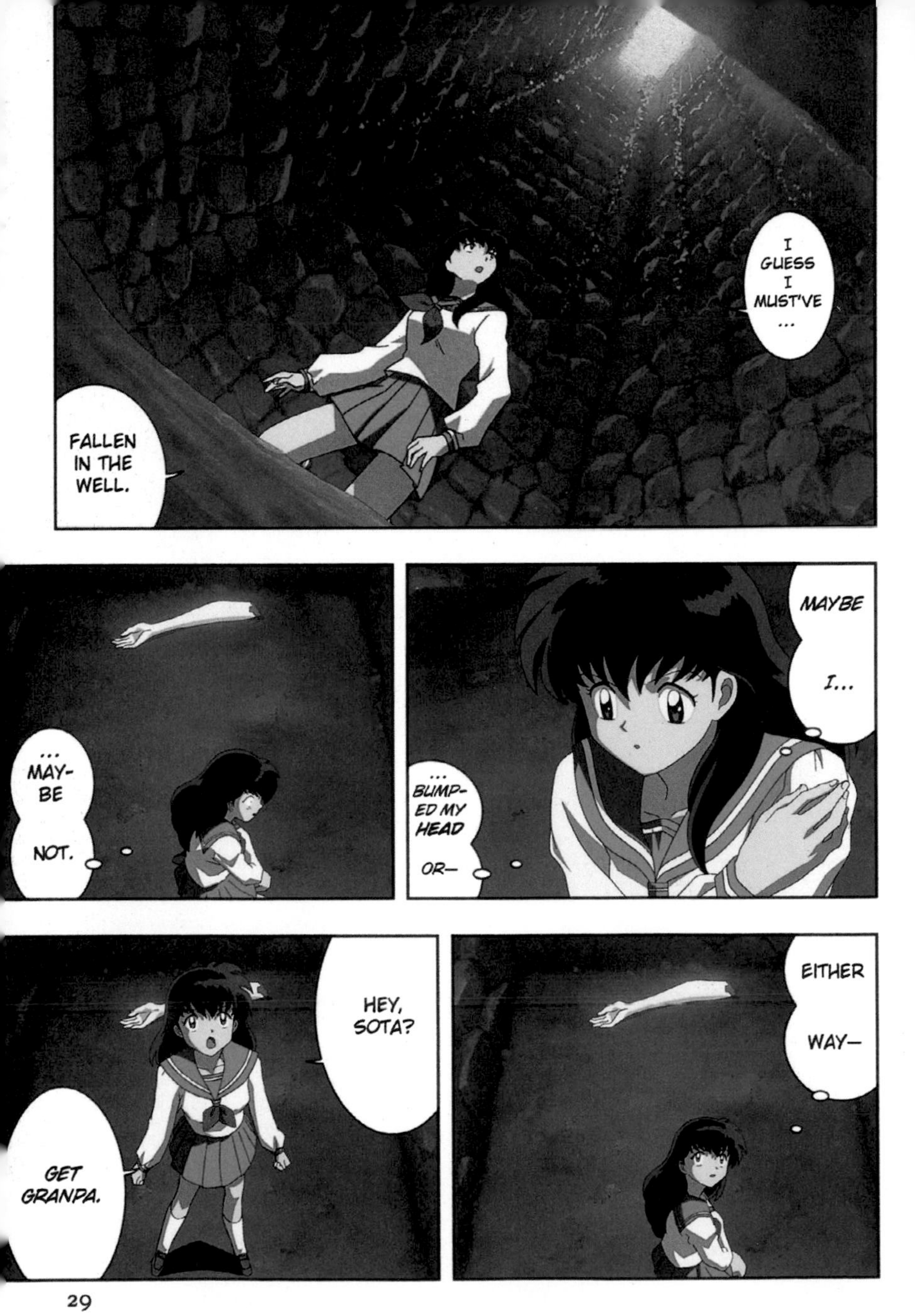
I GUESS I MUST'VE ...
FALLEN IN THE WELL.
MAYBE I...
... BUMPED-ED MY HEAD OR—
... MAY-BE NOT.
EITHER WAY—
HEY, SOTA?
GET GRANPA.

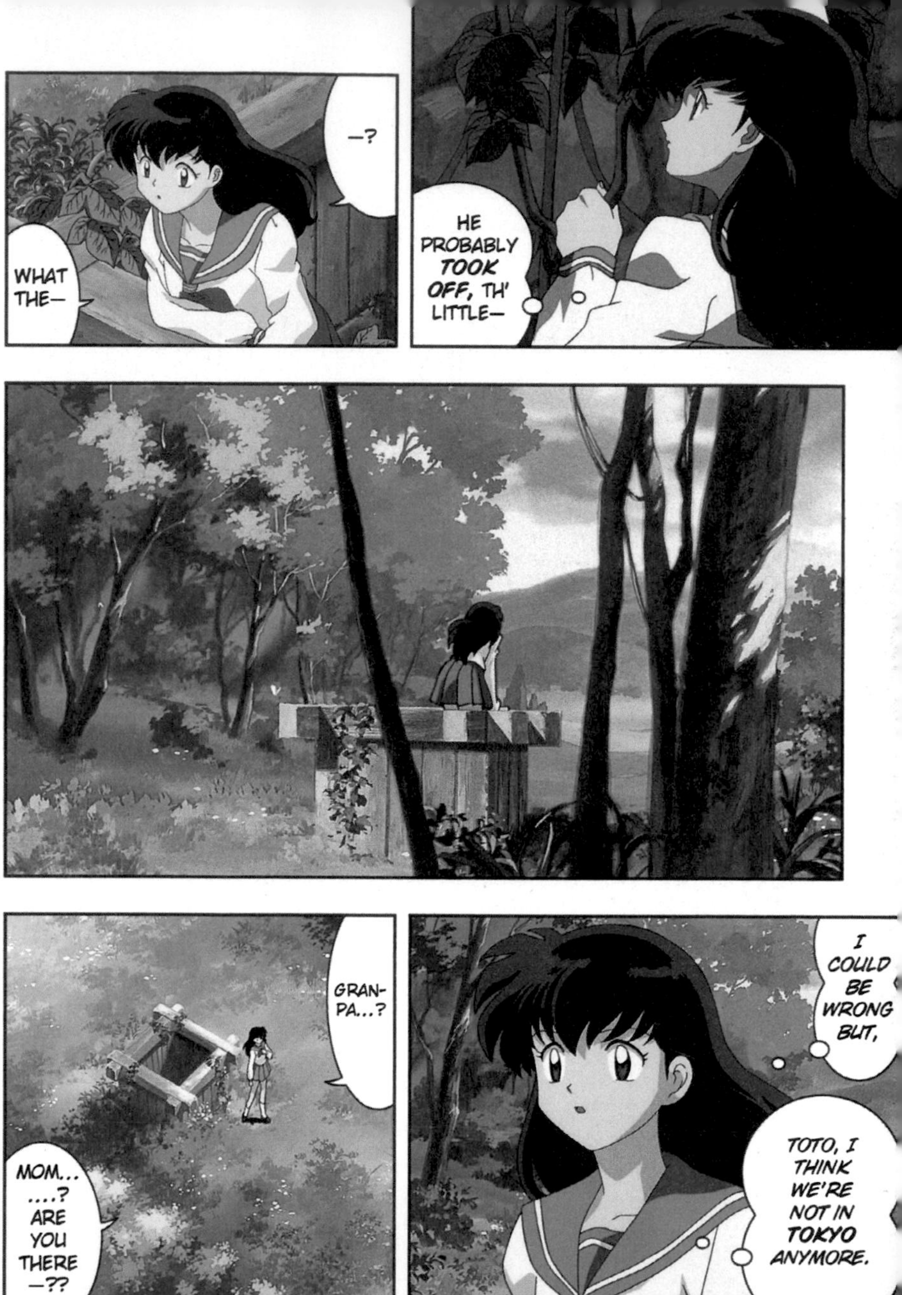
HE PROBABLY TOOK OFF, TH' LITTLE—
—?
WHAT THE—
I COULD BE WRONG BUT,
TOTO, I THINK WE'RE NOT IN TOKYO ANYMORE.
GRAN-PA...?
MOM... ....? ARE YOU THERE —??

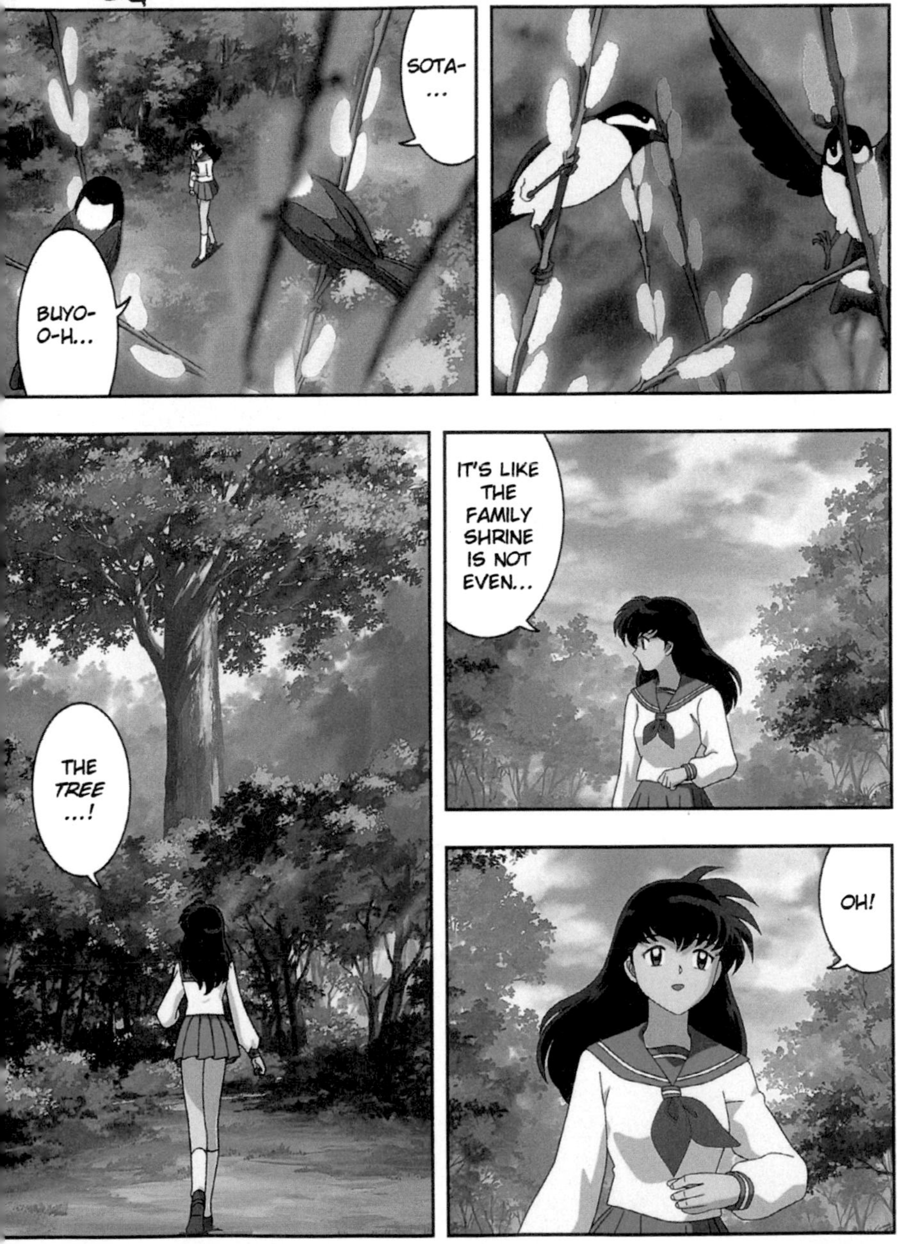
SOTA-...
BUYO-O-H...
IT'S LIKE THE FAMILY SHRINE IS NOT EVEN...
OH!
THE *TREE* ...!

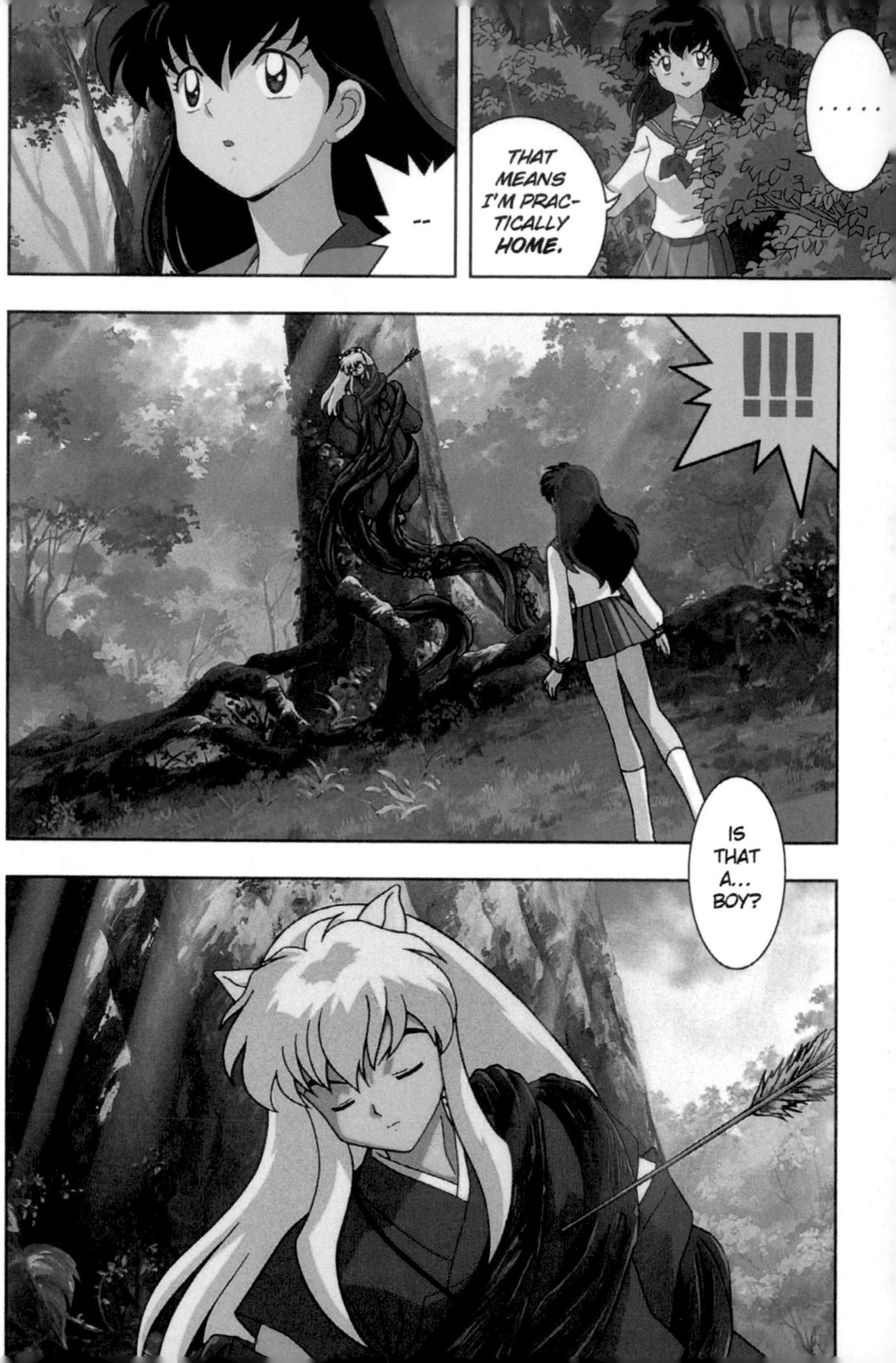
.....
THAT MEANS I'M PRAC-TICALLY HOME.
--
!!!
IS THAT A... BOY?

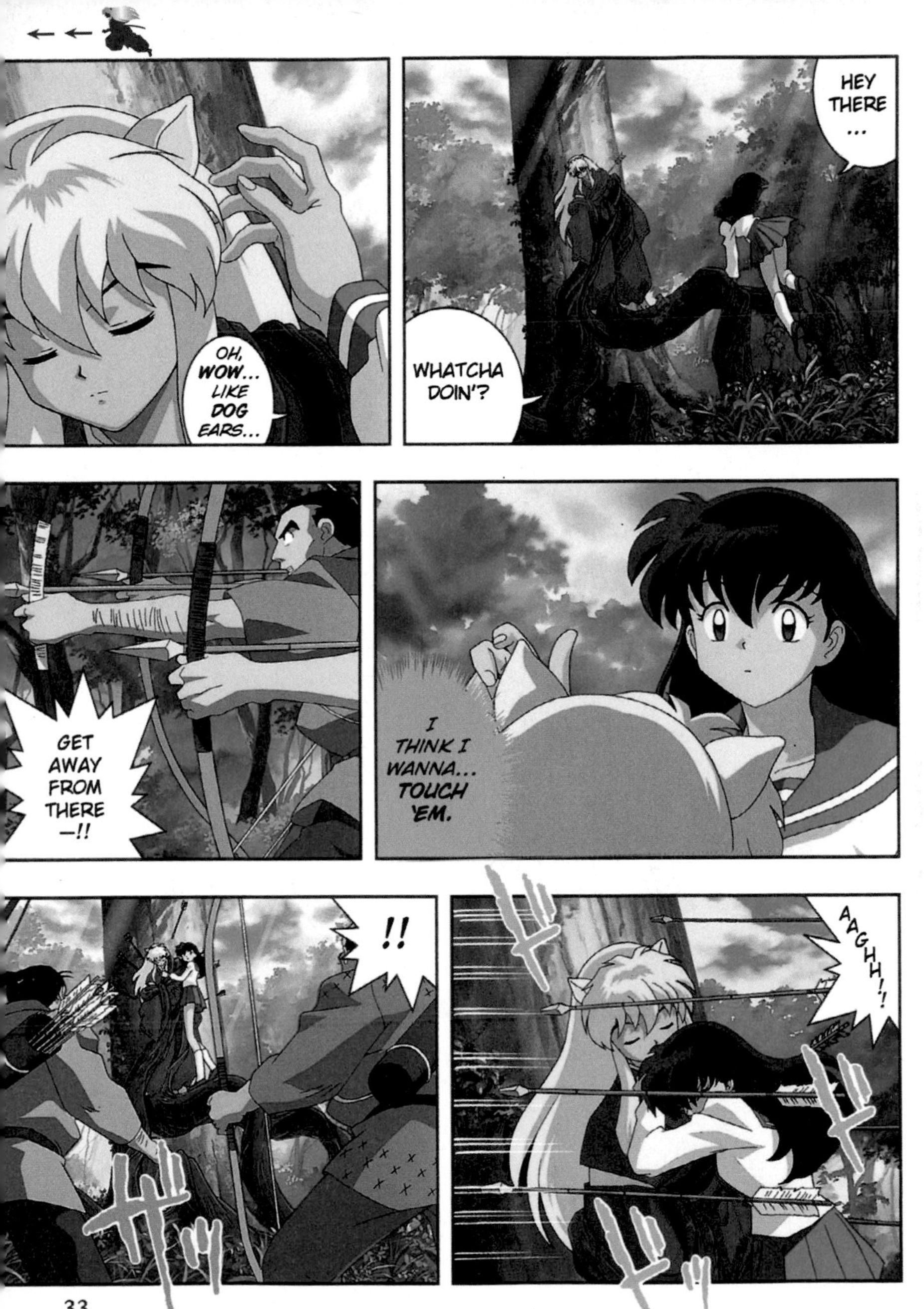
HEY THERE ...
WHATCHA DOIN'?
OH, WOW... LIKE DOG EARS...
I THINK I WANNA... TOUCH 'EM.
GET AWAY FROM THERE —!!
AAGHH!!
!!

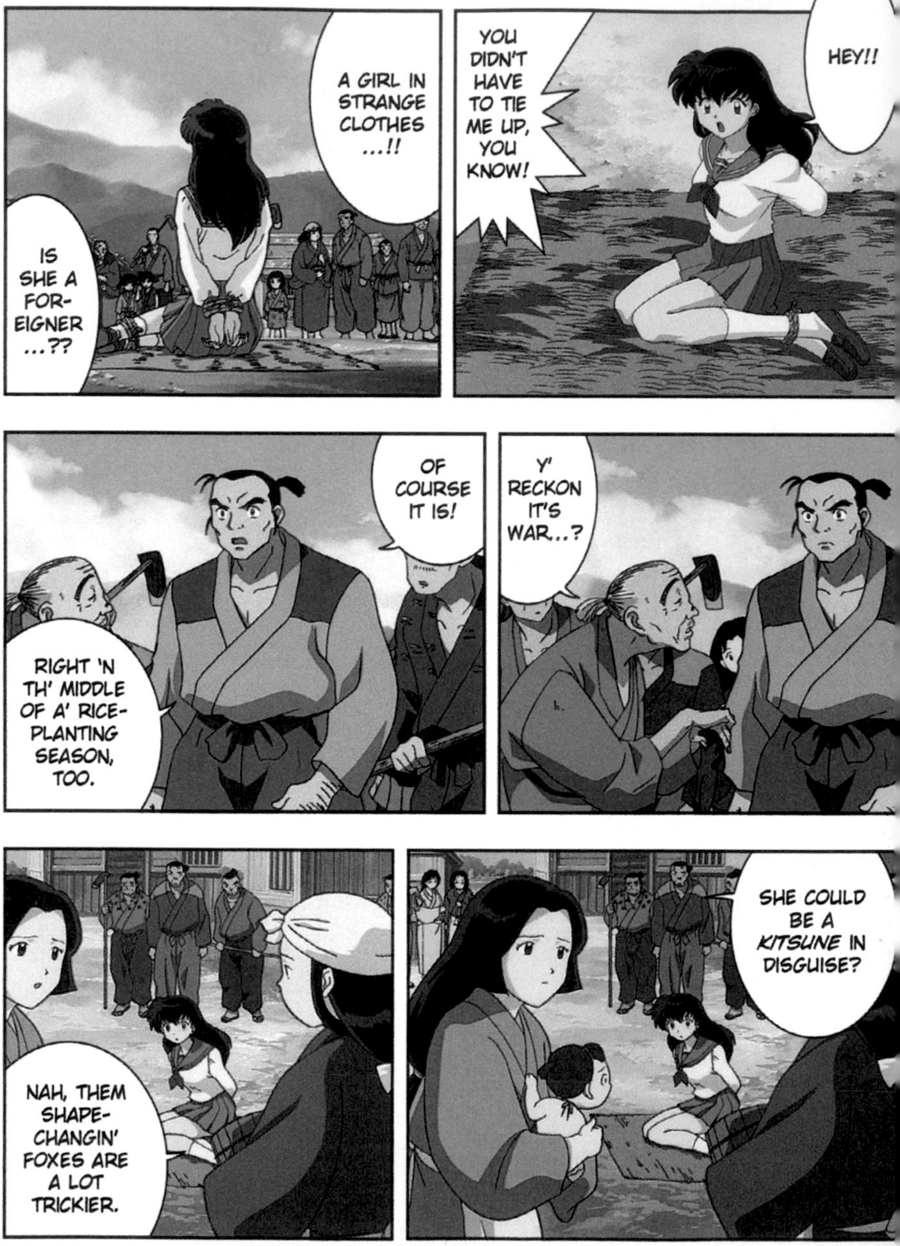
HEY!!
YOU DIDN'T HAVE TO TIE ME UP, YOU KNOW!
A GIRL IN STRANGE CLOTHES ...!!
IS SHE A FOR-EIGNER ...??
Y' RECKON IT'S WAR...?
OF COURSE IT IS!
RIGHT 'N TH' MIDDLE OF A' RICE-PLANTING SEASON, TOO.
SHE COULD BE A *KITSUNE* IN DISGUISE?
NAH, THEM SHAPE-CHANGIN' FOXES ARE A LOT TRICKIER.

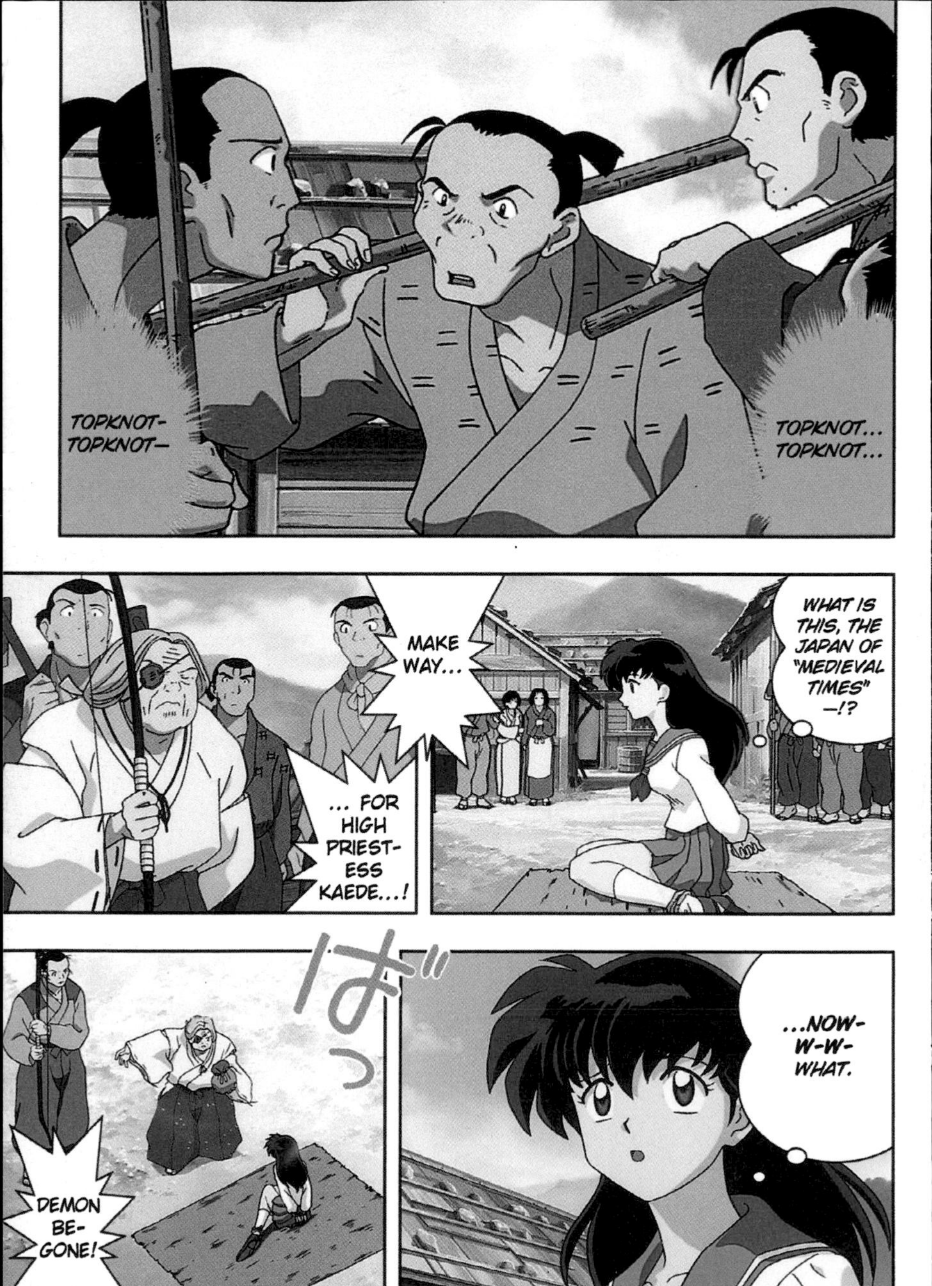
TOPKNOT... TOPKNOT...
TOPKNOT- TOPKNOT—
WHAT IS THIS, THE JAPAN OF "MEDIEVAL TIMES" —!?
MAKE WAY...
... FOR HIGH PRIEST-ESS KAEDE...!
...NOW-W-W-WHAT.
ばっ
DEMON BE-GONE!

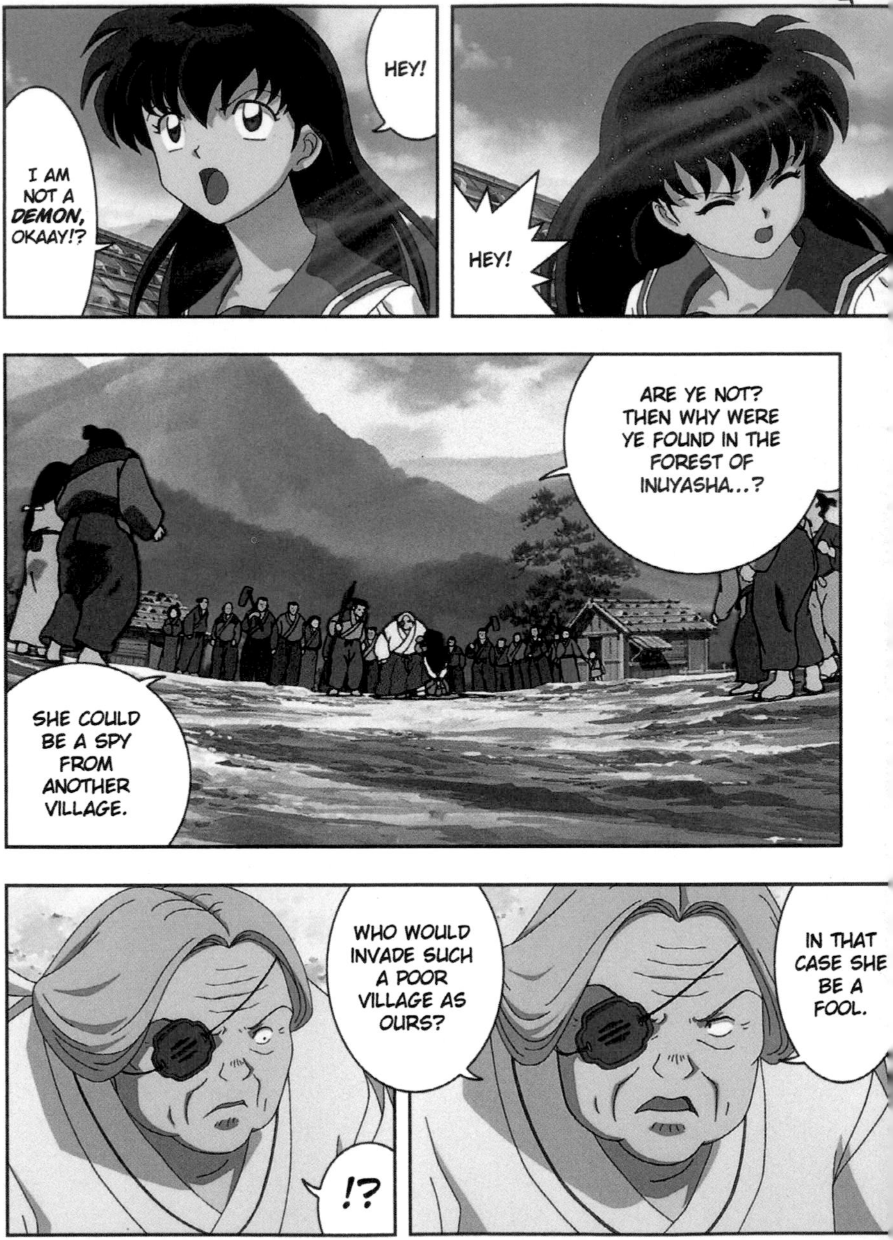

HEY!
HEY!
I AM NOT A *DEMON,* OKAAY!?
ARE YE NOT? THEN WHY WERE YE FOUND IN THE FOREST OF INUYASHA...?
SHE COULD BE A SPY FROM ANOTHER VILLAGE.
IN THAT CASE SHE BE A FOOL.
WHO WOULD INVADE SUCH A POOR VILLAGE AS OURS?
!?

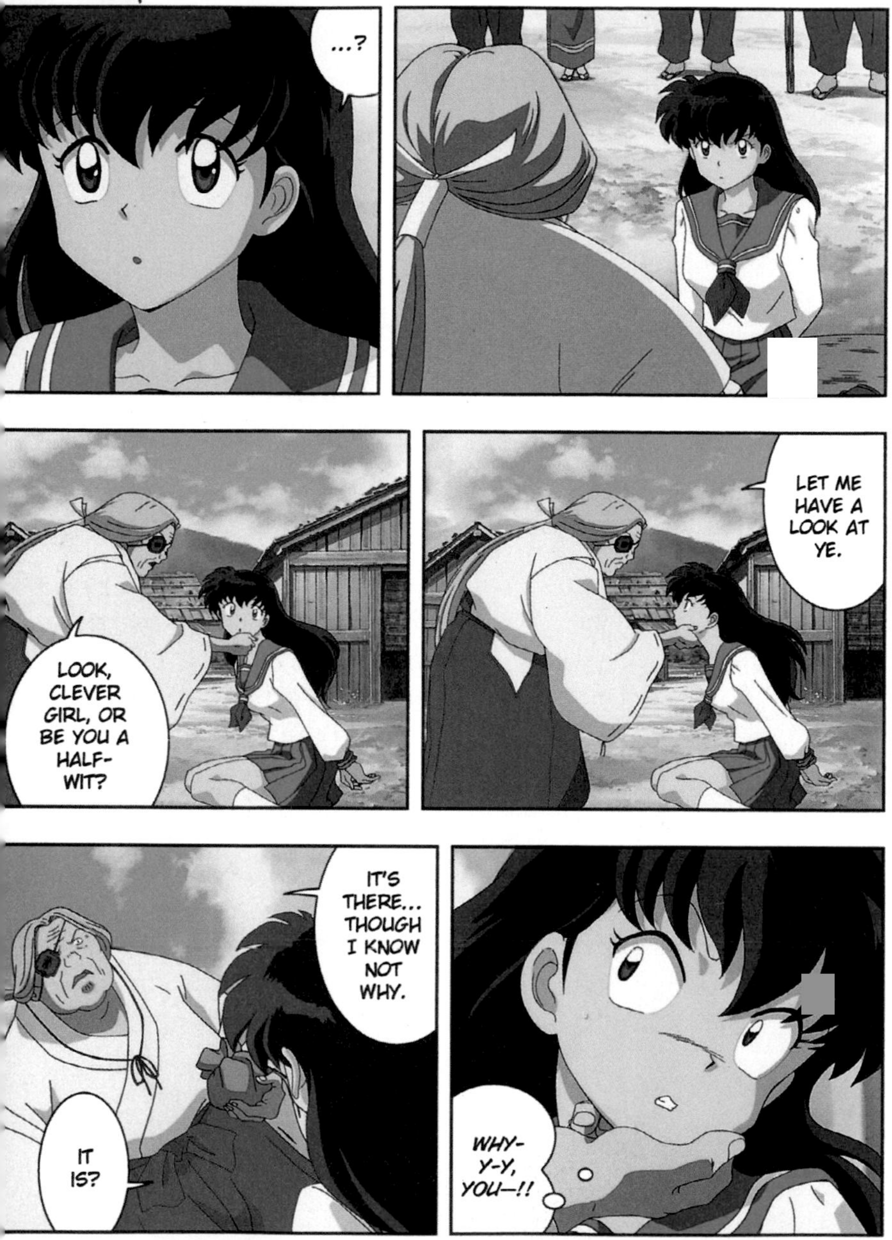
...?
LET ME HAVE A LOOK AT YE.
LOOK, CLEVER GIRL, OR BE YOU A HALF-WIT?
WHY-Y-Y, YOU—!!
IT'S THERE... THOUGH I KNOW NOT WHY.
IT IS?

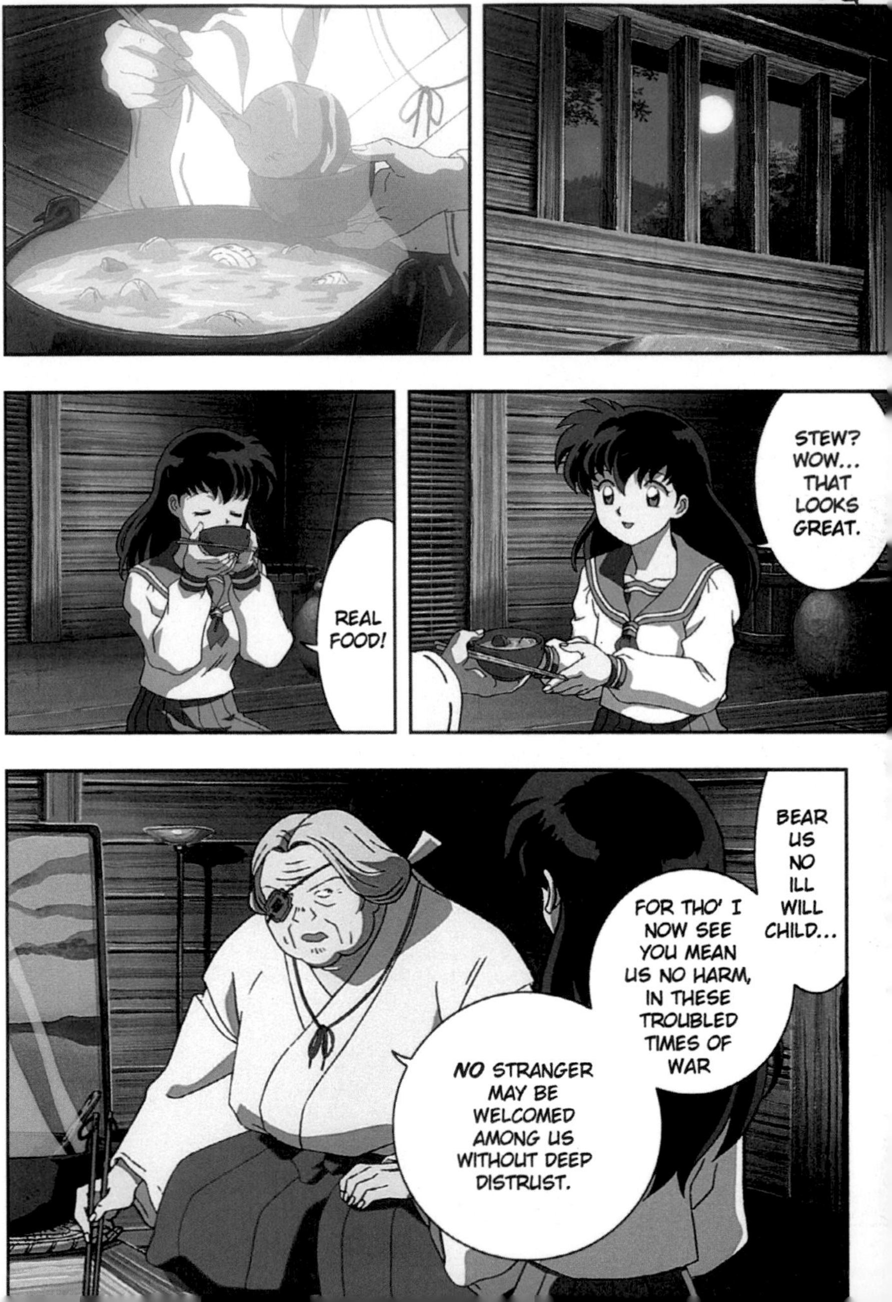
STEW? WOW... THAT LOOKS GREAT.
REAL FOOD!
BEAR US NO ILL WILL CHILD...
FOR THO' I NOW SEE YOU MEAN US NO HARM, IN THESE TROUBLED TIMES OF WAR
NO STRANGER MAY BE WELCOMED AMONG US WITHOUT DEEP DISTRUST.

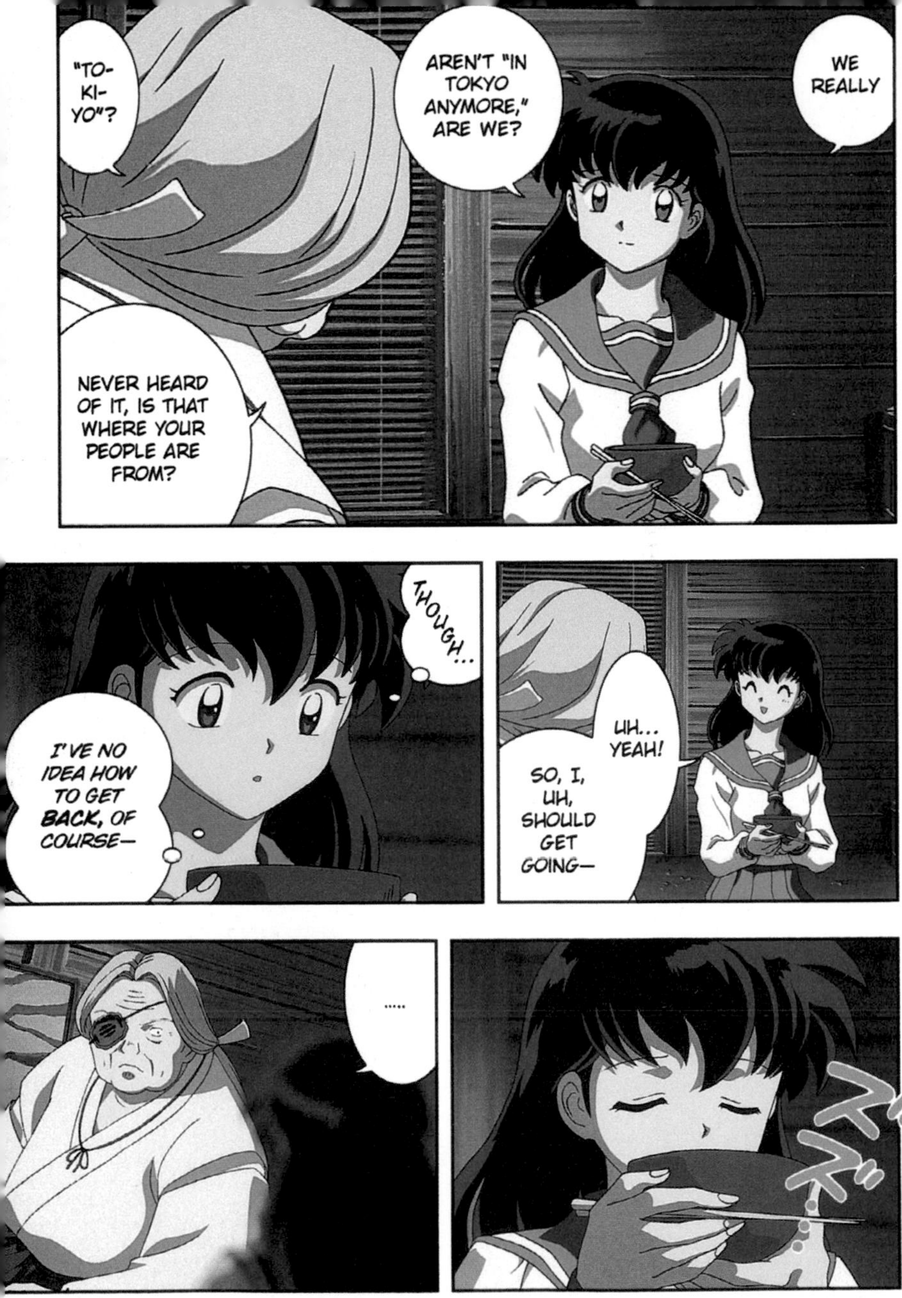

WE REALLY
AREN'T "IN TOKYO ANYMORE," ARE WE?
"TO-KI-YO"?
NEVER HEARD OF IT, IS THAT WHERE YOUR PEOPLE ARE FROM?
UH... YEAH!
SO, I, UH, SHOULD GET GOING—
THOUGH...
I'VE NO IDEA HOW TO GET **BACK,** OF COURSE—
ズズ...
.....

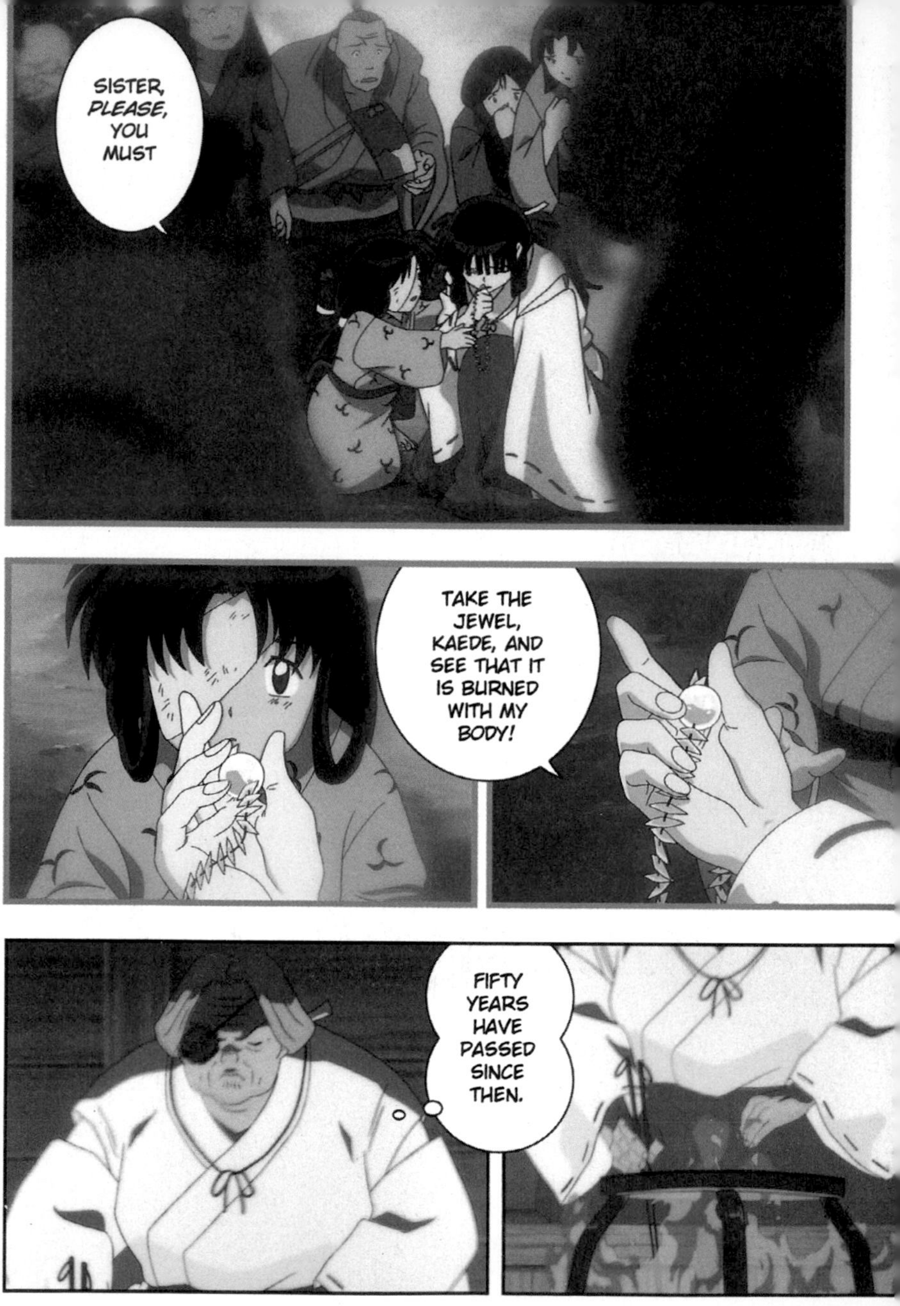
SISTER, *PLEASE,* YOU MUST
TAKE THE JEWEL, KAEDE, AND SEE THAT IT IS BURNED WITH MY BODY!
FIFTY YEARS HAVE PASSED SINCE THEN.

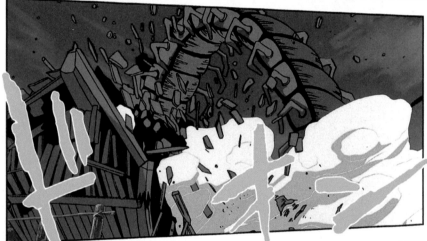

WHAT'S GOING ON!?

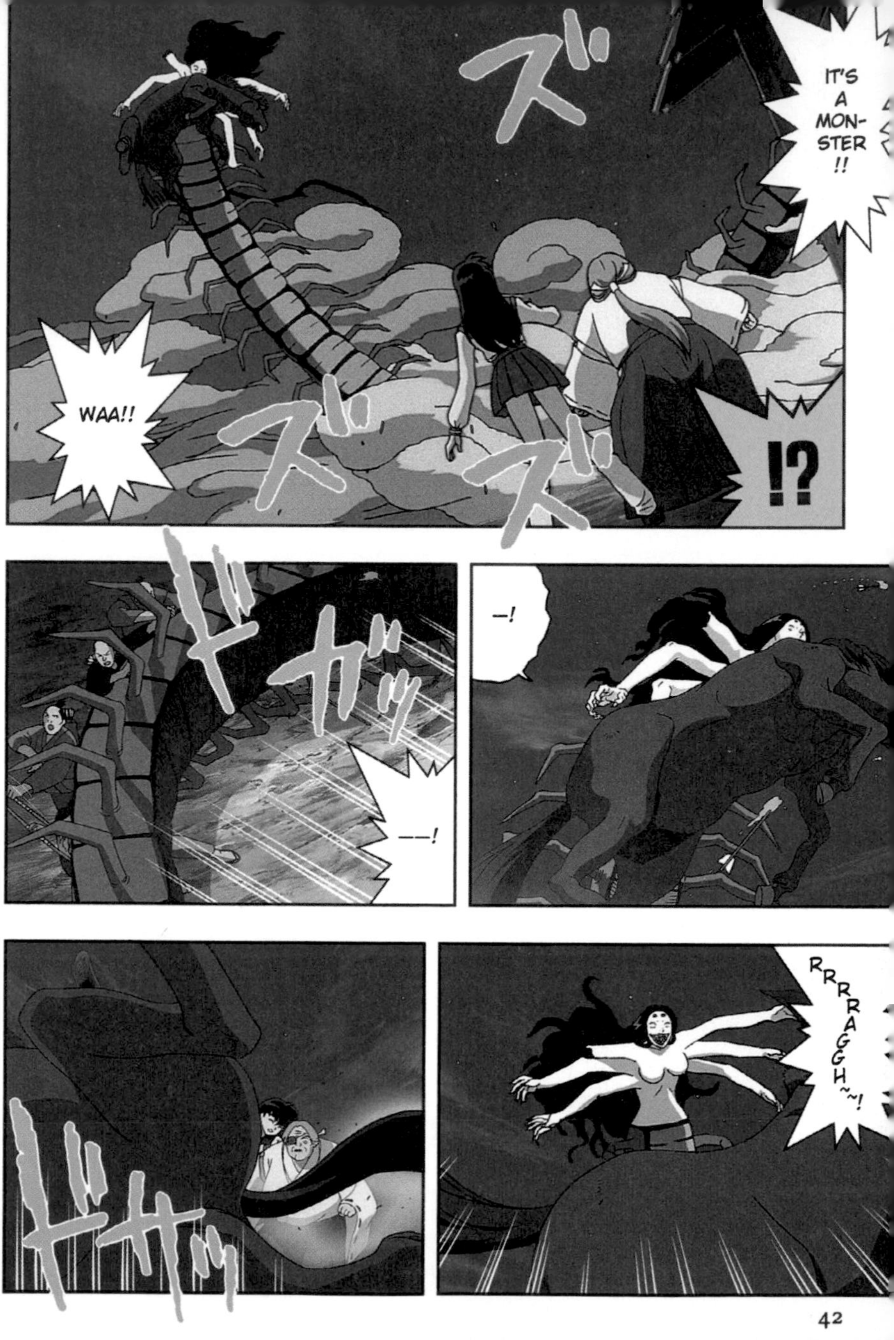
IT'S A MON-STER!!
ズ
!?
ズ
ズ
WAA!!
—!
ドガッ
——!
RRRRRAGGH~~!
ドサッ

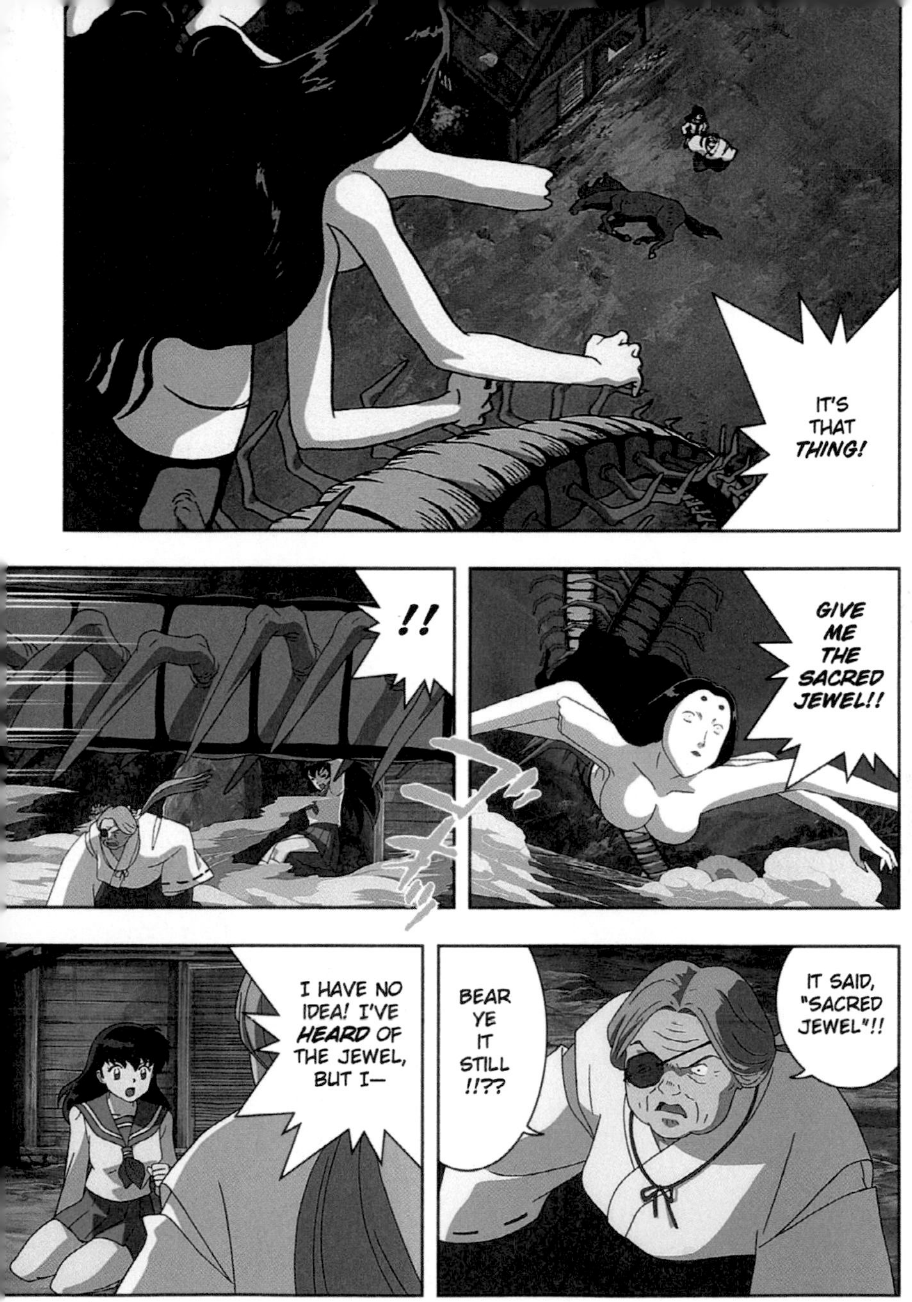
IT'S THAT THING!
GIVE ME THE SACRED JEWEL!!
!!
IT SAID, "SACRED JEWEL"!!
BEAR YE IT STILL !!??
I HAVE NO IDEA! I'VE HEARD OF THE JEWEL, BUT I—

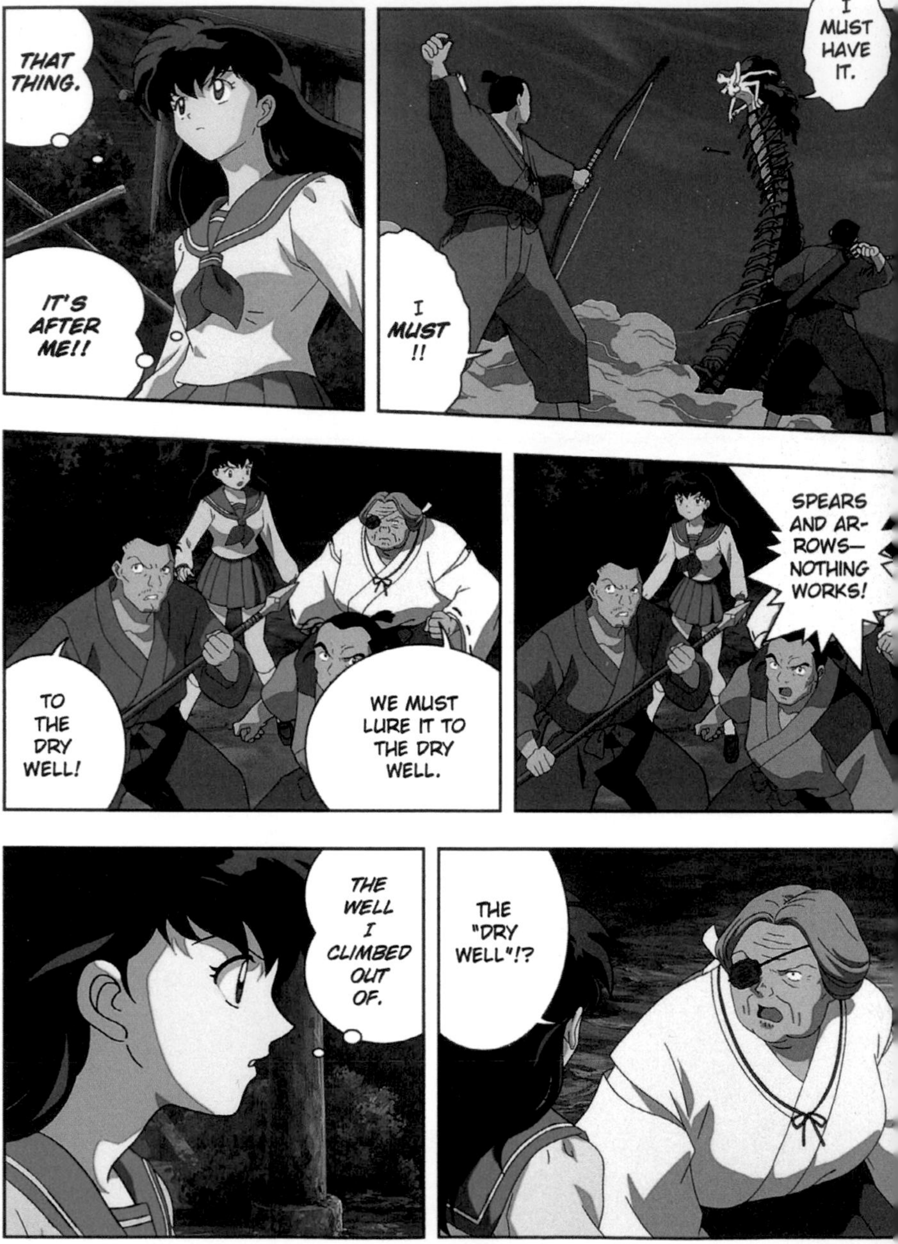
I MUST HAVE IT.
I MUST!!
THAT THING.
IT'S AFTER ME!!
SPEARS AND AR-ROWS—NOTHING WORKS!
WE MUST LURE IT TO THE DRY WELL.
TO THE DRY WELL!
THE "DRY WELL"!?
THE WELL I CLIMBED OUT OF.

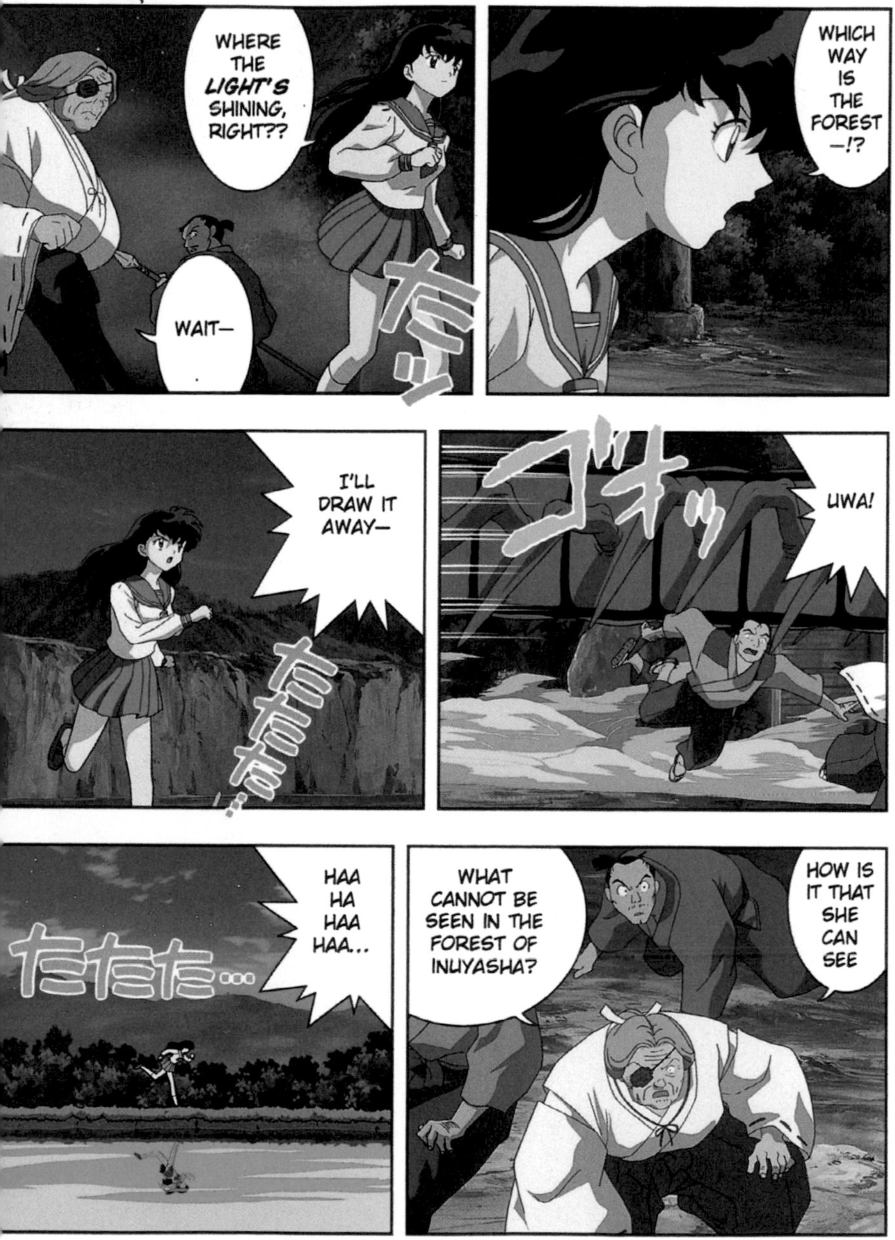
WHICH WAY IS THE FOREST —!?
WHERE THE *LIGHT'S* SHINING, RIGHT??
たッ
WAIT—
ゴオッ
UWA!
I'LL DRAW IT AWAY—
たたたた…
HOW IS IT THAT SHE CAN SEE
WHAT CANNOT BE SEEN IN THE FOREST OF INUYASHA?
HAA HA HAA HAA...
たたたた…

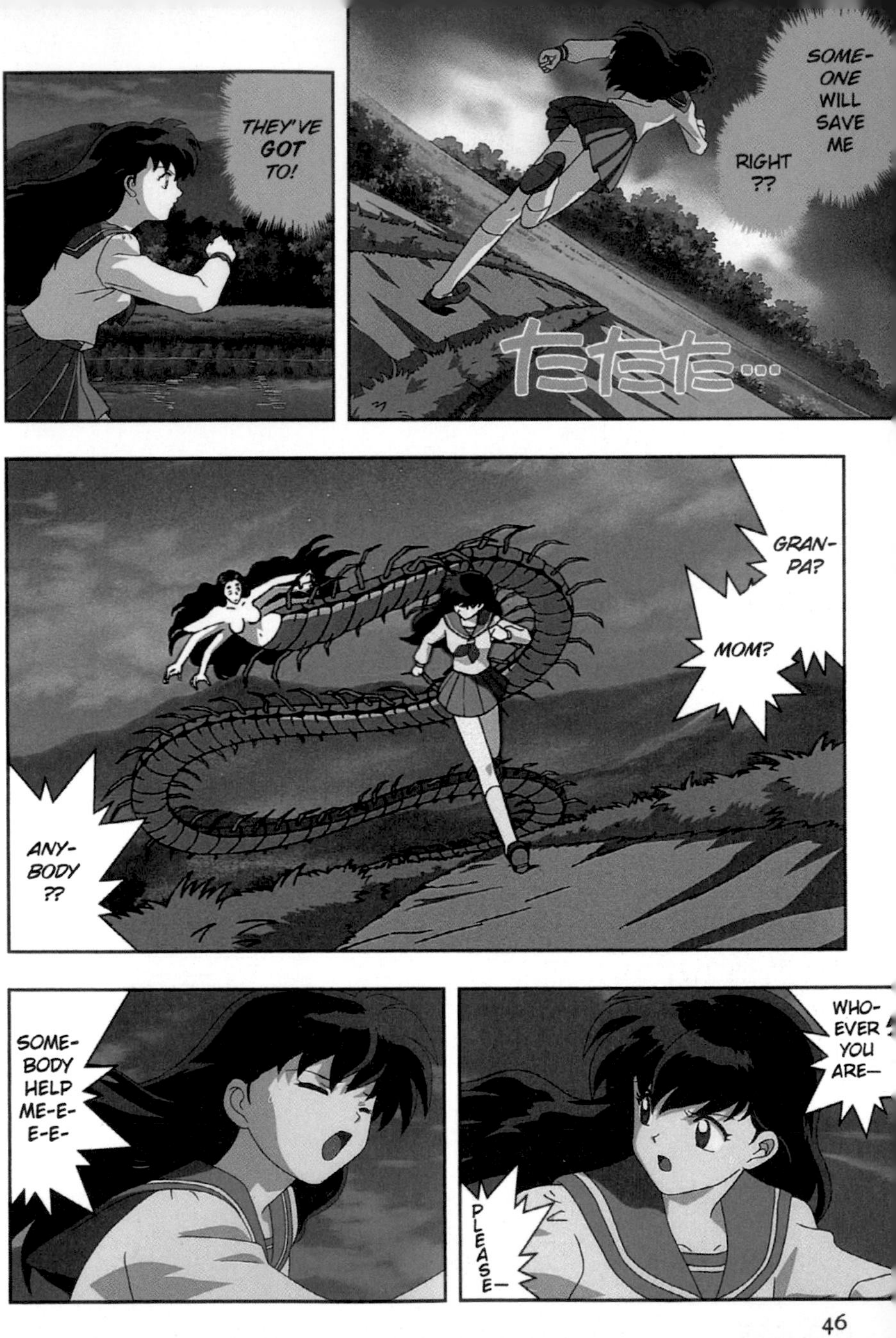
SOME-ONE WILL SAVE ME
RIGHT ??
たたた…
THEY'VE GOT TO!
GRAN-PA?
MOM?
ANY-BODY ??
WHO-EVER YOU ARE—
PLEASE—
SOME-BODY HELP ME-E-E-E-

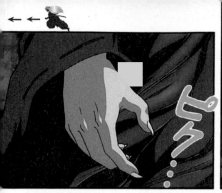

I SMELL IT...

THE **BLOOD** OF THE WOMAN WHO KILLED ME!

AND IT'S COMING CLOSER...

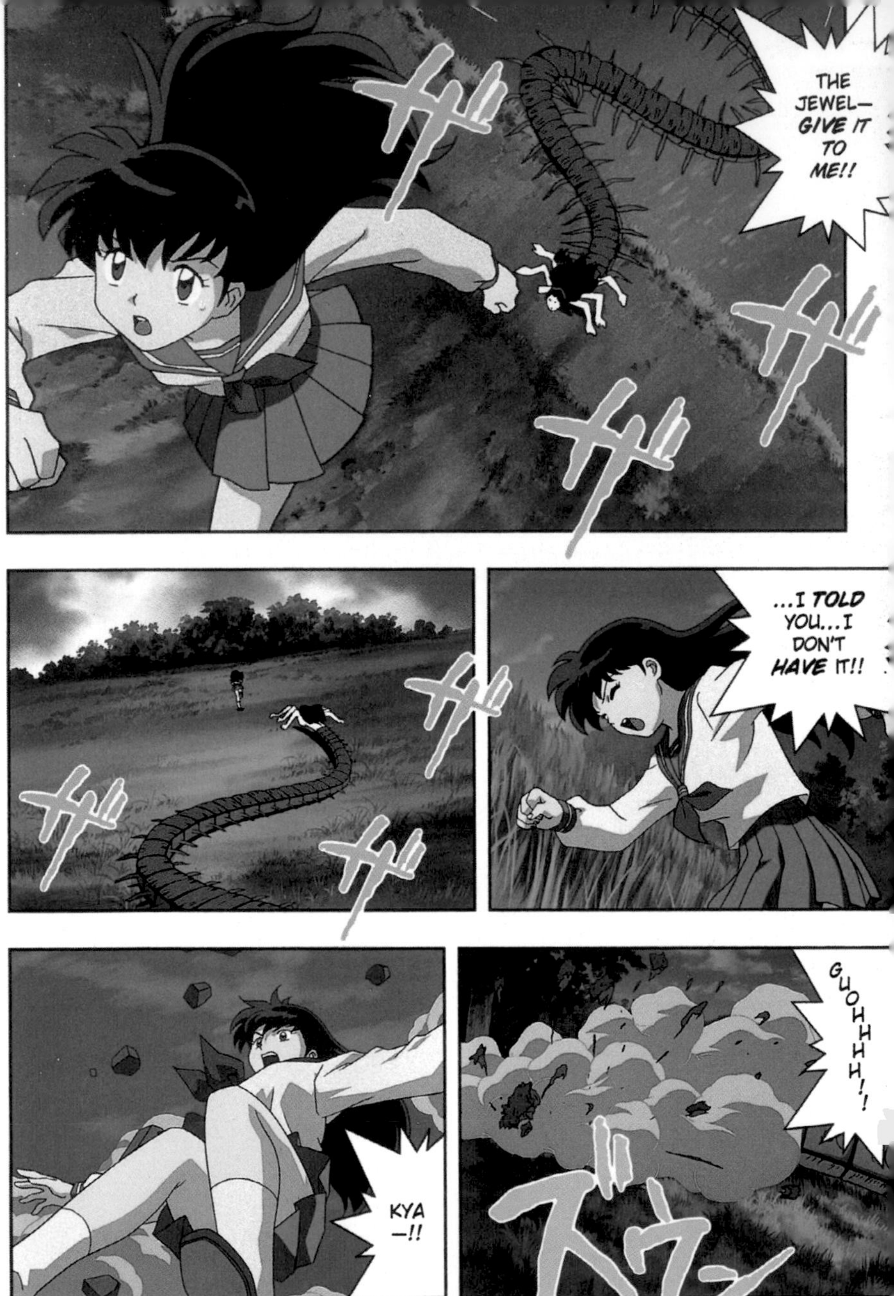
THE JEWEL—GIVE IT TO ME!!
...I TOLD YOU...I DON'T HAVE IT!!
GUOHHHHH!!
KYA—!!

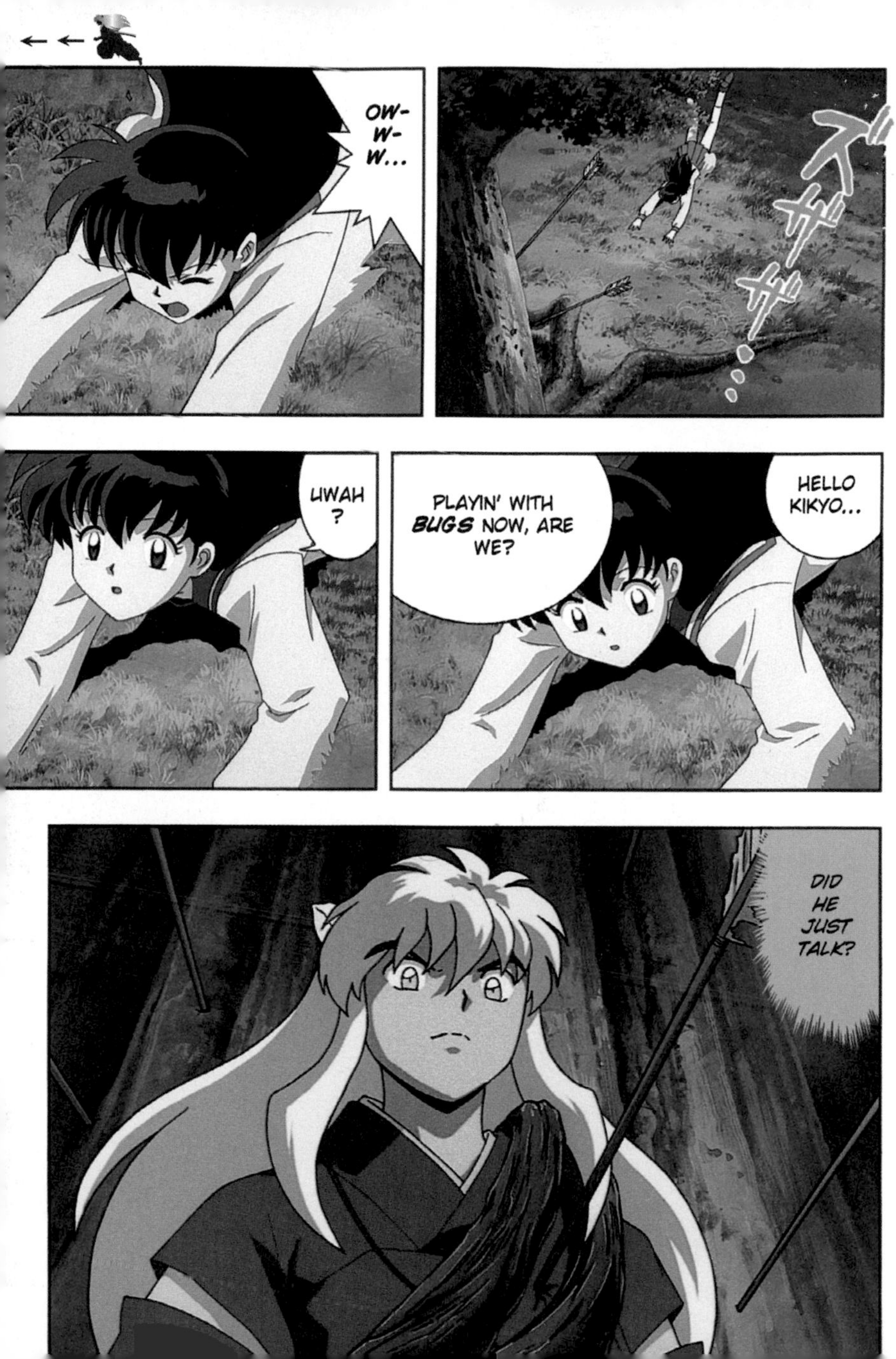
OW-W-W...
HELLO KIKYO...
PLAYIN' WITH BUGS NOW, ARE WE?
UWAH ?
DID HE JUST TALK?

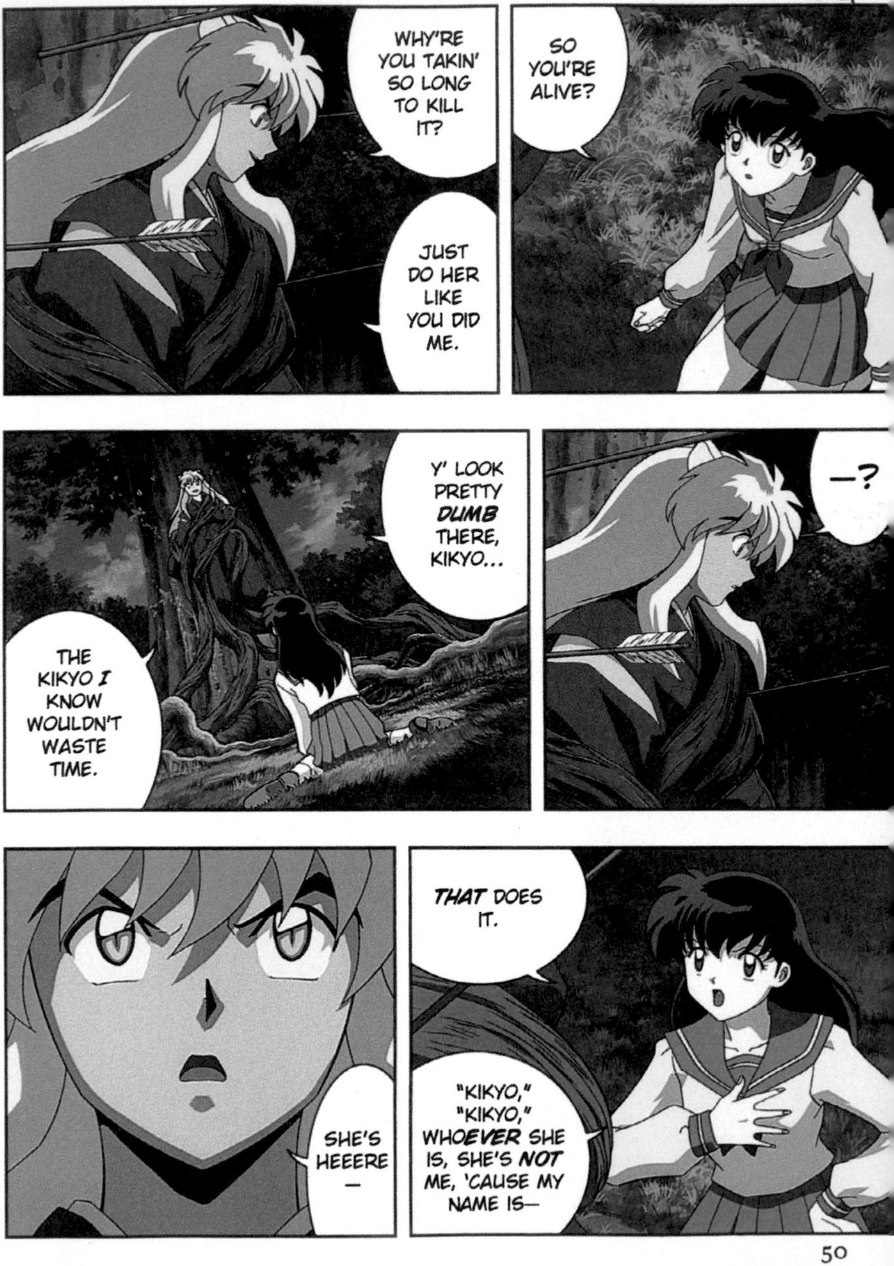
SO YOU'RE ALIVE?
WHY'RE YOU TAKIN' SO LONG TO KILL IT?
JUST DO HER LIKE YOU DID ME.
—?
Y' LOOK PRETTY **DUMB** THERE, KIKYO...
THE KIKYO *I* KNOW WOULDN'T WASTE TIME.
THAT DOES IT.
"KIKYO," "KIKYO," WHO***EVER*** SHE IS, SHE'S ***NOT*** ME, 'CAUSE MY NAME IS—
SHE'S HEEERE—

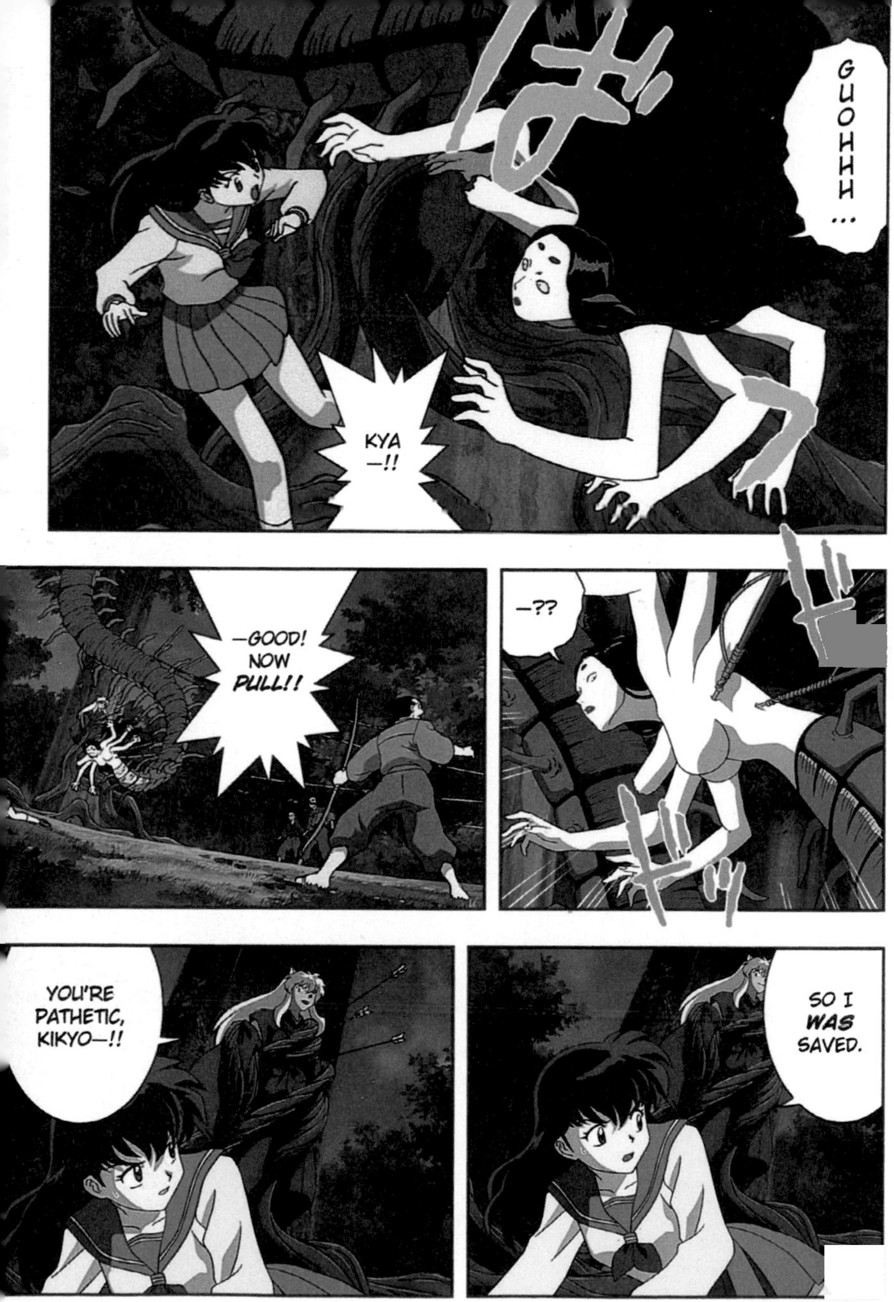
GUOHHH...
KYA—!!
—??
—GOOD! NOW PULL!!
SO I WAS SAVED.
YOU'RE PATHETIC, KIKYO—!!

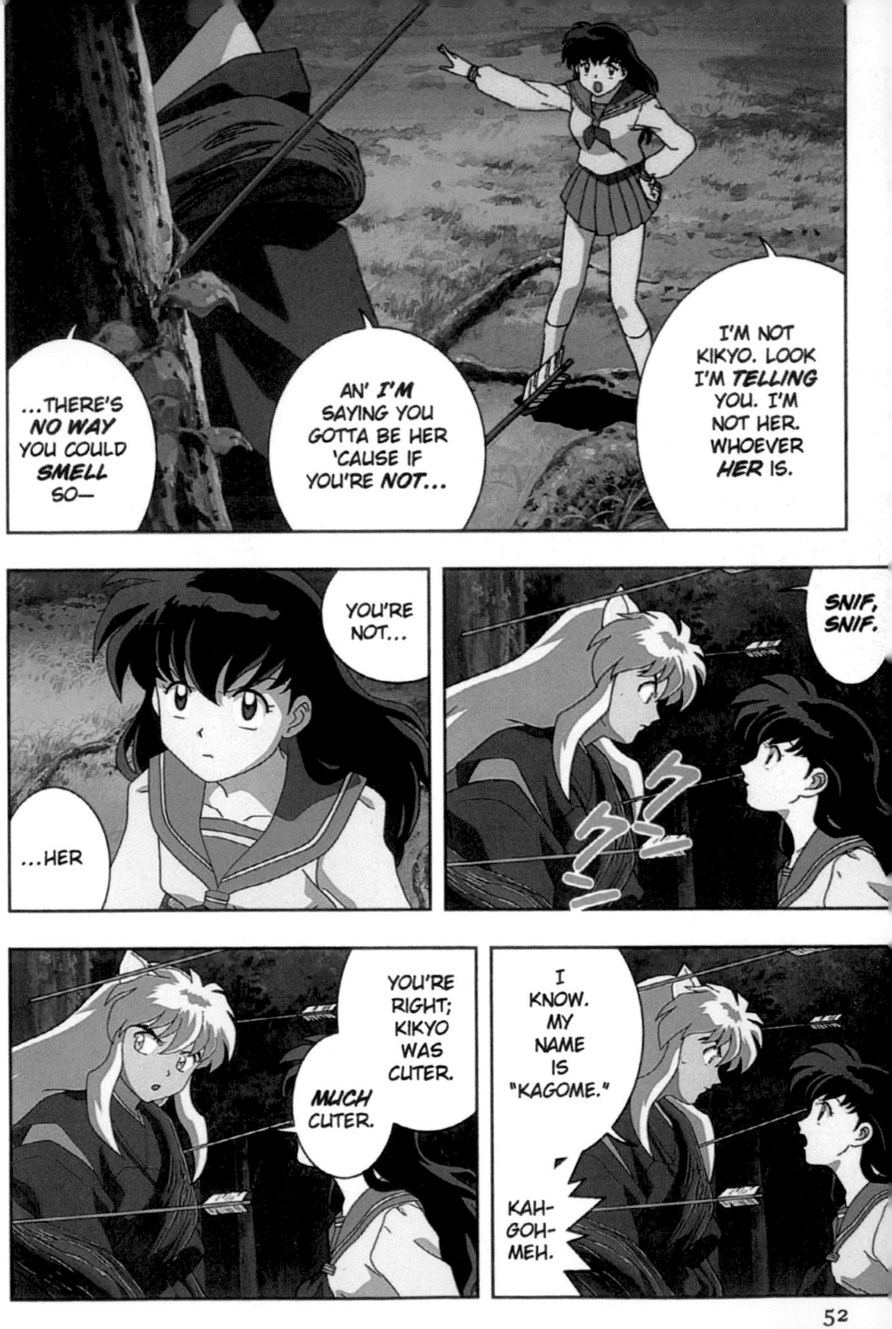
I'M NOT KIKYO. LOOK I'M *TELLING* YOU. I'M NOT HER. WHOEVER *HER* IS.
AN' *I'M* SAYING YOU GOTTA BE HER 'CAUSE IF YOU'RE *NOT*...
...THERE'S *NO WAY* YOU COULD *SMELL* SO—
SNIF, SNIF.
YOU'RE NOT...
...HER
I KNOW. MY NAME IS "KAGOME."
KAH-GOH-MEH.
YOU'RE RIGHT; KIKYO WAS CUTER.
MUCH CUTER.

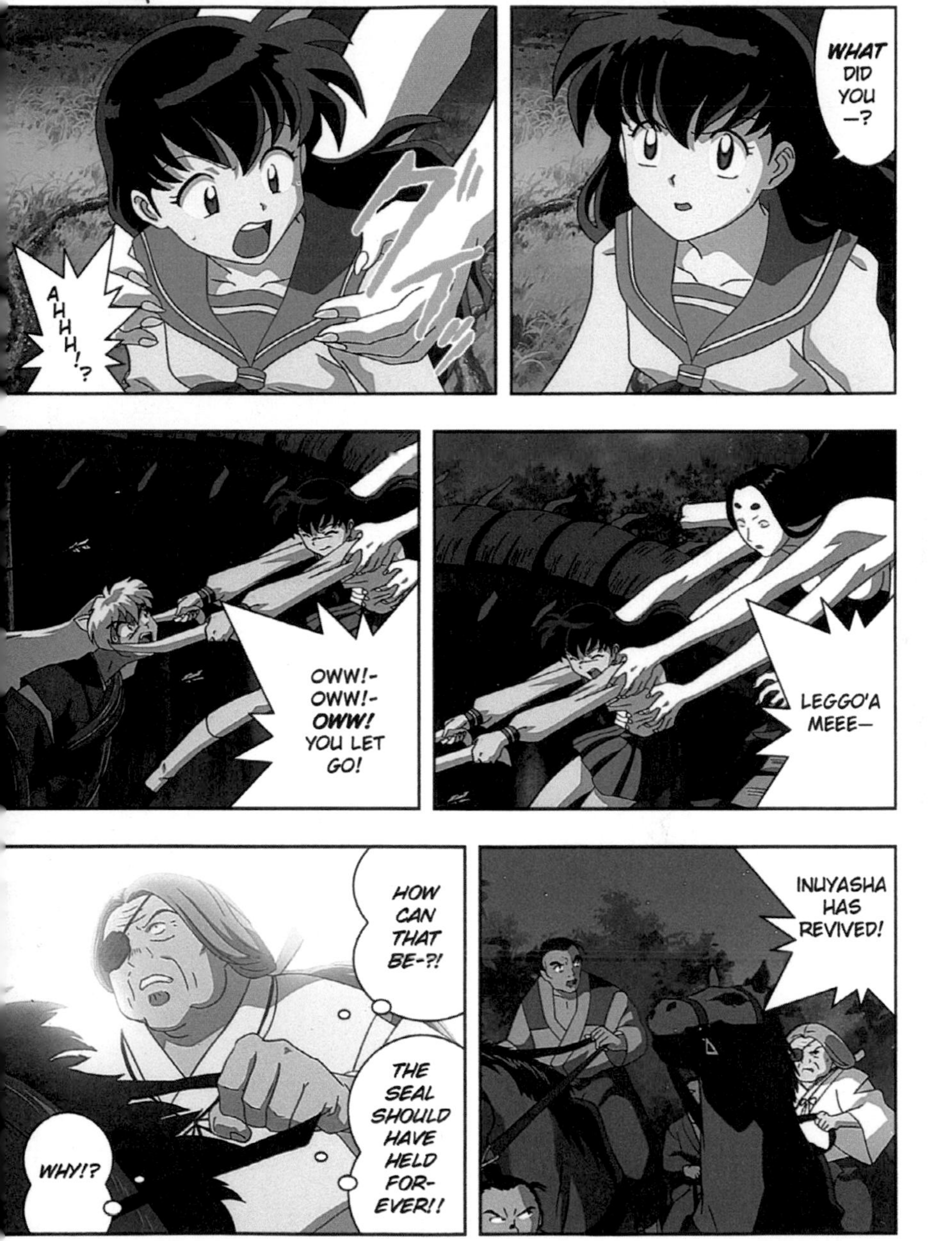
WHAT DID YOU —?
AHHH!?
LEGGO'A MEEE—
OWW!- OWW!- OWW! YOU LET GO!
INUYASHA HAS REVIVED!
HOW CAN THAT BE-?!
THE SEAL SHOULD HAVE HELD FOR-EVER!!
WHY!?

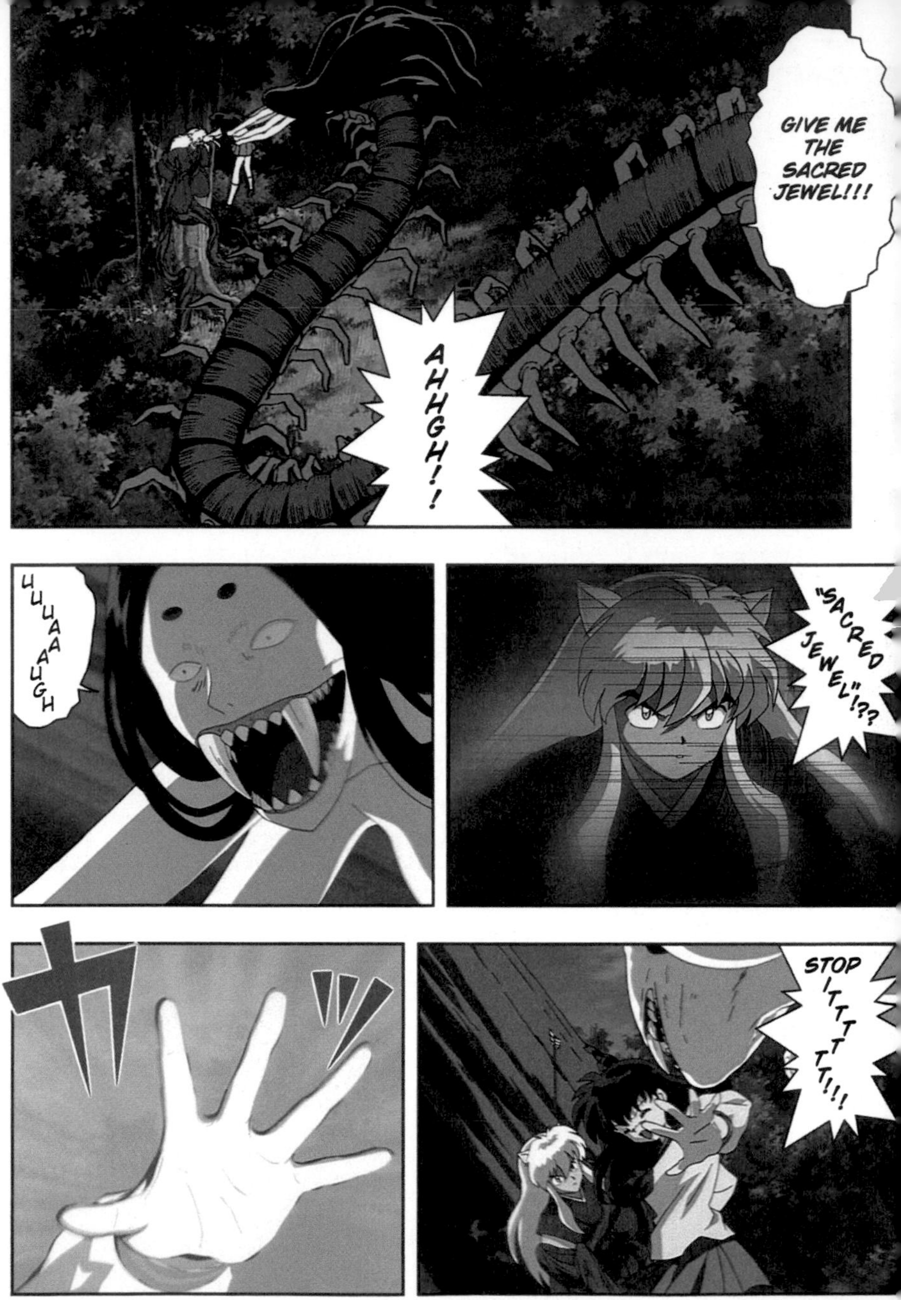
GIVE ME THE SACRED JEWEL!!!
AHHGH!!
"SACRED JEWEL"!??
UUUAAAAUGH
STOP ITTTTTTT!!!

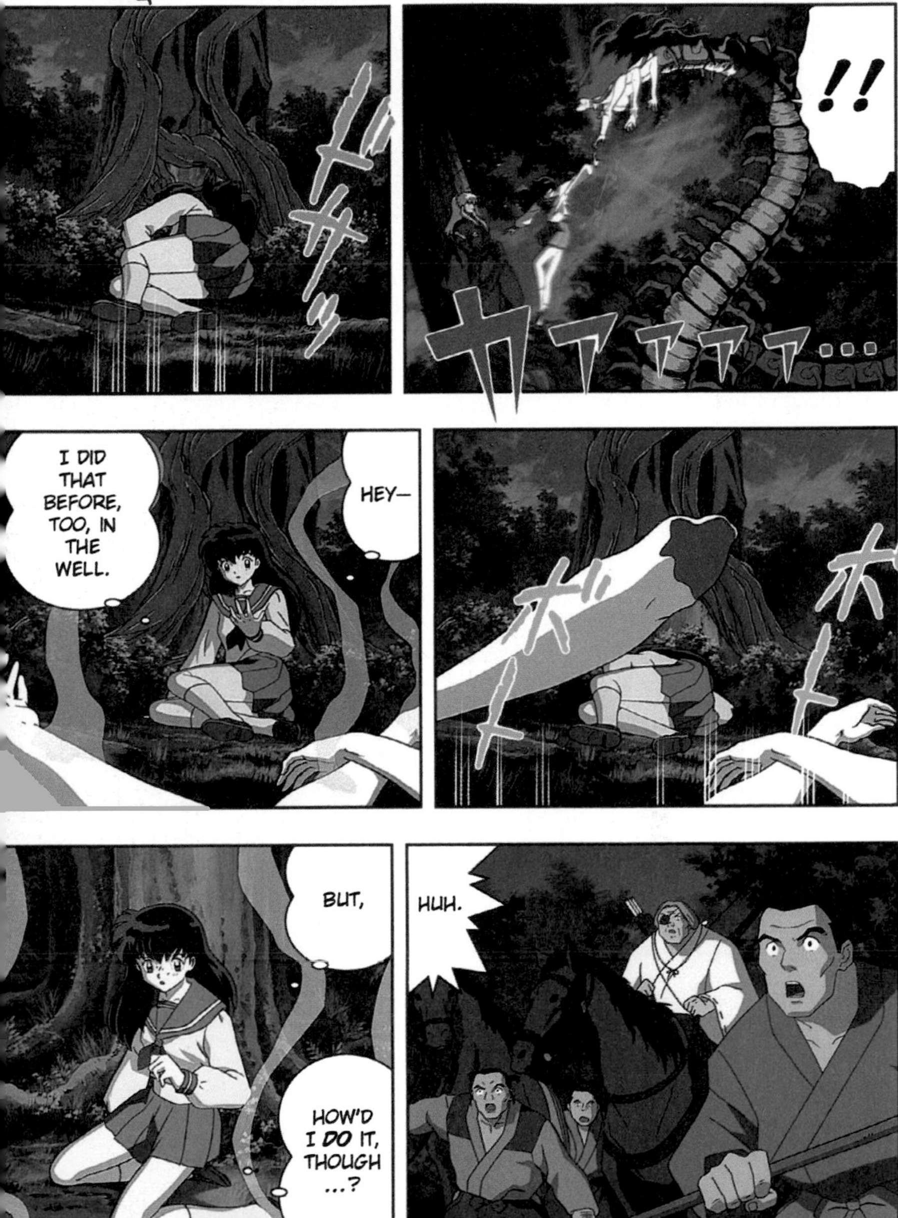
!!
カァァァァ...
ボト
ボト
HEY—
I DID THAT BEFORE, TOO, IN THE WELL.
HUH.
BUT,
HOW'D I *DO* IT, THOUGH ...?

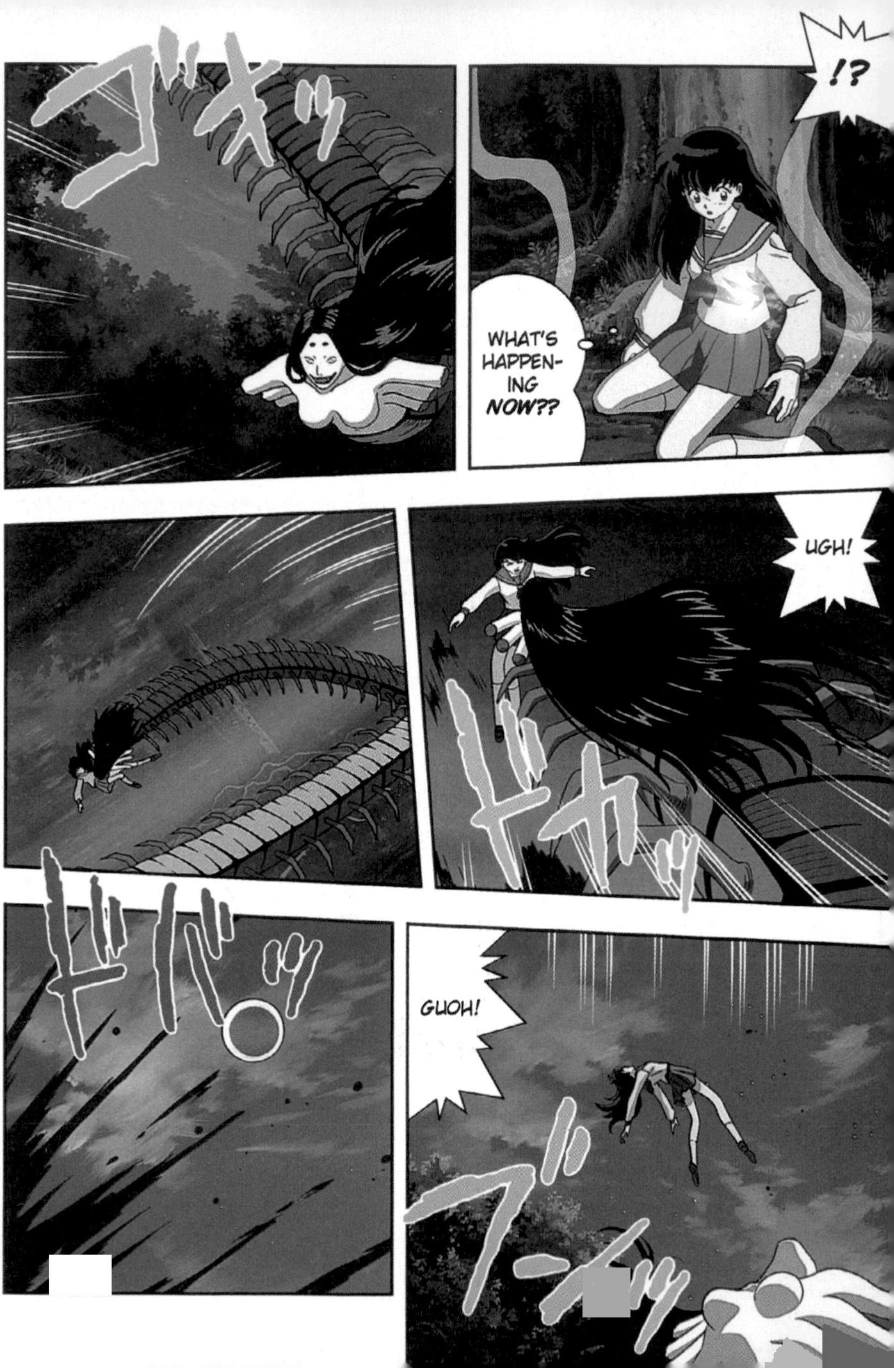
!?
WHAT'S HAPPENING NOW??
UGH!
GUOH!

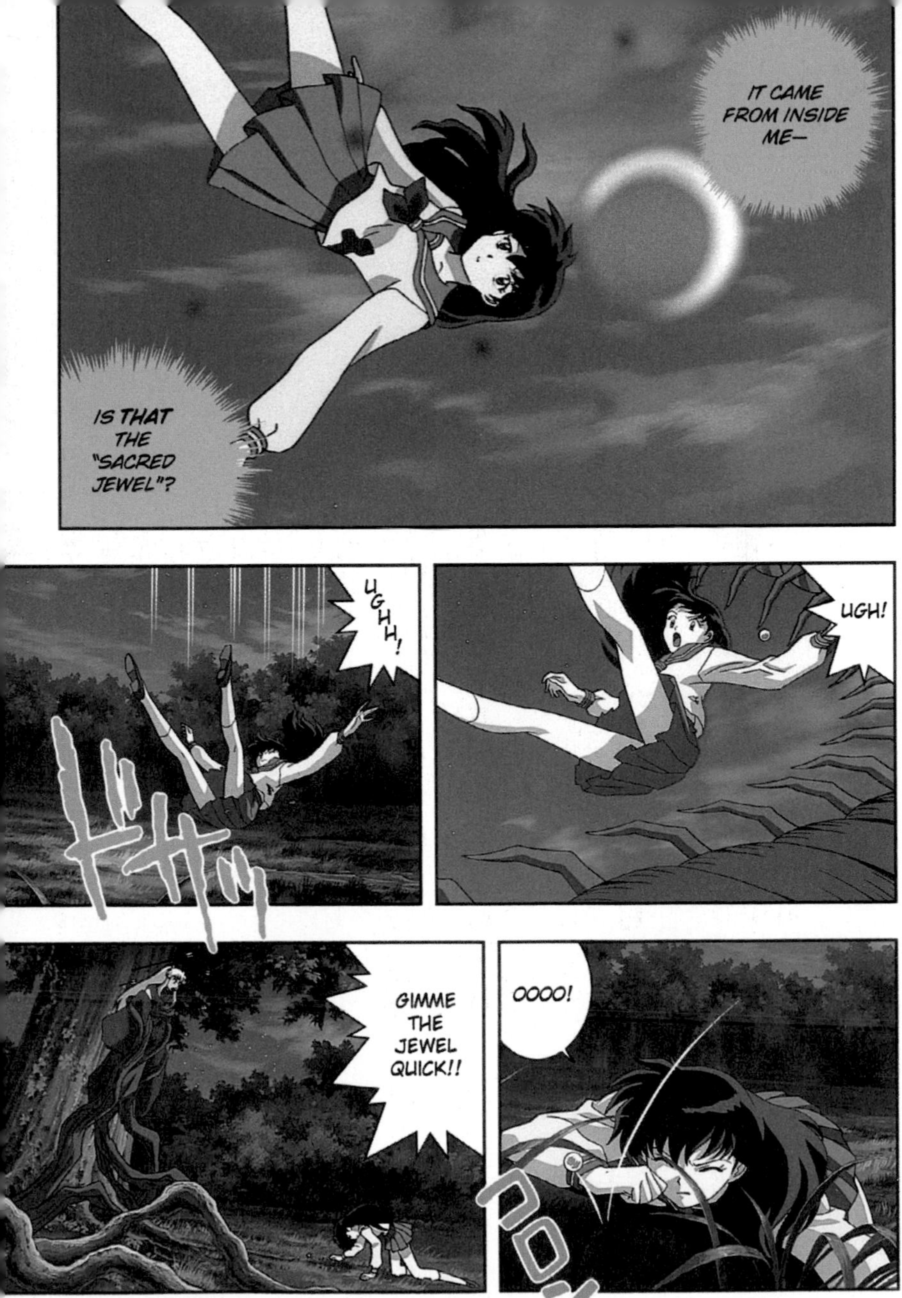
IT CAME FROM INSIDE ME—
IS THAT THE "SACRED JEWEL"?
UGH!
UGHH!
OOOO!
GIMME THE JEWEL QUICK!!

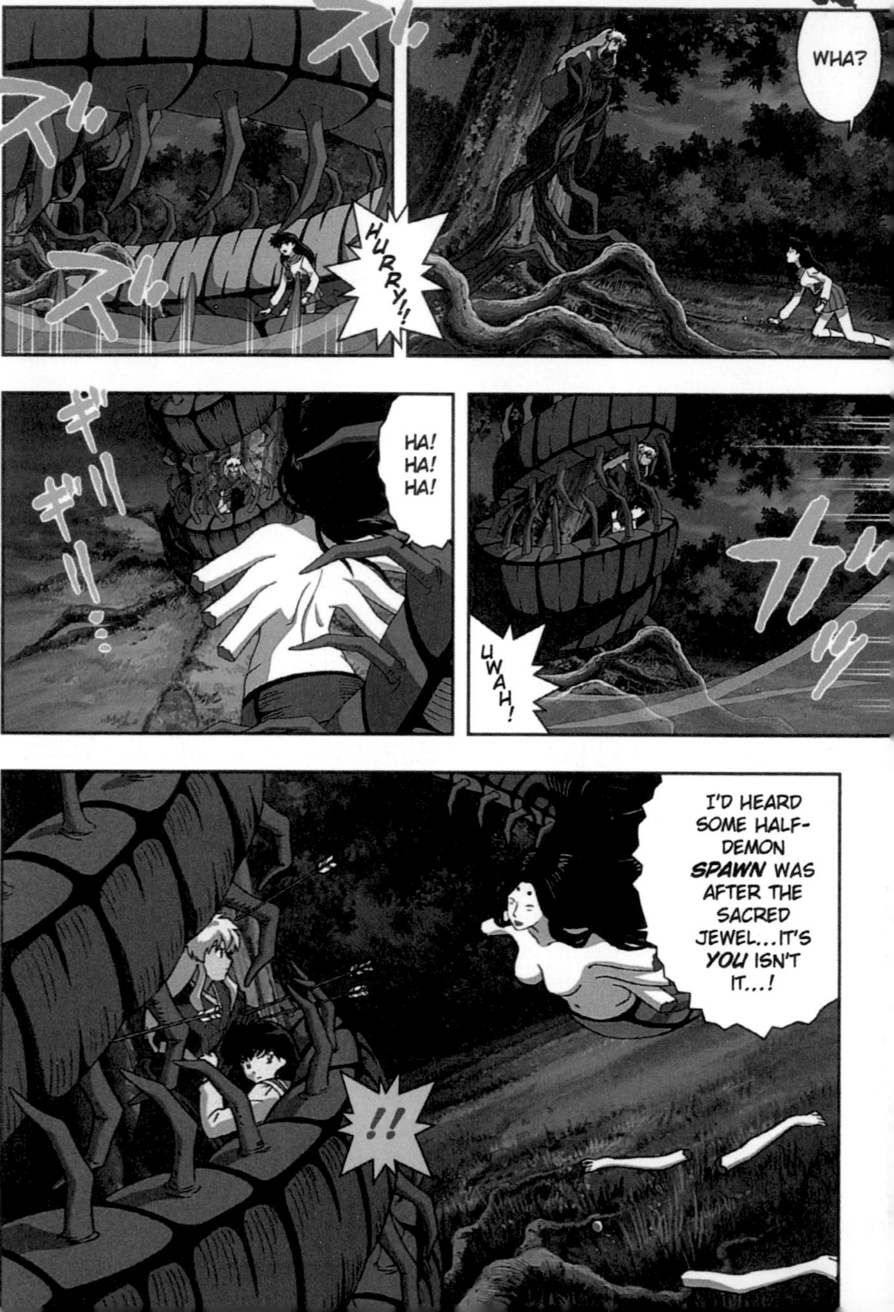
WHA?
HURRY!!
UWAH!
ガッ
HA! HA! HA!
ギリギリ…
I'D HEARD SOME HALF-DEMON SPAWN WAS AFTER THE SACRED JEWEL…IT'S YOU ISN'T IT…!
!!

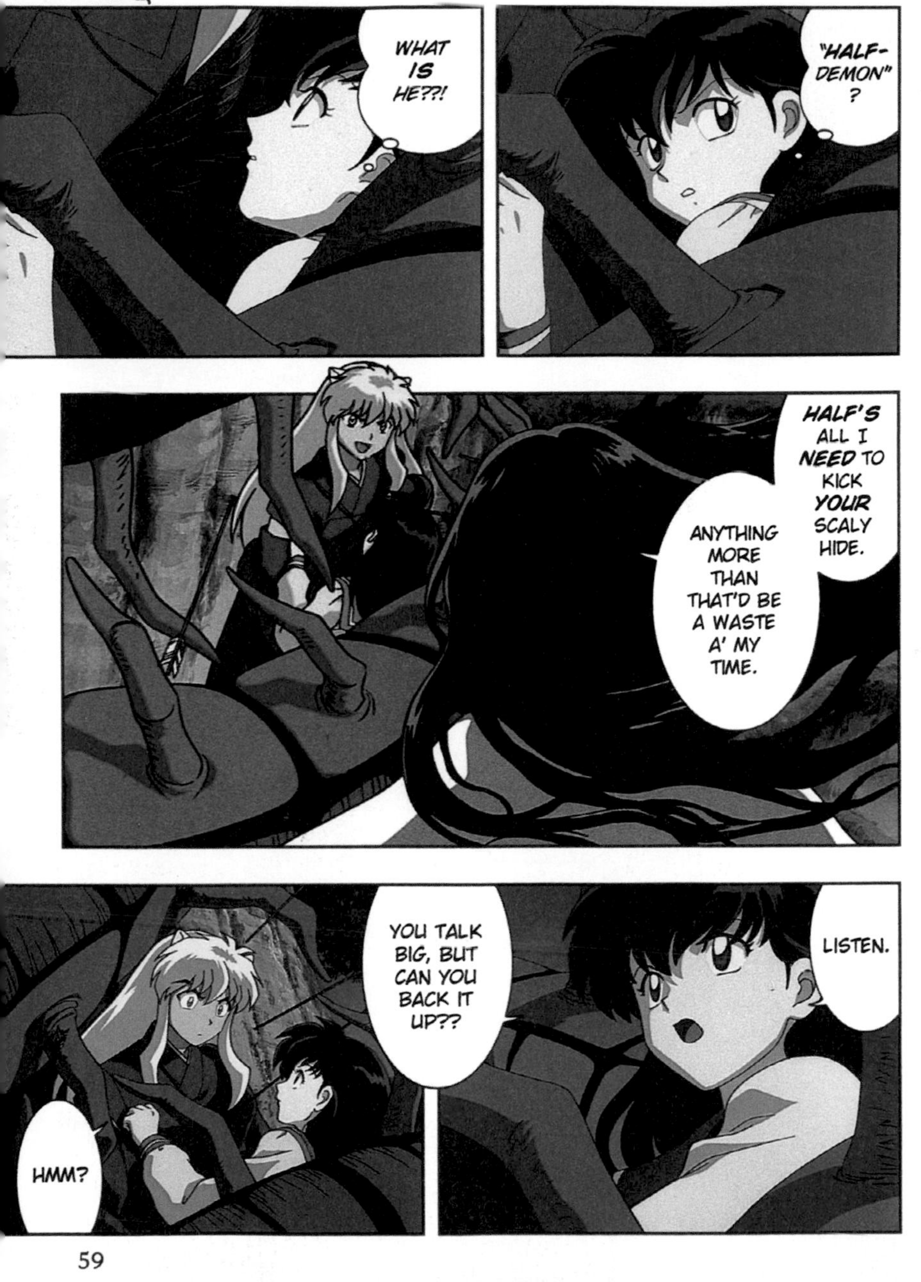
"HALF-DEMON"?
WHAT IS HE??!
HALF'S ALL I NEED TO KICK YOUR SCALY HIDE.
ANYTHING MORE THAN THAT'D BE A WASTE A' MY TIME.
LISTEN.
YOU TALK BIG, BUT CAN YOU BACK IT UP??
HMM?

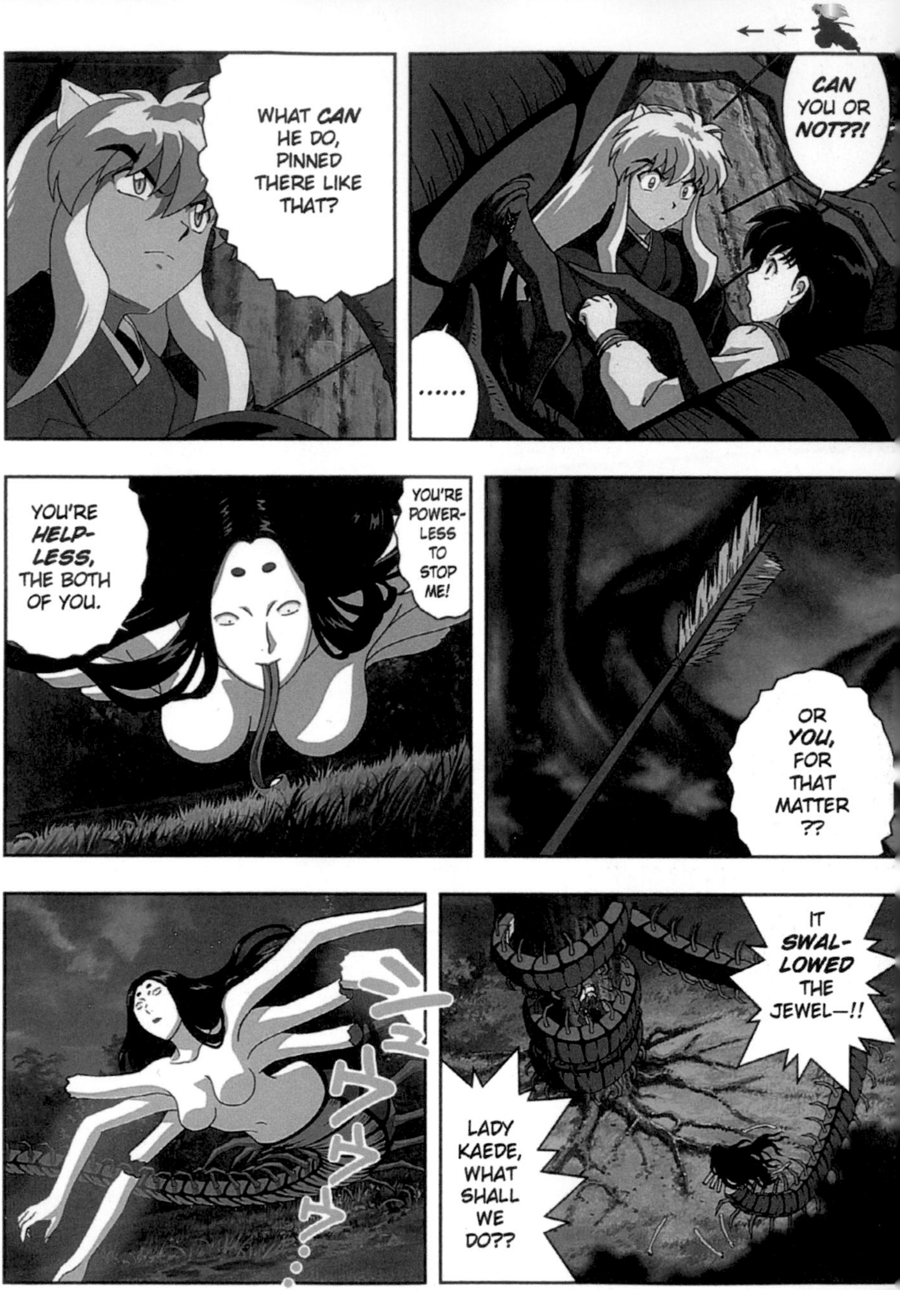
CAN YOU OR NOT??!
......
WHAT CAN HE DO, PINNED THERE LIKE THAT?
OR YOU, FOR THAT MATTER ??
YOU'RE POWERLESS TO STOP ME!
YOU'RE HELPLESS, THE BOTH OF YOU.
IT SWALLOWED THE JEWEL—!!
LADY KAEDE, WHAT SHALL WE DO??

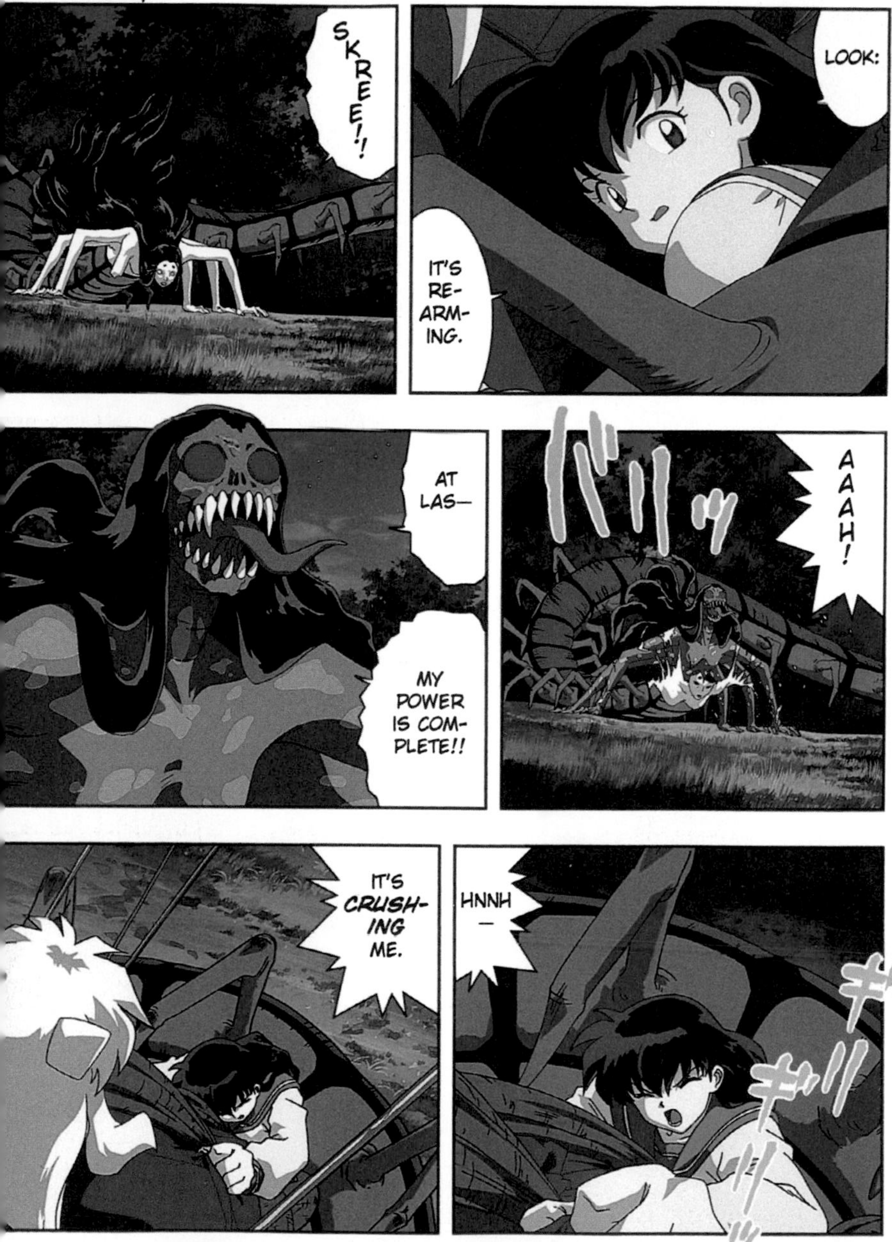
LOOK:
IT'S RE-ARMING.
SKREE!!
バリッ
AAAAH!
AT LAS—
MY POWER IS COMPLETE!!
HNNH—
ギリギリ
IT'S *CRUSHING* ME.

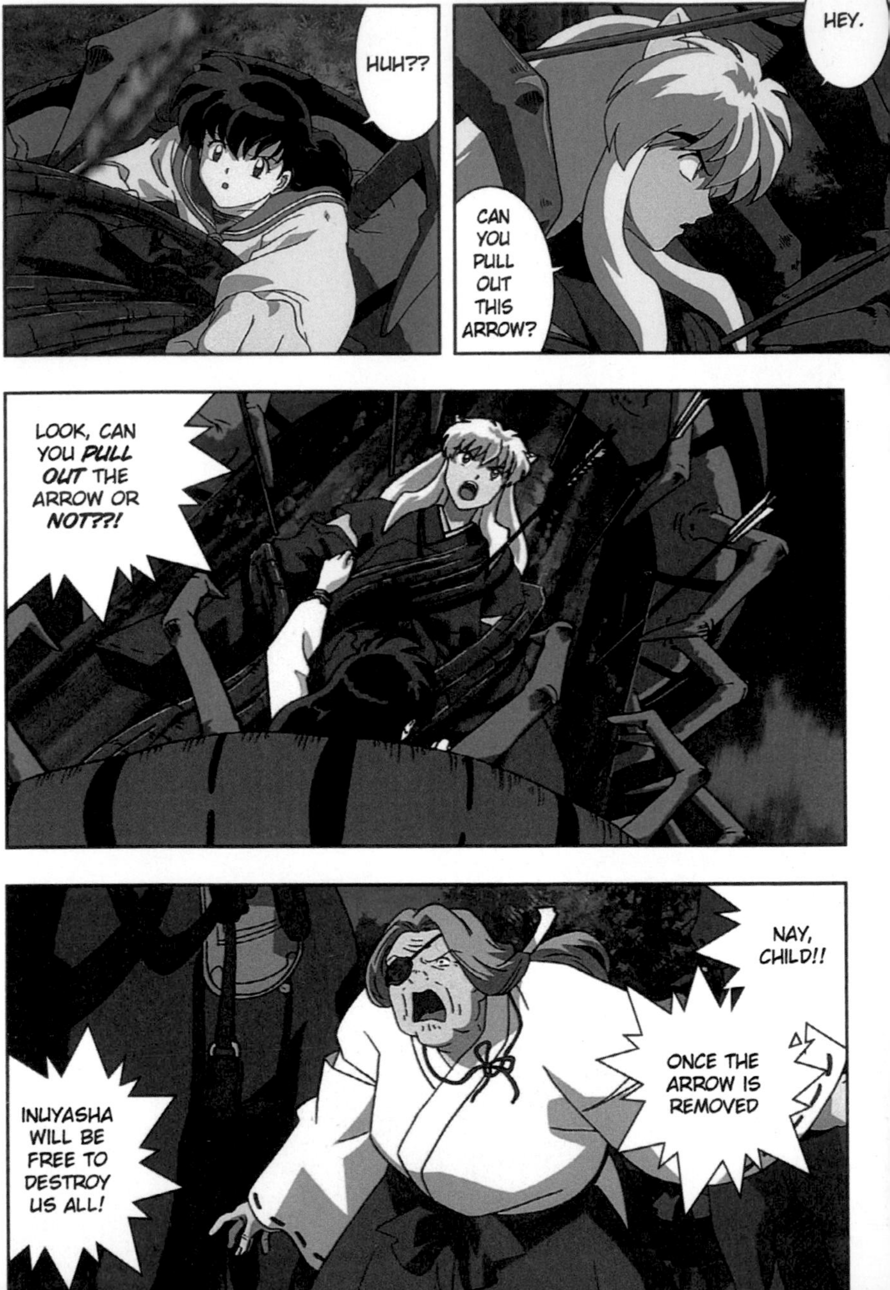
HEY.
CAN YOU PULL OUT THIS ARROW?
HUH??
LOOK, CAN YOU PULL OUT THE ARROW OR NOT??!
NAY, CHILD!!
ONCE THE ARROW IS REMOVED
INUYASHA WILL BE FREE TO DESTROY US ALL!

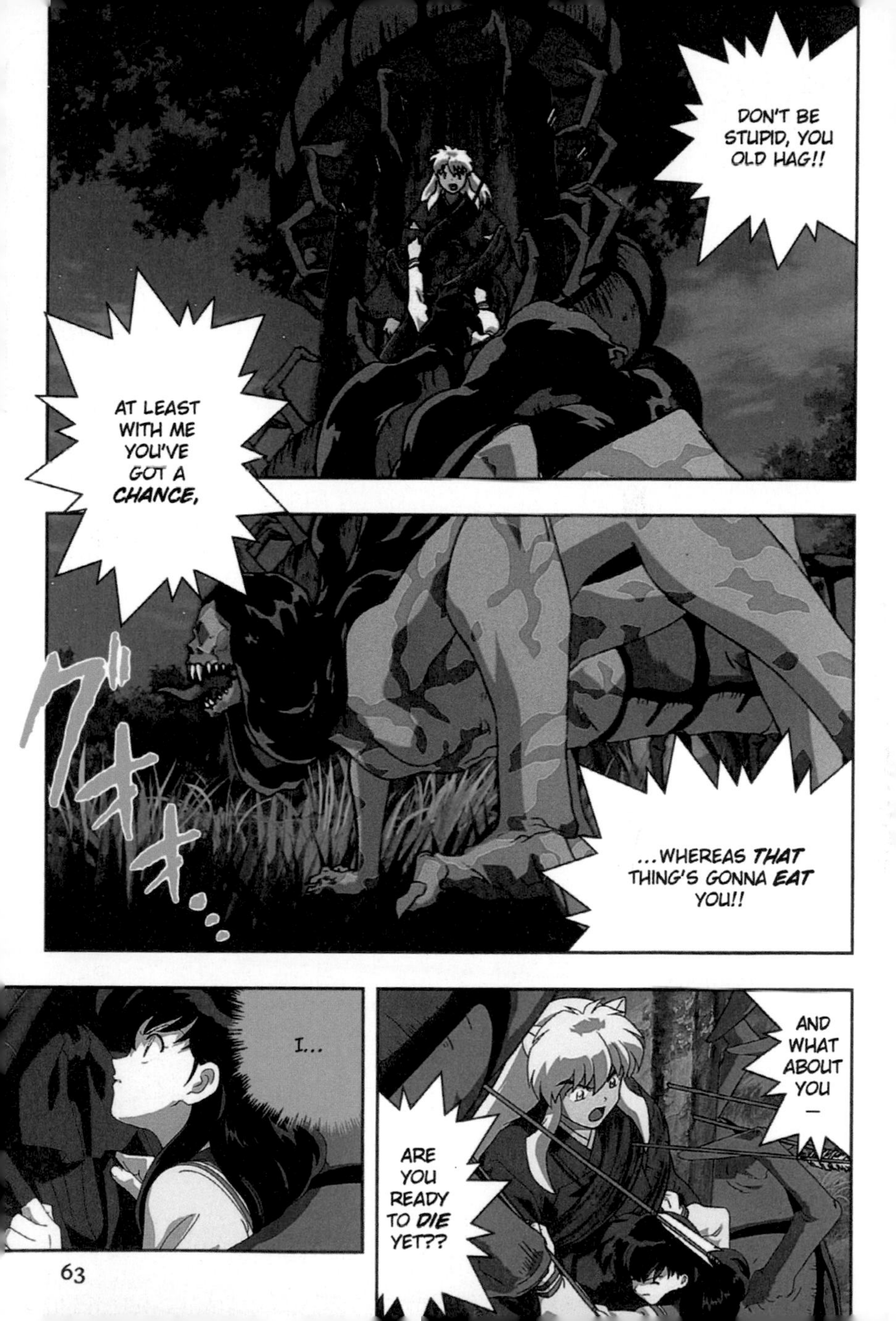
DON'T BE STUPID, YOU OLD HAG!!
AT LEAST WITH ME YOU'VE GOT A *CHANCE,*
...WHEREAS *THAT* THING'S GONNA *EAT* YOU!!
グォォ...
AND WHAT ABOUT YOU —
ARE YOU READY TO *DIE* YET??
I...

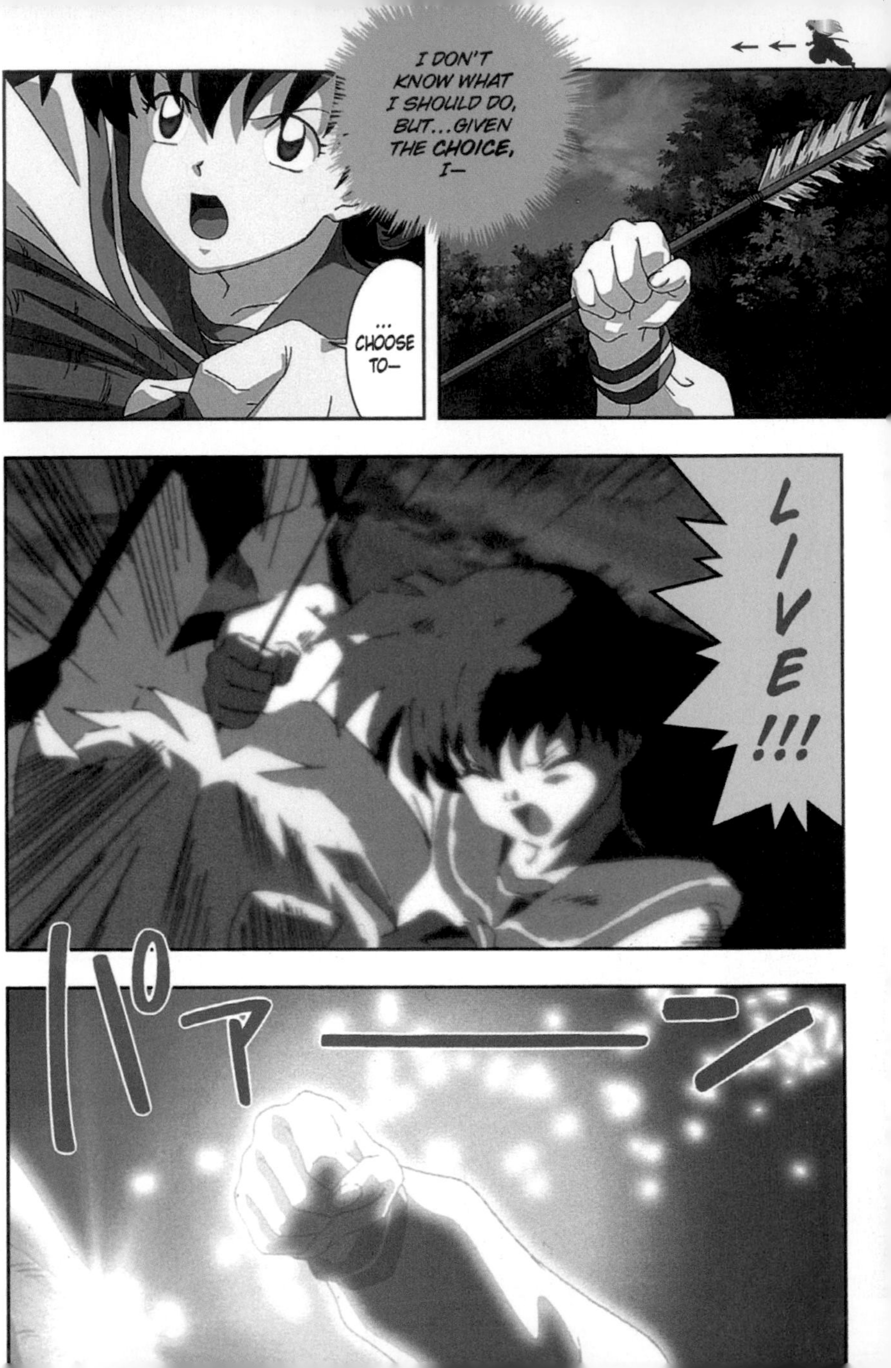
I DON'T KNOW WHAT I SHOULD DO, BUT...GIVEN THE CHOICE, I—
...CHOOSE TO—
LIVE!!!
パァーーーン

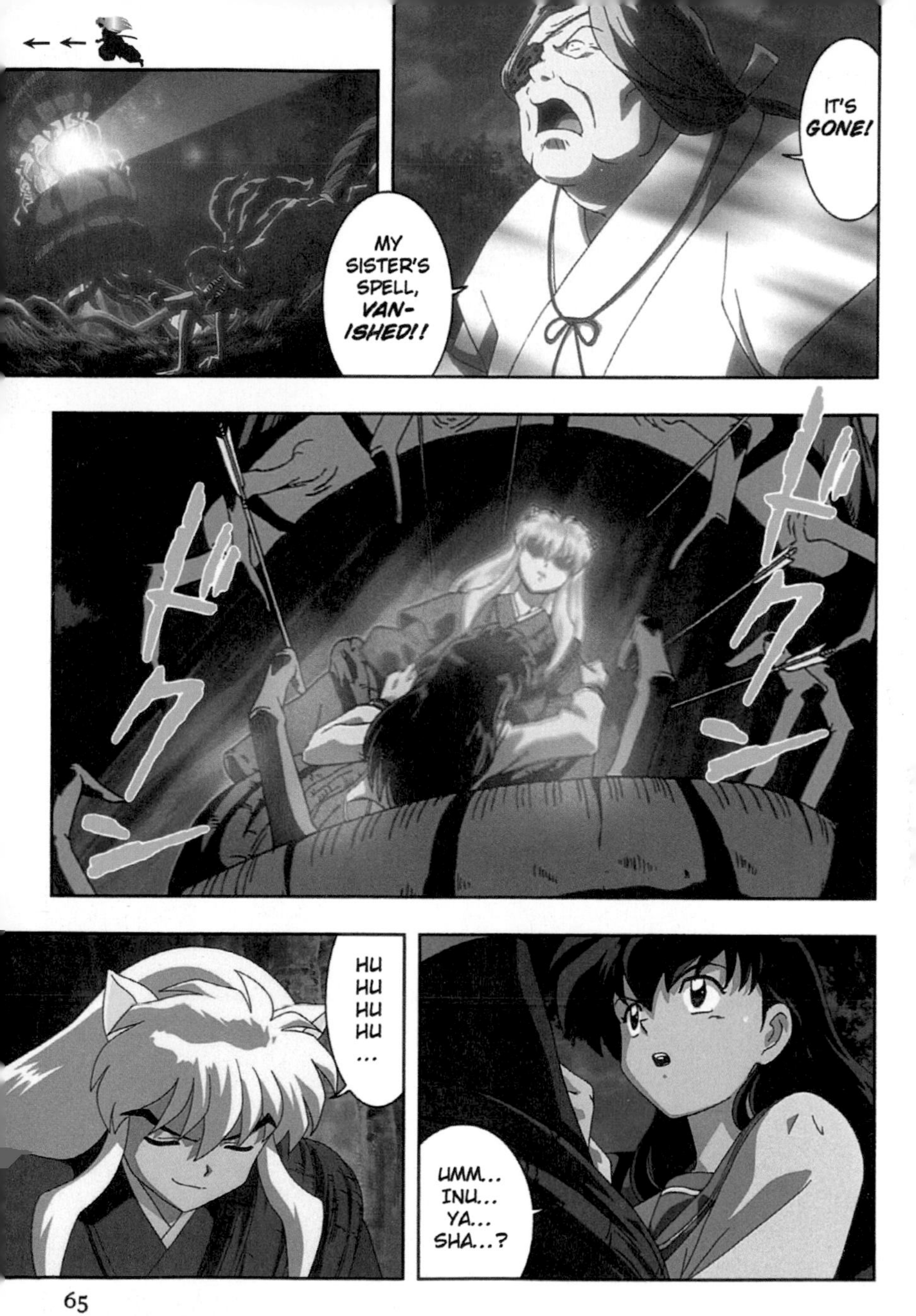
IT'S GONE!
MY SISTER'S SPELL, VAN-ISHED!!
ドクン
ドクン
UMM.. INU... YA... SHA...?
HU HU HU HU ...

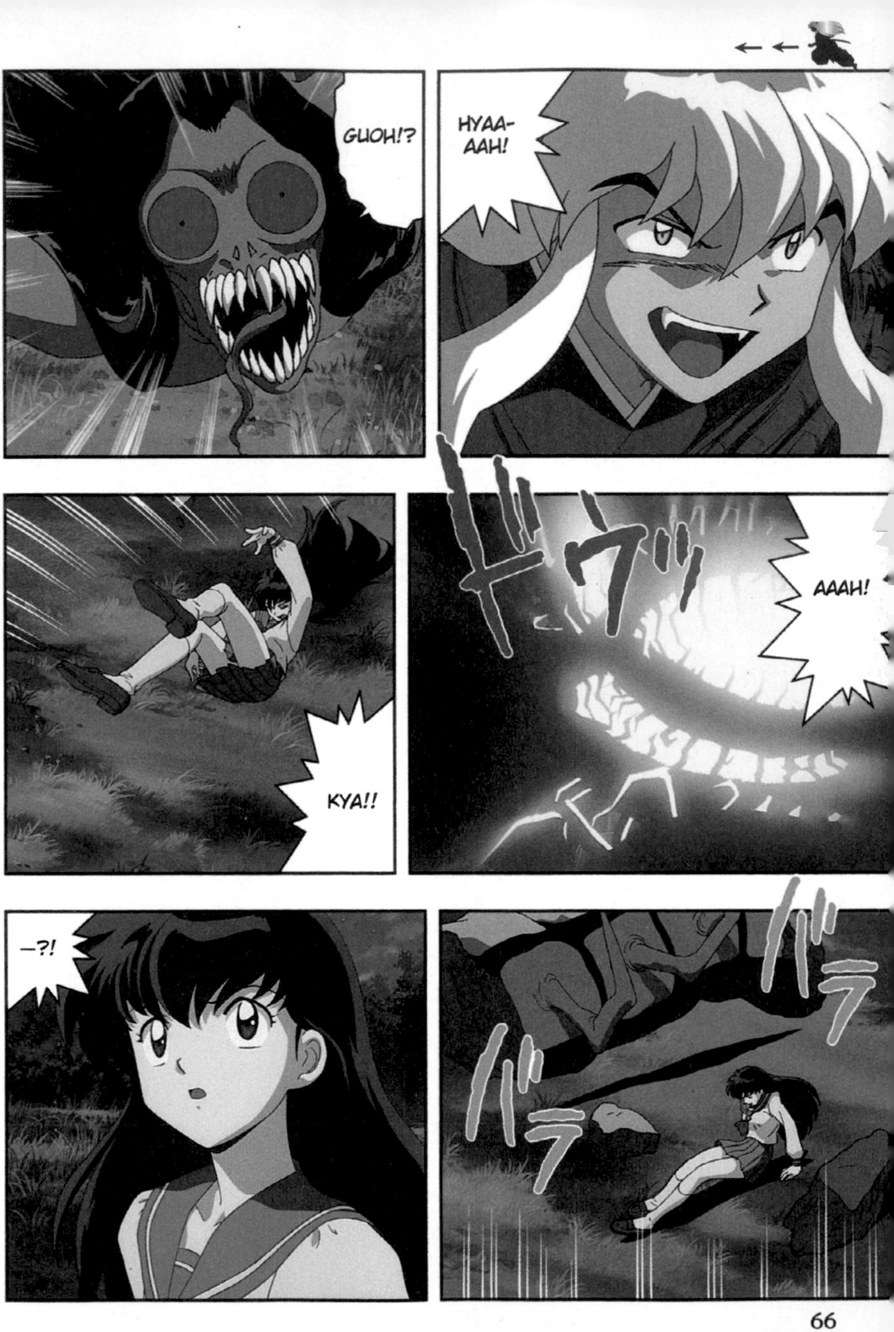
HYAA-AAH!
GUOH!?
ドウッ
AAAH!
KYA!!
バラ
バラ
—?!

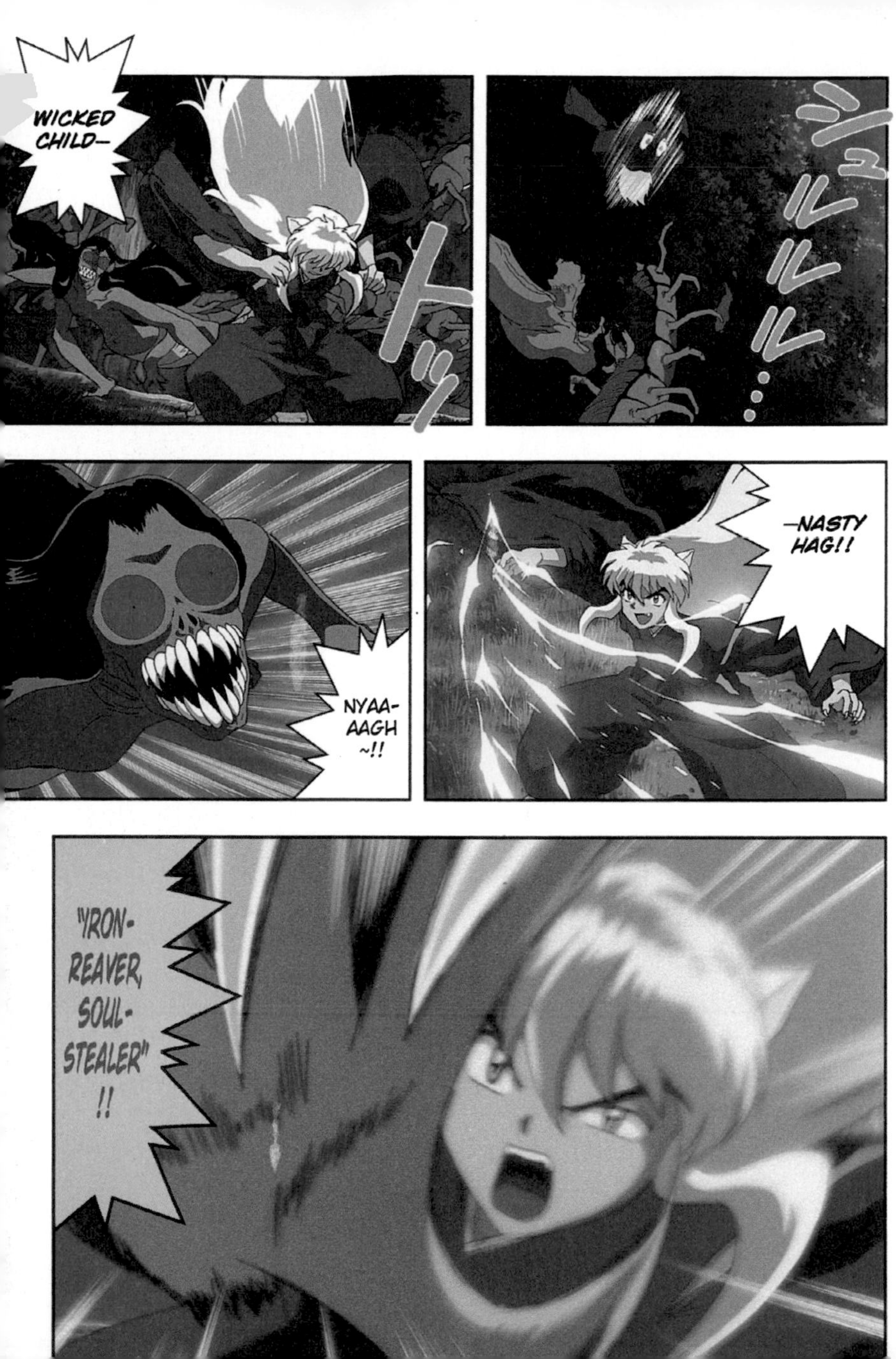
シュルルル…
WICKED CHILD—
トッ
—NASTY HAG!!
NYAA-AAGH ~!!
"IRON-REAVER, SOUL-STEALER" !!

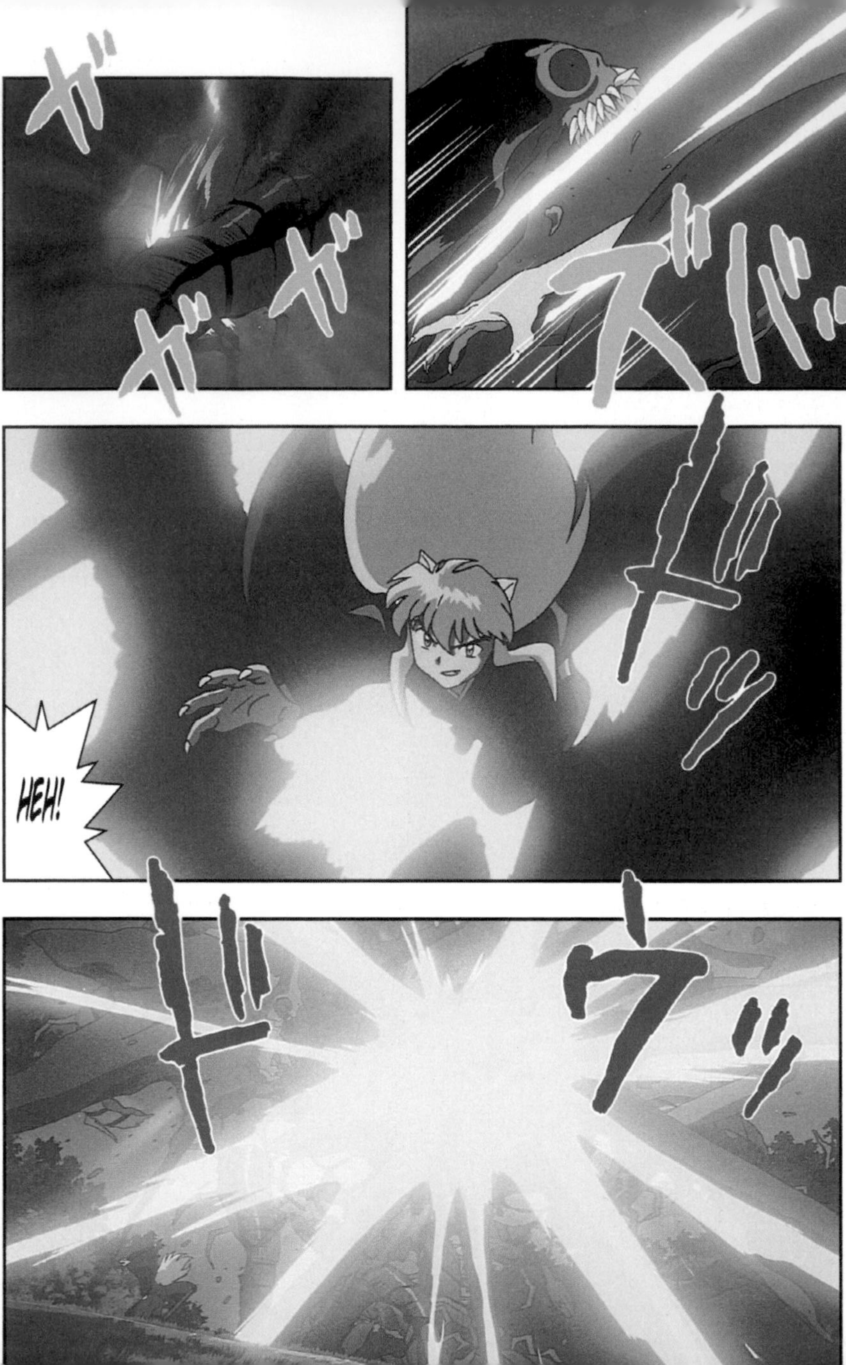
ズバッ
ガガガ
ドッ
HEH!
ドウッ

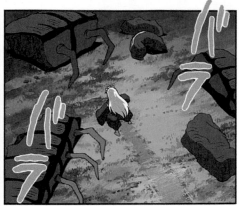

HE *IS* STRONG.

WELL, NOW I KNOW.

IT'S STILL MOVING !!

AAAH!

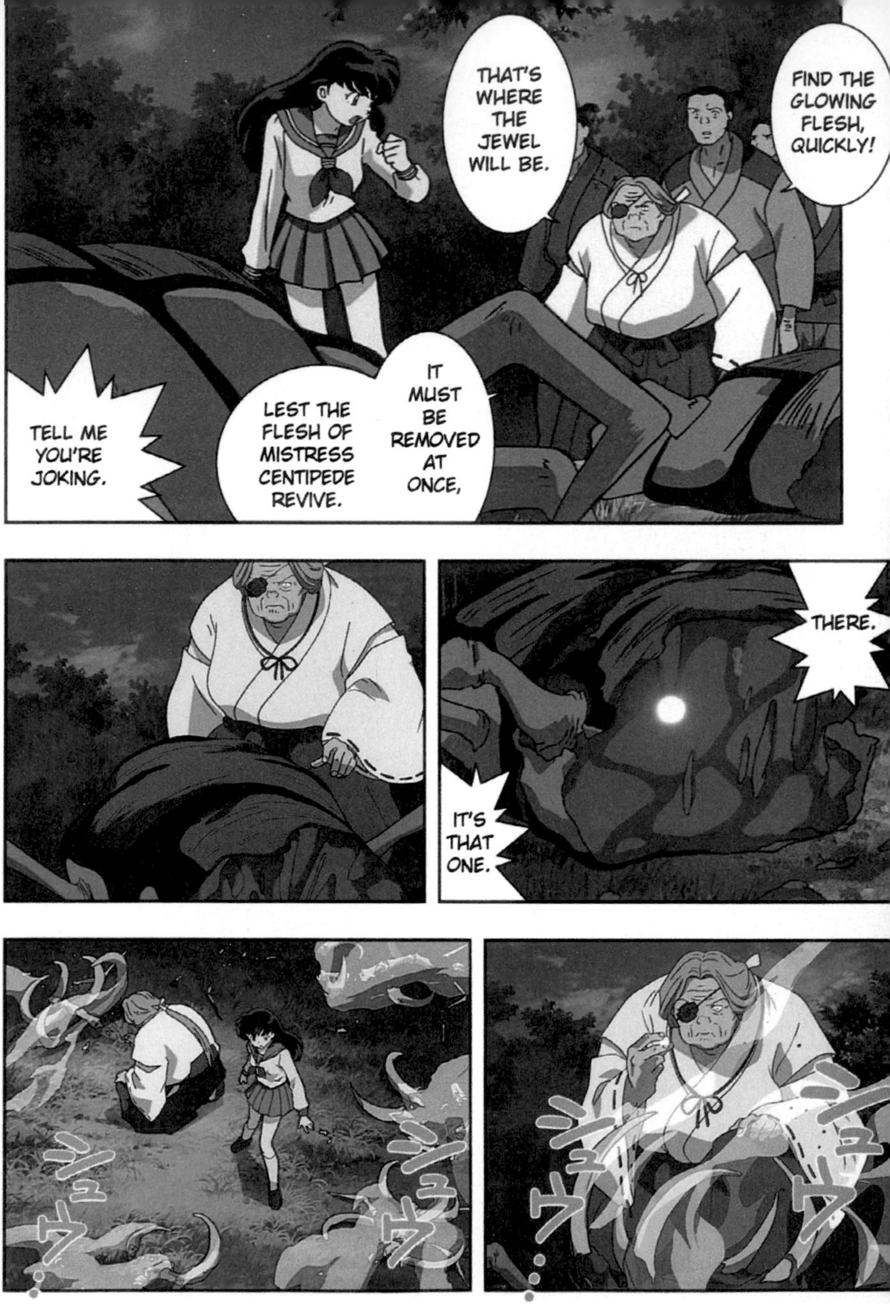
FIND THE GLOWING FLESH, QUICKLY!
THAT'S WHERE THE JEWEL WILL BE.
IT MUST BE REMOVED AT ONCE,
LEST THE FLESH OF MISTRESS CENTIPEDE REVIVE.
TELL ME YOU'RE JOKING.
THERE.
IT'S THAT ONE.
シュウ…
シュウ…
シュウ…
シュウ…

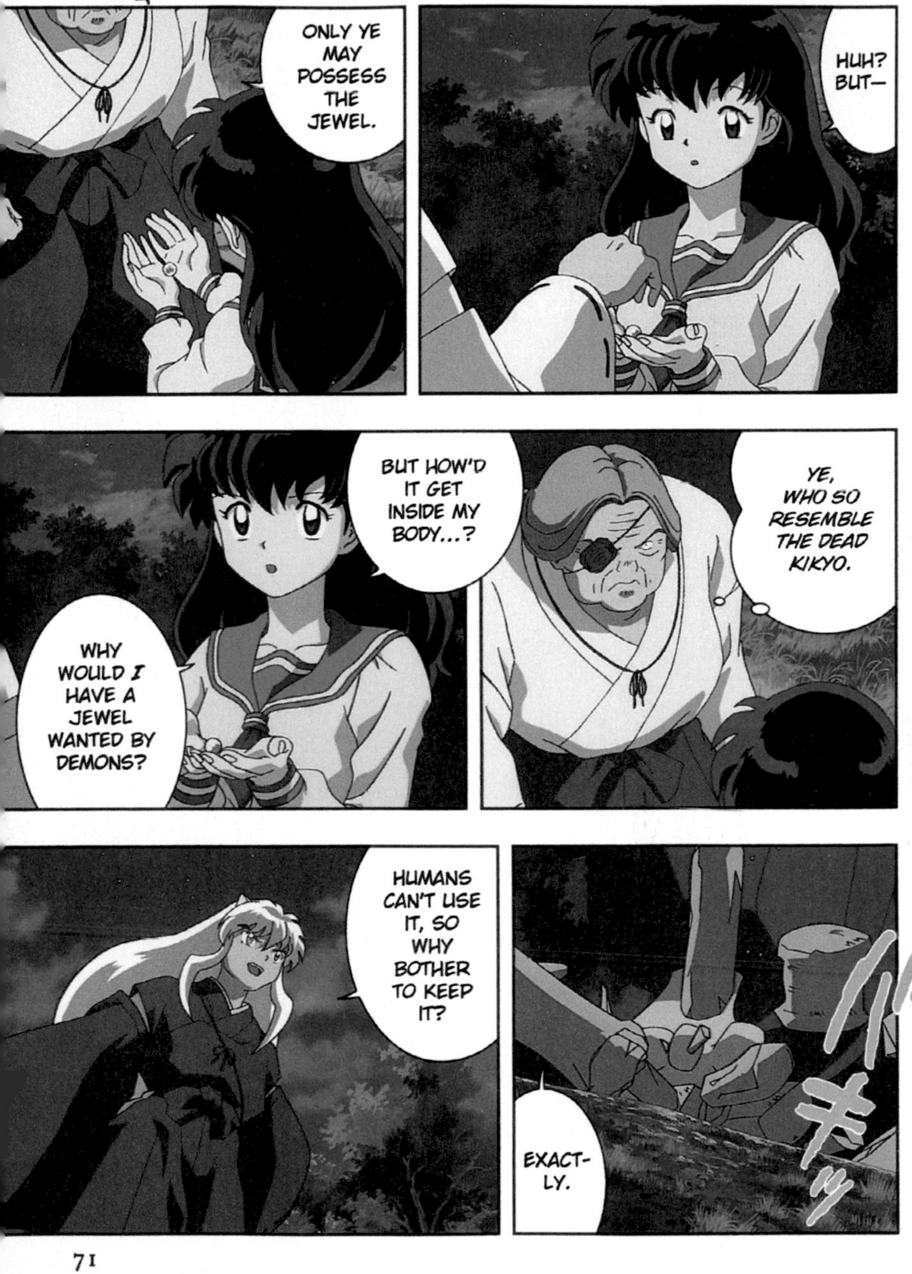
HUH? BUT—
ONLY YE MAY POSSESS THE JEWEL.
YE, WHO SO RESEMBLE THE DEAD KIKYO.
BUT HOW'D IT GET INSIDE MY BODY...?
WHY WOULD I HAVE A JEWEL WANTED BY DEMONS?
EXACT-LY.
HUMANS CAN'T USE IT, SO WHY BOTHER TO KEEP IT?

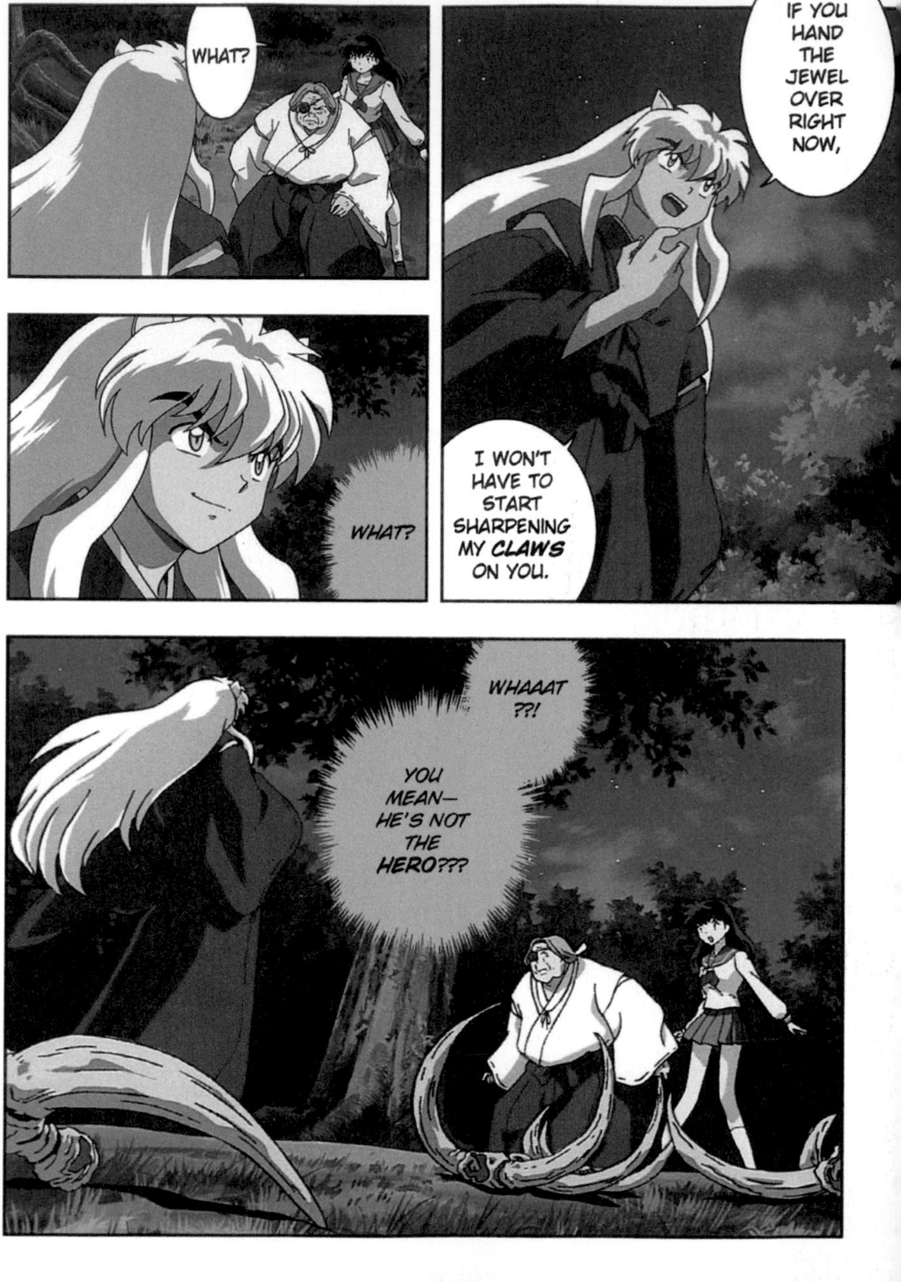
IF YOU HAND THE JEWEL OVER RIGHT NOW,
I WON'T HAVE TO START SHARPENING MY **CLAWS** ON YOU.
WHAT?
WHAT?
WHAAAT ??!
YOU MEAN— HE'S NOT THE **HERO**???

2
Seekers of the Sacred Jewel

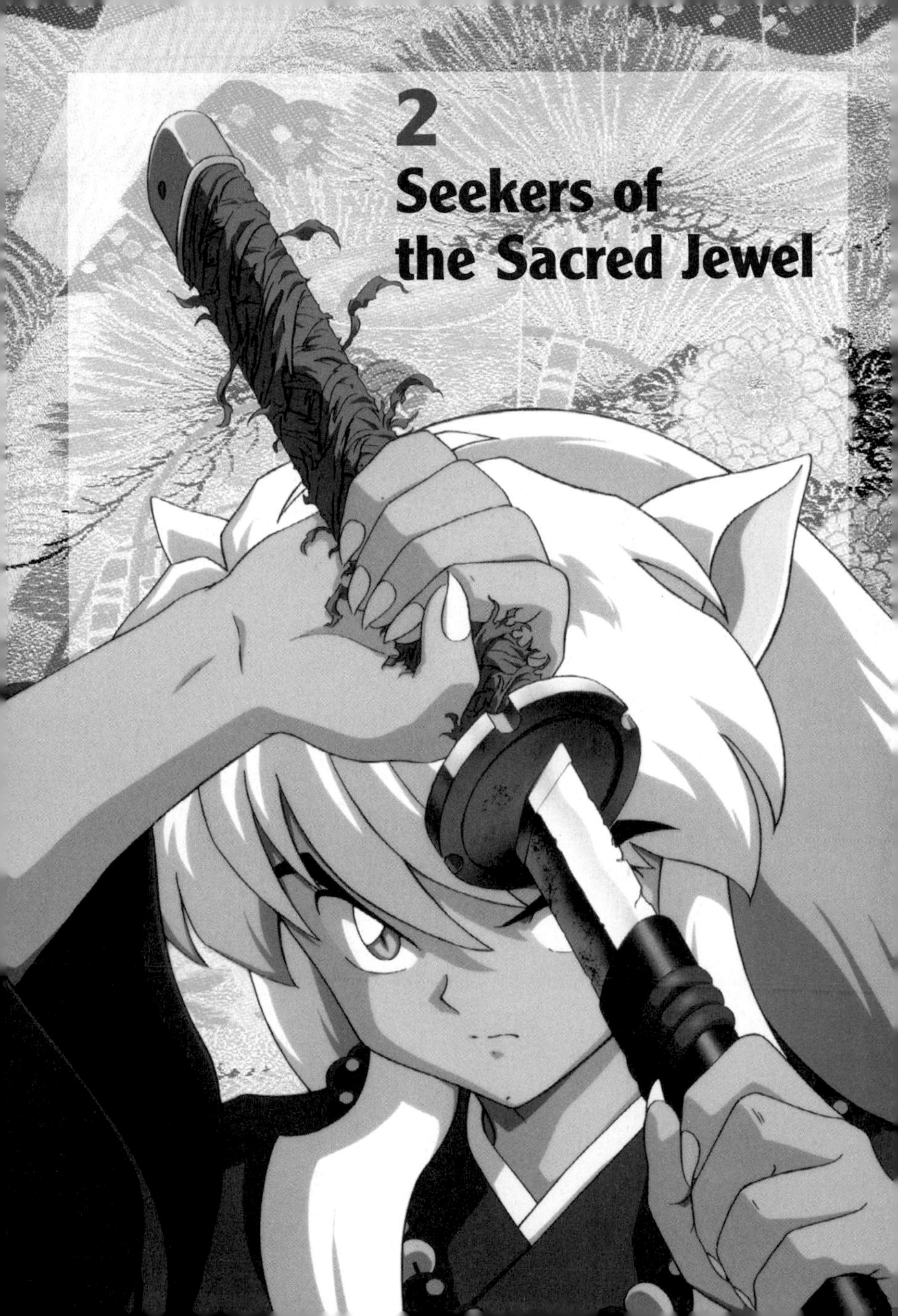

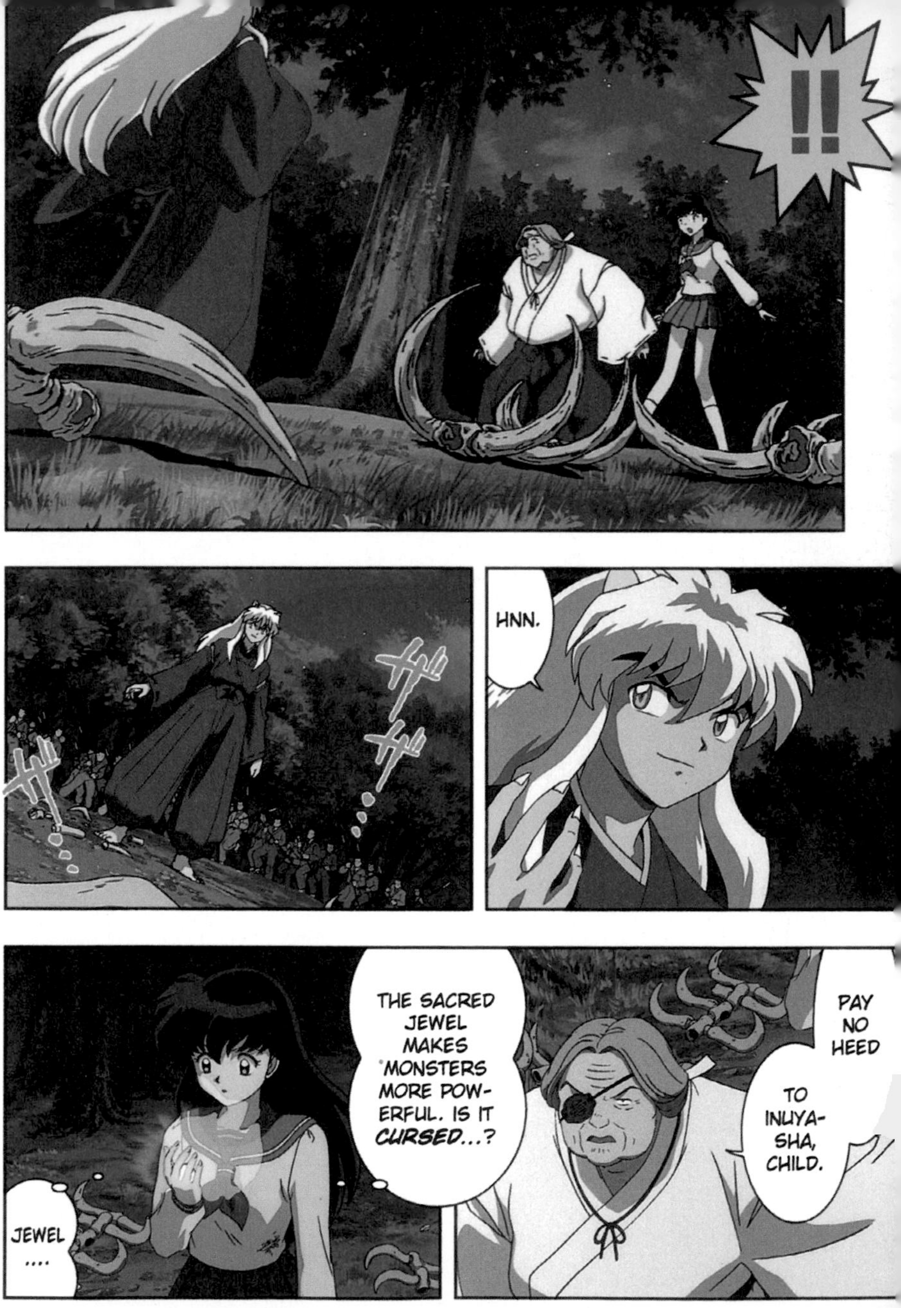
!!
HNN.
PAY NO HEED TO INUYA-SHA, CHILD.
THE SACRED JEWEL MAKES MONSTERS MORE POW-ERFUL. IS IT CURSED...?
JEWEL ....

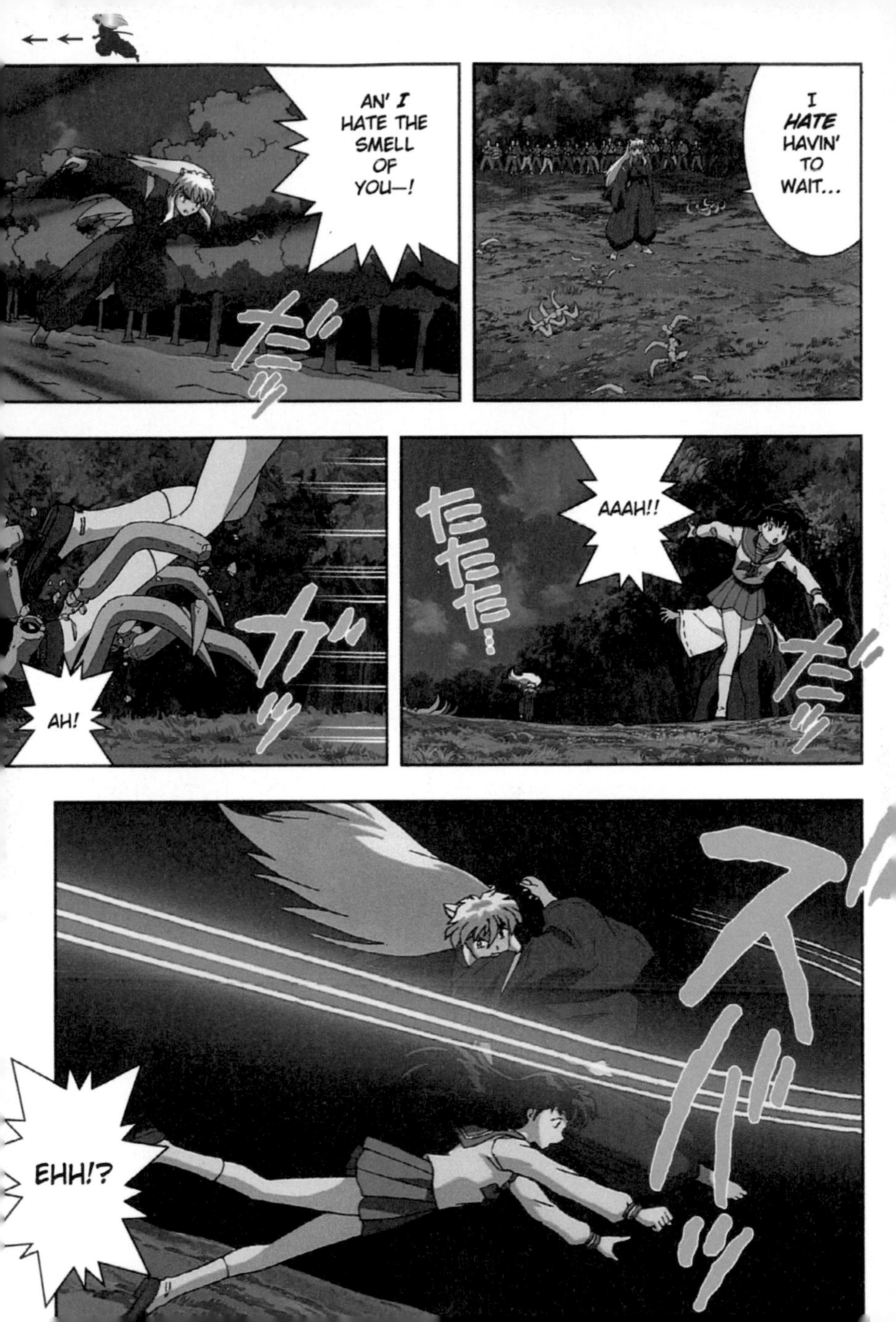
I HATE HAVIN' TO WAIT...
AN' I HATE THE SMELL OF YOU—!
だッ
AAAH!!
たたた…
だッ
ガッ
AH!
ズザッ
EHH!?

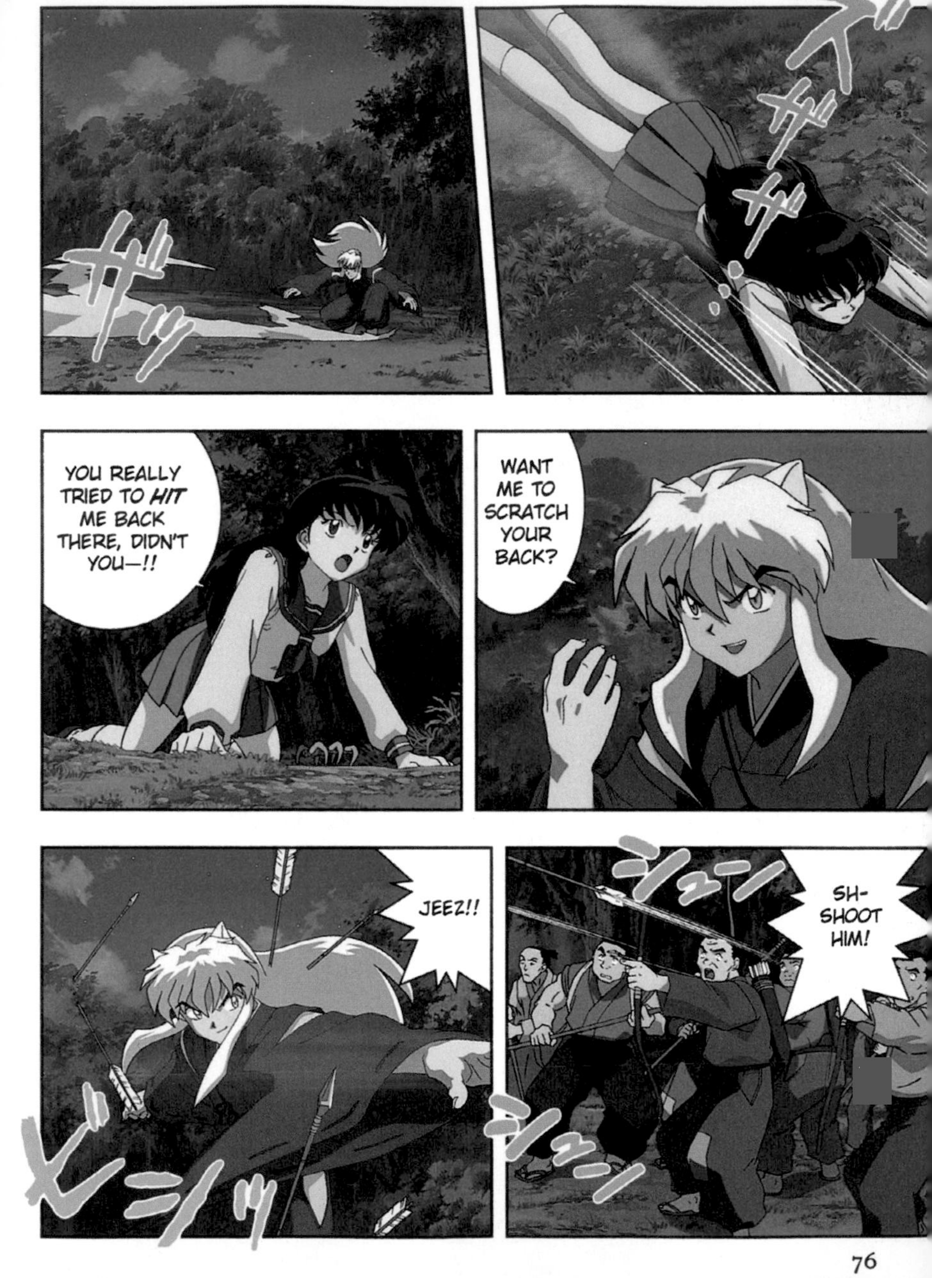
WANT ME TO SCRATCH YOUR BACK?
YOU REALLY TRIED TO *HIT* ME BACK THERE, DIDN'T YOU—!!
SH- SHOOT HIM!
JEEZ!!

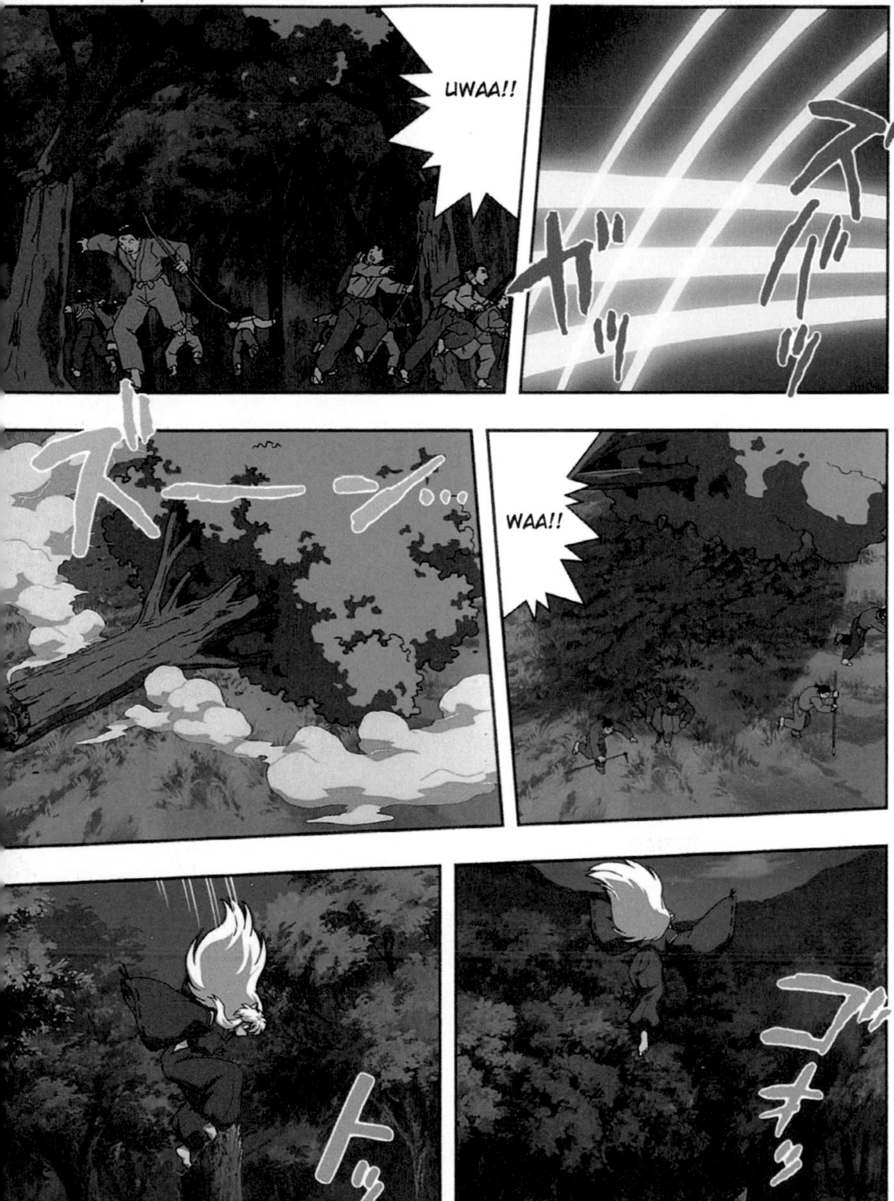
ズバッ
ガッ
UWAA!!
WAA!!
ズーン…
ゴキッ
トッ

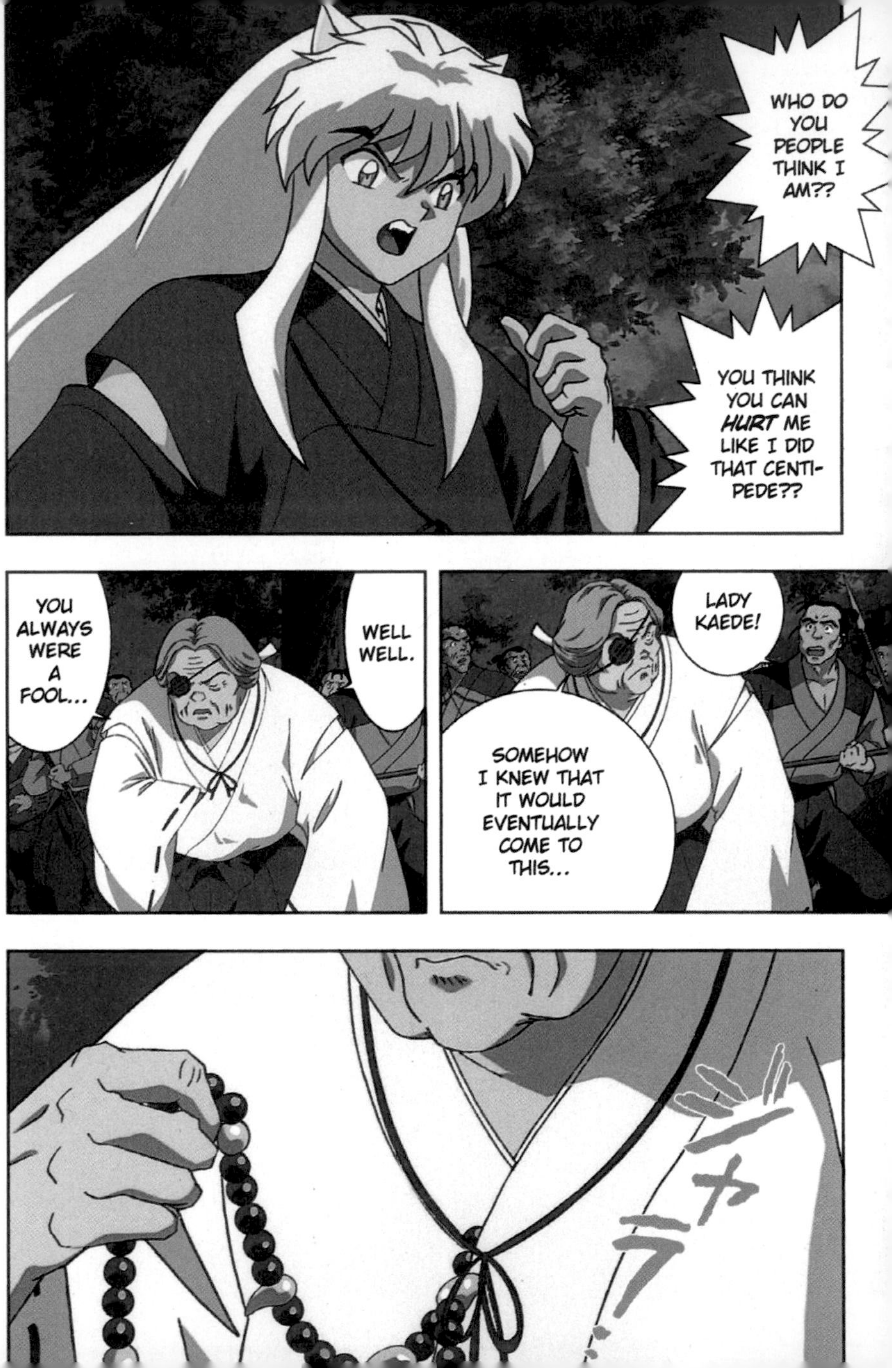
WHO DO YOU PEOPLE THINK I AM??
YOU THINK YOU CAN **HURT** ME LIKE I DID THAT CENTI-PEDE??
LADY KAEDE!
SOMEHOW I KNEW THAT IT WOULD EVENTUALLY COME TO THIS...
WELL WELL.
YOU ALWAYS WERE A FOOL...
ジャラ

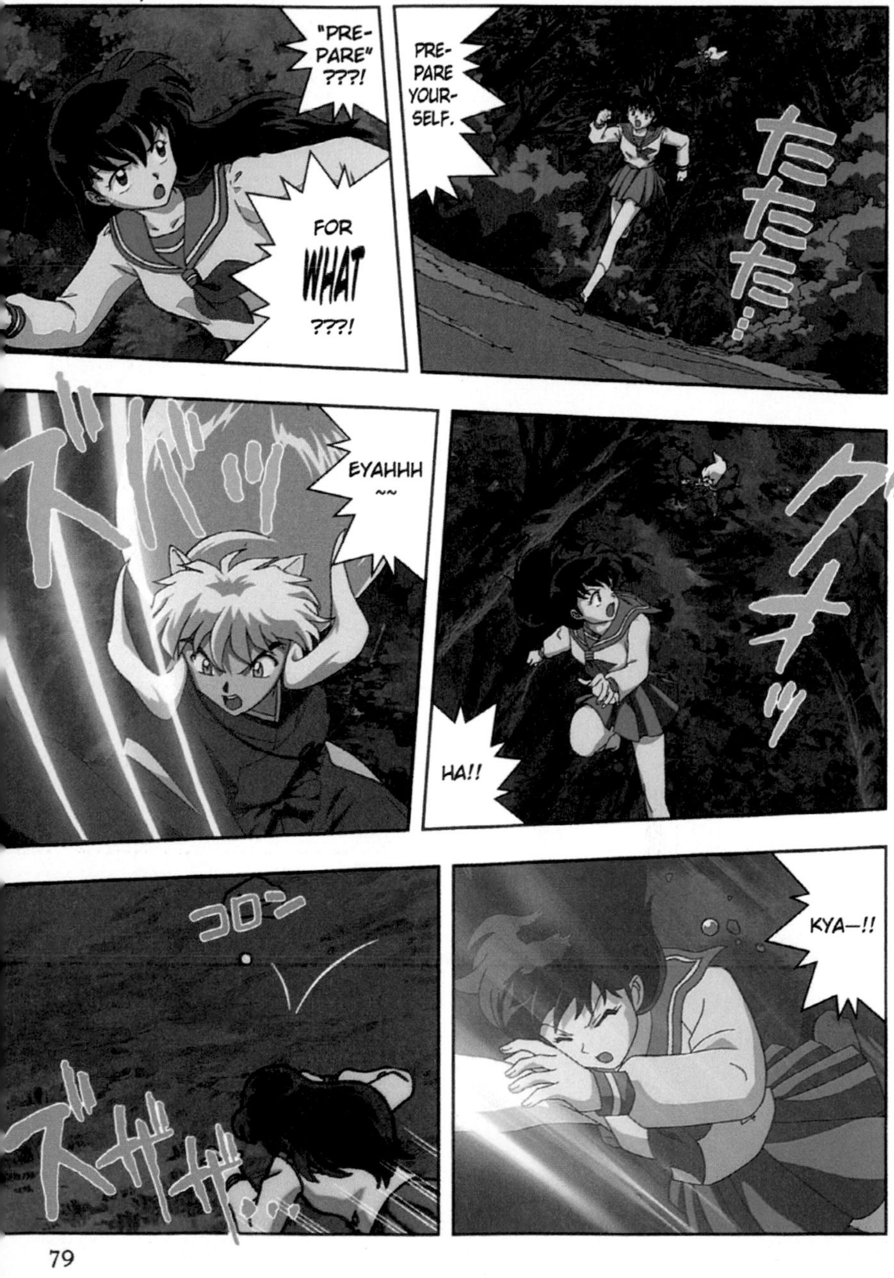
PRE-PARE YOUR-SELF.
たたた…
"PRE-PARE" ???!
FOR WHAT ???!
HA!!
EYAHHH ~~
ズバッ
KYA—!!
コロン
ズザザ…

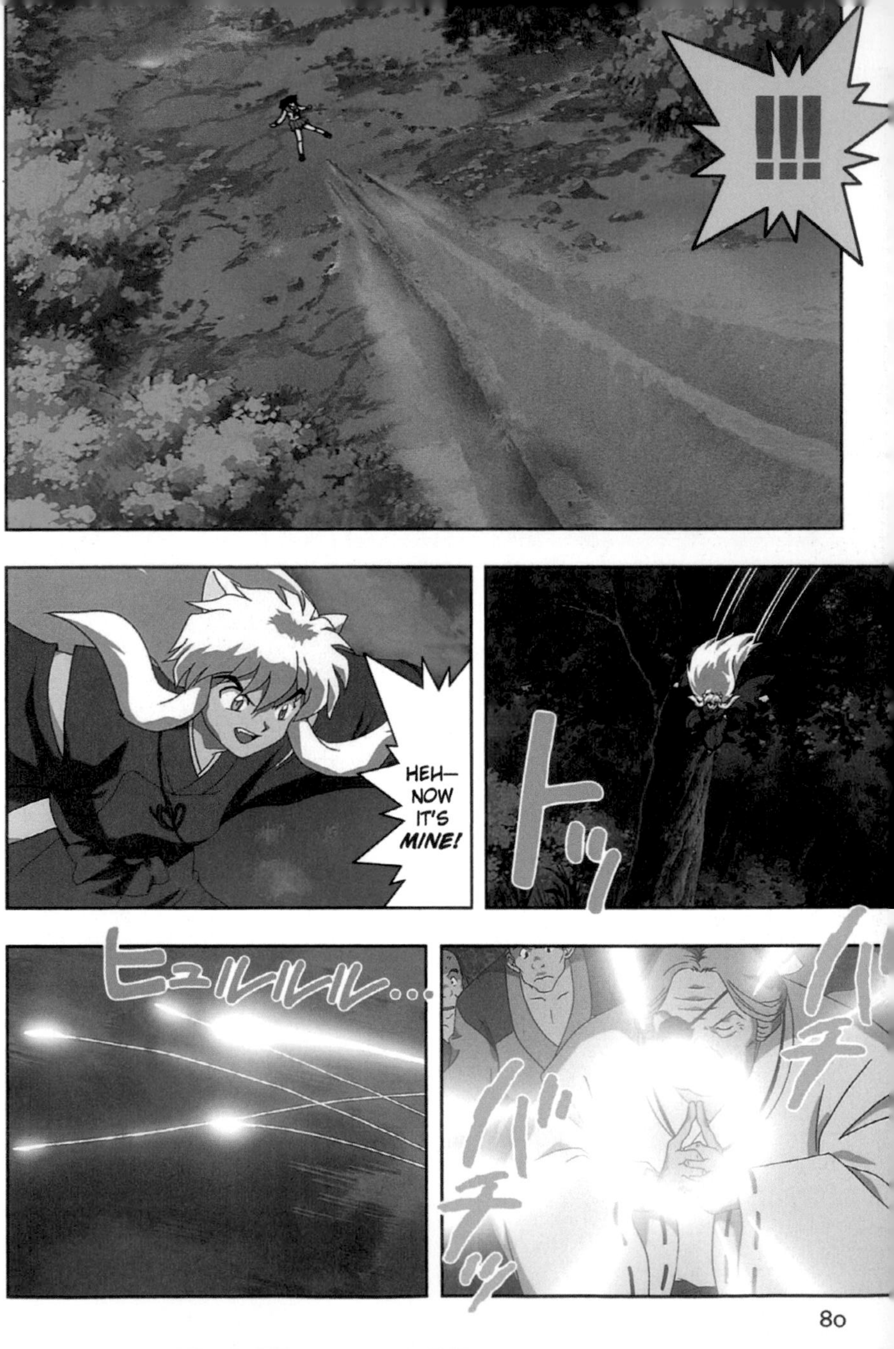
!!!
トッ
HEH— NOW IT'S MINE!
バチ
バチッ
ヒュルルルル...

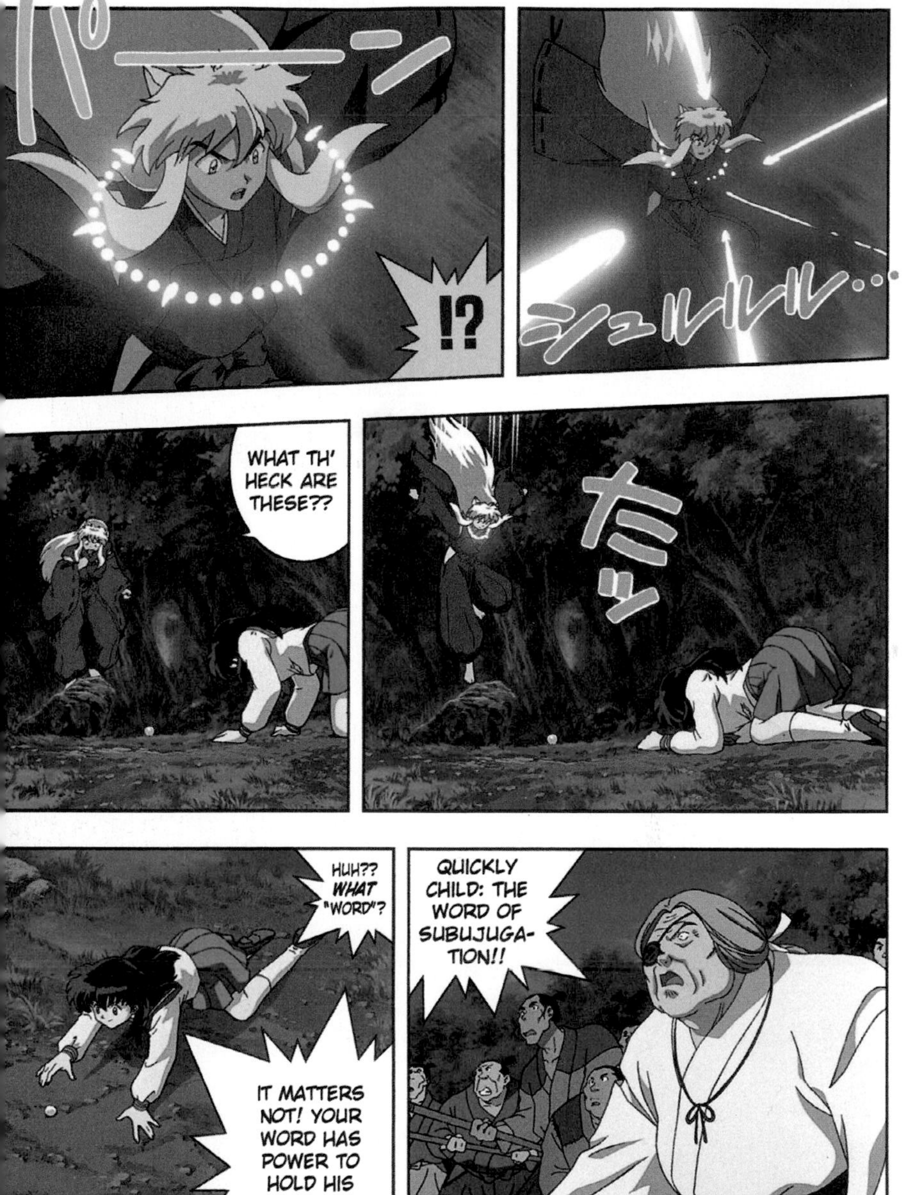
シュルルルル…
パーン
!?
タッ
WHAT TH' HECK ARE THESE??
QUICKLY CHILD: THE WORD OF SUBUJUGA-TION!!
HUH?? WHAT "WORD"?
IT MATTERS NOT! YOUR WORD HAS POWER TO HOLD HIS SPIRIT!

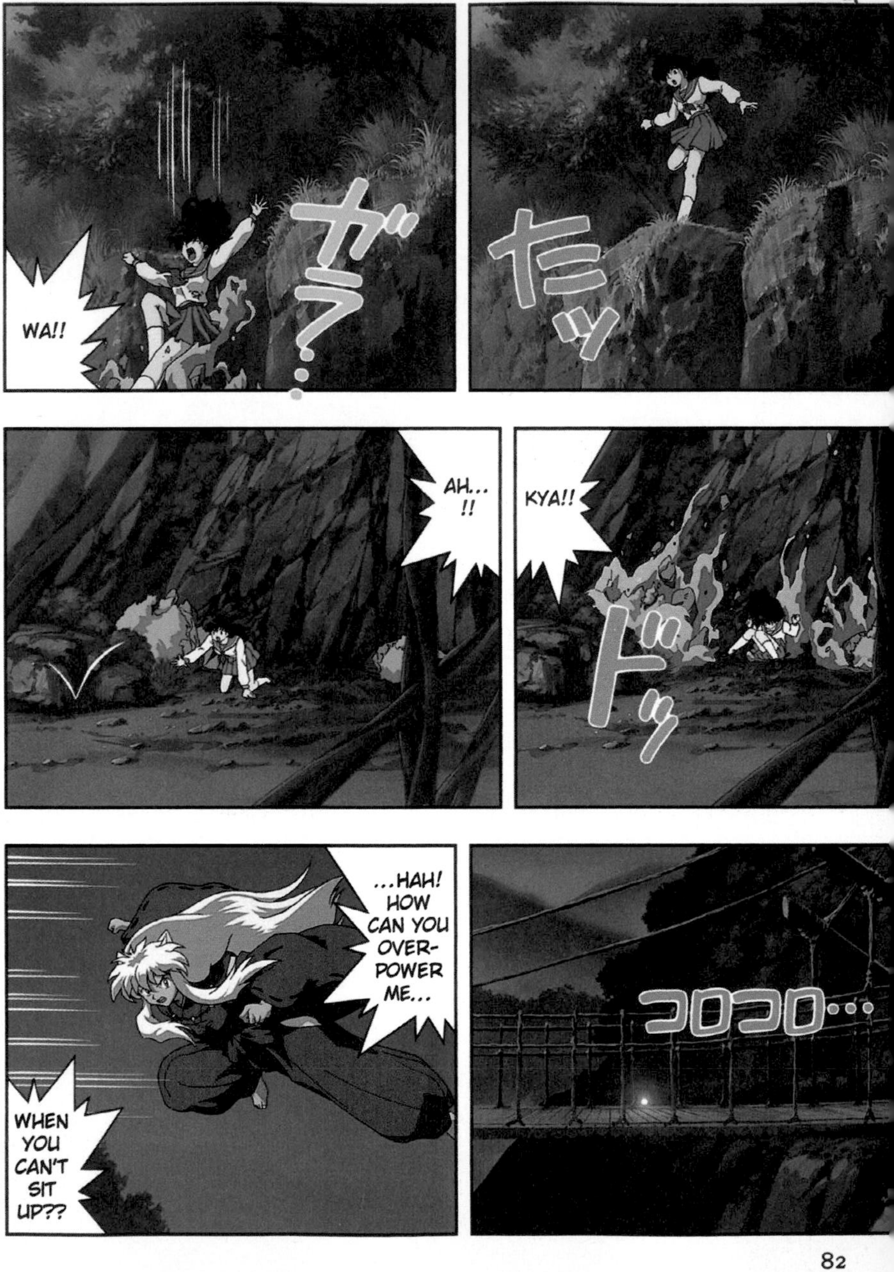
タッ
ガラ…
WA!!
KYA!!
ドッ
AH... !!
コロコロ…
...HAH! HOW CAN YOU OVER-POWER ME...
WHEN YOU CAN'T SIT UP??

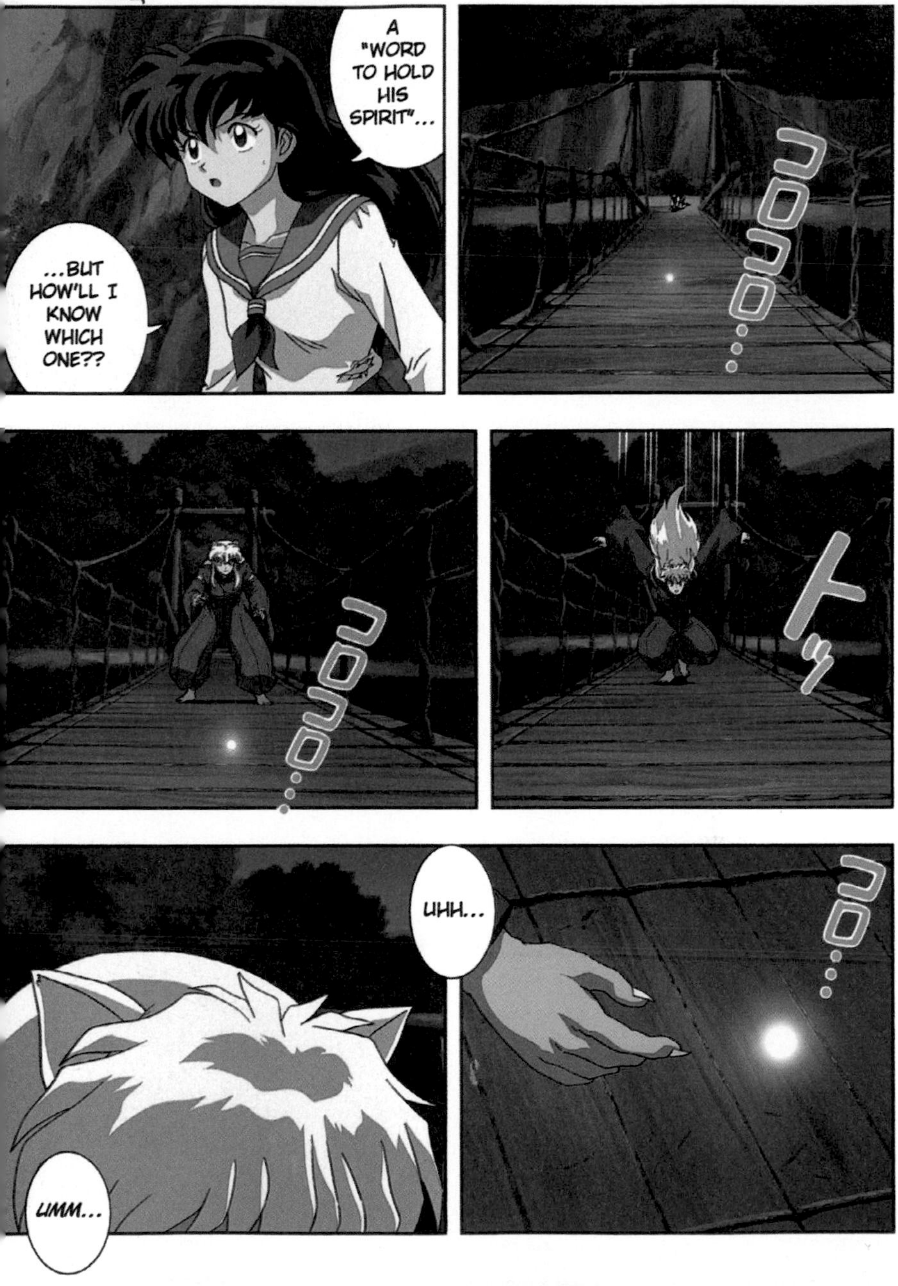
コロコロ…
A "WORD TO HOLD HIS SPIRIT"…
…BUT HOW'LL I KNOW WHICH ONE??
トッ
コロコロ…
UHH…
コロ…
UMM…

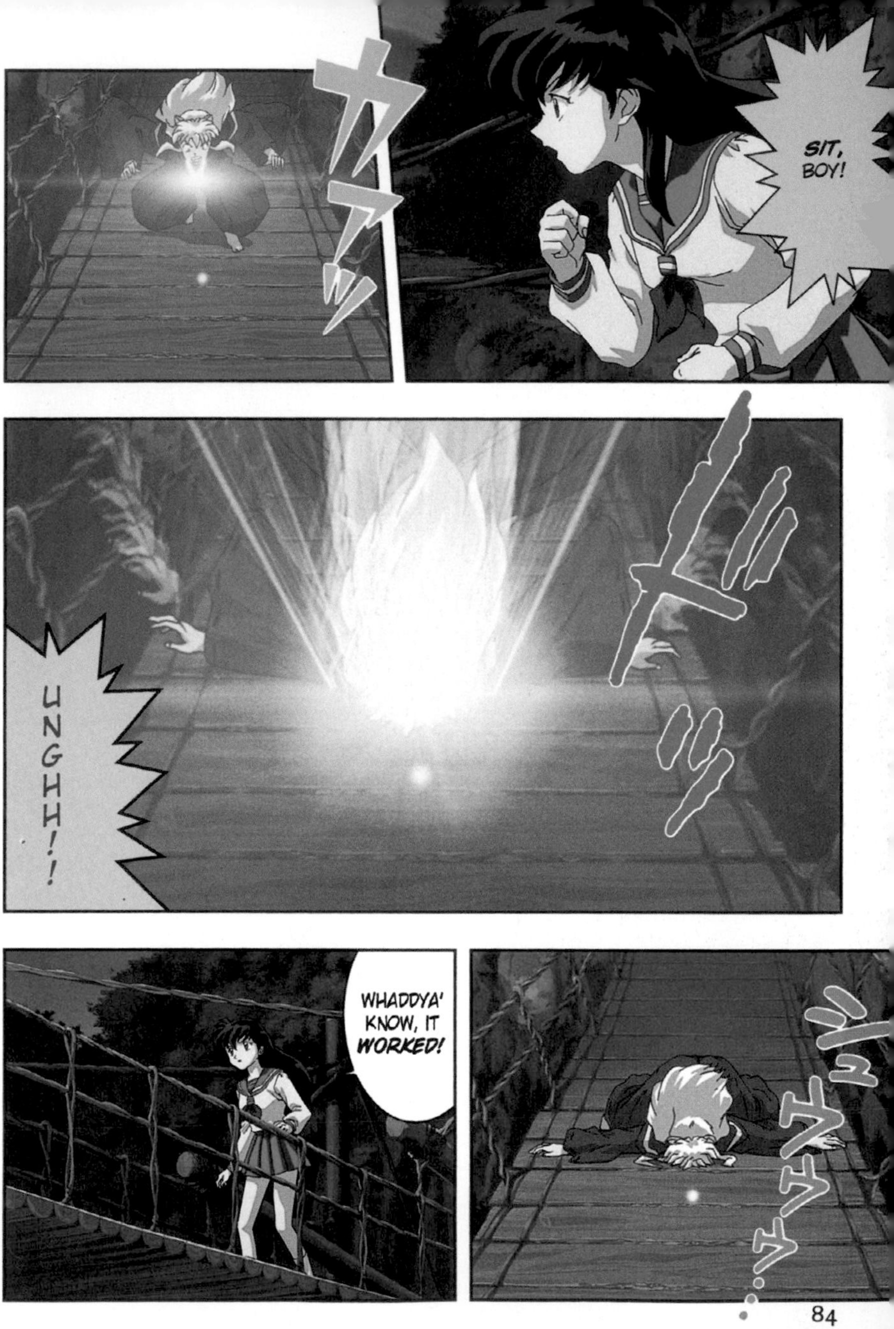
SIT, BOY!
UNGHH!!
WHADDYA' KNOW, IT WORKED!

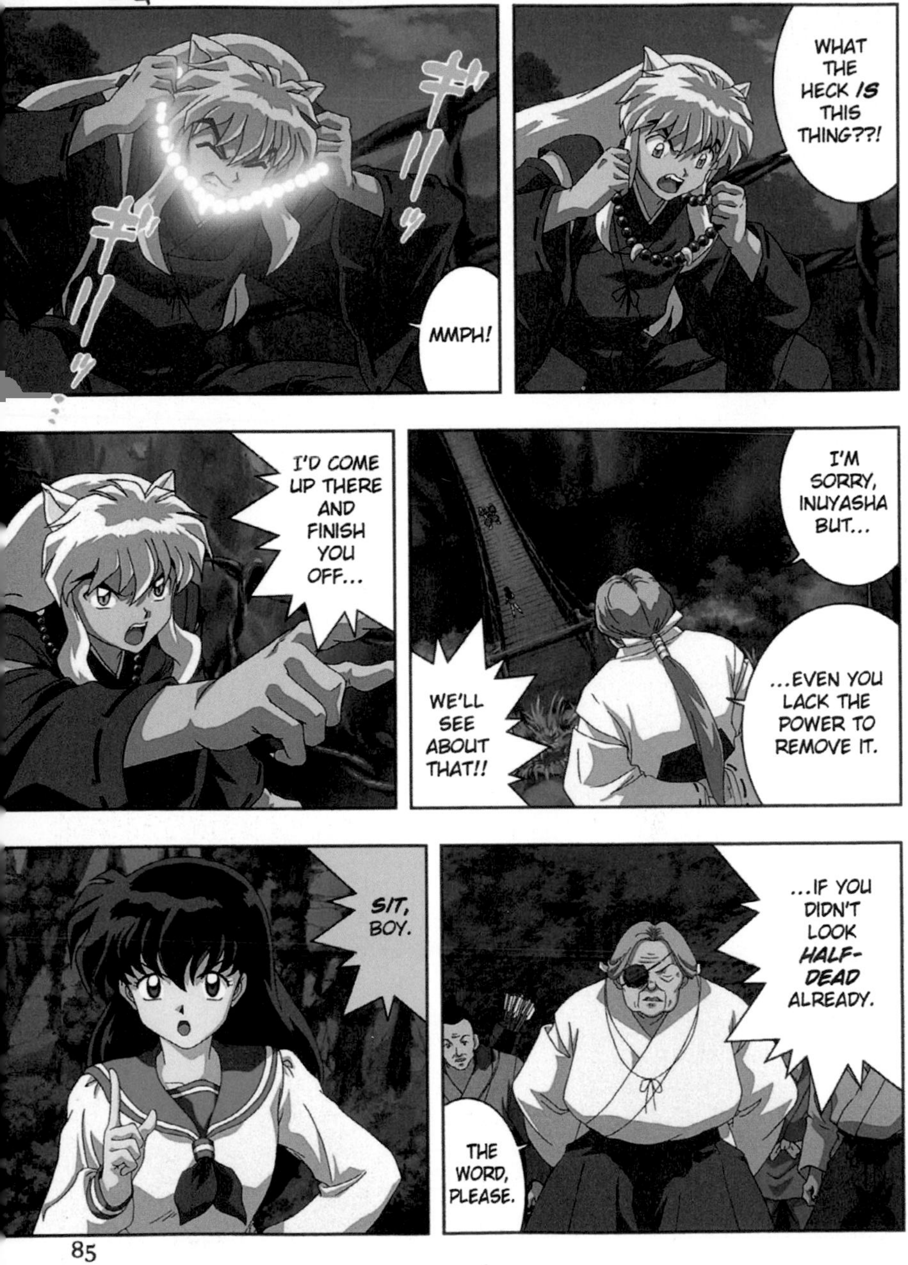
WHAT THE HECK *IS* THIS THING??!
ギリッ
ギリッ
MMPH!
I'M SORRY, INUYASHA BUT...
...EVEN YOU LACK THE POWER TO REMOVE IT.
WE'LL SEE ABOUT THAT!!
I'D COME UP THERE AND FINISH YOU OFF...
...IF YOU DIDN'T LOOK *HALF-DEAD* ALREADY.
THE WORD, PLEASE.
SIT, BOY.

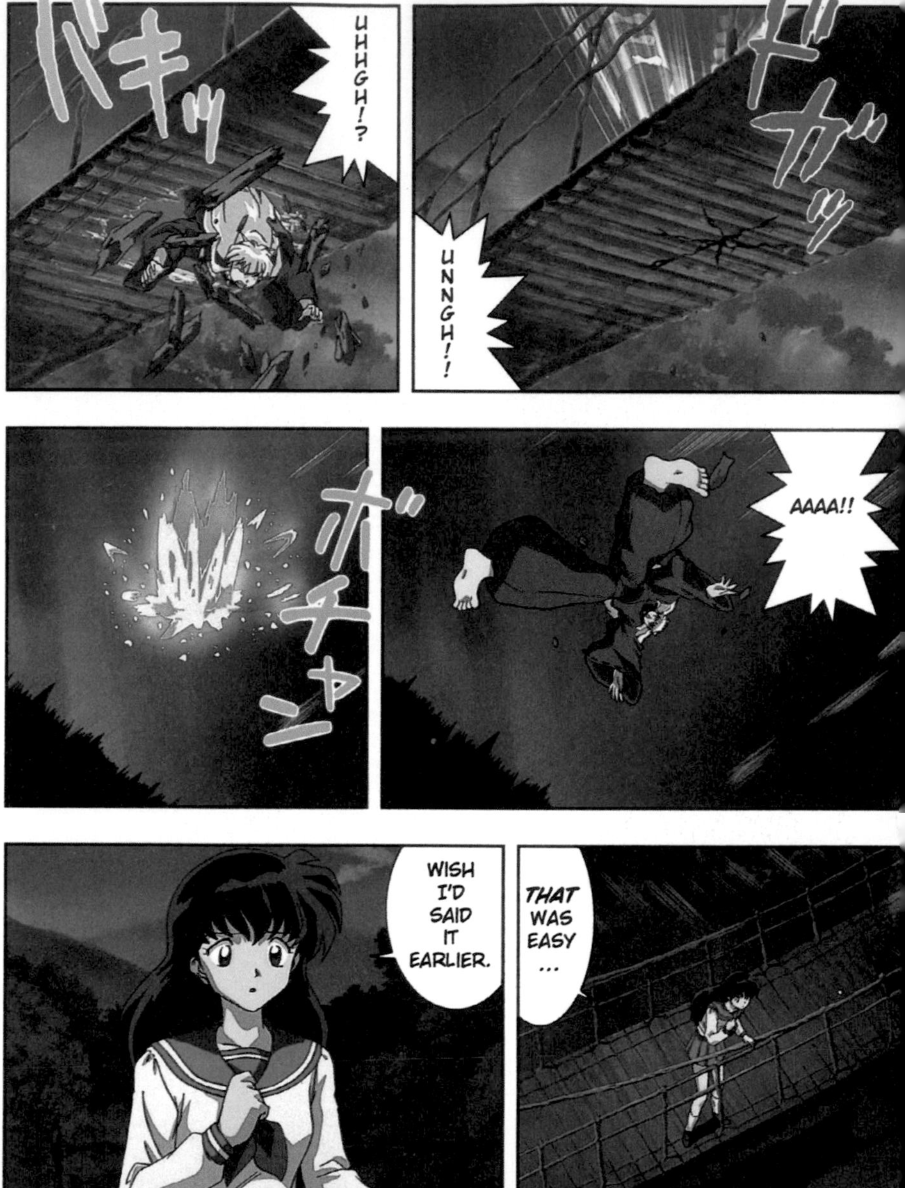
ドガッ
UNNGH!!
バキッ
UHHGH!?
AAAA!!
ボチャン
THAT WAS EASY...
WISH I'D SAID IT EARLIER.

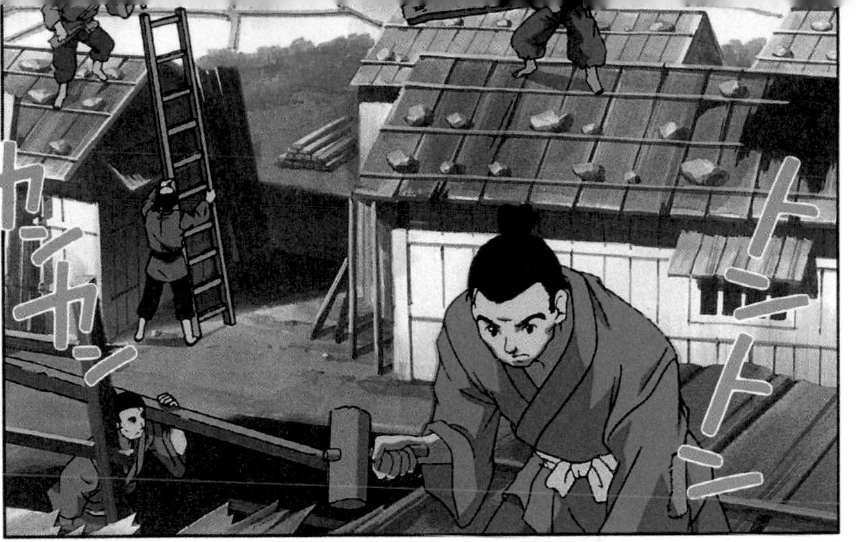
トントン
カーンカーン

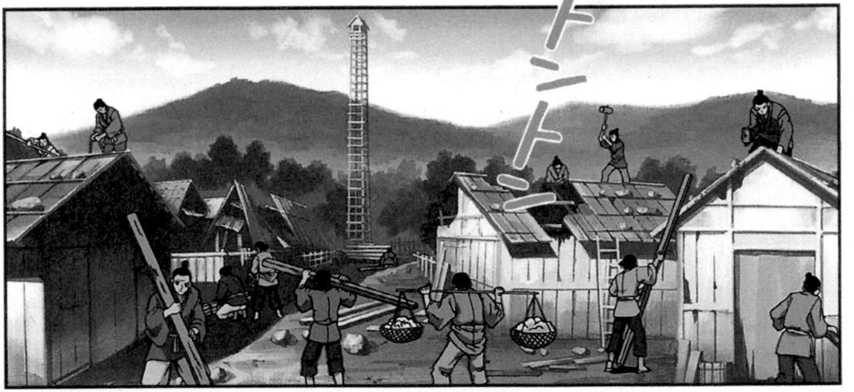
トントン

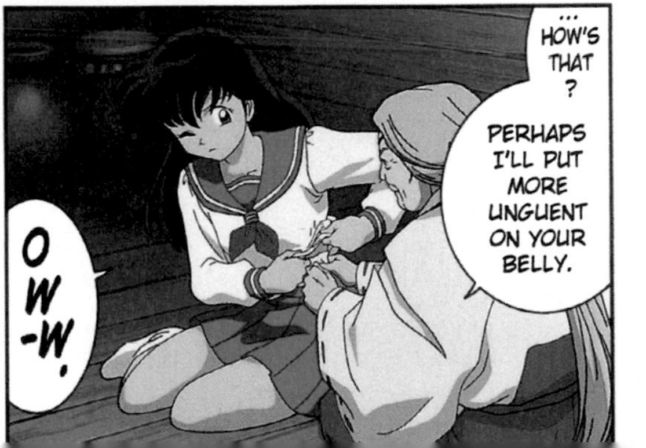
...HOW'S THAT?
PERHAPS I'LL PUT MORE UNGUENT ON YOUR BELLY.
OW-W.

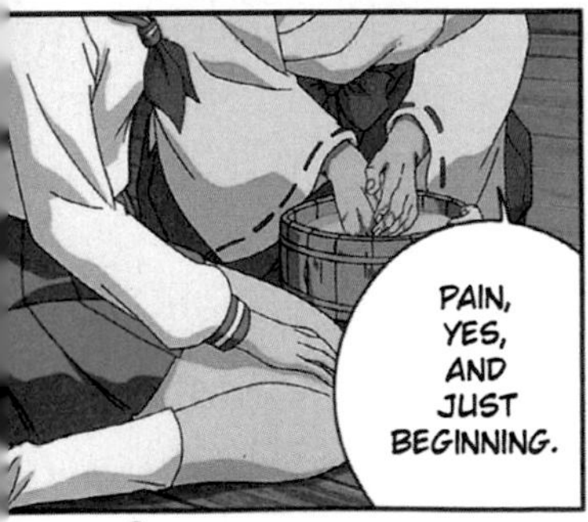
PAIN, YES, AND JUST BEGINNING.

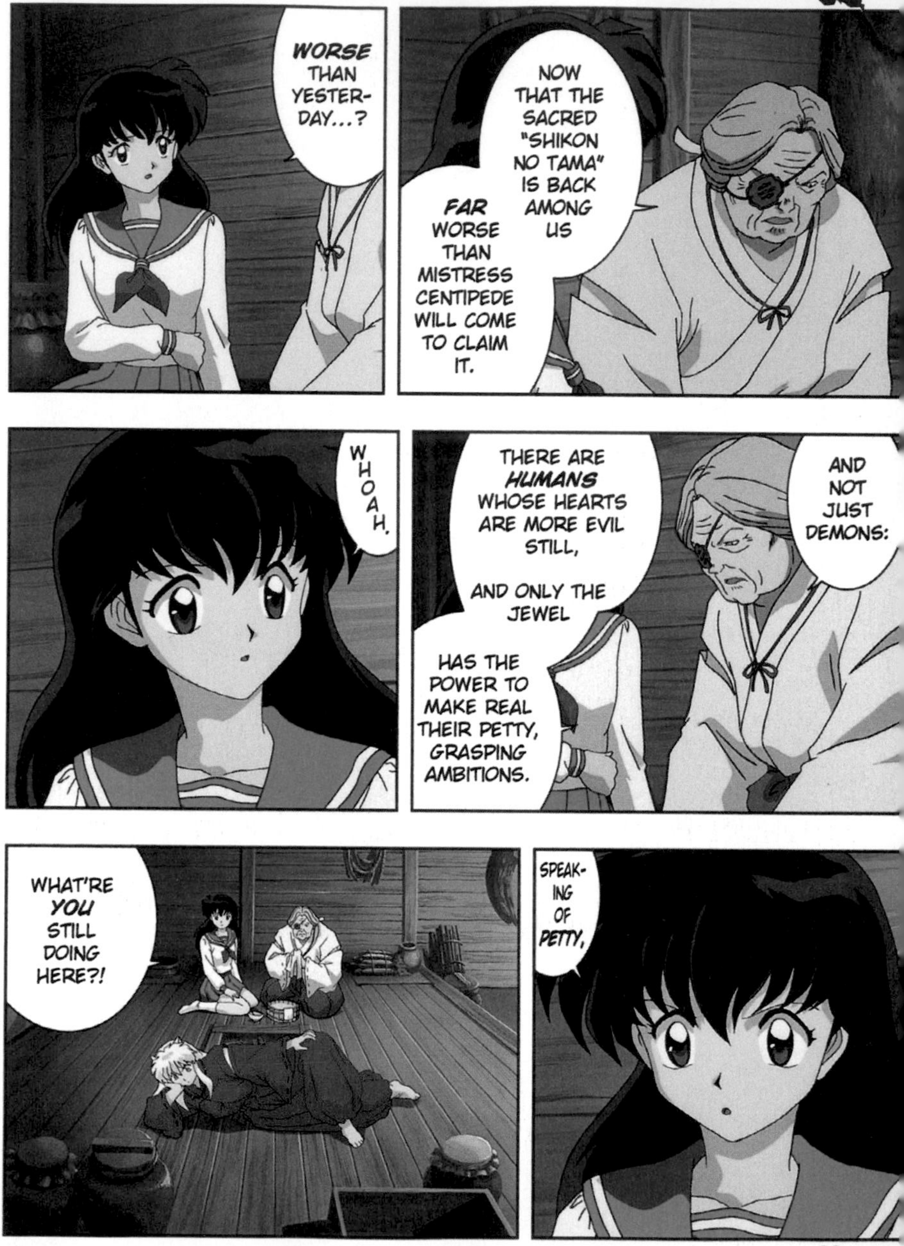
NOW THAT THE SACRED "SHIKON NO TAMA" IS BACK AMONG US
FAR WORSE THAN MISTRESS CENTIPEDE WILL COME TO CLAIM IT.
WORSE THAN YESTER-DAY...?
AND NOT JUST DEMONS:
THERE ARE HUMANS WHOSE HEARTS ARE MORE EVIL STILL,
AND ONLY THE JEWEL
HAS THE POWER TO MAKE REAL THEIR PETTY, GRASPING AMBITIONS.
WHOAH.
SPEAK-ING OF PETTY,
WHAT'RE YOU STILL DOING HERE?!

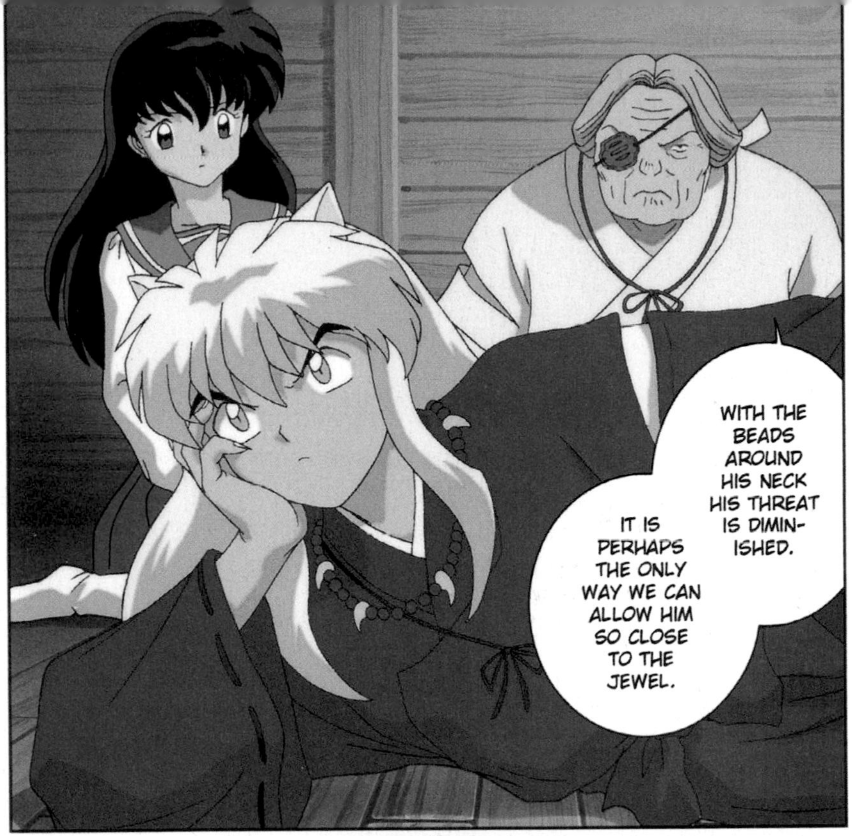
WITH THE BEADS AROUND HIS NECK HIS THREAT IS DIMIN-ISHED.
IT IS PERHAPS THE ONLY WAY WE CAN ALLOW HIM SO CLOSE TO THE JEWEL.

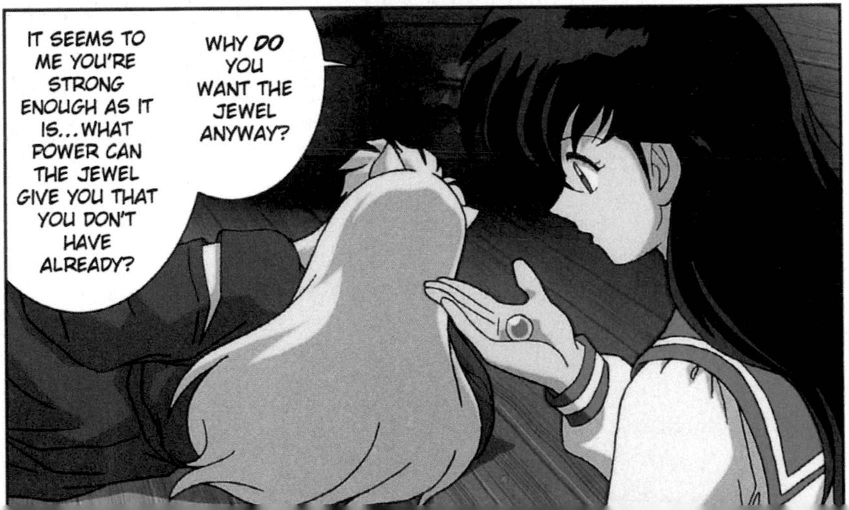
WHY *DO* YOU WANT THE JEWEL ANYWAY?
IT SEEMS TO ME YOU'RE STRONG ENOUGH AS IT IS...WHAT POWER CAN THE JEWEL GIVE YOU THAT YOU DON'T HAVE ALREADY?

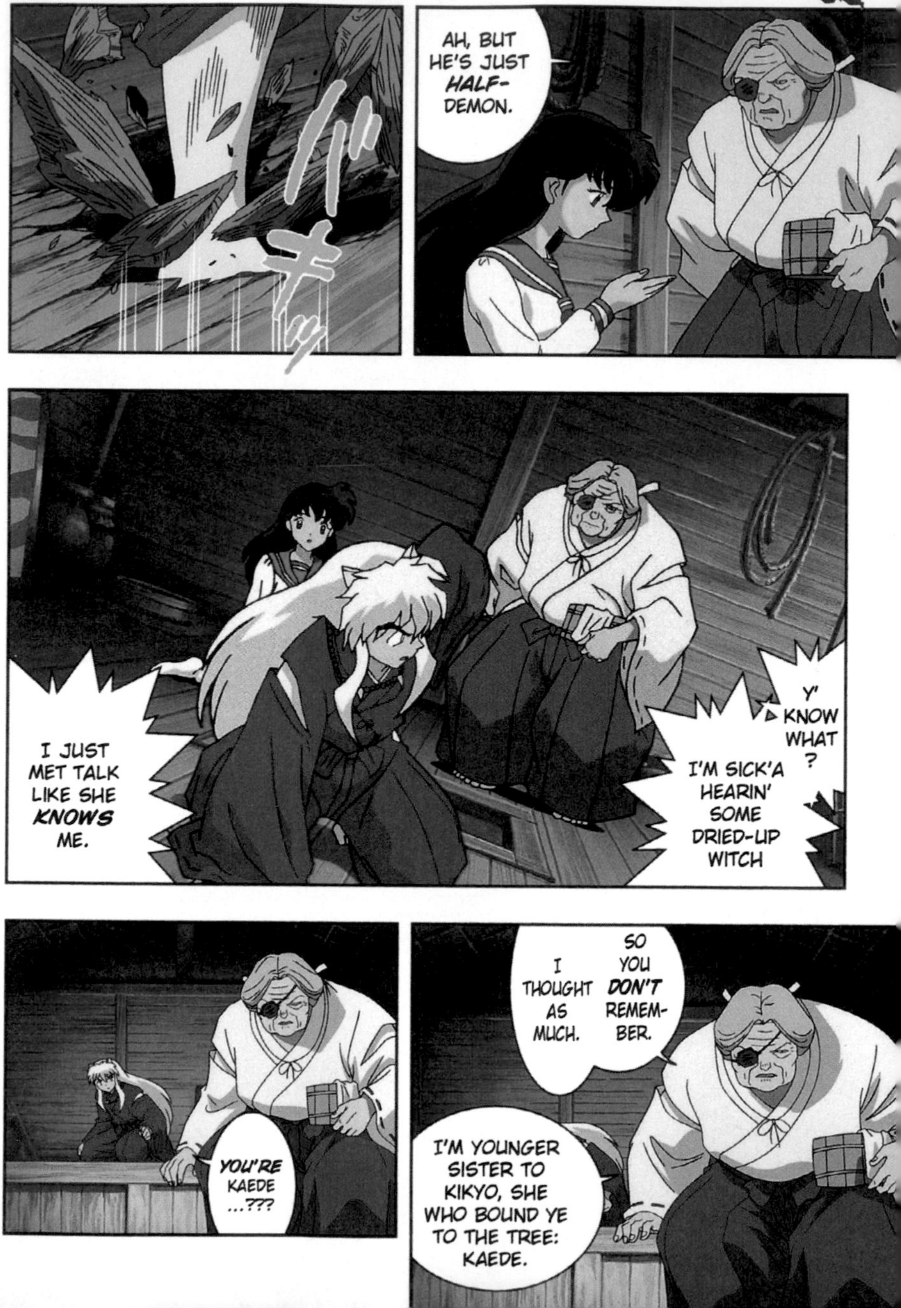
AH, BUT HE'S JUST HALF-DEMON.
Y' KNOW WHAT?
I'M SICK'A HEARIN' SOME DRIED-UP WITCH
I JUST MET TALK LIKE SHE KNOWS ME.
SO YOU DON'T REMEMBER.
I THOUGHT AS MUCH.
I'M YOUNGER SISTER TO KIKYO, SHE WHO BOUND YE TO THE TREE: KAEDE.
YOU'RE KAEDE ...???

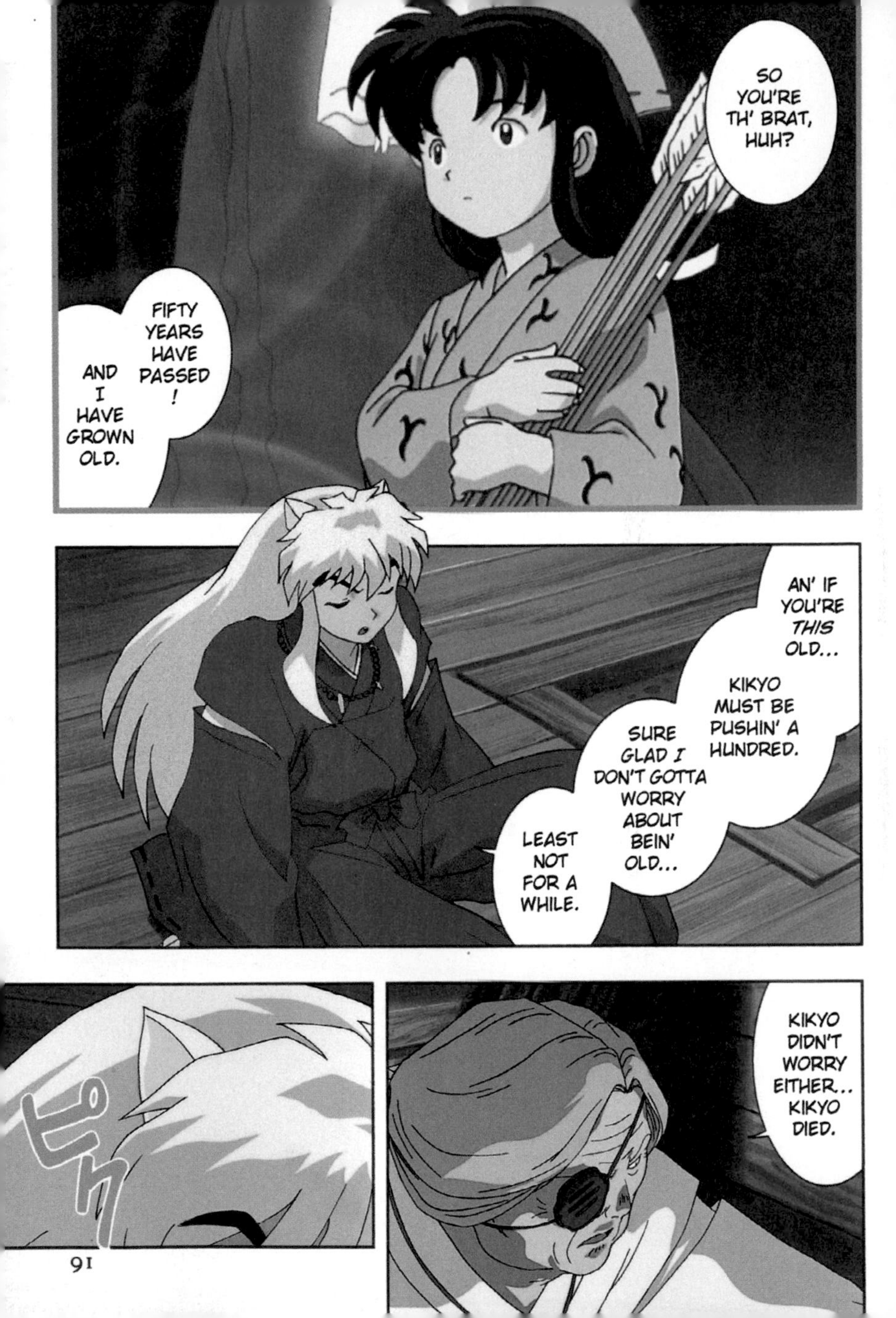
SO YOU'RE TH' BRAT, HUH?
FIFTY YEARS HAVE PASSED!
AND I HAVE GROWN OLD.
AN' IF YOU'RE *THIS* OLD...
KIKYO MUST BE PUSHIN' A HUNDRED.
SURE GLAD *I* DON'T GOTTA WORRY ABOUT BEIN' OLD...
LEAST NOT FOR A WHILE.
KIKYO DIDN'T WORRY EITHER... KIKYO DIED.
ピク

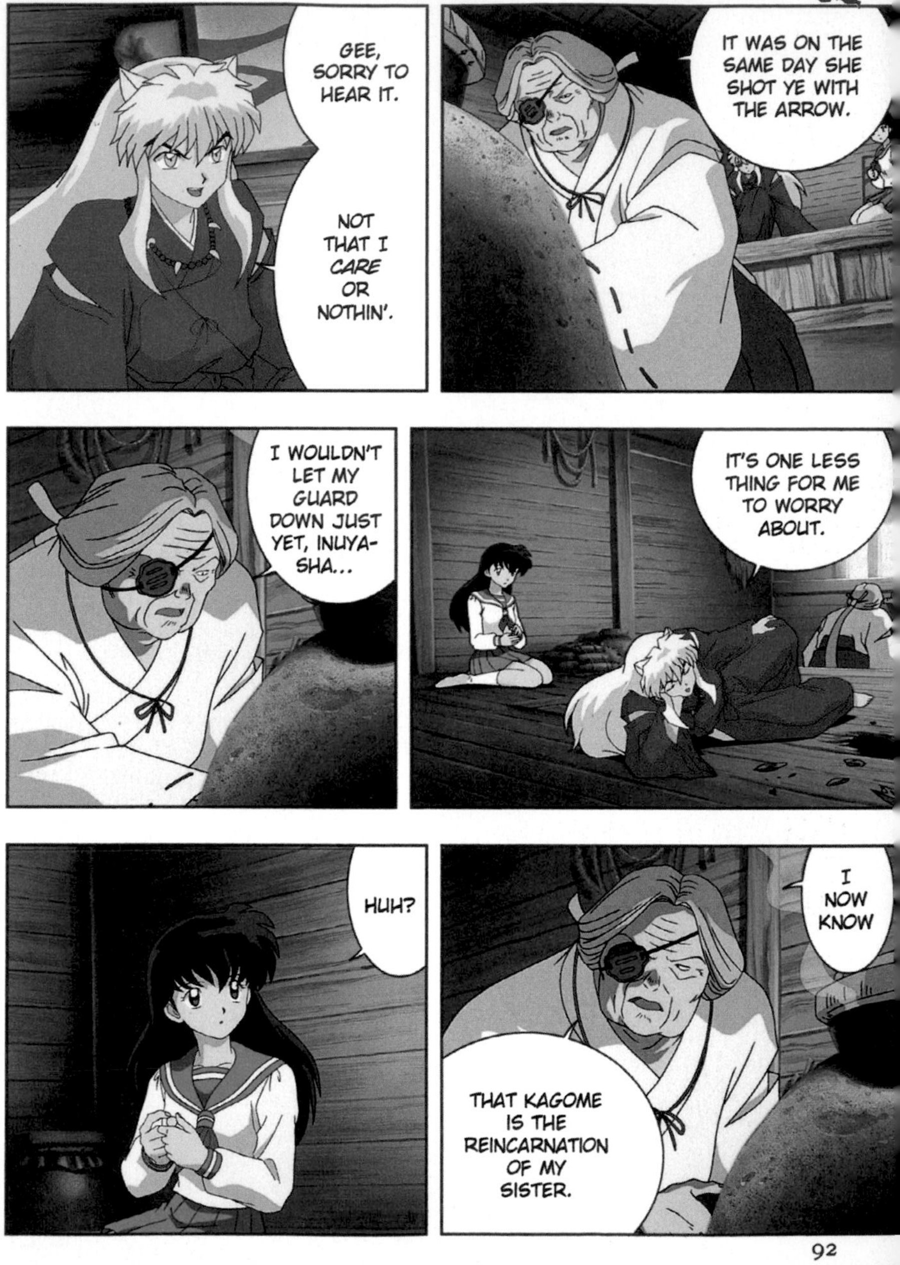
IT WAS ON THE SAME DAY SHE SHOT YE WITH THE ARROW.
GEE, SORRY TO HEAR IT.
NOT THAT I *CARE* OR NOTHIN'.
IT'S ONE LESS THING FOR ME TO WORRY ABOUT.
I WOULDN'T LET MY GUARD DOWN JUST YET, INUYA-SHA...
I NOW KNOW
THAT KAGOME IS THE REINCARNATION OF MY SISTER.
HUH?

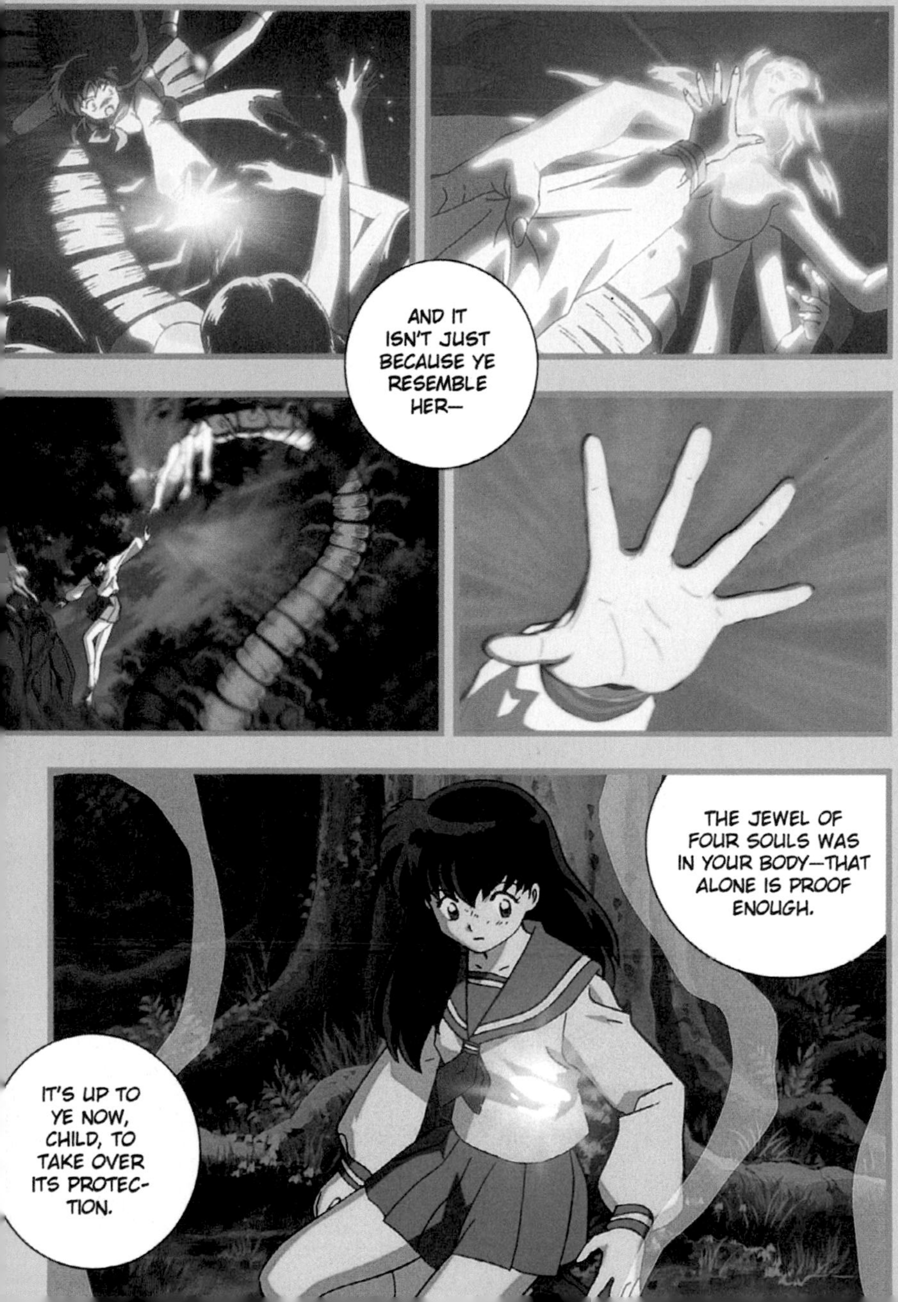
AND IT ISN'T JUST BECAUSE YE RESEMBLE HER—
THE JEWEL OF FOUR SOULS WAS IN YOUR BODY—THAT ALONE IS PROOF ENOUGH.
IT'S UP TO YE NOW, CHILD, TO TAKE OVER ITS PROTEC-TION.

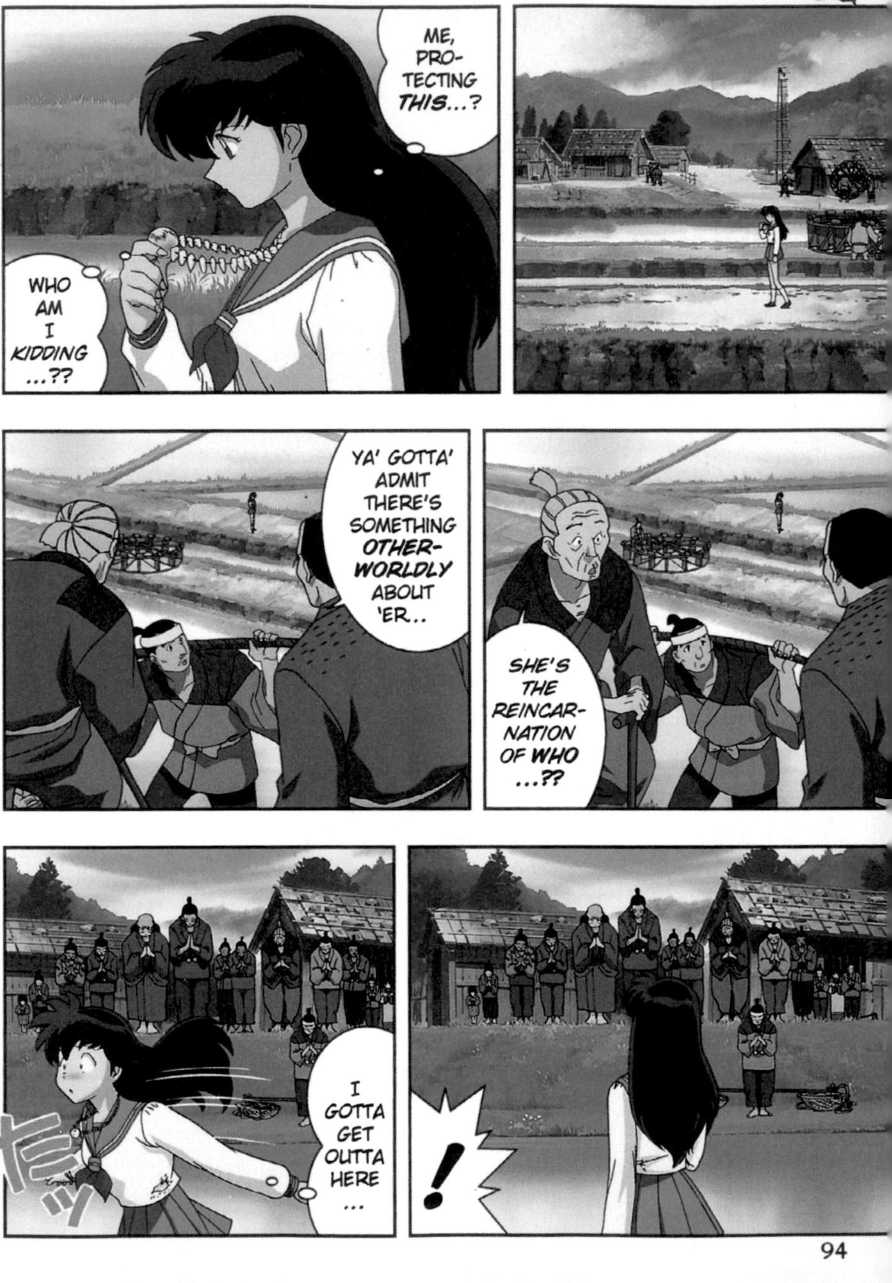
ME, PROTECTING THIS...?
WHO AM I KIDDING ...??
SHE'S THE REINCARNATION OF WHO ...??
YA' GOTTA' ADMIT THERE'S SOMETHING OTHER-WORLDLY ABOUT 'ER..
!
I GOTTA GET OUTTA HERE ...

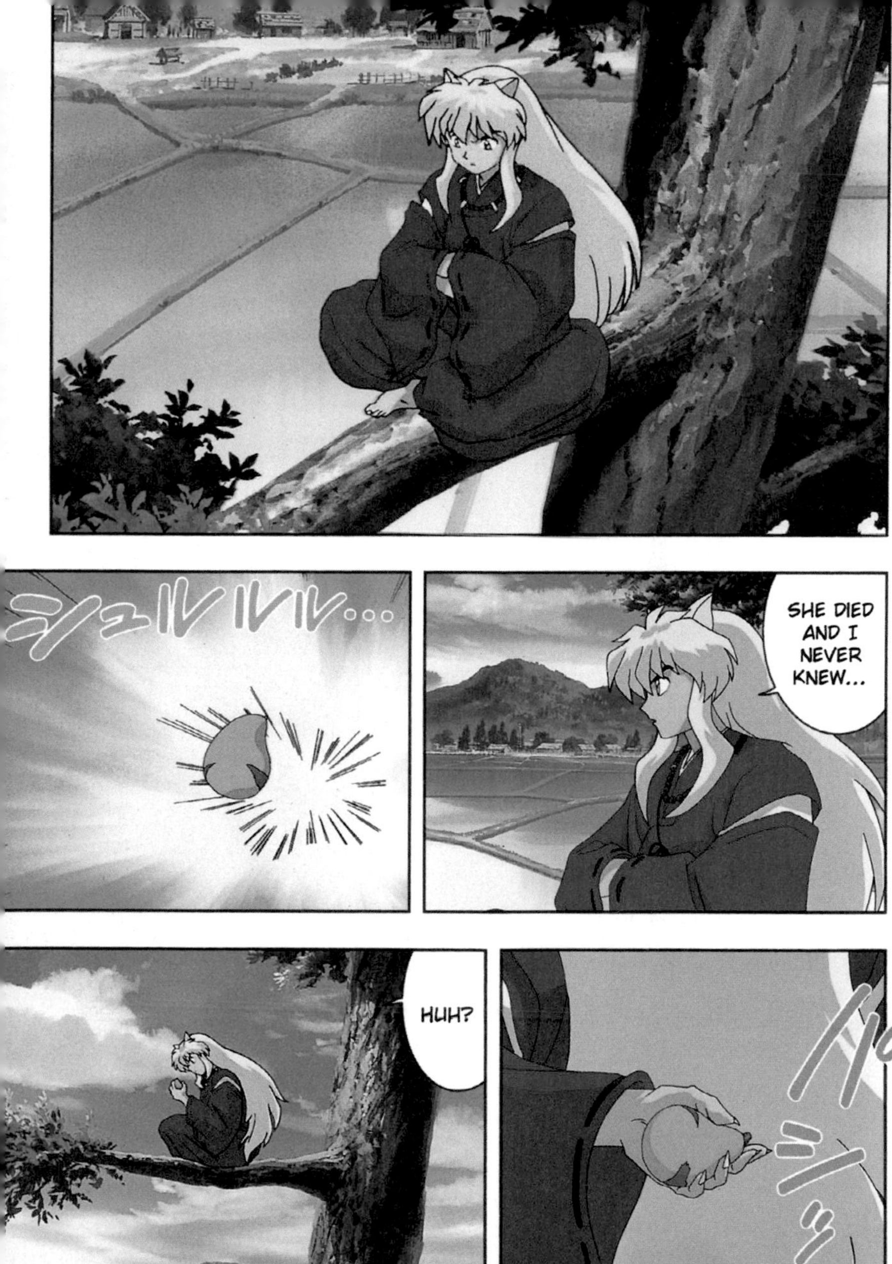
SHE DIED AND I NEVER KNEW...
シュルルルル...
パシッ
HUH?

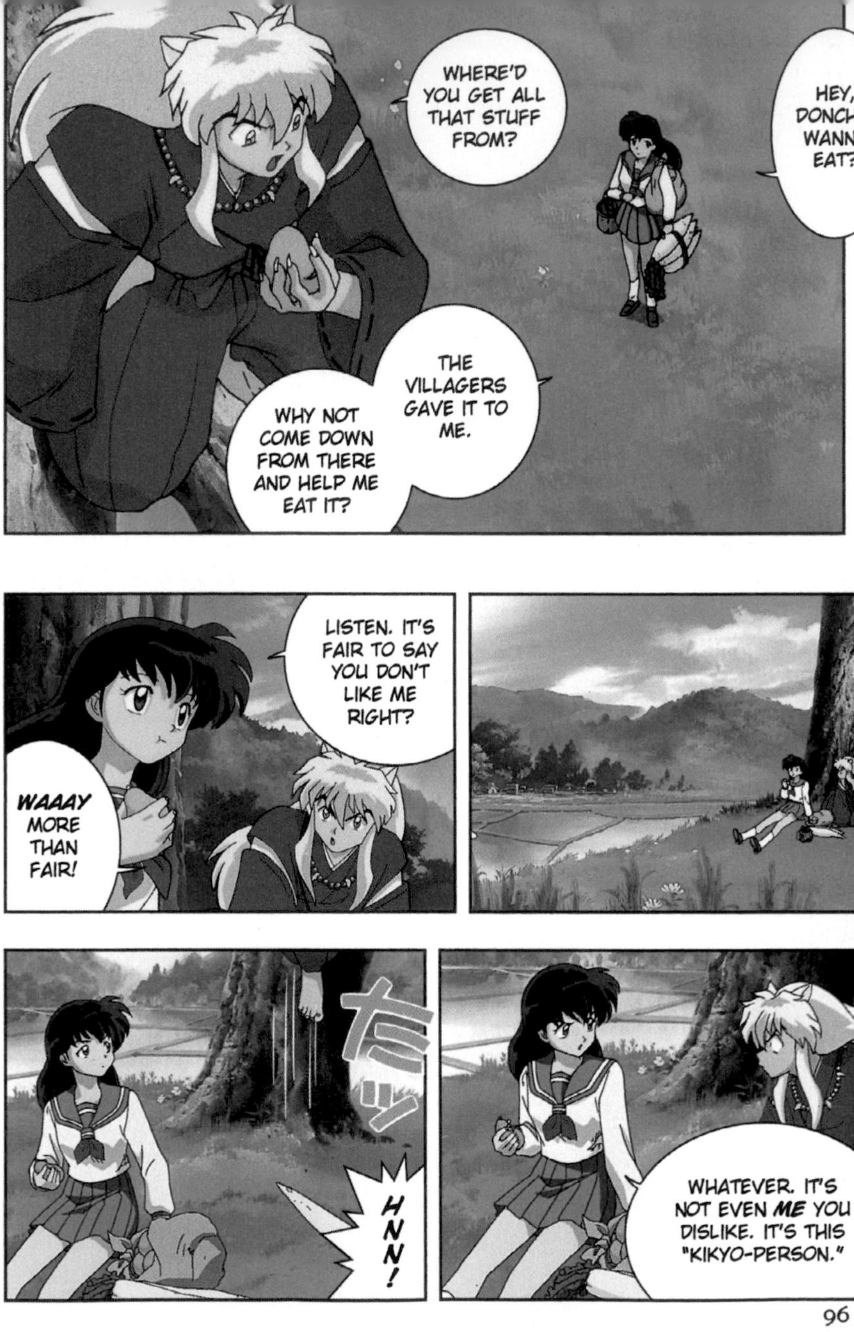
HEY, DONCHA' WANNA EAT?
WHERE'D YOU GET ALL THAT STUFF FROM?
THE VILLAGERS GAVE IT TO ME.
WHY NOT COME DOWN FROM THERE AND HELP ME EAT IT?
LISTEN. IT'S FAIR TO SAY YOU DON'T LIKE ME RIGHT?
WAAAY MORE THAN FAIR!
WHATEVER. IT'S NOT EVEN ME YOU DISLIKE. IT'S THIS "KIKYO-PERSON."
たッ
HNN!

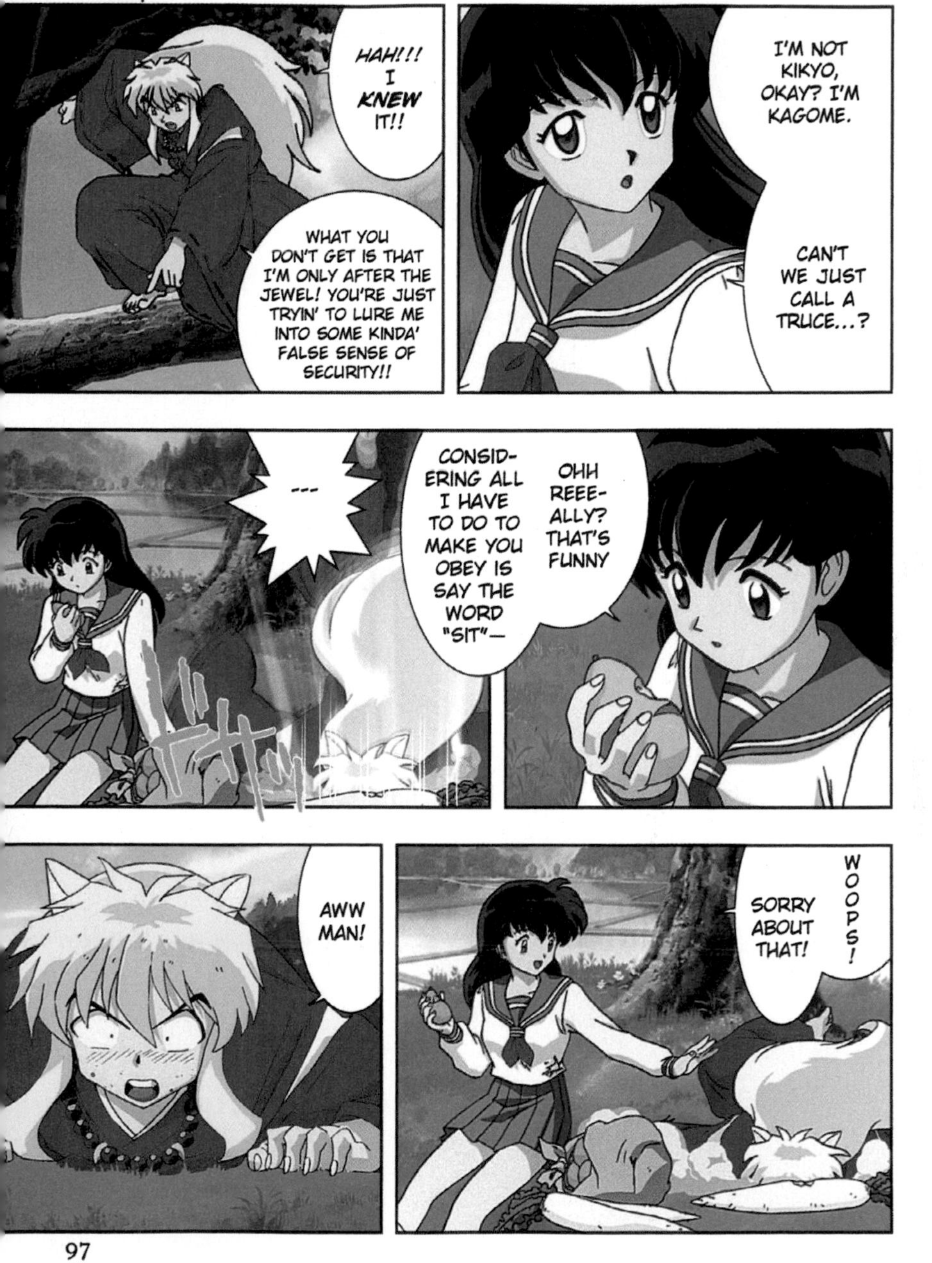
I'M NOT KIKYO, OKAY? I'M KAGOME.
CAN'T WE JUST CALL A TRUCE...?
HAH!!! I **KNEW** IT!!
WHAT YOU DON'T GET IS THAT I'M ONLY AFTER THE JEWEL! YOU'RE JUST TRYIN' TO LURE ME INTO SOME KINDA' FALSE SENSE OF SECURITY!!
OHH REEE-ALLY? THAT'S FUNNY
CONSID-ERING ALL I HAVE TO DO TO MAKE YOU OBEY IS SAY THE WORD "SIT"—

WOOPS!
SORRY ABOUT THAT!
AWW MAN!

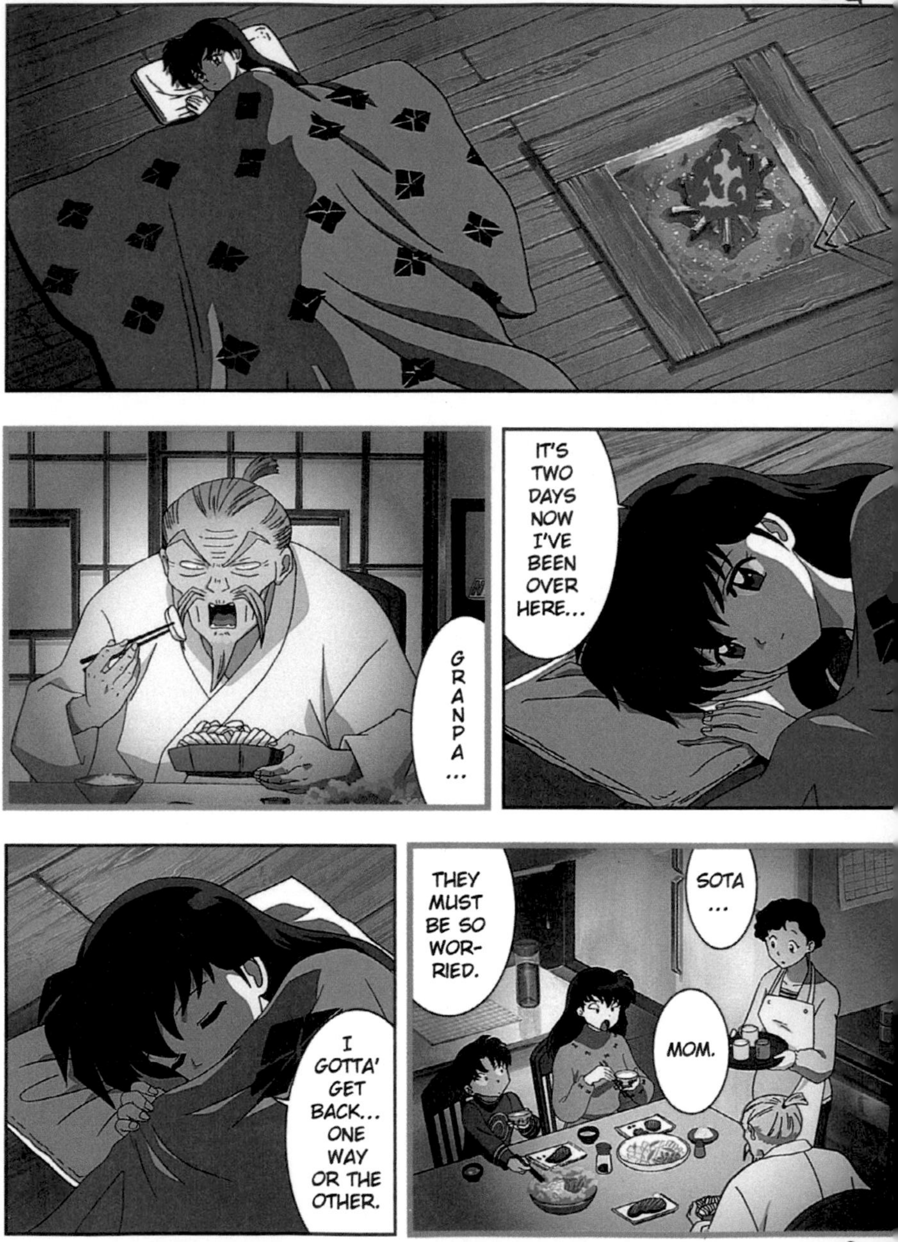
IT'S TWO DAYS NOW I'VE BEEN OVER HERE...
GRANPA...
SOTA...
MOM.
THEY MUST BE SO WORRIED.
I GOTTA' GET BACK... ONE WAY OR THE OTHER.

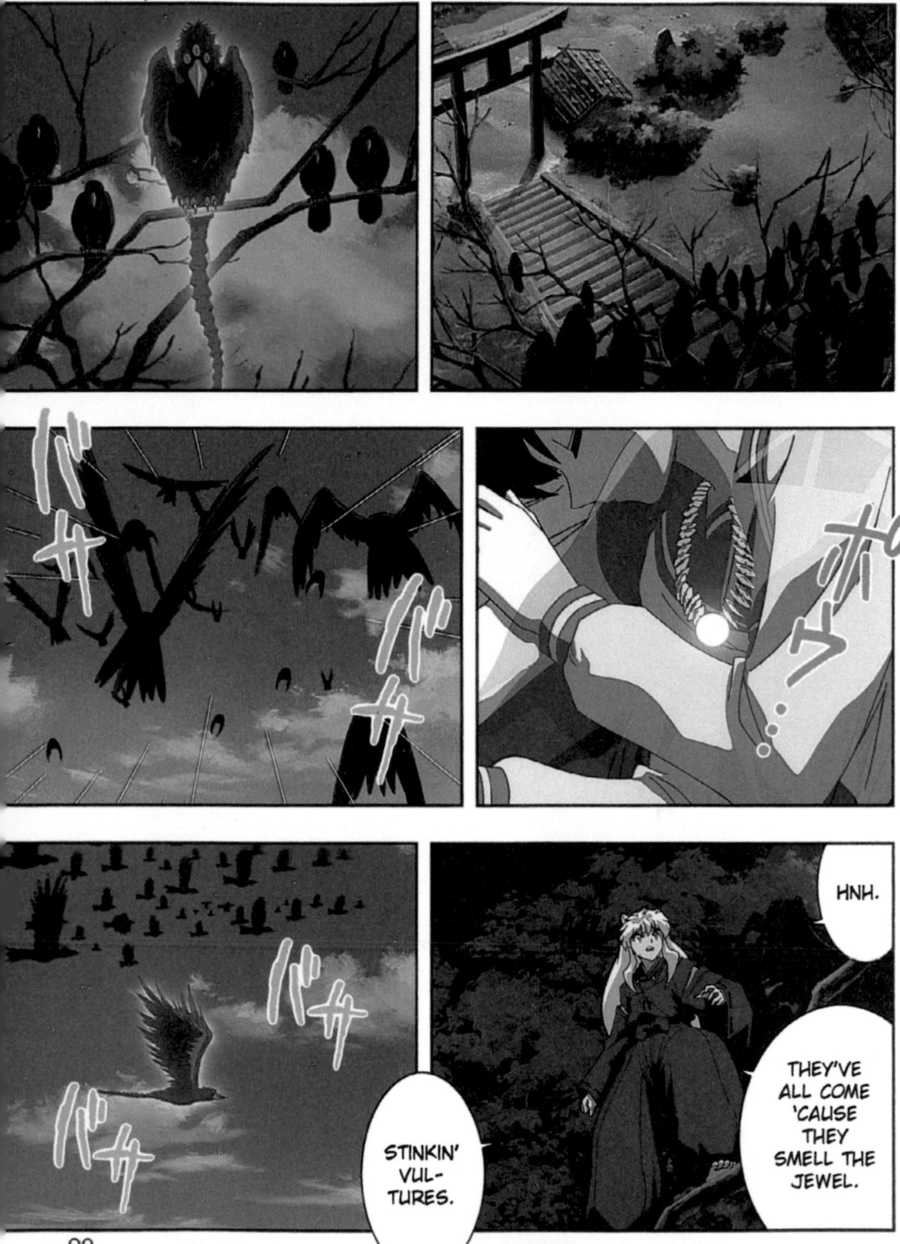
ポウ…
バサ
バサ
バサ
バサ
HNH.
THEY'VE ALL COME 'CAUSE THEY SMELL THE JEWEL.
STINKIN' VUL-TURES.

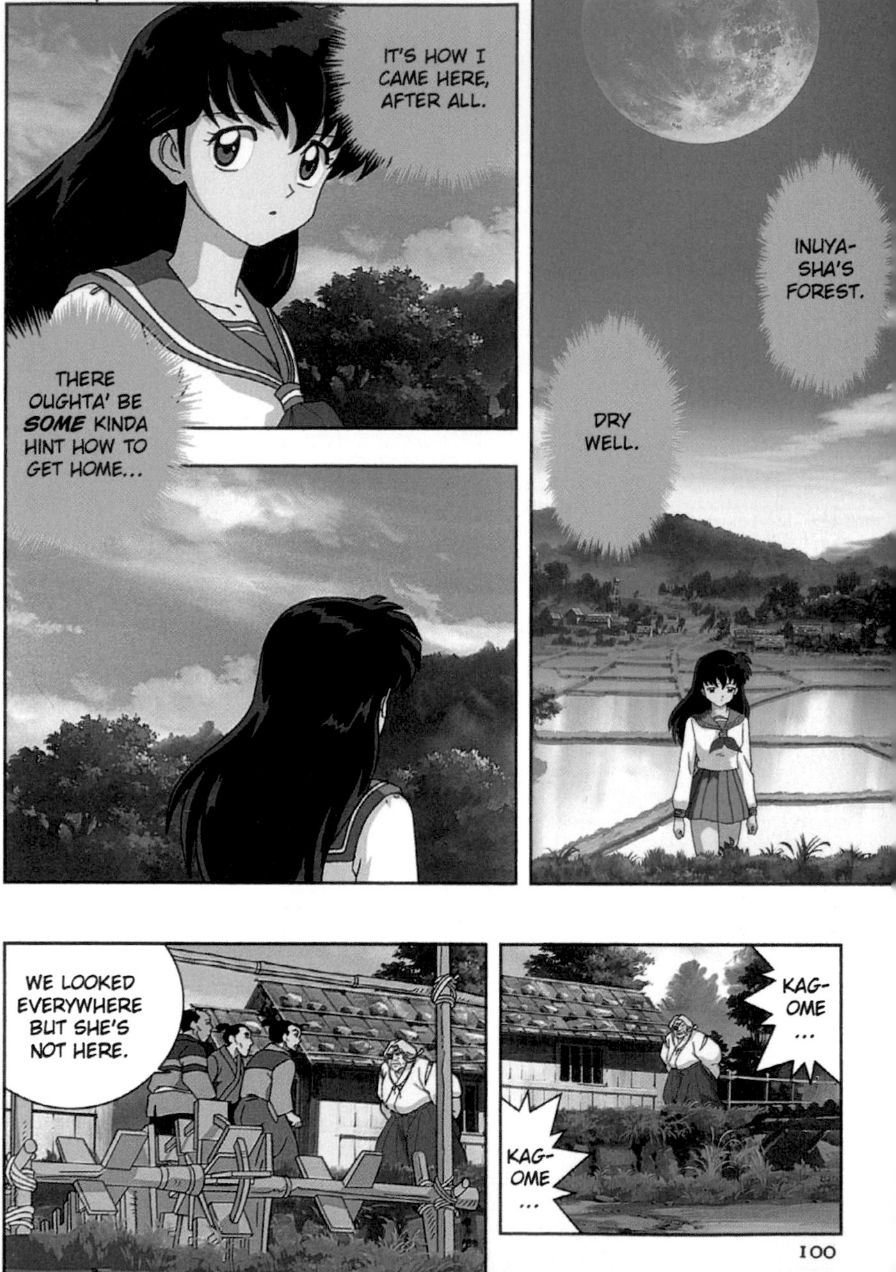
INUYA-SHA'S FOREST.
DRY WELL.
IT'S HOW I CAME HERE, AFTER ALL.
THERE OUGHTA' BE SOME KINDA HINT HOW TO GET HOME...
KAG-OME ...
KAG-OME ...
WE LOOKED EVERYWHERE BUT SHE'S NOT HERE.

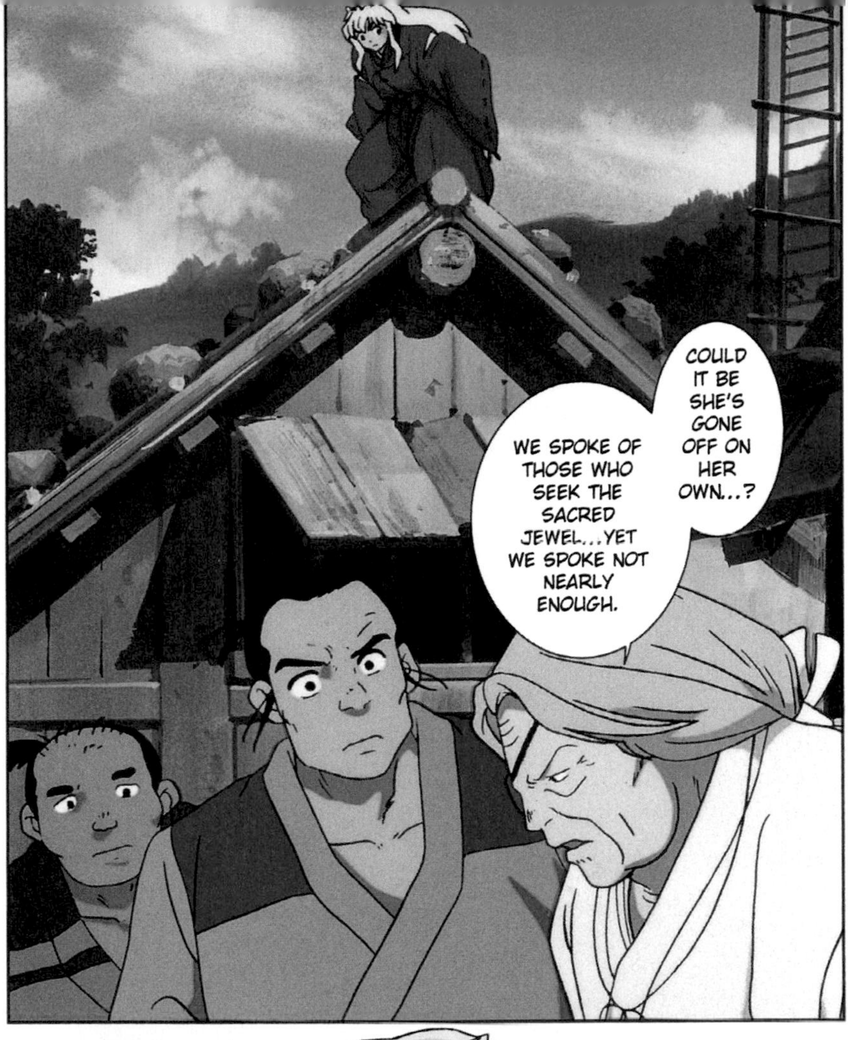
COULD IT BE SHE'S GONE OFF ON HER OWN...?
WE SPOKE OF THOSE WHO SEEK THE SACRED JEWEL...YET WE SPOKE NOT NEARLY ENOUGH.

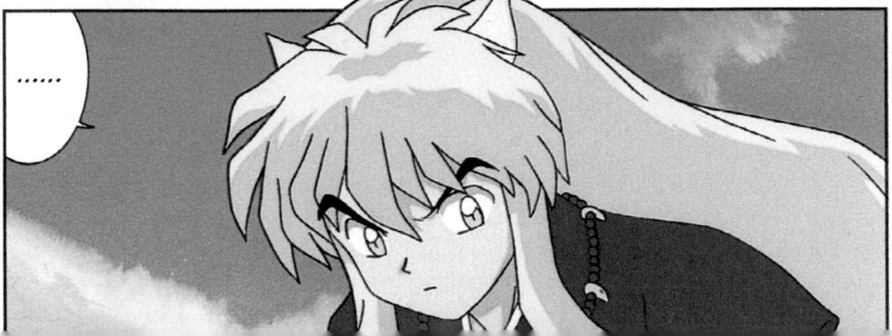
......

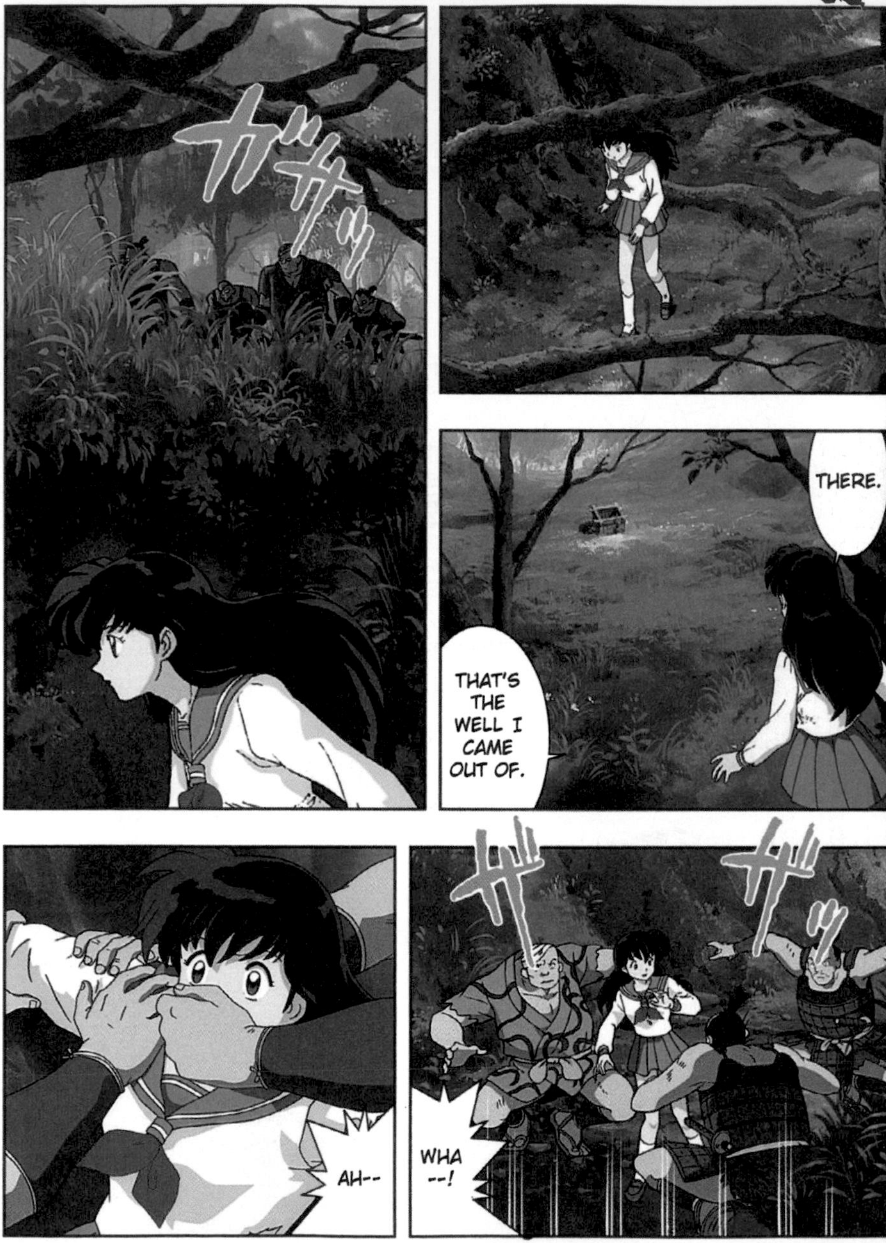
THERE.
THAT'S THE WELL I CAME OUT OF.
ガサッ
ザ
ザッ
WHA --!
AH--

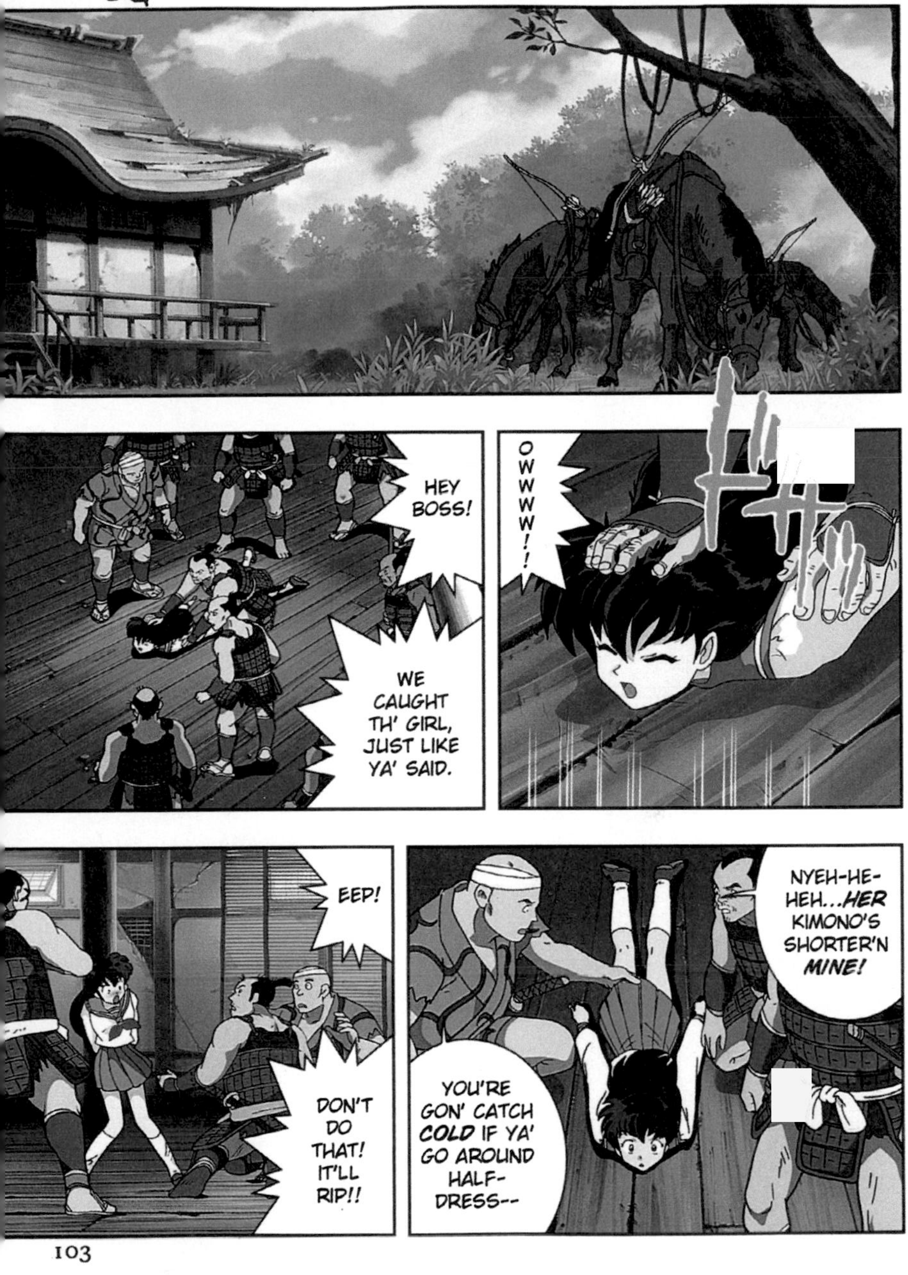
OWWWWW!!
HEY BOSS!
WE CAUGHT TH' GIRL, JUST LIKE YA' SAID.
NYEH-HE-HEH...HER KIMONO'S SHORTER'N MINE!
YOU'RE GON' CATCH COLD IF YA' GO AROUND HALF-DRESS--
EEP!
DON'T DO THAT! IT'LL RIP!!

HAN'
O'ER THE
JEWEL—
RIGHT
NOW.

AAAHGH!!

!?

HEY
BOSS!

TRY TAKIN'
HER HEAD
OFF IN ONE
SWING LIKE A
DANDYLION...!

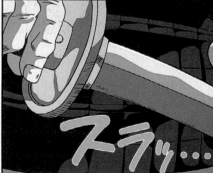

スラッ...

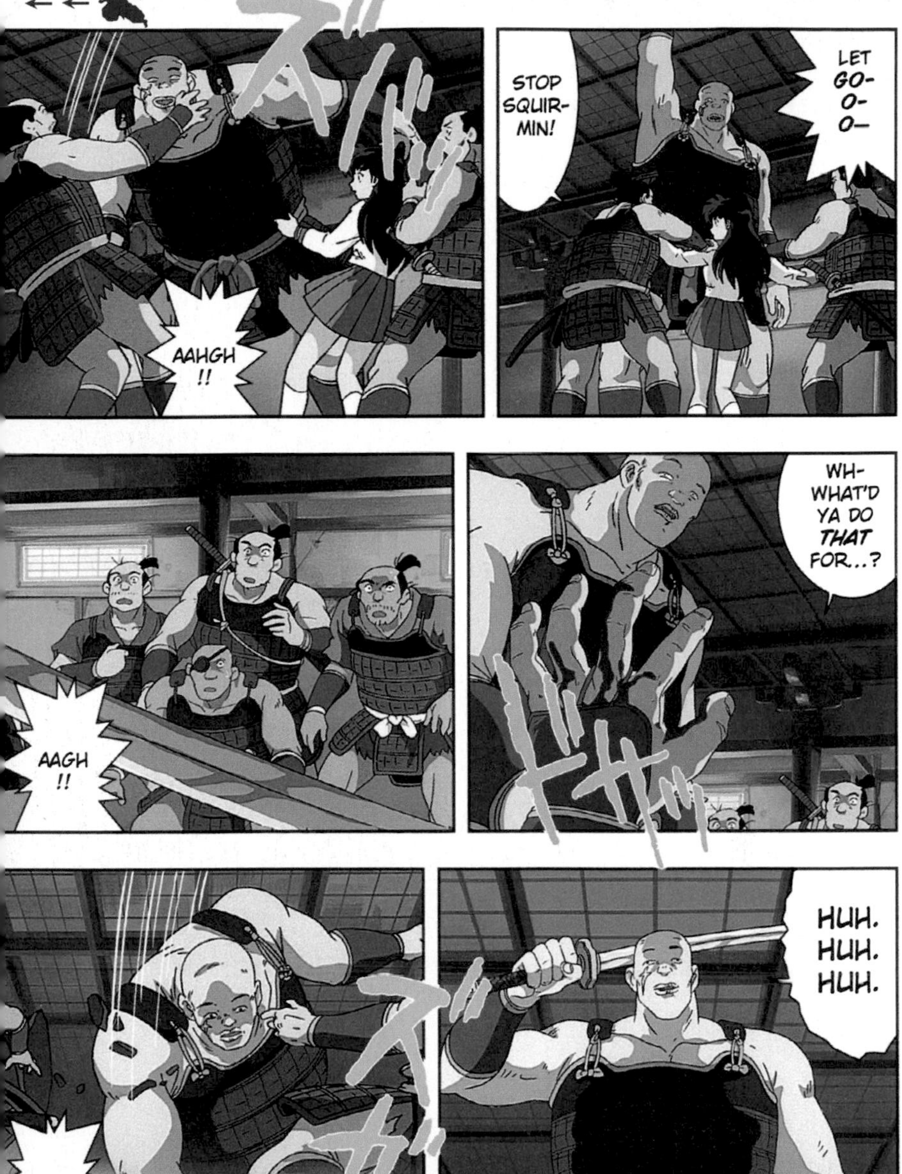
LET GO-O-O-
STOP SQUIRMIN!
ズドッ
AAHGH !!
WH-WHAT'D YA DO *THAT* FOR...?
ドサッ
AAGH !!
HUH. HUH. HUH.
ズガッ
AAAHH !

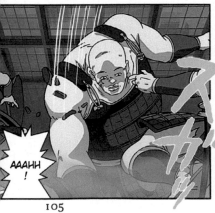

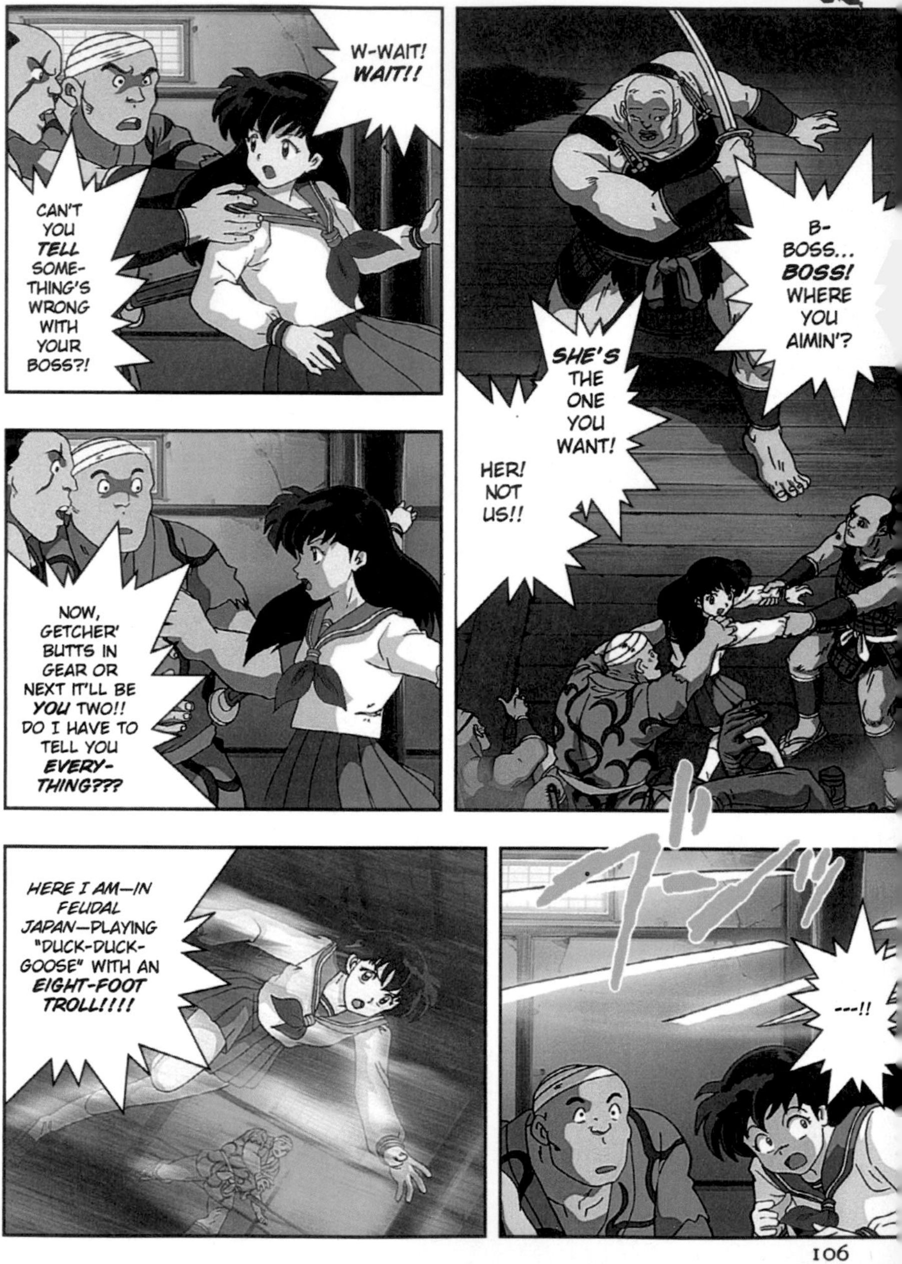
B-BOSS... BOSS! WHERE YOU AIMIN'?
SHE'S THE ONE YOU WANT!
HER! NOT US!!
W-WAIT! WAIT!!
CAN'T YOU TELL SOMETHING'S WRONG WITH YOUR BOSS?!
NOW, GETCHER' BUTTS IN GEAR OR NEXT IT'LL BE YOU TWO!! DO I HAVE TO TELL YOU EVERYTHING???
---!!
HERE I AM—IN FEUDAL JAPAN—PLAYING "DUCK-DUCK-GOOSE" WITH AN EIGHT-FOOT TROLL!!!!

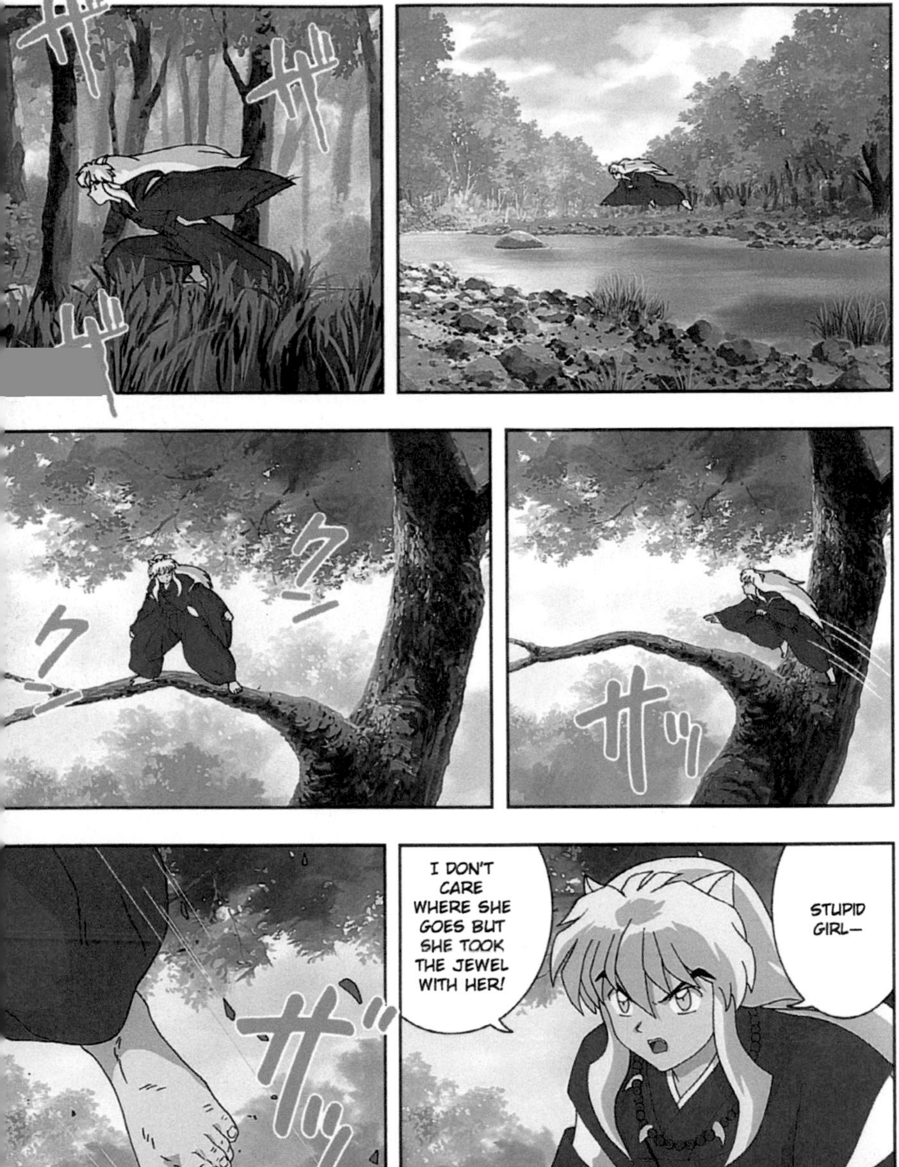
ザ
ザ
ザ
ザッ
ク
クー
STUPID GIRL—
I DON'T CARE WHERE SHE GOES BUT SHE TOOK THE JEWEL WITH HER!
ザッ

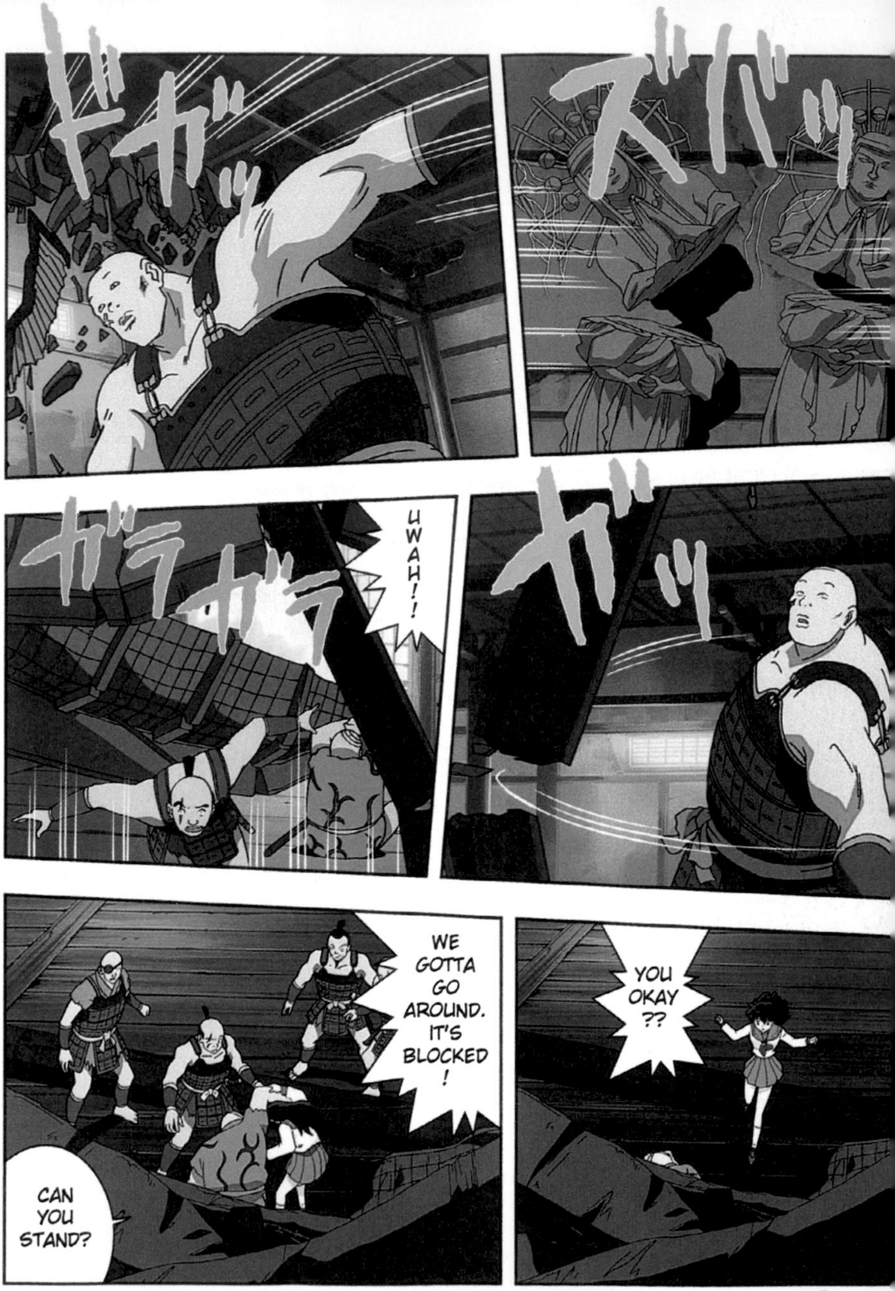
ズバッ
ドガッ
ガッ
ガラガラ
UWAH!!
YOU OKAY??
WE GOTTA GO AROUND. IT'S BLOCKED!
CAN YOU STAND?

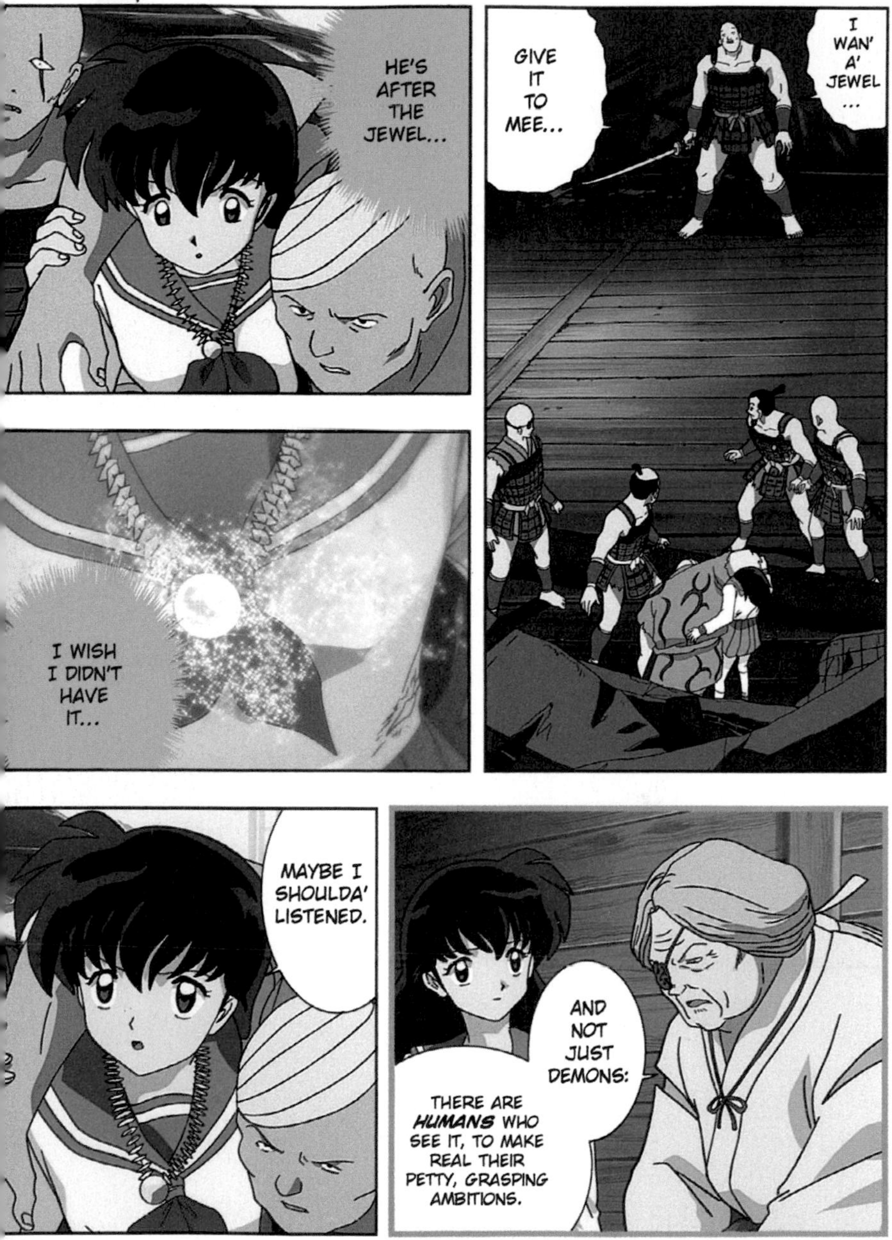
I WAN' A' JEWEL...
GIVE IT TO MEE...
HE'S AFTER THE JEWEL...
I WISH I DIDN'T HAVE IT...
AND NOT JUST DEMONS:
THERE ARE ***HUMANS*** WHO SEE IT, TO MAKE REAL THEIR PETTY, GRASPING AMBITIONS.
MAYBE I SHOULDA' LISTENED.

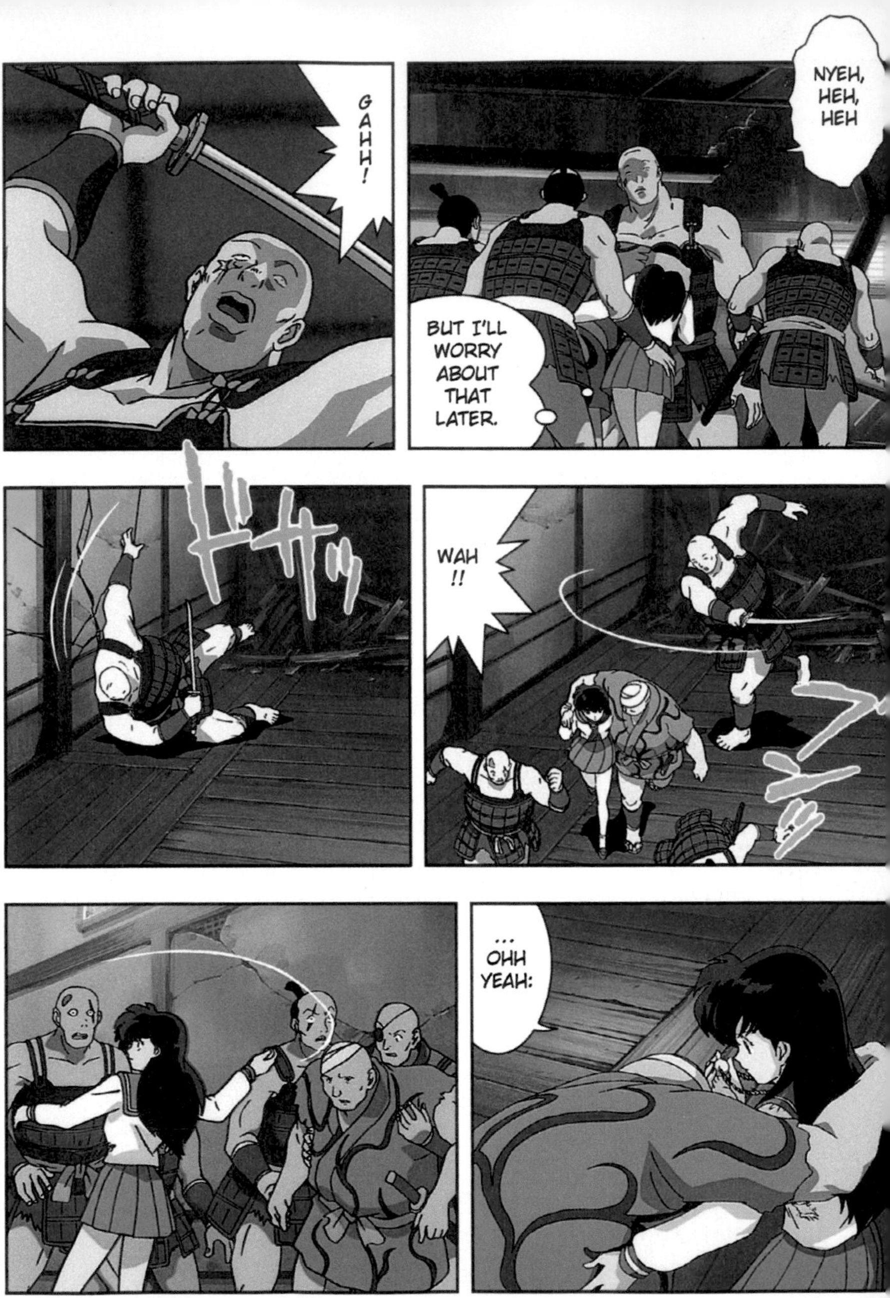
NYEH, HEH, HEH
BUT I'LL WORRY ABOUT THAT LATER.
GAHH!
WAH !!
ドサッ
... OHH YEAH:

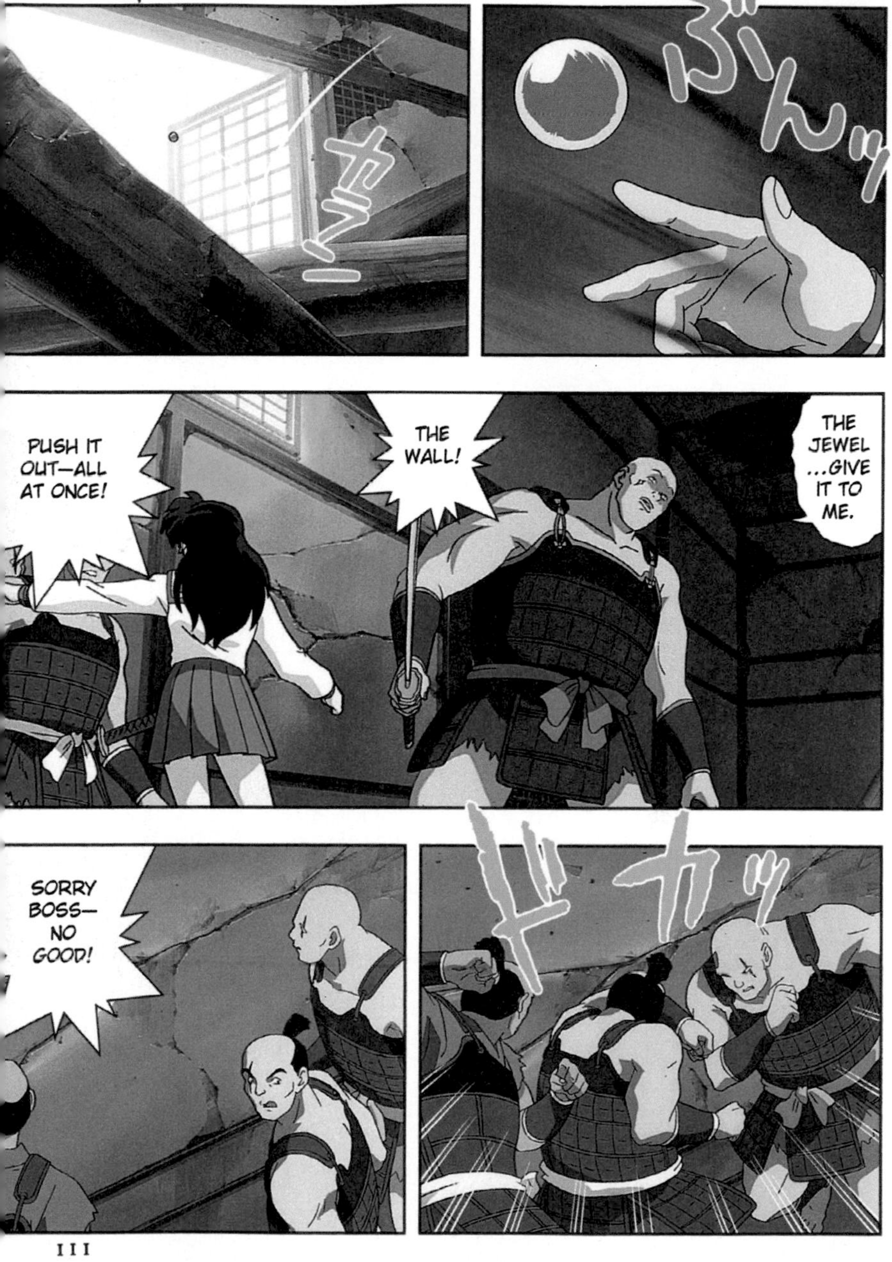
ぶんッ
カラー
THE JEWEL ...GIVE IT TO ME.
THE WALL!
PUSH IT OUT—ALL AT ONCE!
ドカッ
SORRY BOSS—NO GOOD!

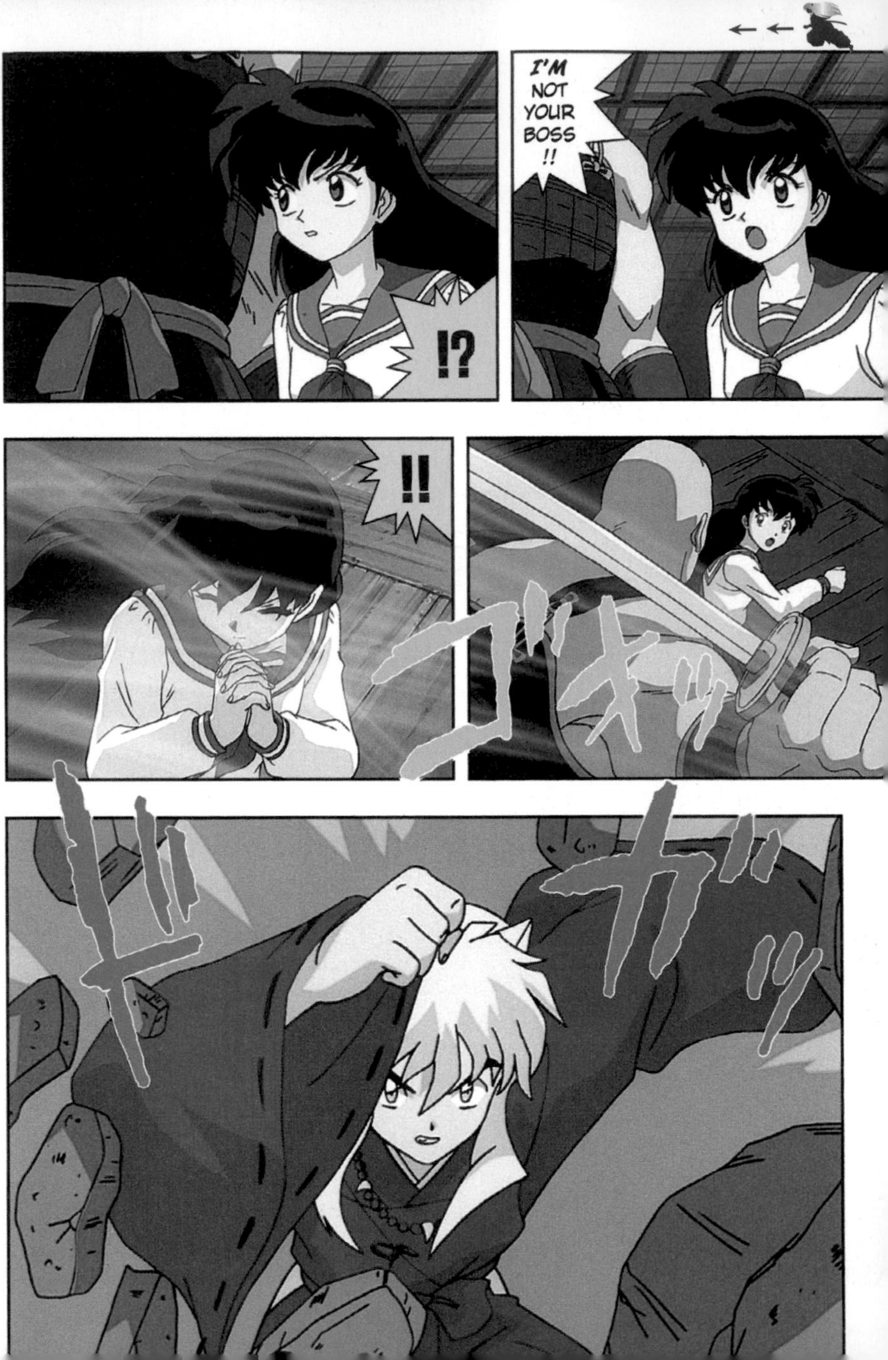
I'M NOT YOUR BOSS !!
!?
!!

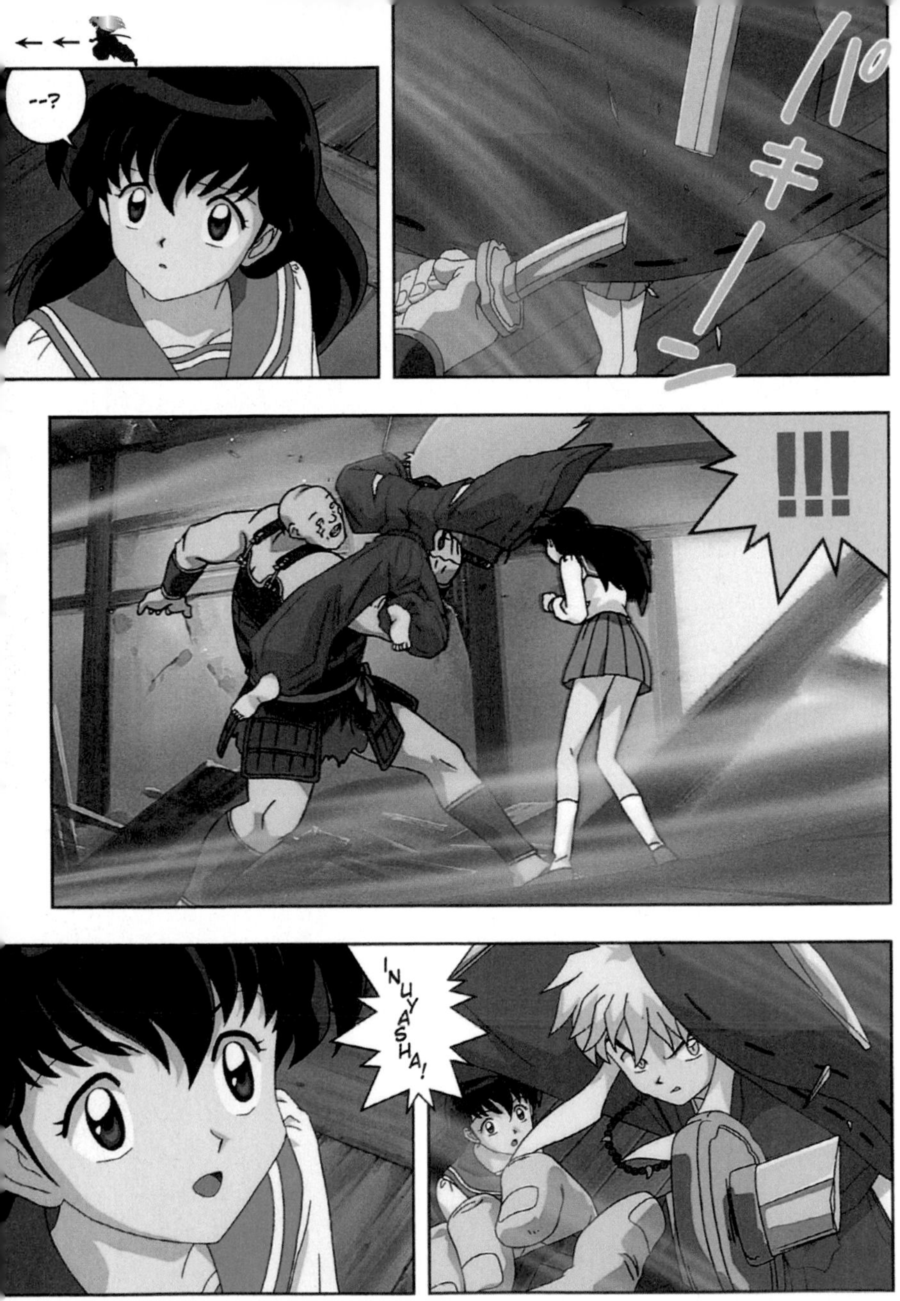
パキーン
--?
!!!
INUYASHA!

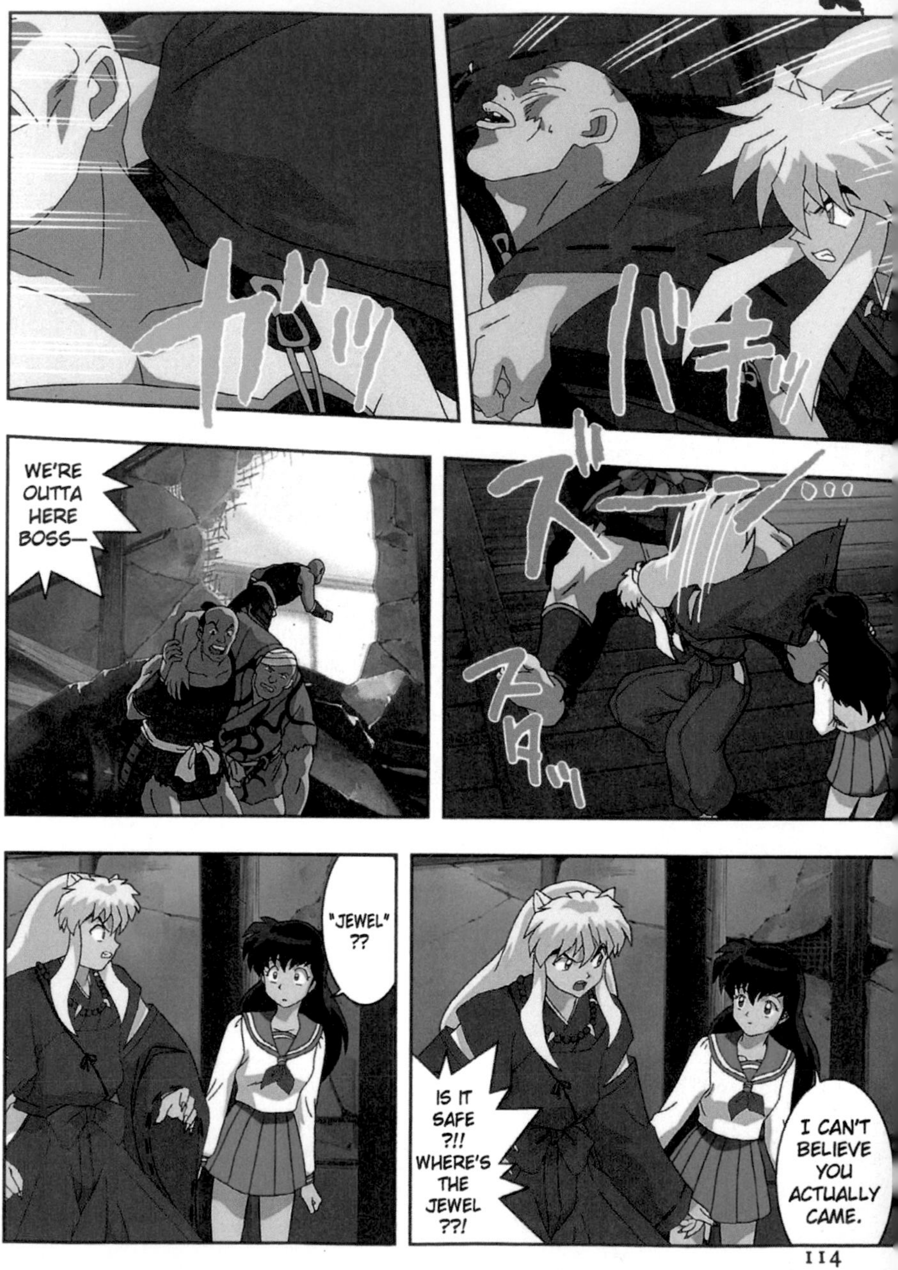
バキッ
ガッ
ズーン…
スタッ
WE'RE OUTTA HERE BOSS—
I CAN'T BELIEVE YOU ACTUALLY CAME.
IS IT SAFE ?!! WHERE'S THE JEWEL ??!
"JEWEL" ??

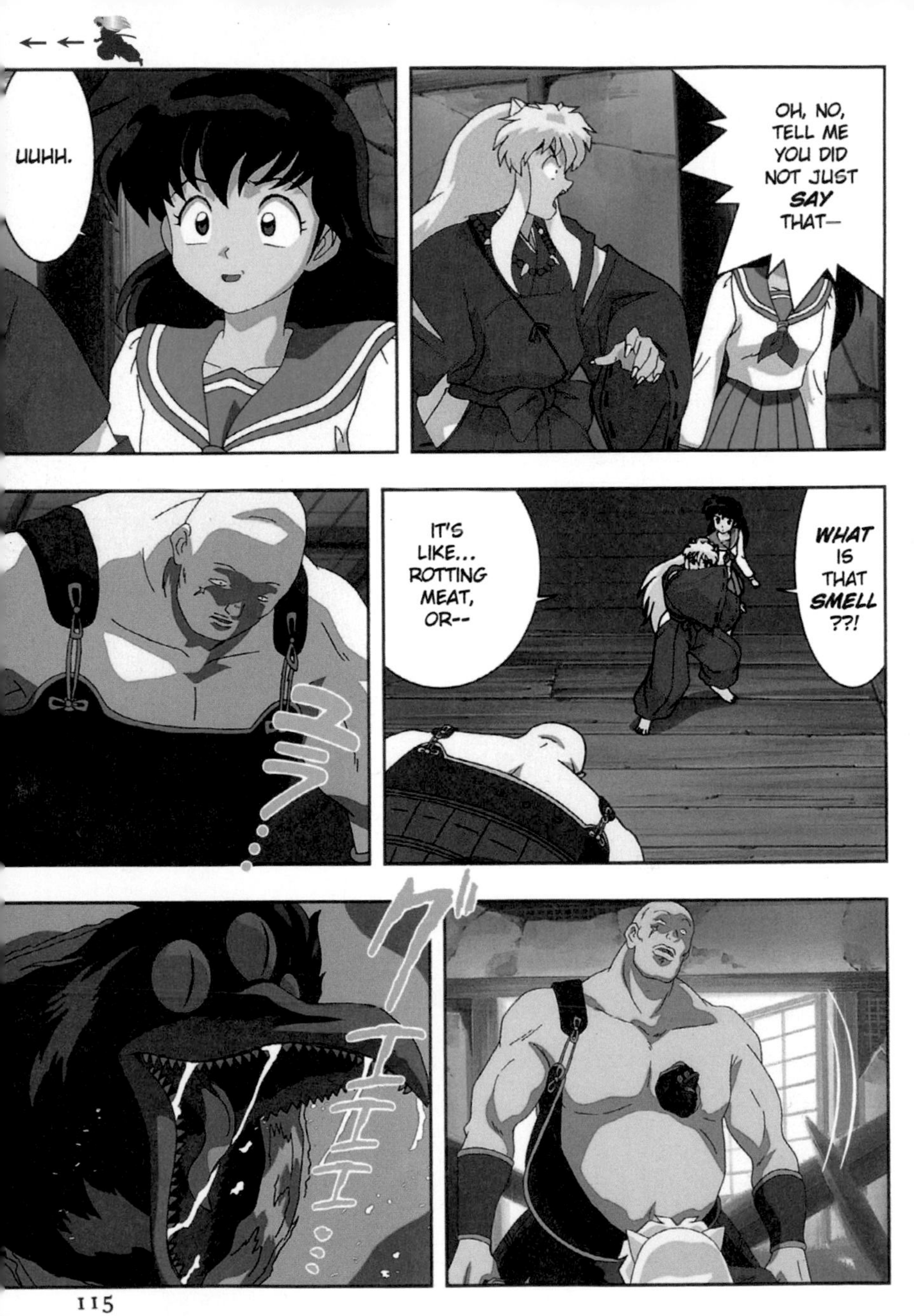
OH, NO, TELL ME YOU DID NOT JUST **SAY** THAT—
UUHH.
WHAT IS THAT **SMELL** ??!
IT'S LIKE... ROTTING MEAT, OR--

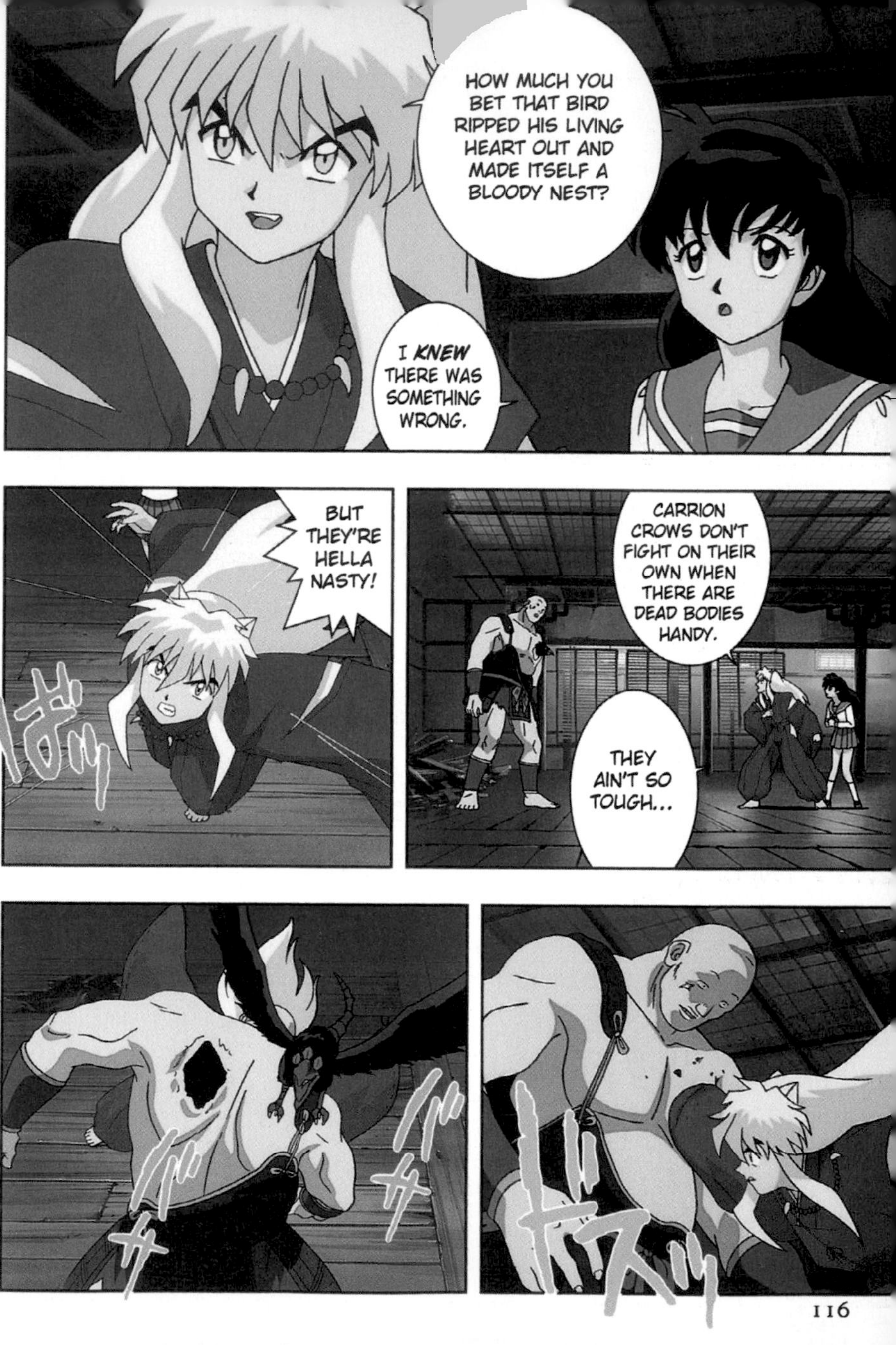
HOW MUCH YOU BET THAT BIRD RIPPED HIS LIVING HEART OUT AND MADE ITSELF A BLOODY NEST?
I *KNEW* THERE WAS SOMETHING WRONG.
CARRION CROWS DON'T FIGHT ON THEIR OWN WHEN THERE ARE DEAD BODIES HANDY.
THEY AIN'T SO TOUGH...
BUT THEY'RE HELLA NASTY!
ばッ
ドスッ
ザザ

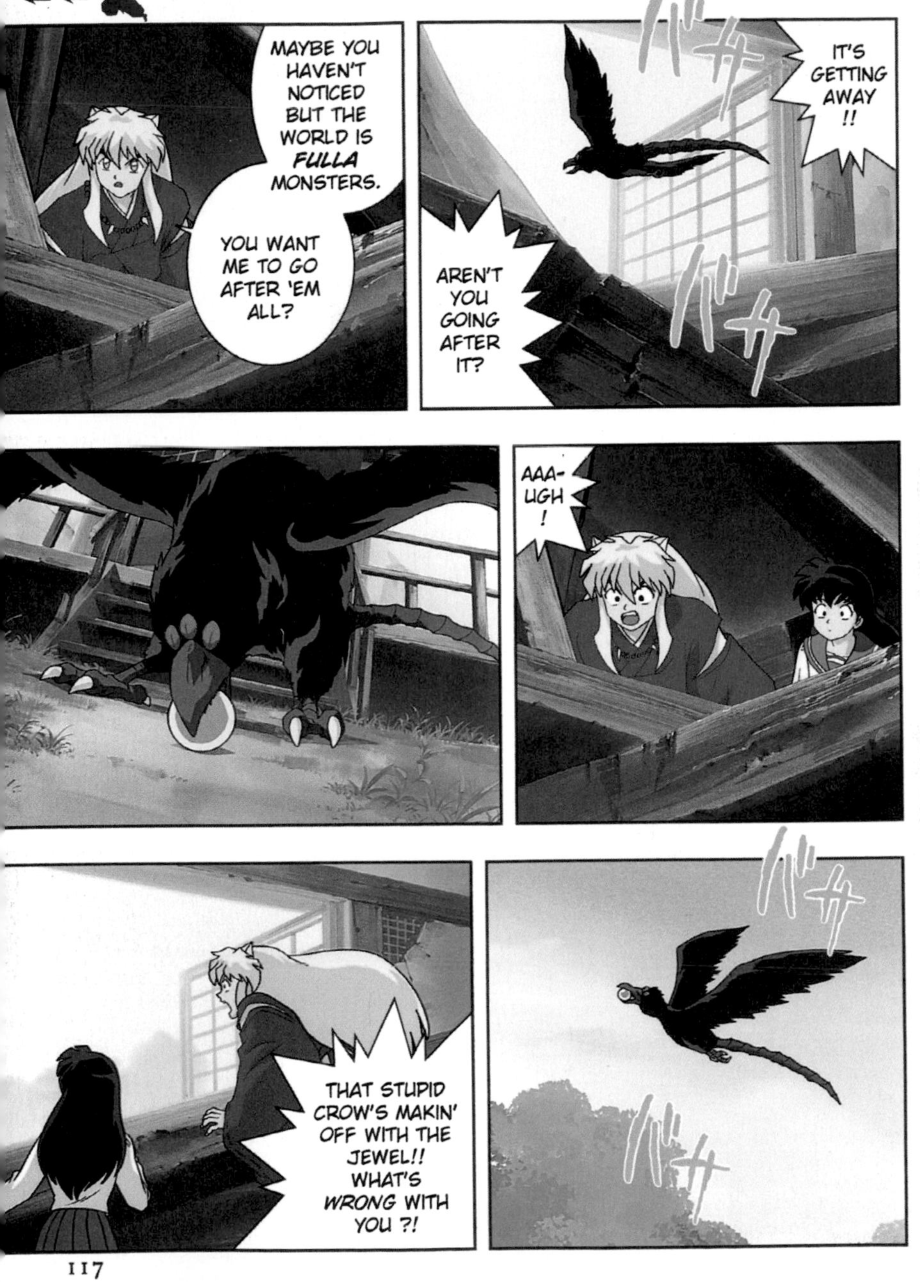
バサ
IT'S GETTING AWAY !!
AREN'T YOU GOING AFTER IT?
バサ
MAYBE YOU HAVEN'T NOTICED BUT THE WORLD IS FULLA MONSTERS.
YOU WANT ME TO GO AFTER 'EM ALL?
AAA-UGH !
バサ
バサ
THAT STUPID CROW'S MAKIN' OFF WITH THE JEWEL!! WHAT'S WRONG WITH YOU ?!

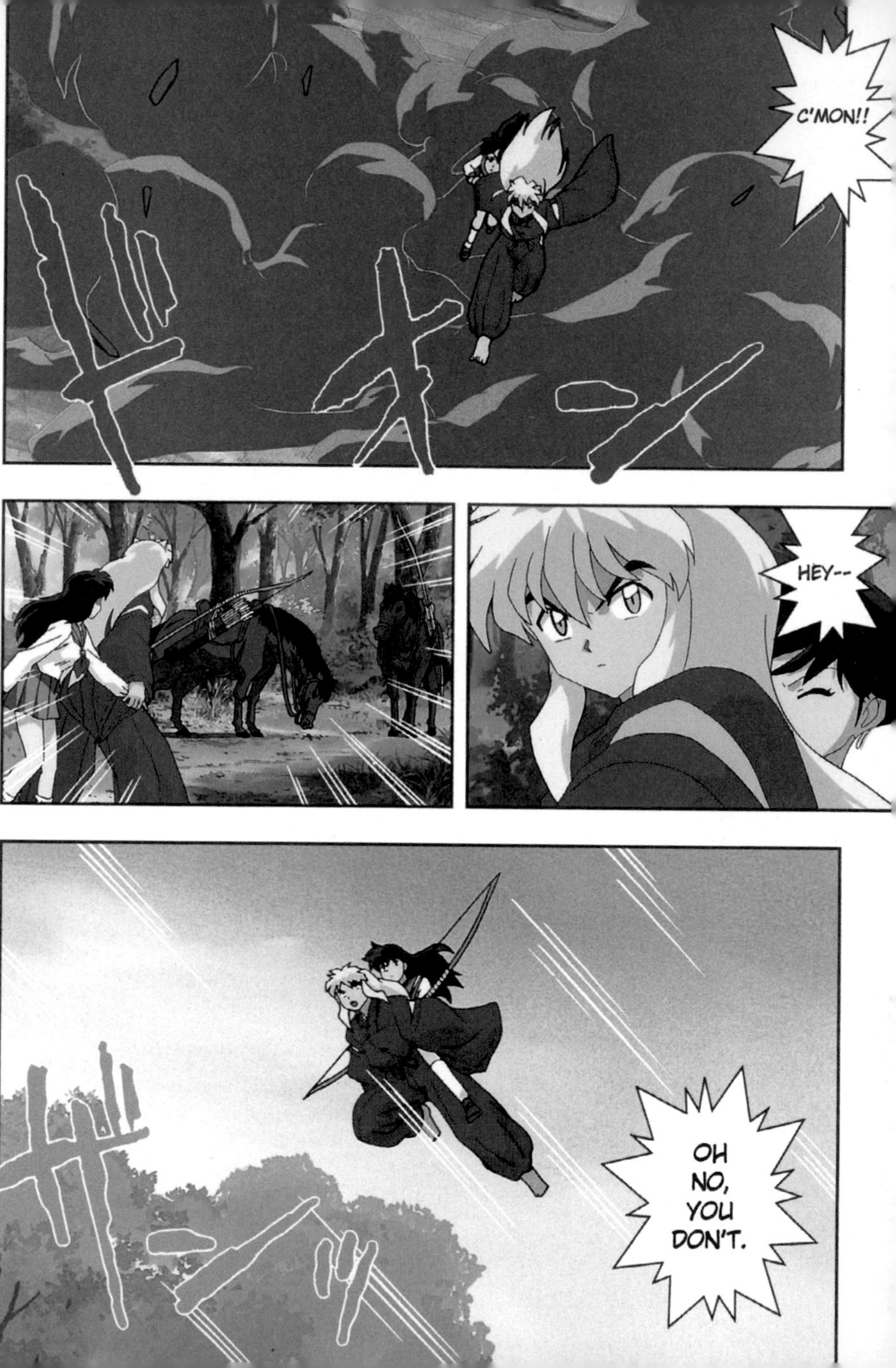
C'MON!!
HEY--
OH NO, YOU DON'T.

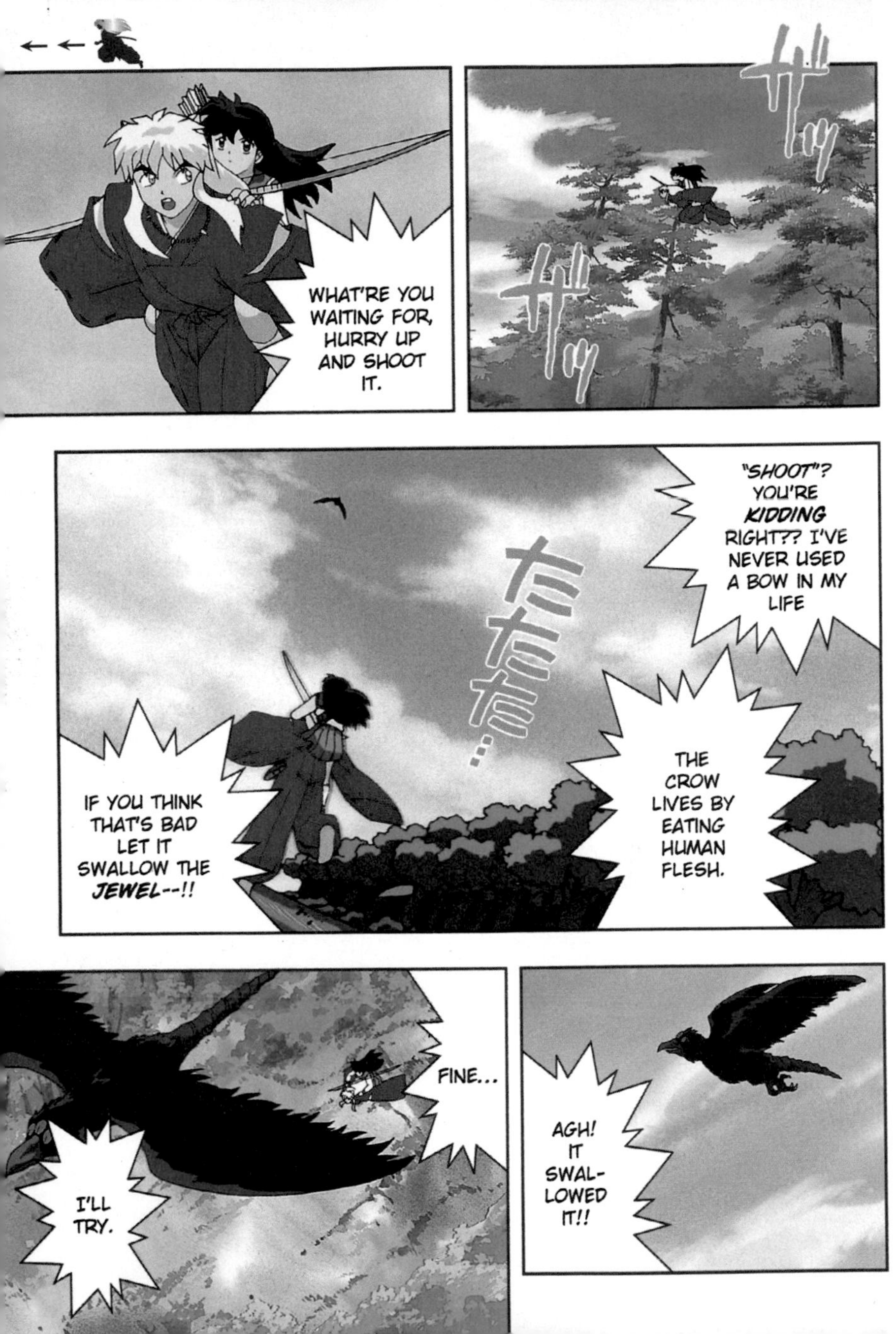
ザッ
ザッ
WHAT'RE YOU WAITING FOR, HURRY UP AND SHOOT IT.
"SHOOT"? YOU'RE KIDDING RIGHT?? I'VE NEVER USED A BOW IN MY LIFE
たたた…
THE CROW LIVES BY EATING HUMAN FLESH.
IF YOU THINK THAT'S BAD LET IT SWALLOW THE JEWEL--!!
AGH! IT SWAL-LOWED IT!!
FINE...
I'LL TRY.

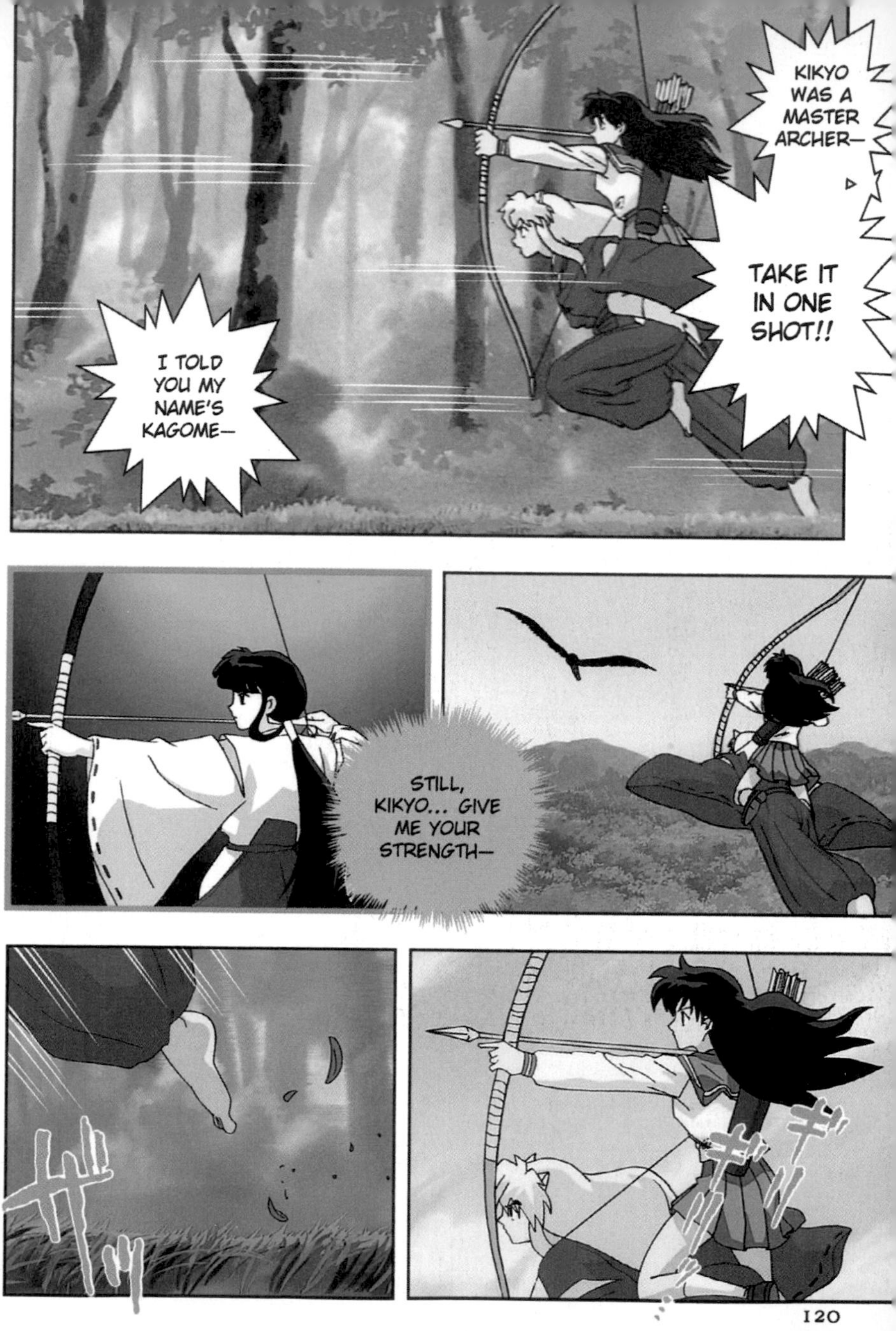
KIKYO WAS A MASTER ARCHER—
TAKE IT IN ONE SHOT!!
I TOLD YOU MY NAME'S KAGOME—
STILL, KIKYO... GIVE ME YOUR STRENGTH—

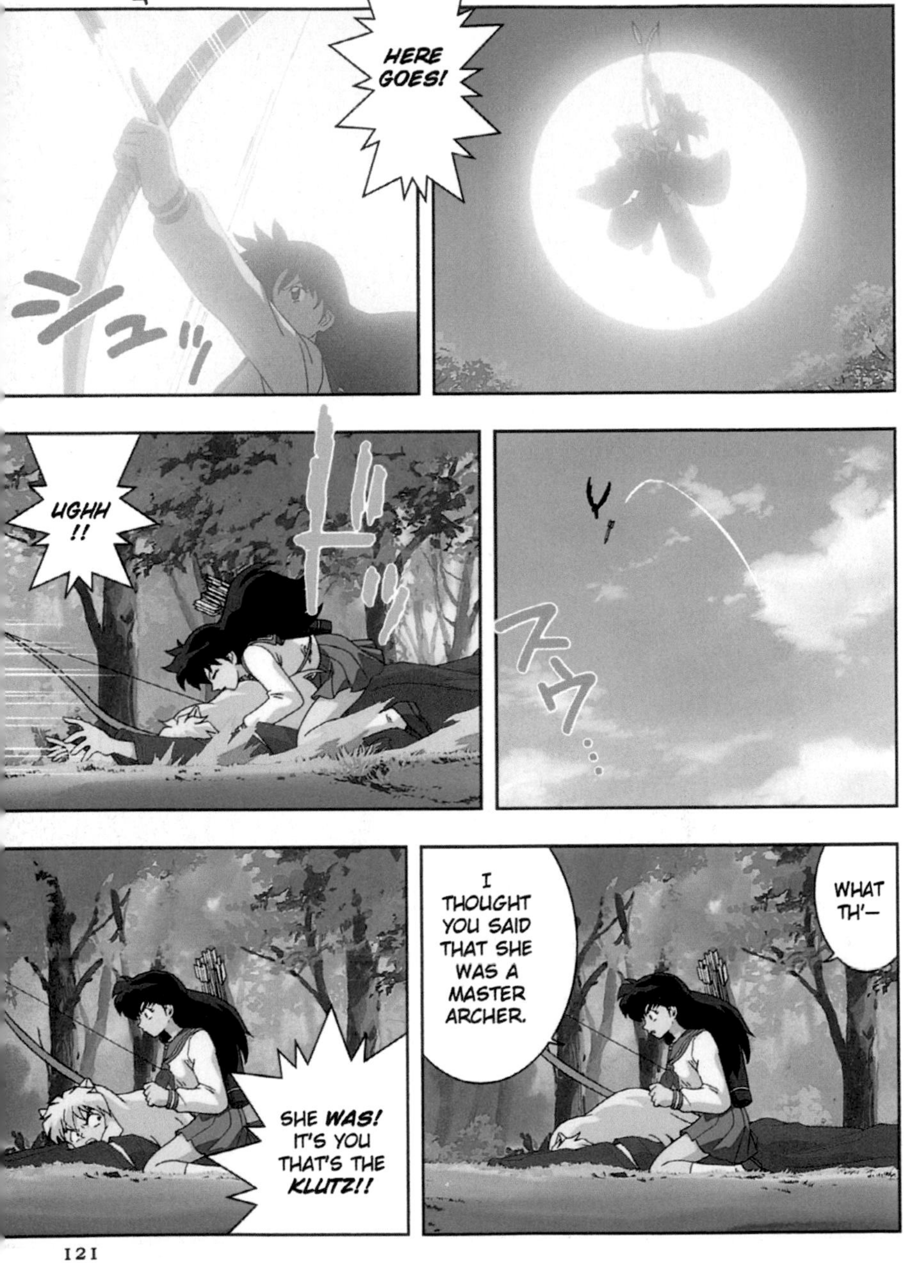
HERE GOES!
シュッ
スゥ…
UGHH !!
ドッ
WHAT TH'—
I THOUGHT YOU SAID THAT SHE WAS A MASTER ARCHER.
SHE WAS! IT'S YOU THAT'S THE KLUTZ!!

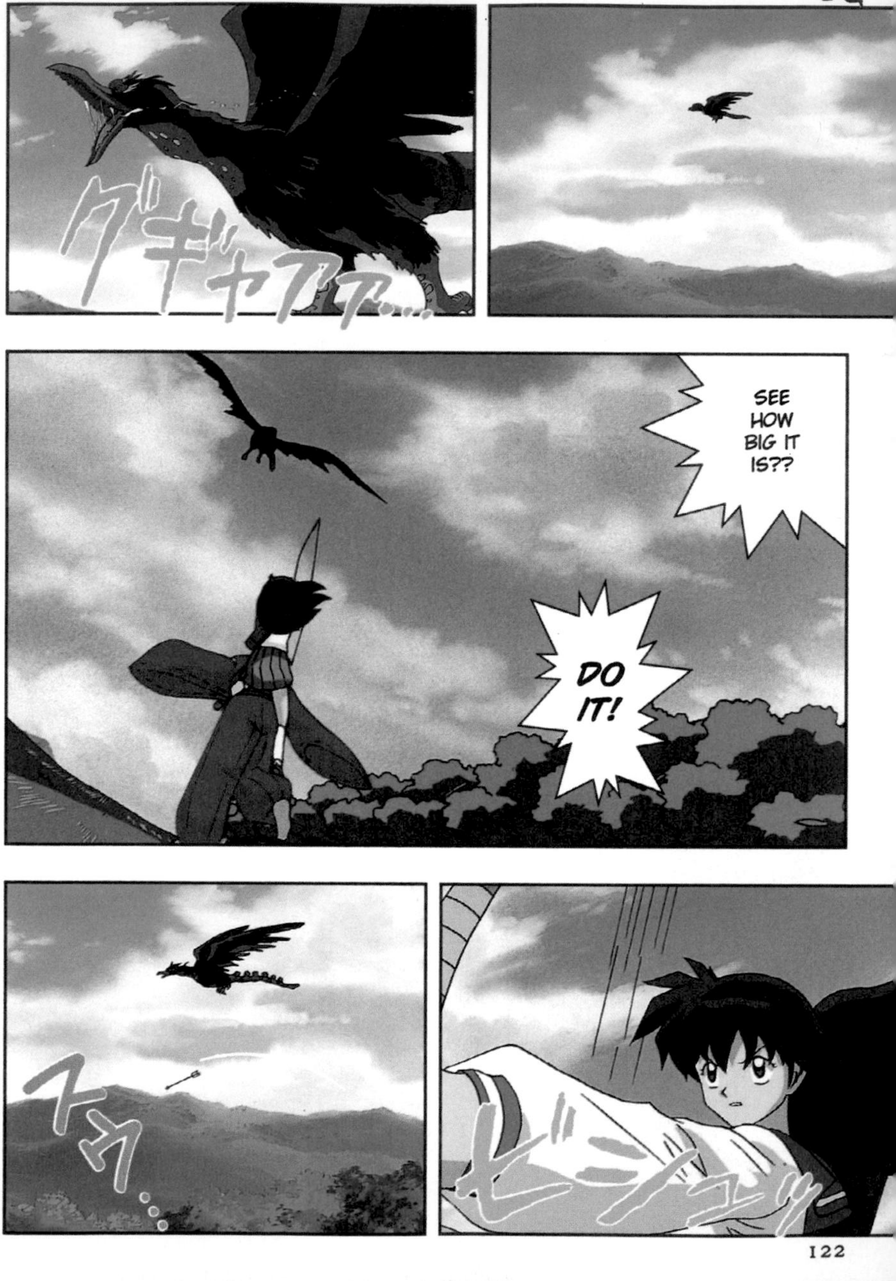

グギャアア…
SEE HOW BIG IT IS??
DO IT!
ビシュッ
スゥ…

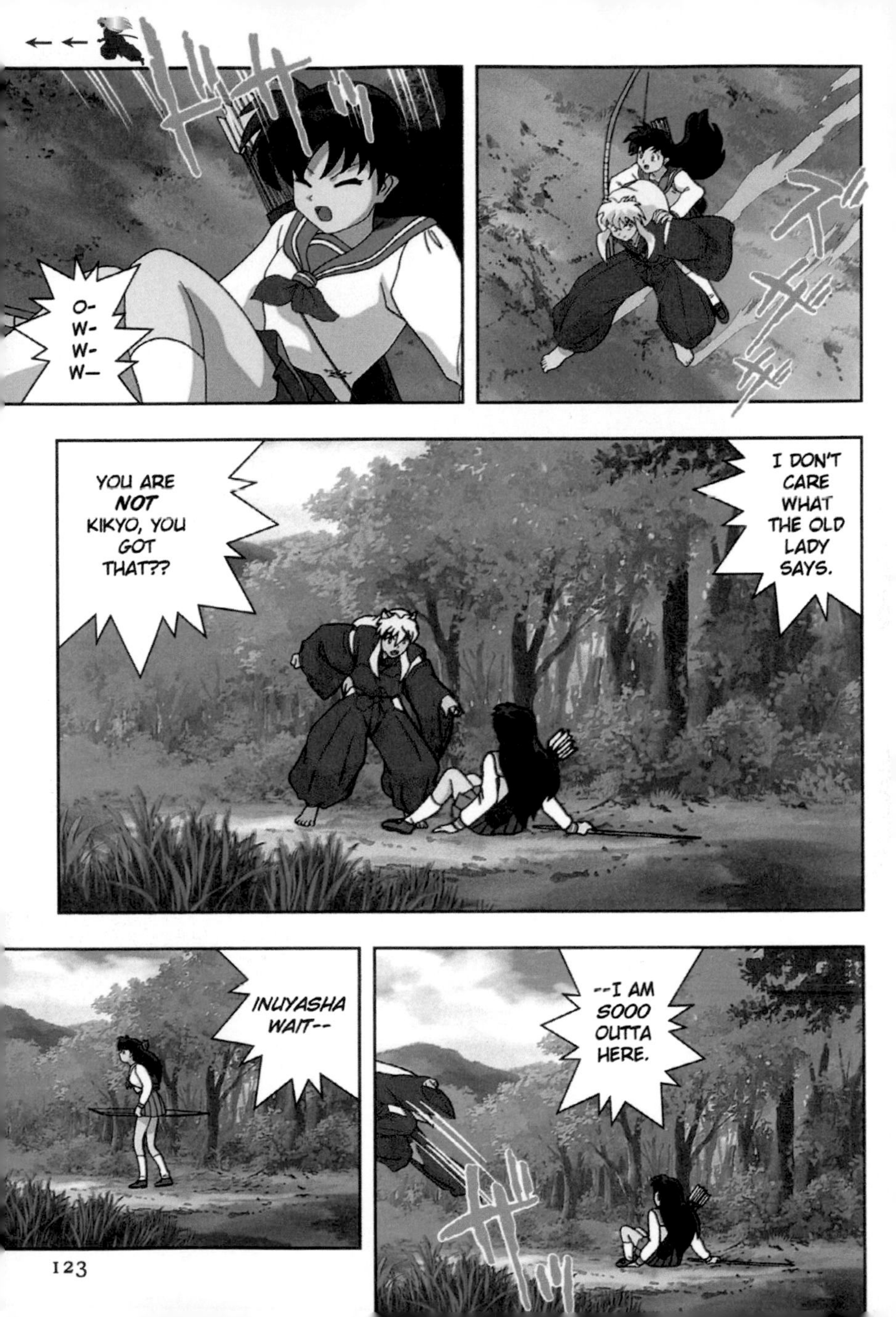
O-W-W-W—
I DON'T CARE WHAT THE OLD LADY SAYS.
YOU ARE **NOT** KIKYO, YOU GOT THAT??
--I AM SOOO OUTTA HERE.
INUYASHA WAIT--

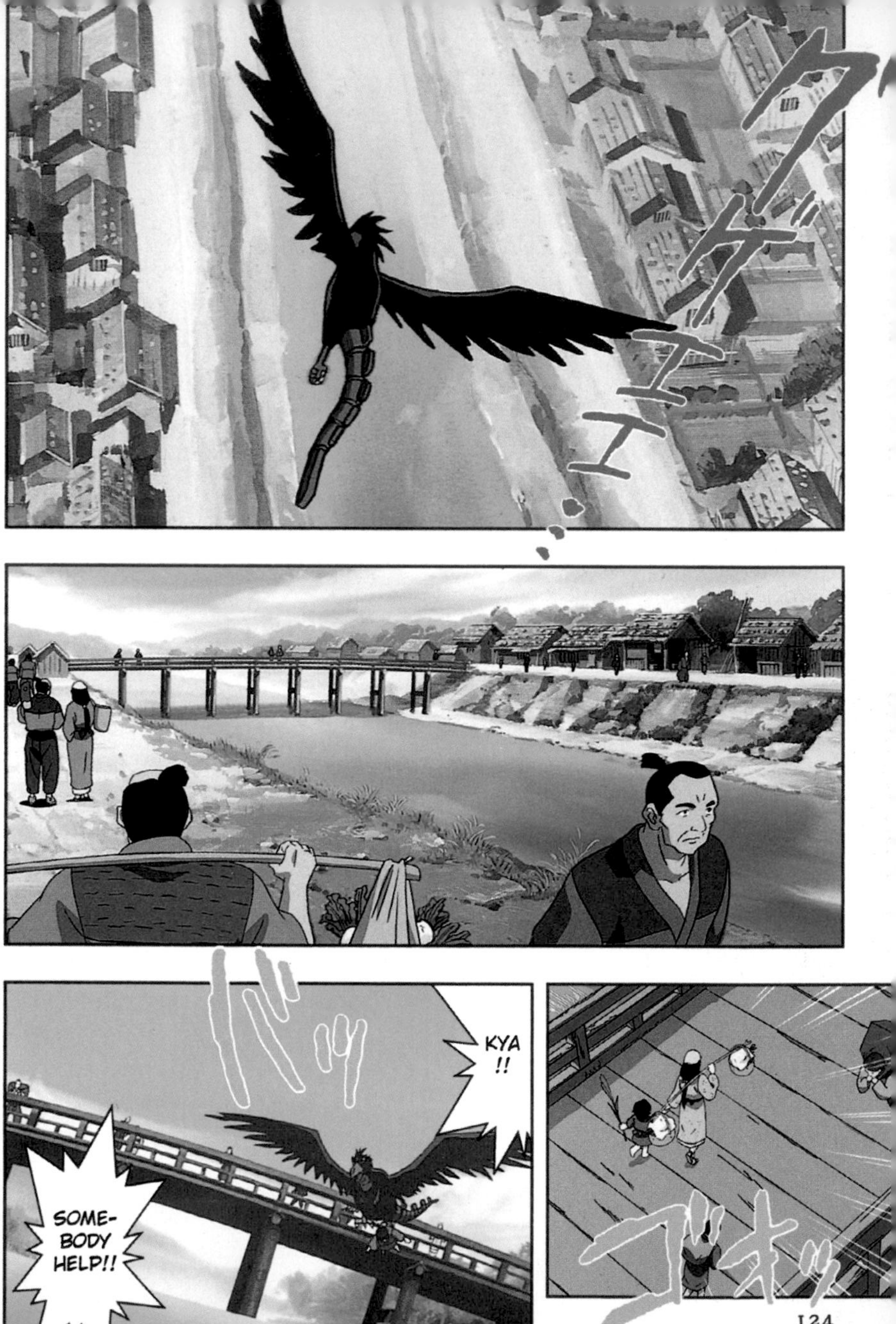

クゲェェ
ゴオッ
KYA !!
バッ
SOME-BODY HELP!!

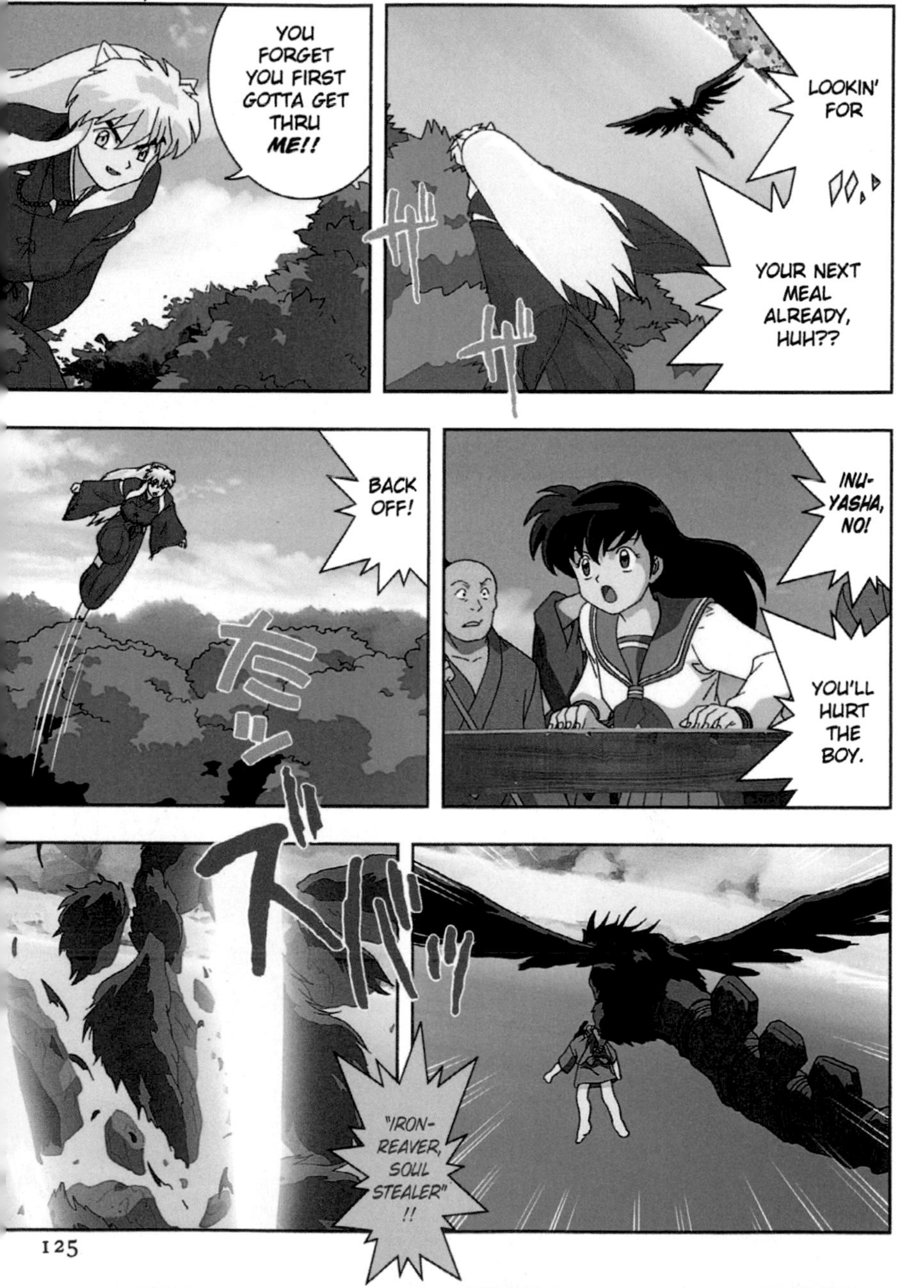
LOOKIN' FOR
YOUR NEXT MEAL ALREADY, HUH??
ザ ザ
YOU FORGET YOU FIRST GOTTA GET THRU ME!!
INU-YASHA, NO!
YOU'LL HURT THE BOY.
BACK OFF!
ダッ
ズバッ
"IRON-REAVER, SOUL STEALER" !!

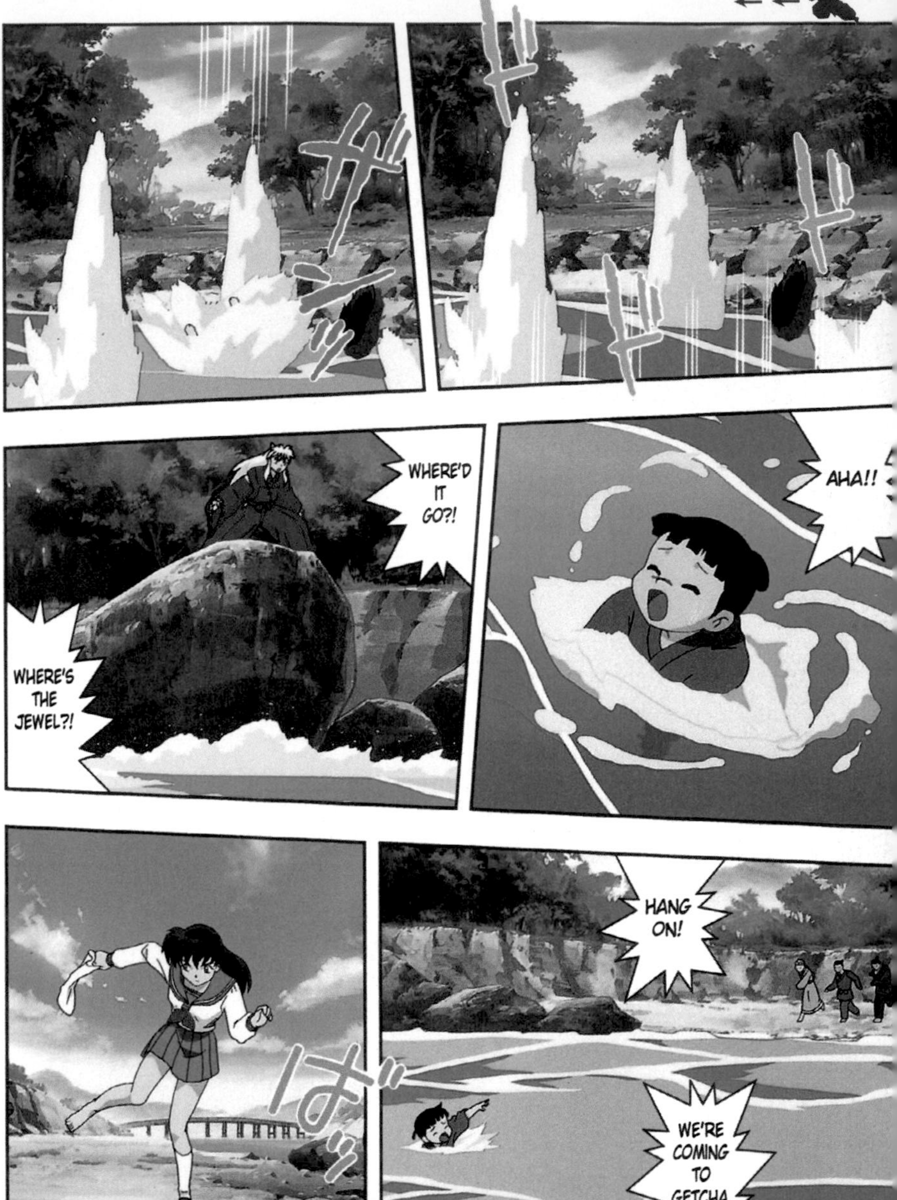
AHA!!
WHERE'D IT GO?!
WHERE'S THE JEWEL?!
HANG ON!
WE'RE COMING TO GETCHA, KID.

HELLP
!

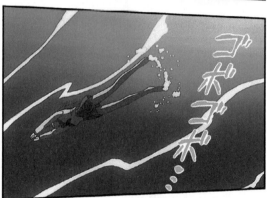

I'M SO
GLAD I
TOOK
LESSONS.

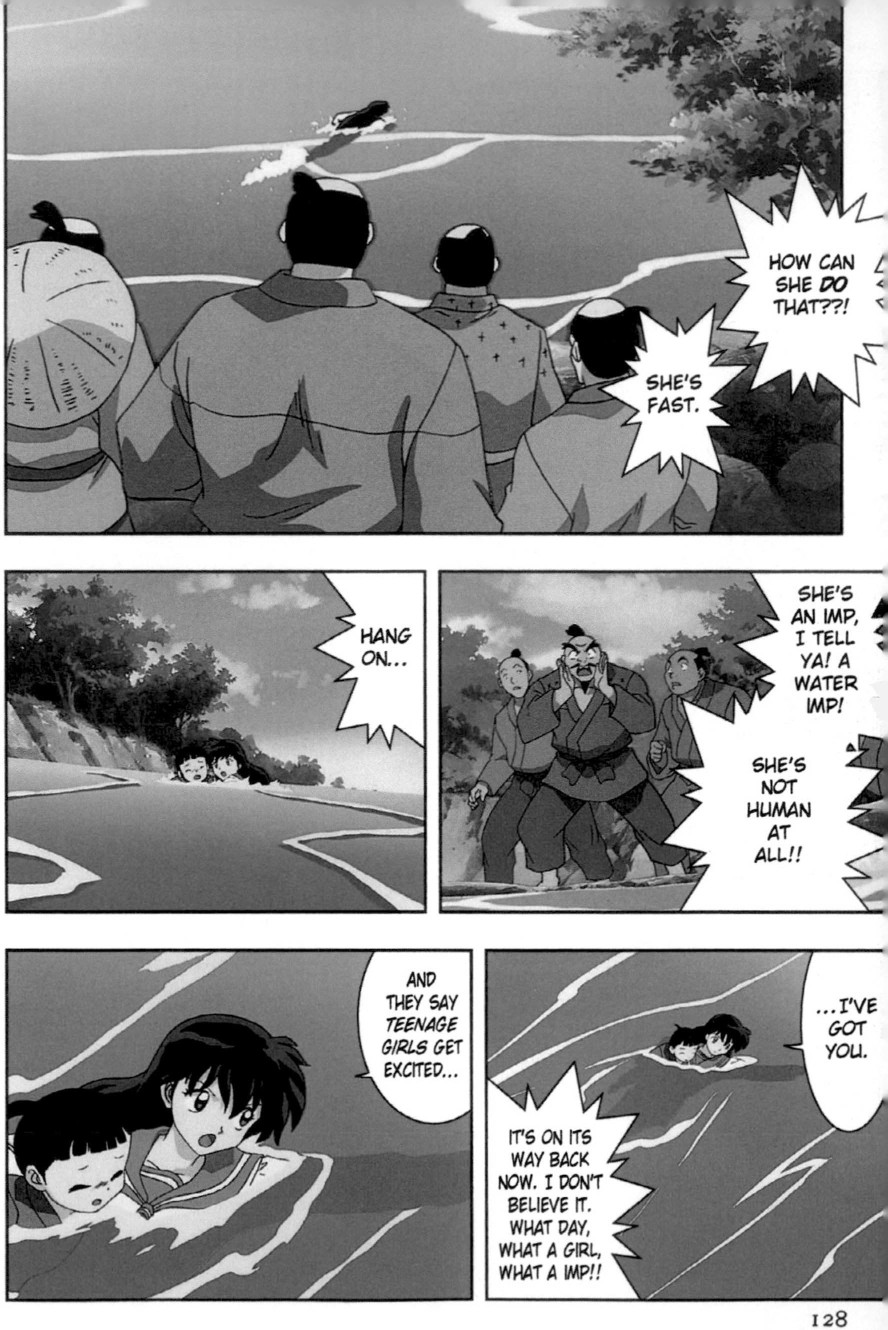
HOW CAN SHE *DO* THAT??!
SHE'S FAST.
SHE'S AN IMP, I TELL YA! A WATER IMP!
SHE'S NOT HUMAN AT ALL!!
HANG ON...
...I'VE GOT YOU.
IT'S ON ITS WAY BACK NOW. I DON'T BELIEVE IT. WHAT DAY, WHAT A GIRL, WHAT A IMP!!
AND THEY SAY *TEENAGE GIRLS* GET EXCITED...

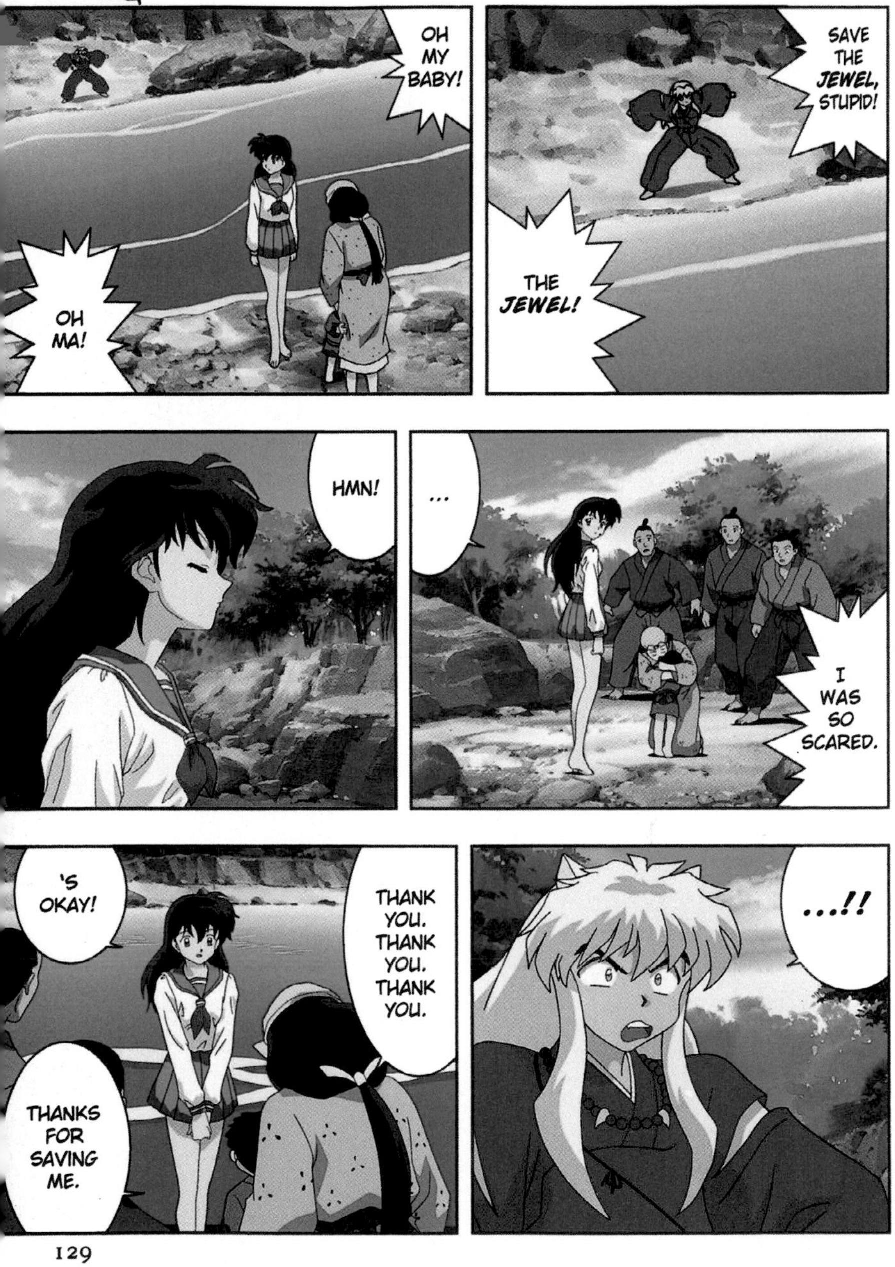
SAVE THE JEWEL, STUPID!
THE JEWEL!
OH MY BABY!
OH MA!
...
I WAS SO SCARED.
HMN!
...!!
THANK YOU. THANK YOU. THANK YOU.
'S OKAY!
THANKS FOR SAVING ME.

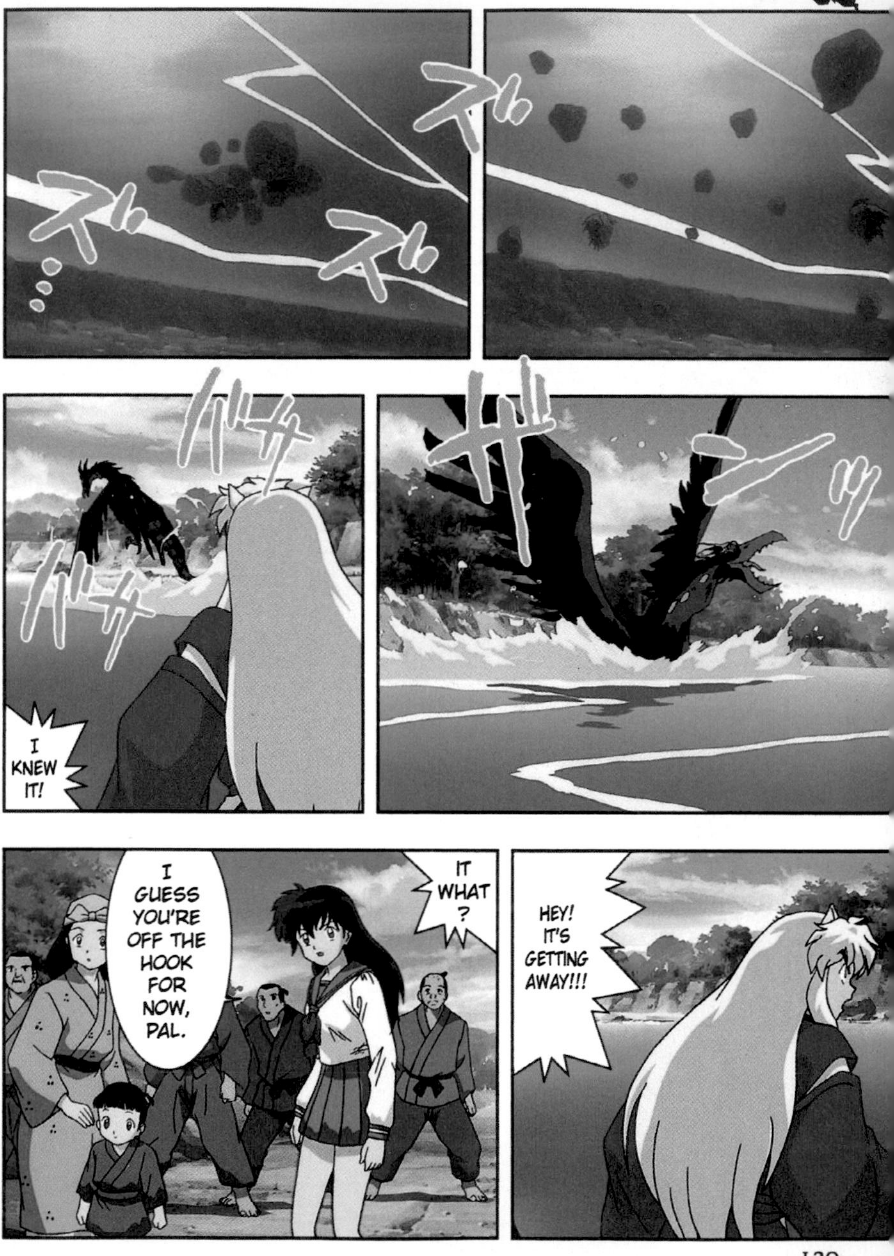
ザーンッ
バサ
バサ
I KNEW IT!
HEY! IT'S GETTING AWAY!!!
IT WHAT?
I GUESS YOU'RE OFF THE HOOK FOR NOW, PAL.

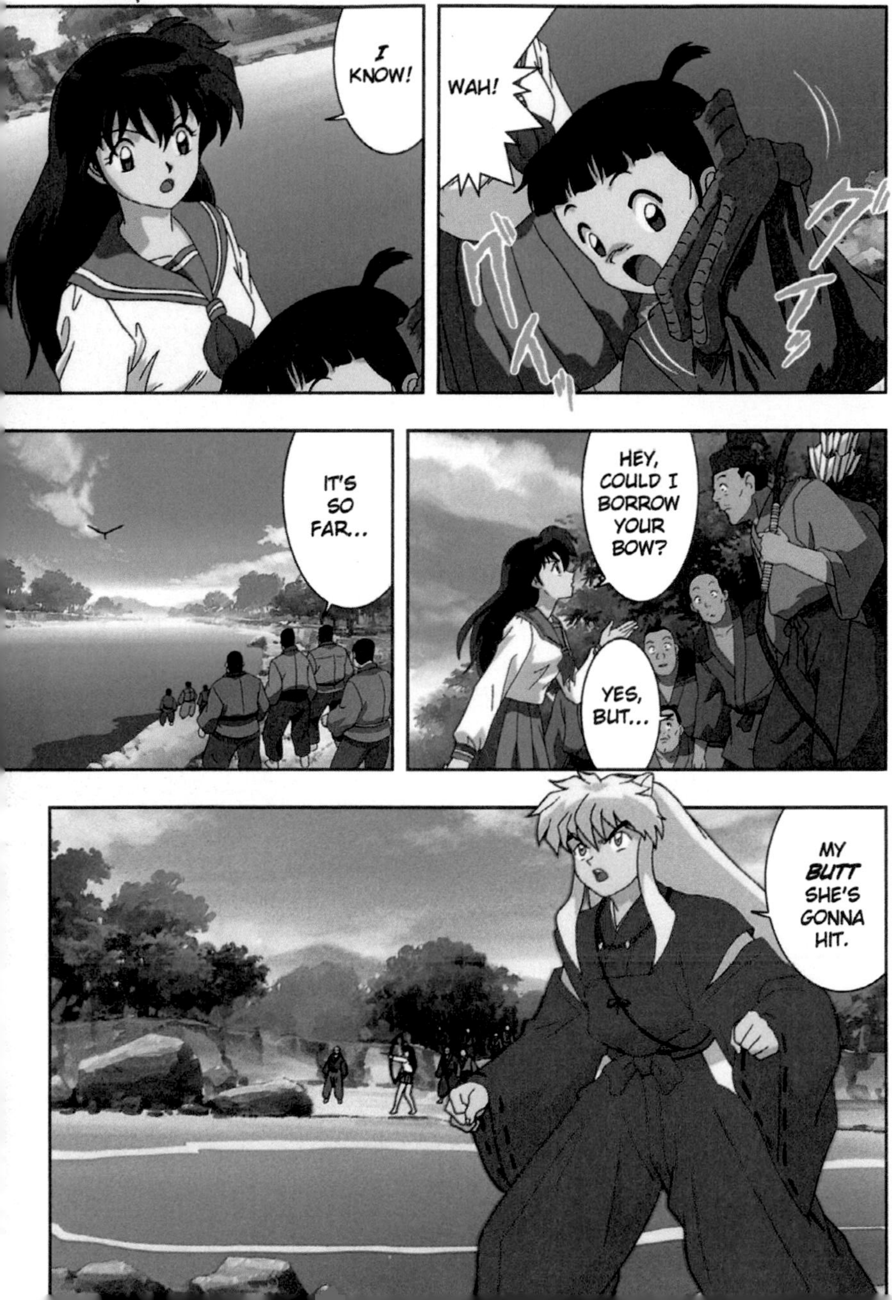
WAH!
I KNOW!
HEY, COULD I BORROW YOUR BOW?
YES, BUT...
IT'S SO FAR...
MY *BUTT* SHE'S GONNA HIT.

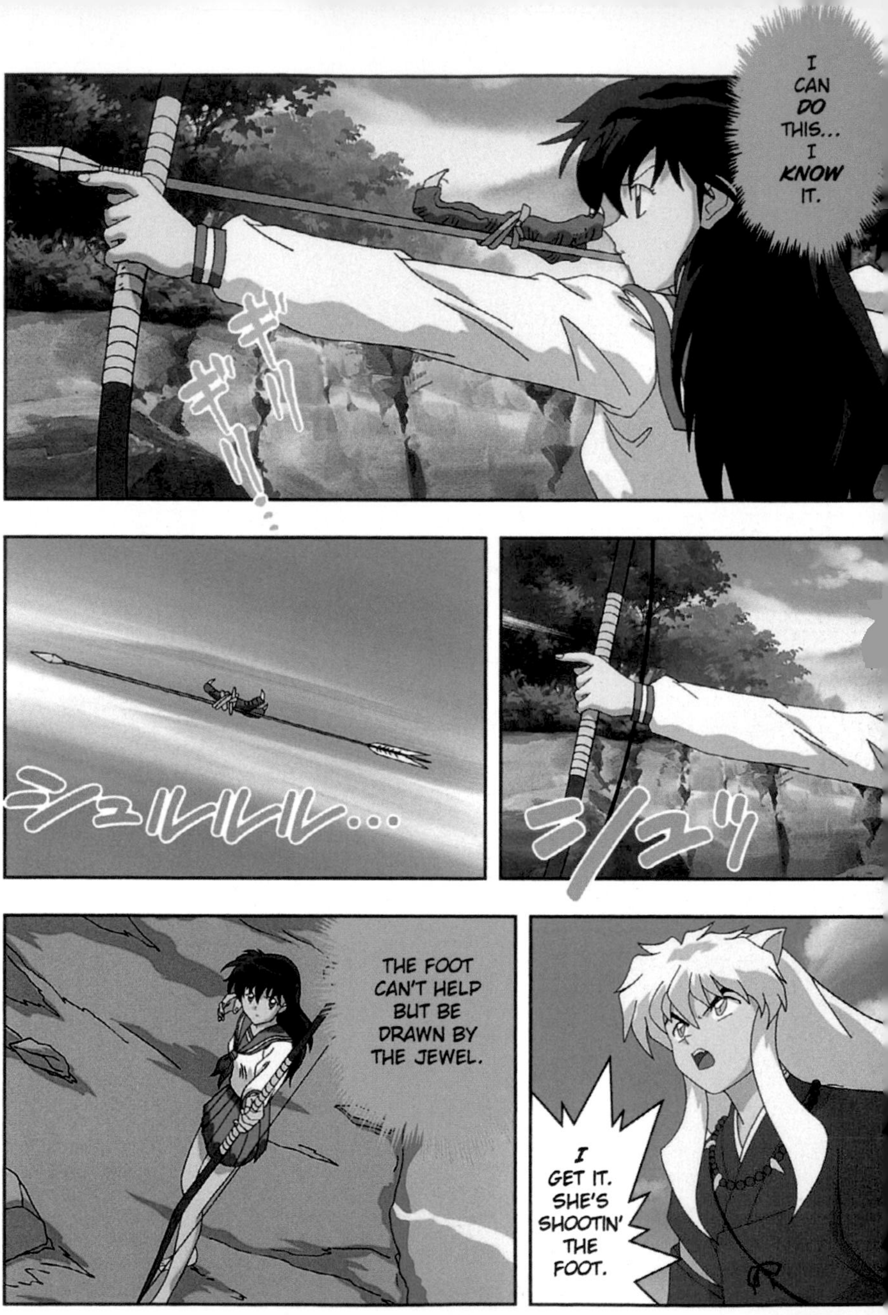
I CAN DO THIS... I KNOW IT.
ギリギリ...
シュッ
シュルルルル...
I GET IT. SHE'S SHOOTIN' THE FOOT.
THE FOOT CAN'T HELP BUT BE DRAWN BY THE JEWEL.

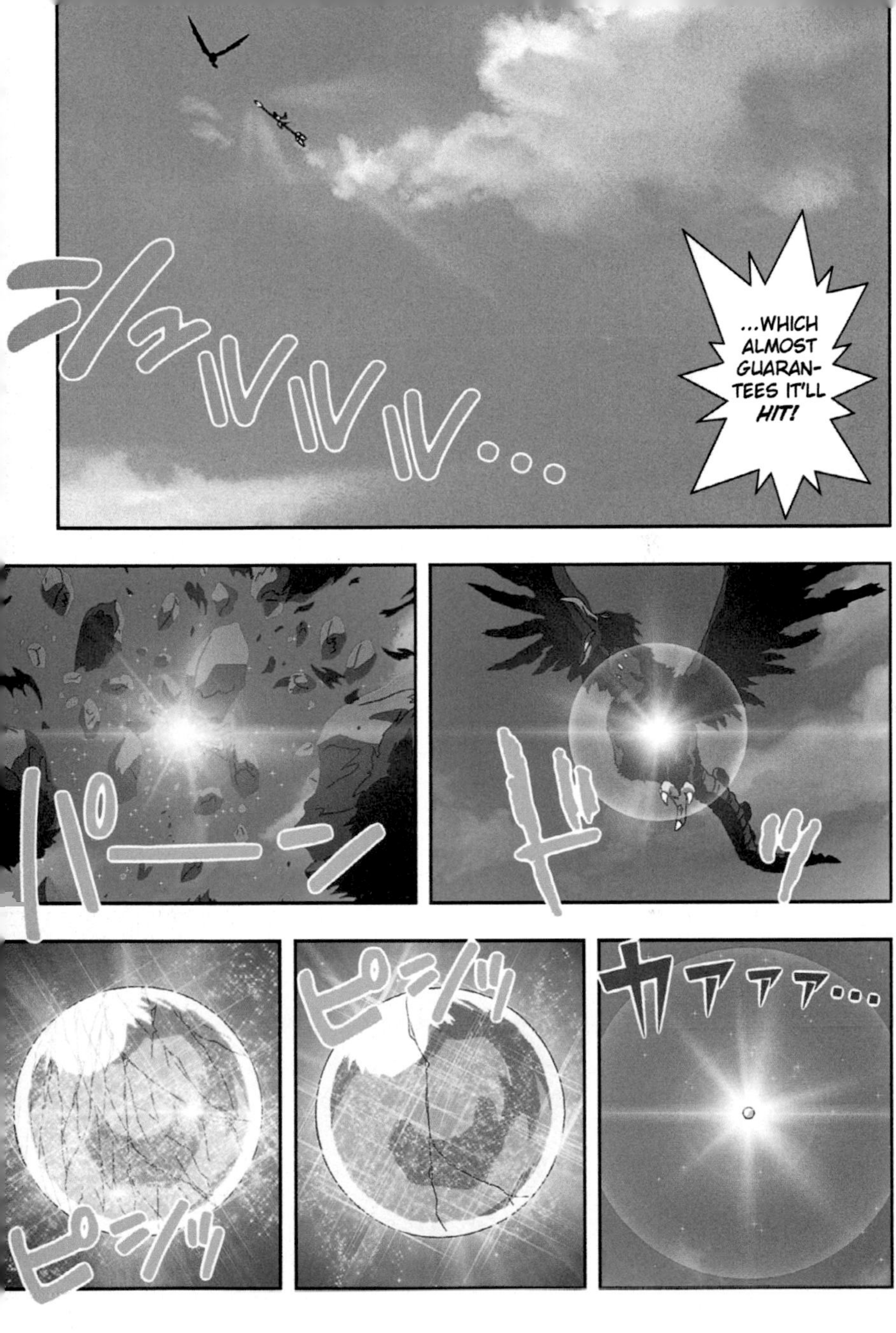
...WHICH ALMOST GUARAN- TEES IT'LL *HIT!*
シュルルル...
ドッ
パーン
カァァァ...
ピシッ
ピシッ

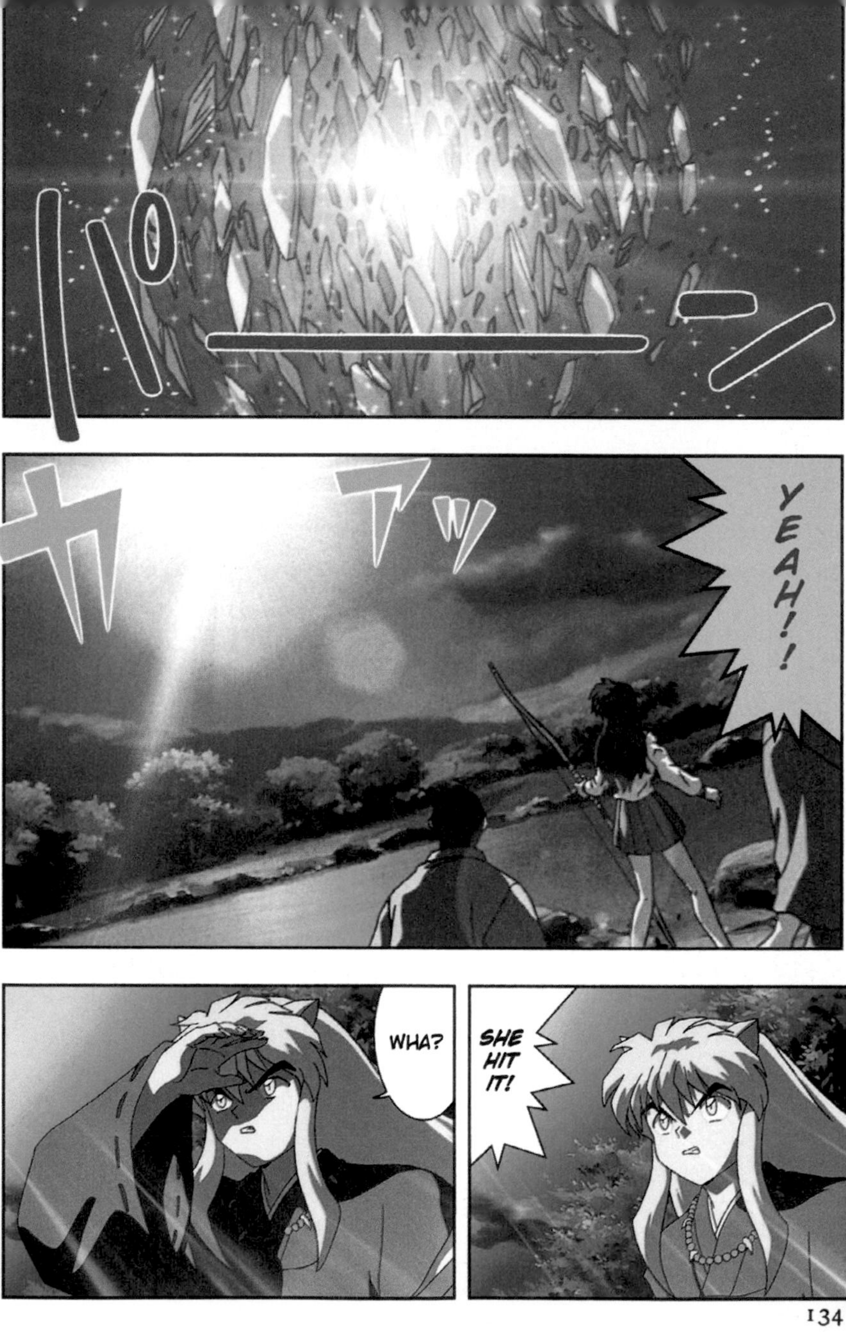
パーーー
カアッ
YEAH!!
SHE HIT IT!
WHA?

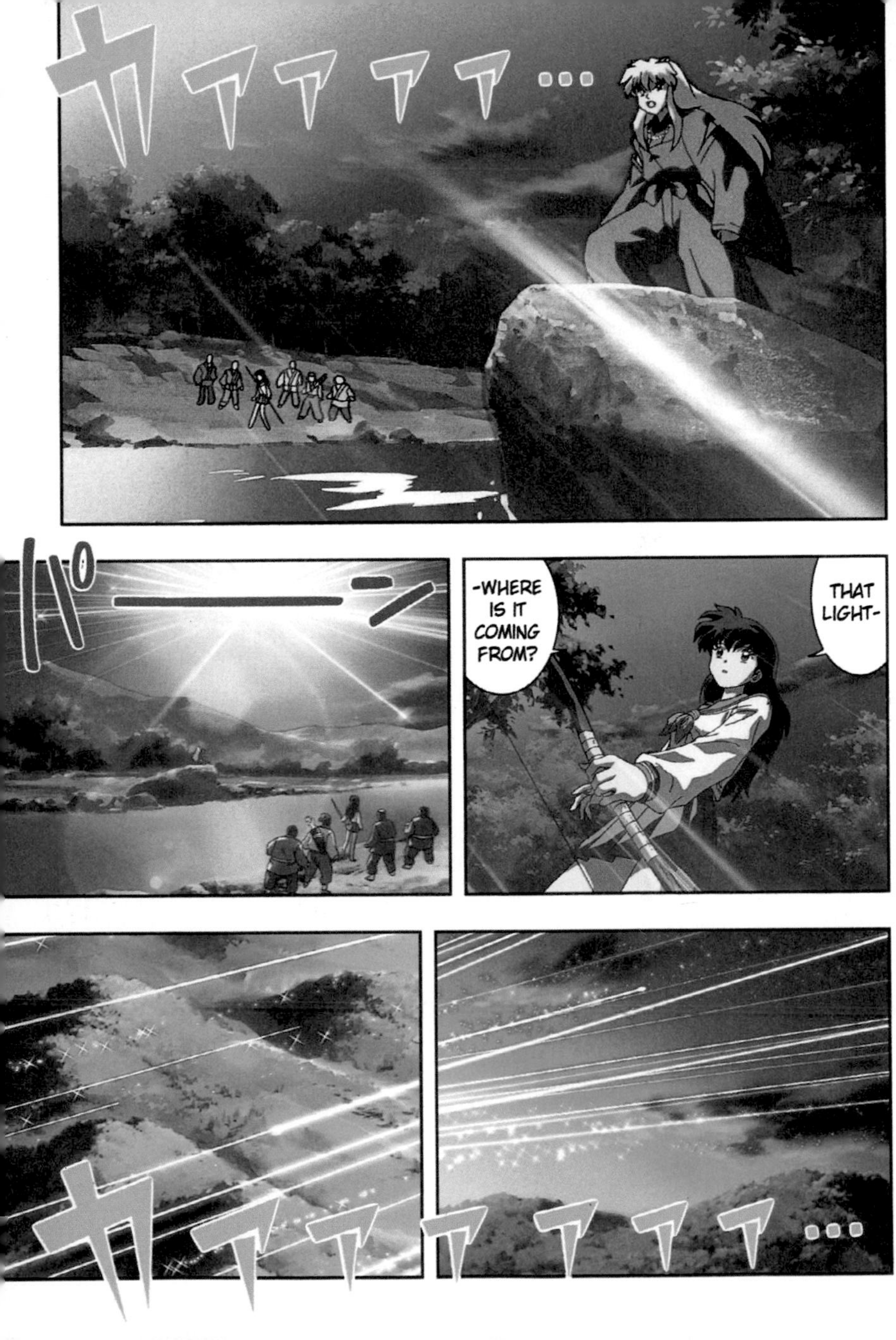

カァァァァ…
THAT LIGHT-
-WHERE IS IT COMING FROM?
カァァァァァァァ…

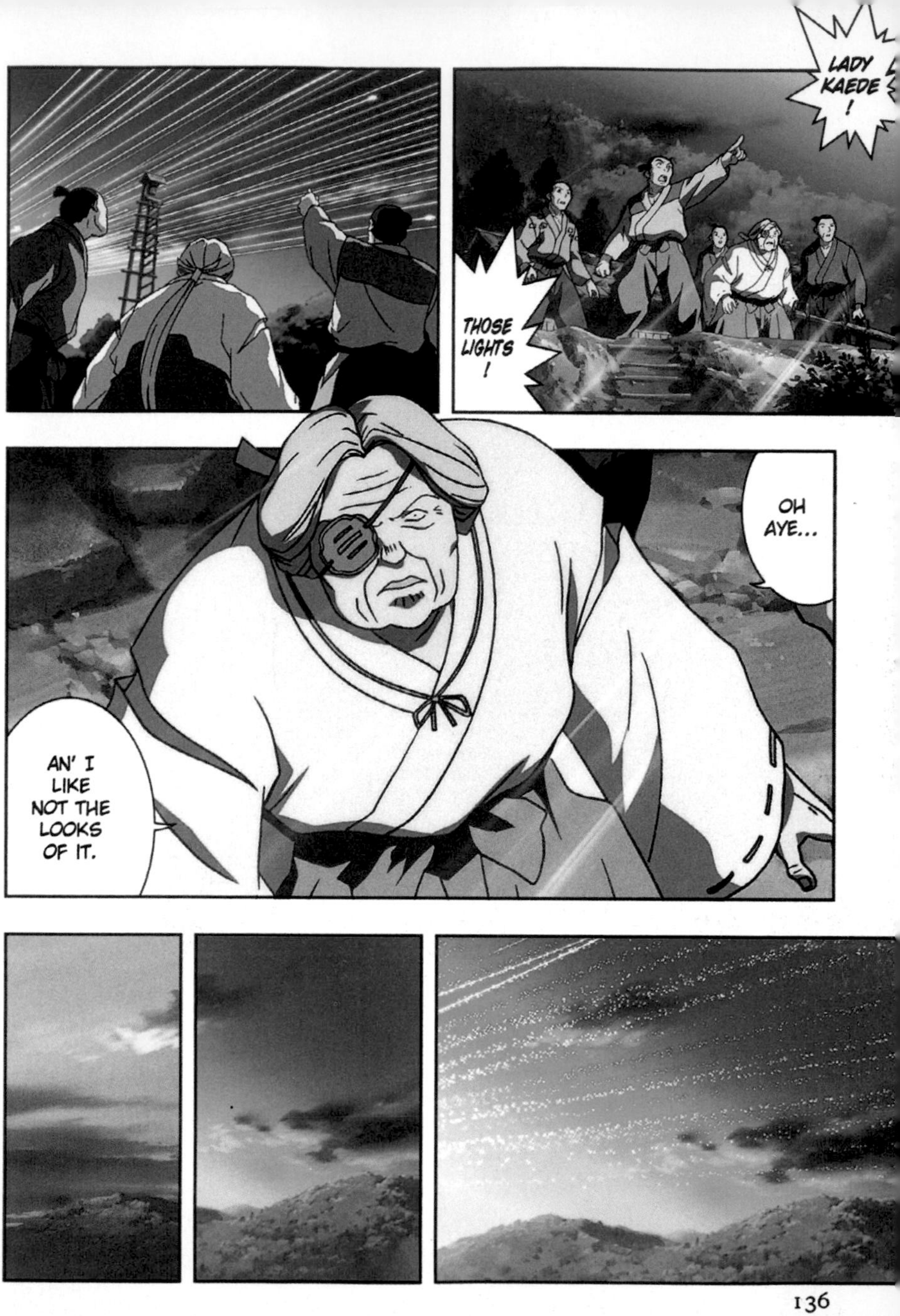
LADY KAEDE !
THOSE LIGHTS !
OH AYE...
AN' I LIKE NOT THE LOOKS OF IT.

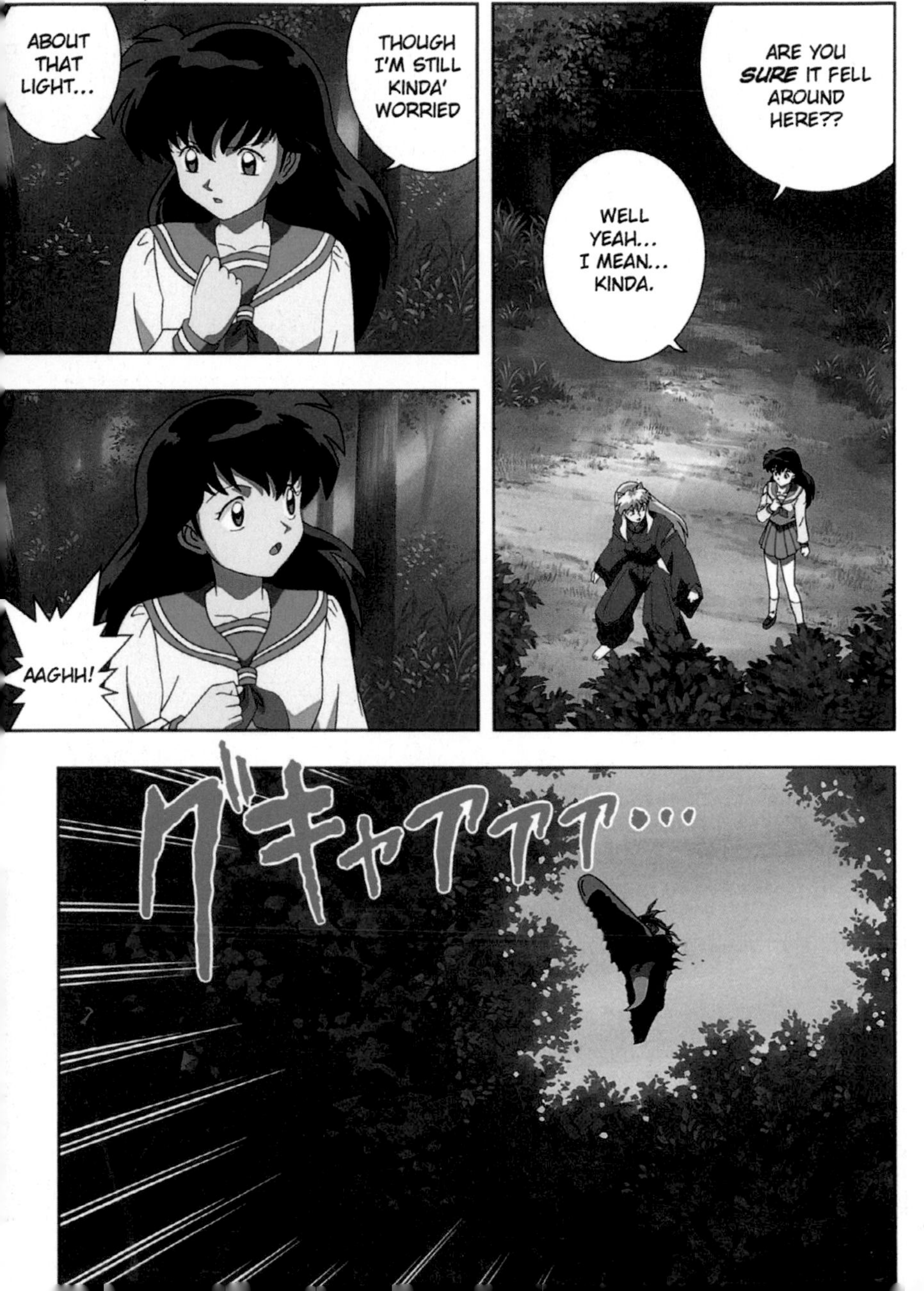
ARE YOU SURE IT FELL AROUND HERE??
WELL YEAH... I MEAN... KINDA.
THOUGH I'M STILL KINDA' WORRIED
ABOUT THAT LIGHT...
AAGHH!
グキャアアア…

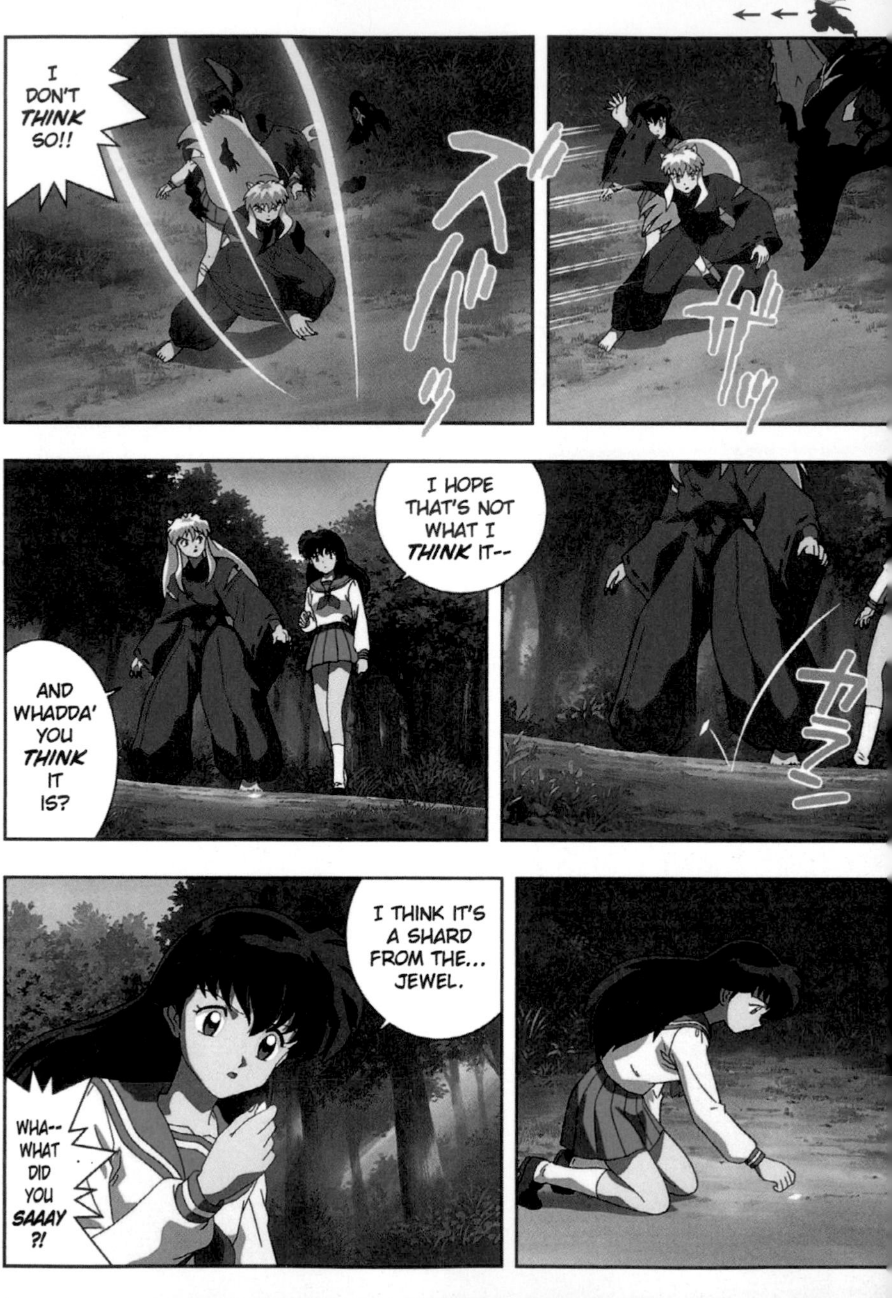
I DON'T THINK SO!!
I HOPE THAT'S NOT WHAT I THINK IT--
AND WHADDA' YOU THINK IT IS?
I THINK IT'S A SHARD FROM THE... JEWEL.
WHA-- WHAT DID YOU SAAAY?!

3

Down the Rabbit Hole and Back Again

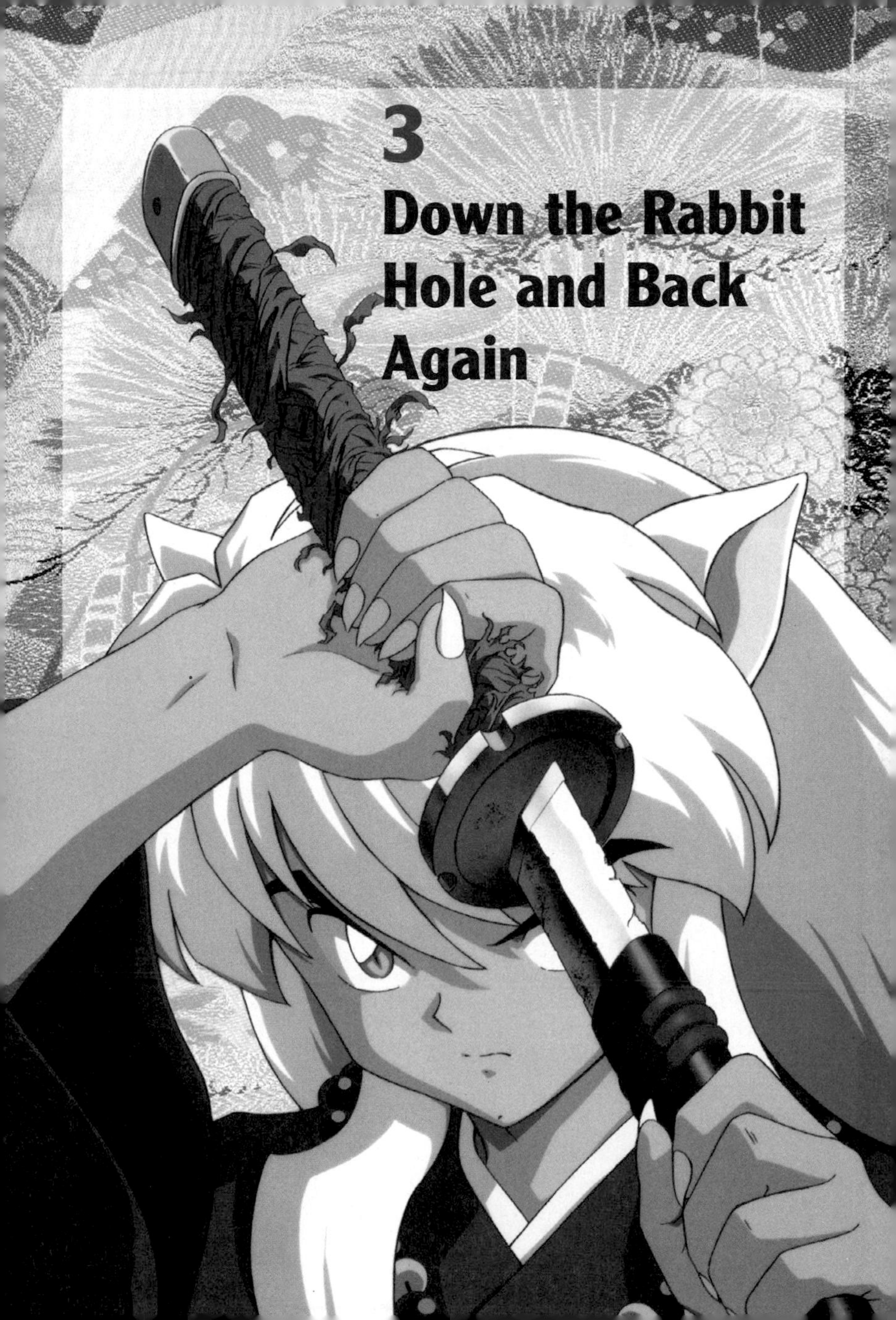

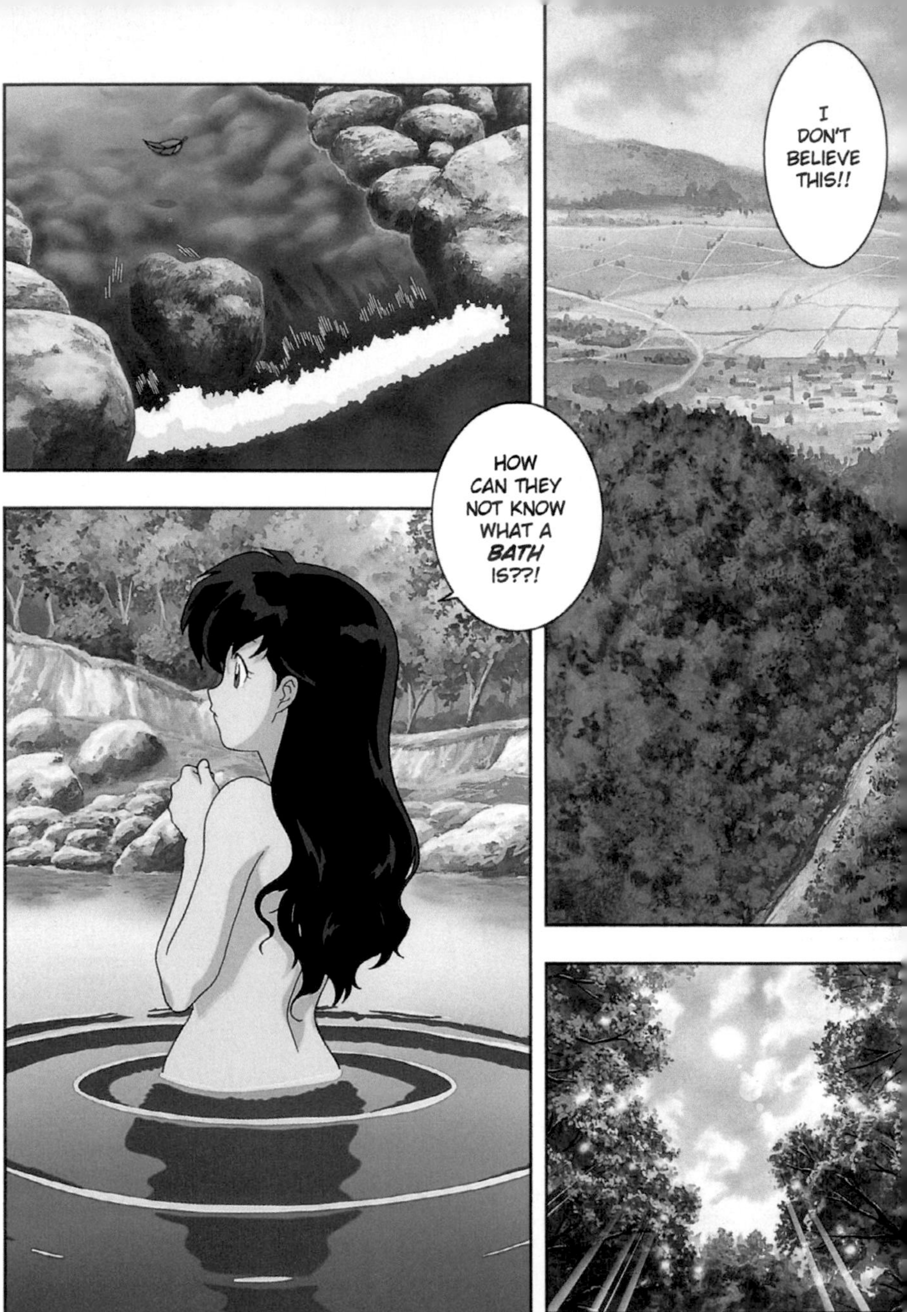
I DON'T BELIEVE THIS!!
HOW CAN THEY NOT KNOW WHAT A ***BATH*** IS??!

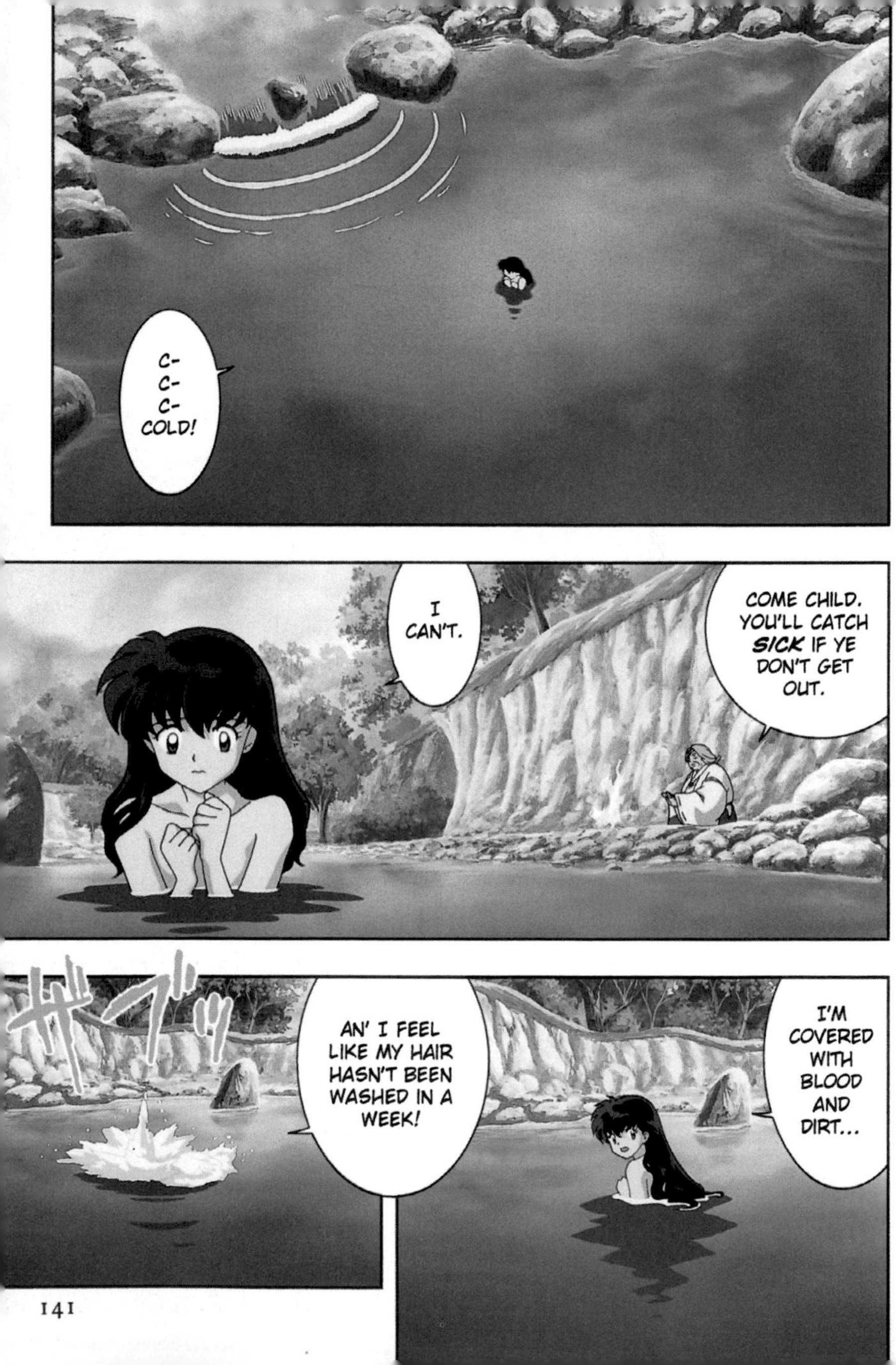
C- C- C- COLD!
COME CHILD. YOU'LL CATCH SICK IF YE DON'T GET OUT.
I CAN'T.
I'M COVERED WITH BLOOD AND DIRT...
AN' I FEEL LIKE MY HAIR HASN'T BEEN WASHED IN A WEEK!
ザブッ

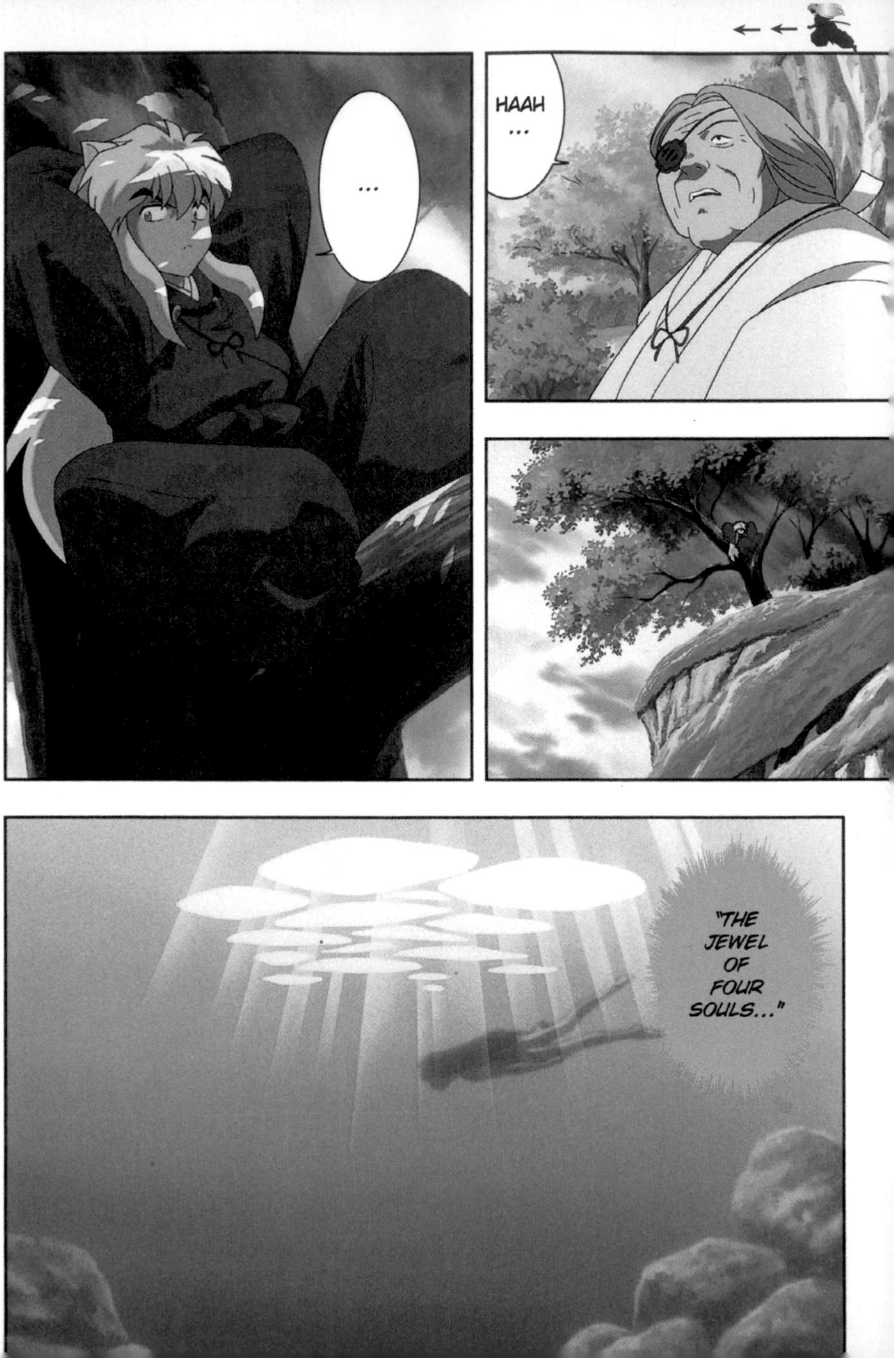
HAAH ...
...
"THE JEWEL OF FOUR SOULS..."

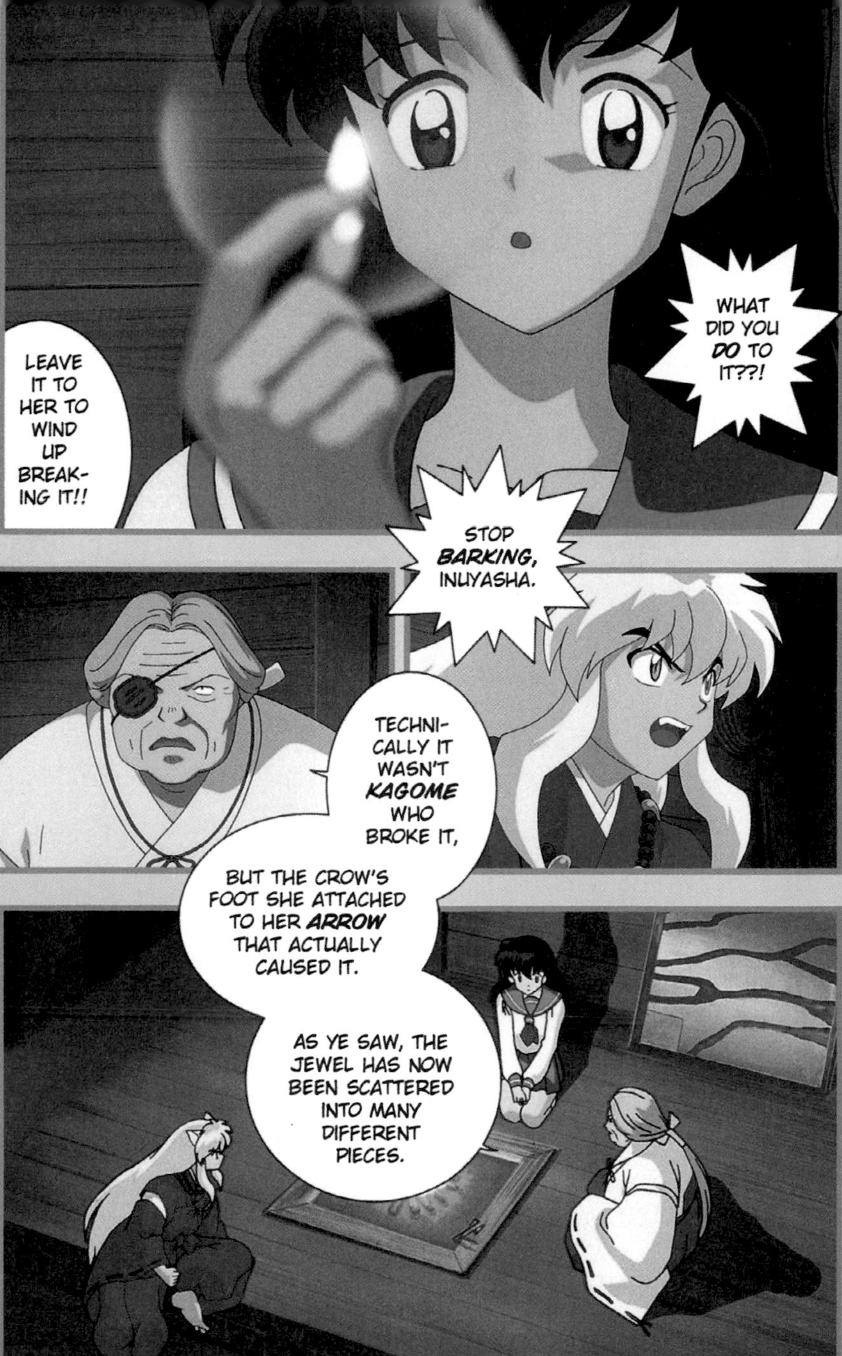
WHAT DID YOU DO TO IT??!
LEAVE IT TO HER TO WIND UP BREAKING IT!!
STOP BARKING, INUYASHA.
TECHNICALLY IT WASN'T KAGOME WHO BROKE IT,
BUT THE CROW'S FOOT SHE ATTACHED TO HER ARROW THAT ACTUALLY CAUSED IT.
AS YE SAW, THE JEWEL HAS NOW BEEN SCATTERED INTO MANY DIFFERENT PIECES.

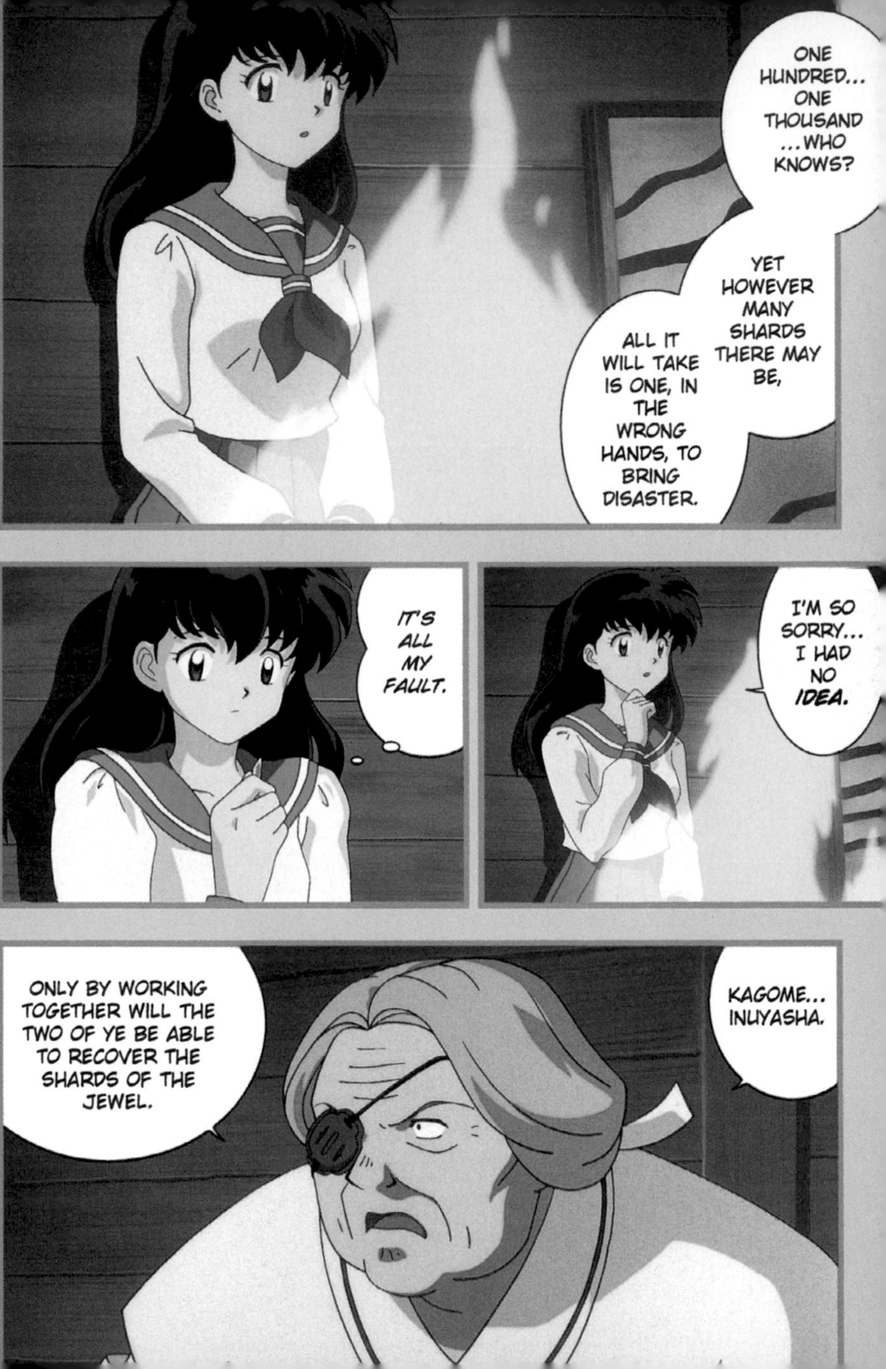
ONE HUNDRED... ONE THOUSAND ...WHO KNOWS?
YET HOWEVER MANY SHARDS THERE MAY BE,
ALL IT WILL TAKE IS ONE, IN THE WRONG HANDS, TO BRING DISASTER.
I'M SO SORRY... I HAD NO *IDEA.*
IT'S ALL MY FAULT.
KAGOME... INUYASHA.
ONLY BY WORKING TOGETHER WILL THE TWO OF YE BE ABLE TO RECOVER THE SHARDS OF THE JEWEL.

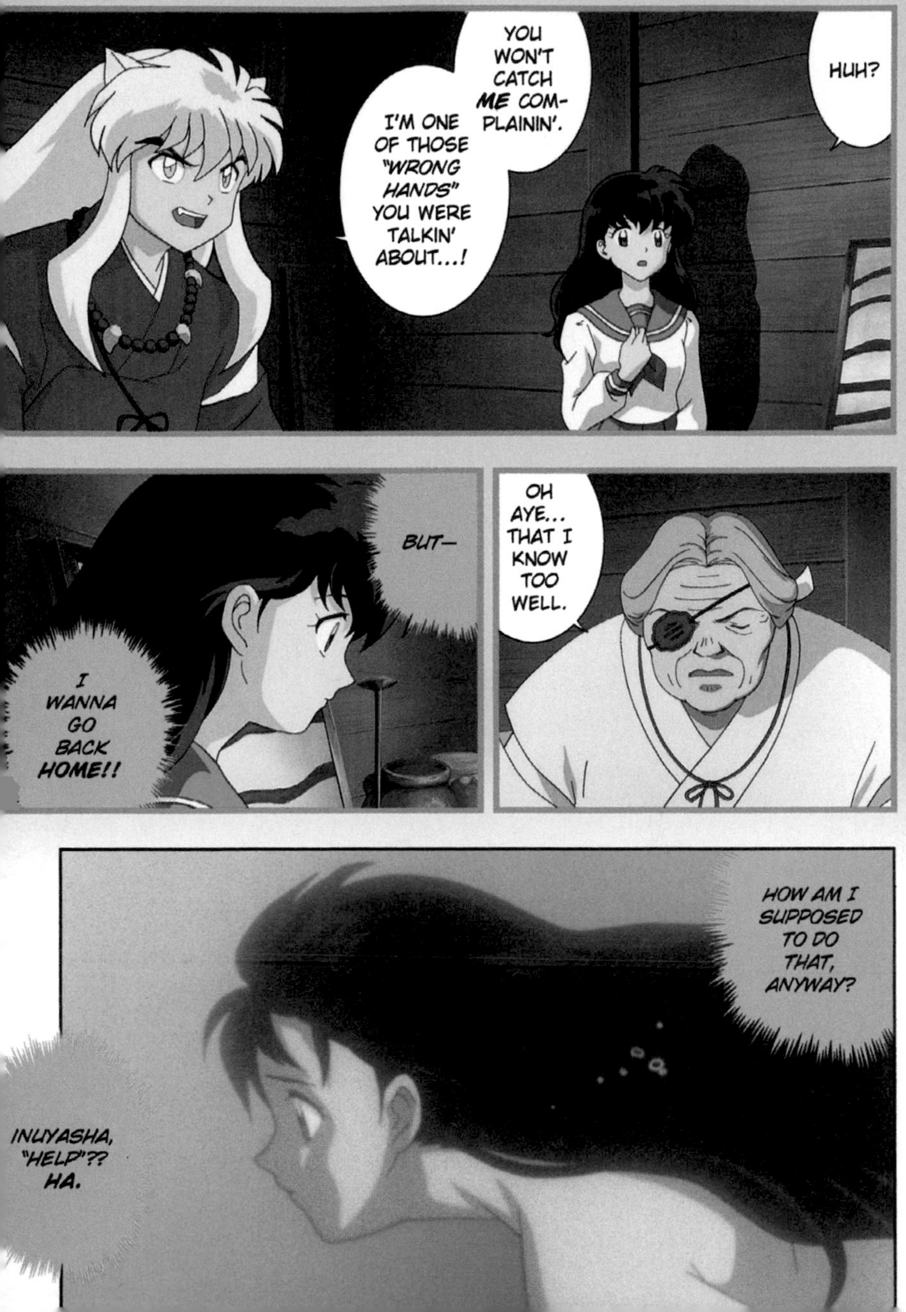
HUH?
YOU WON'T CATCH ME COM-PLAININ'.
I'M ONE OF THOSE "WRONG HANDS" YOU WERE TALKIN' ABOUT...!
OH AYE... THAT I KNOW TOO WELL.
BUT—
I WANNA GO BACK HOME!!
HOW AM I SUPPOSED TO DO THAT, ANYWAY?
INUYASHA, "HELP"?? HA.

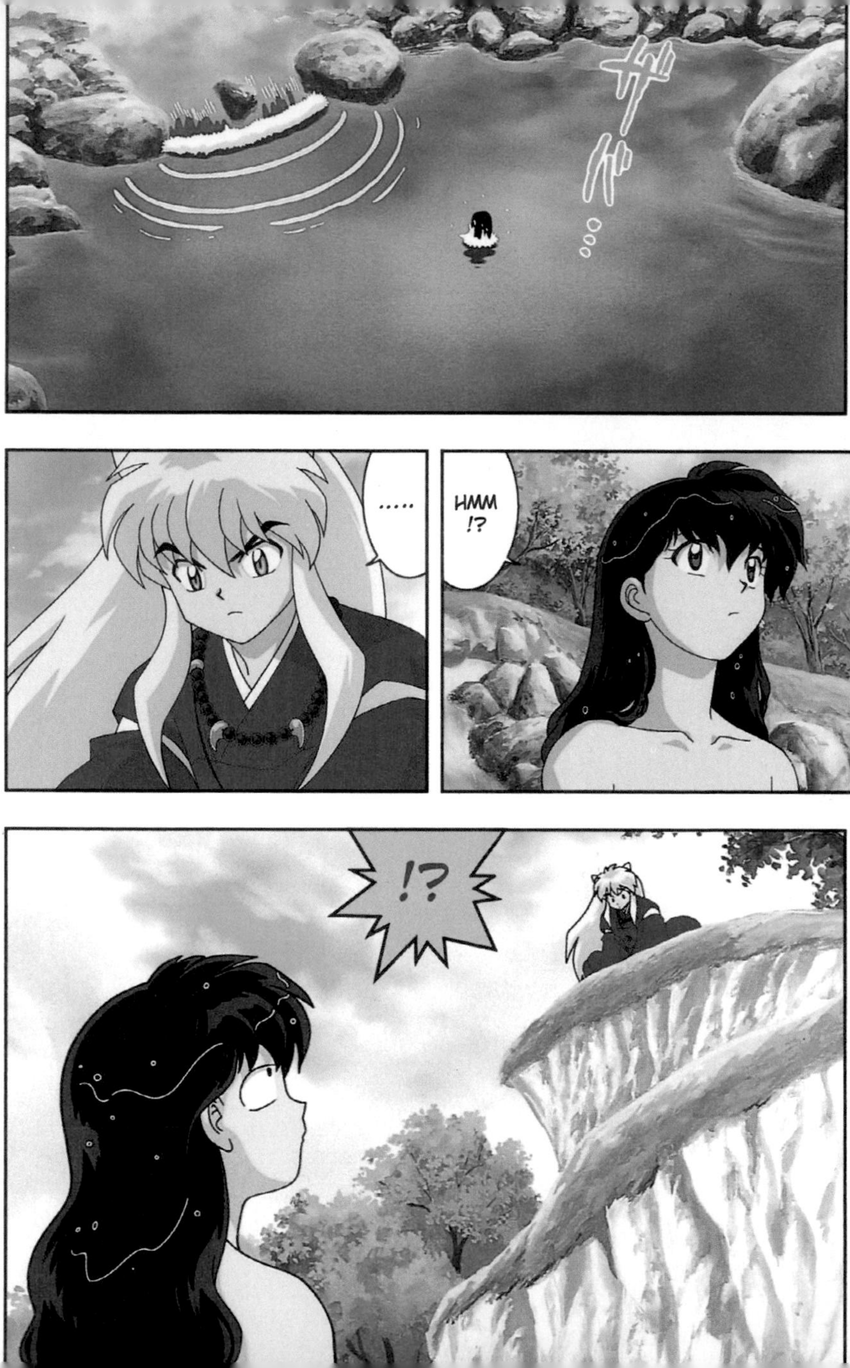
HMM !?
.....
!?

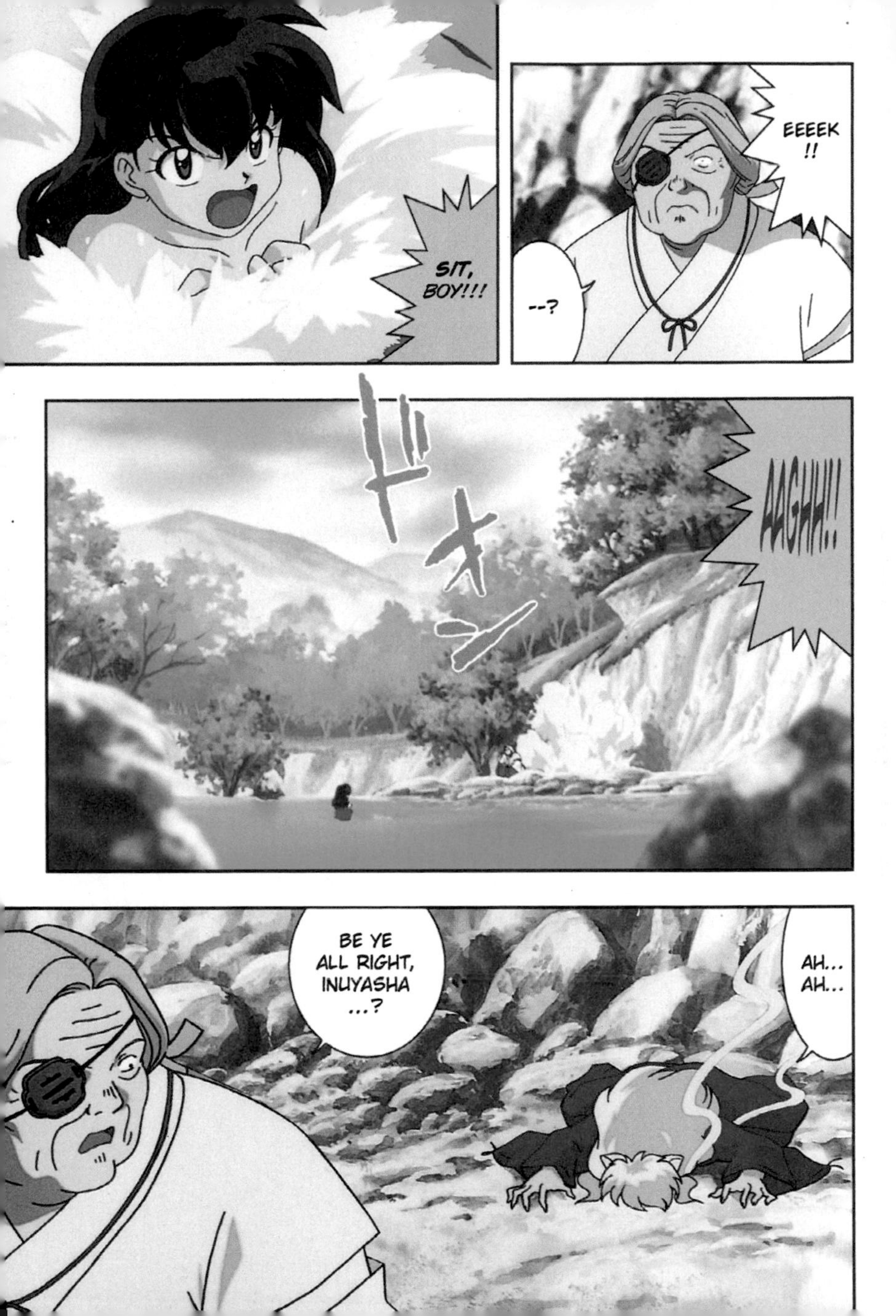
EEEEK !!
--?
SIT, BOY!!!
AAGHH!!
ドオン
AH... AH...
BE YE ALL RIGHT, INUYASHA ...?

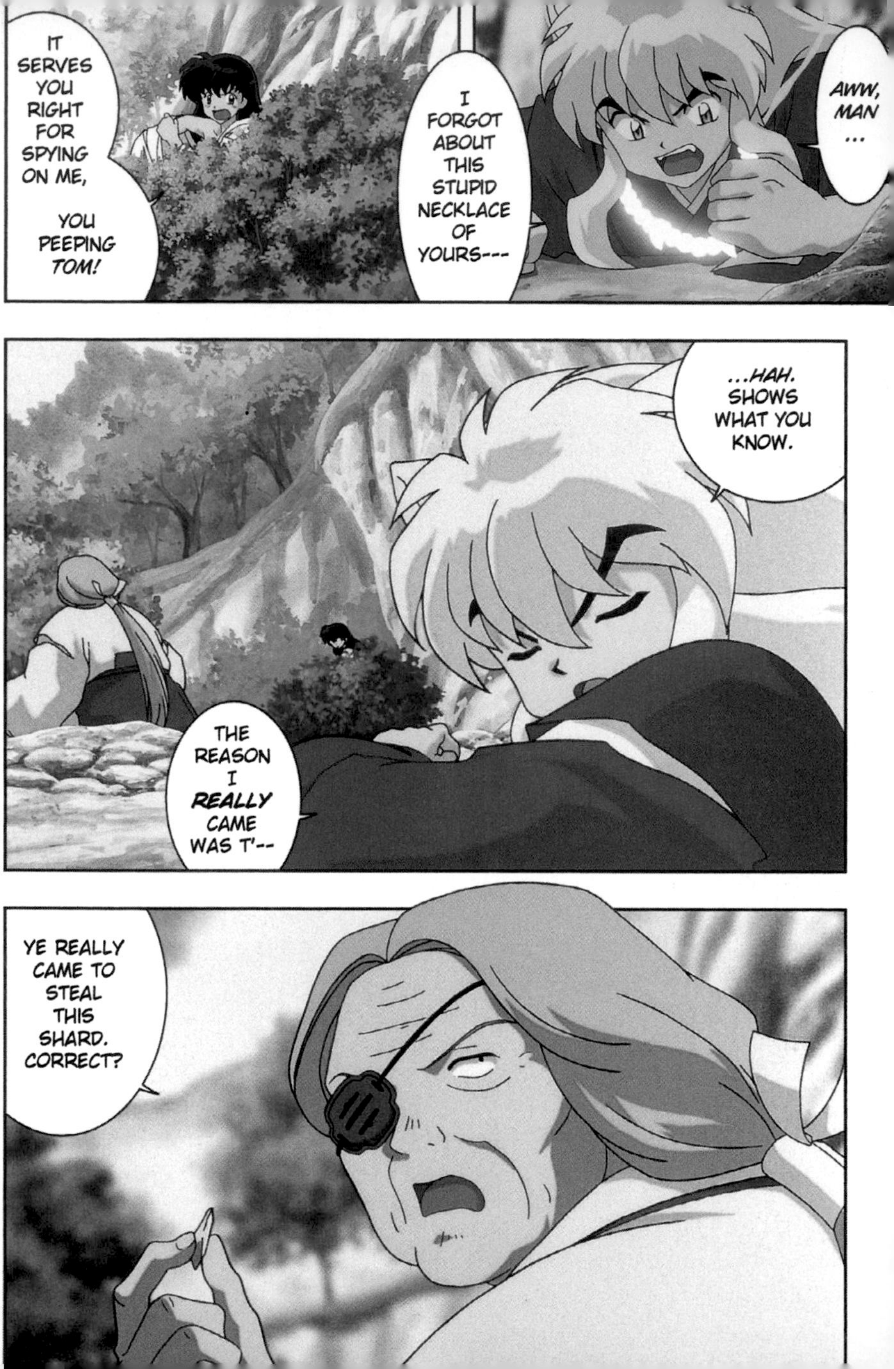
AWW, MAN ...
I FORGOT ABOUT THIS STUPID NECKLACE OF YOURS---
IT SERVES YOU RIGHT FOR SPYING ON ME,
YOU PEEPING TOM!
...HAH. SHOWS WHAT YOU KNOW.
THE REASON I REALLY CAME WAS T'--
YE REALLY CAME TO STEAL THIS SHARD. CORRECT?

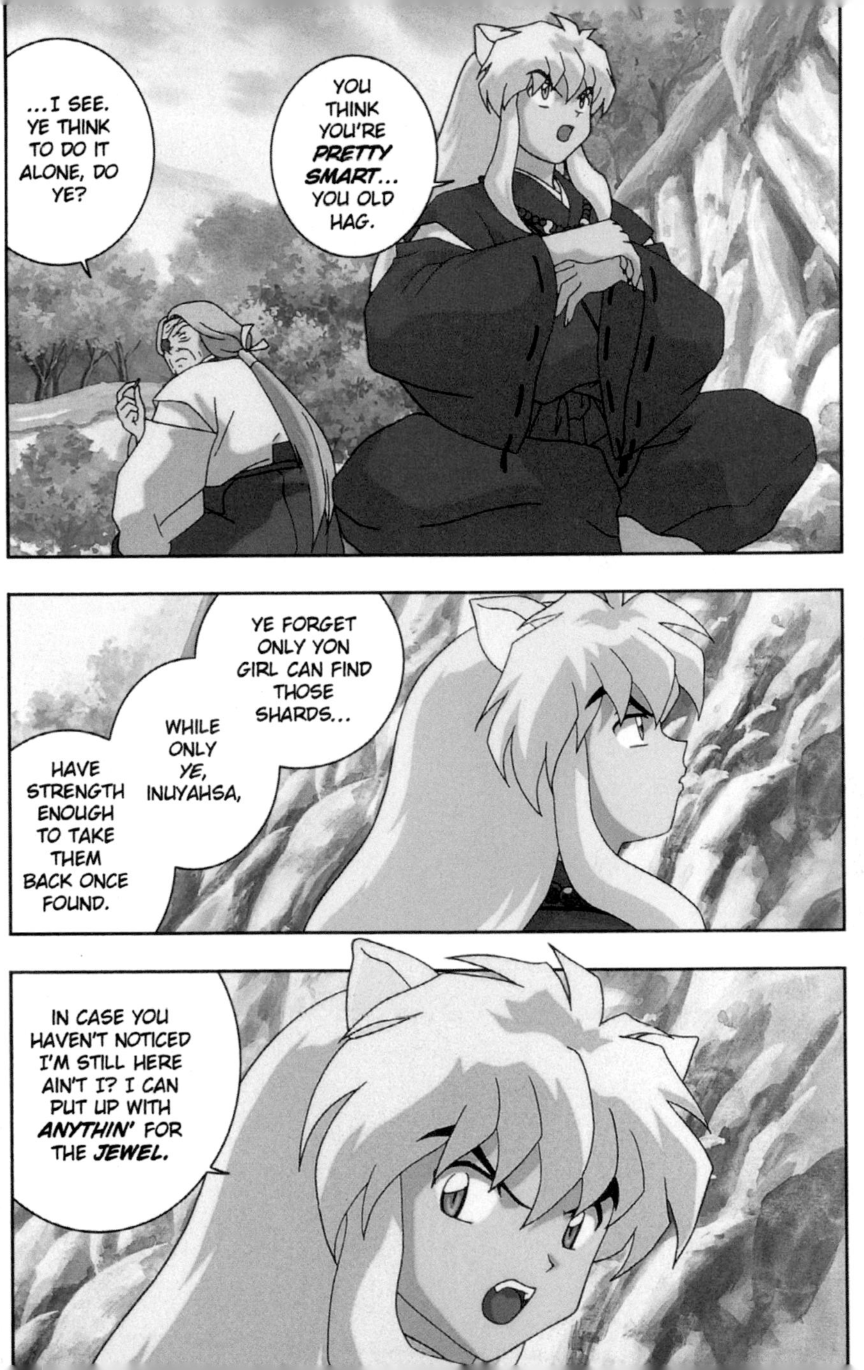
YOU THINK YOU'RE PRETTY SMART... YOU OLD HAG.
...I SEE. YE THINK TO DO IT ALONE, DO YE?
YE FORGET ONLY YON GIRL CAN FIND THOSE SHARDS...
WHILE ONLY YE, INUYAHSA,
HAVE STRENGTH ENOUGH TO TAKE THEM BACK ONCE FOUND.
IN CASE YOU HAVEN'T NOTICED I'M STILL HERE AIN'T I? I CAN PUT UP WITH ANYTHIN' FOR THE JEWEL.

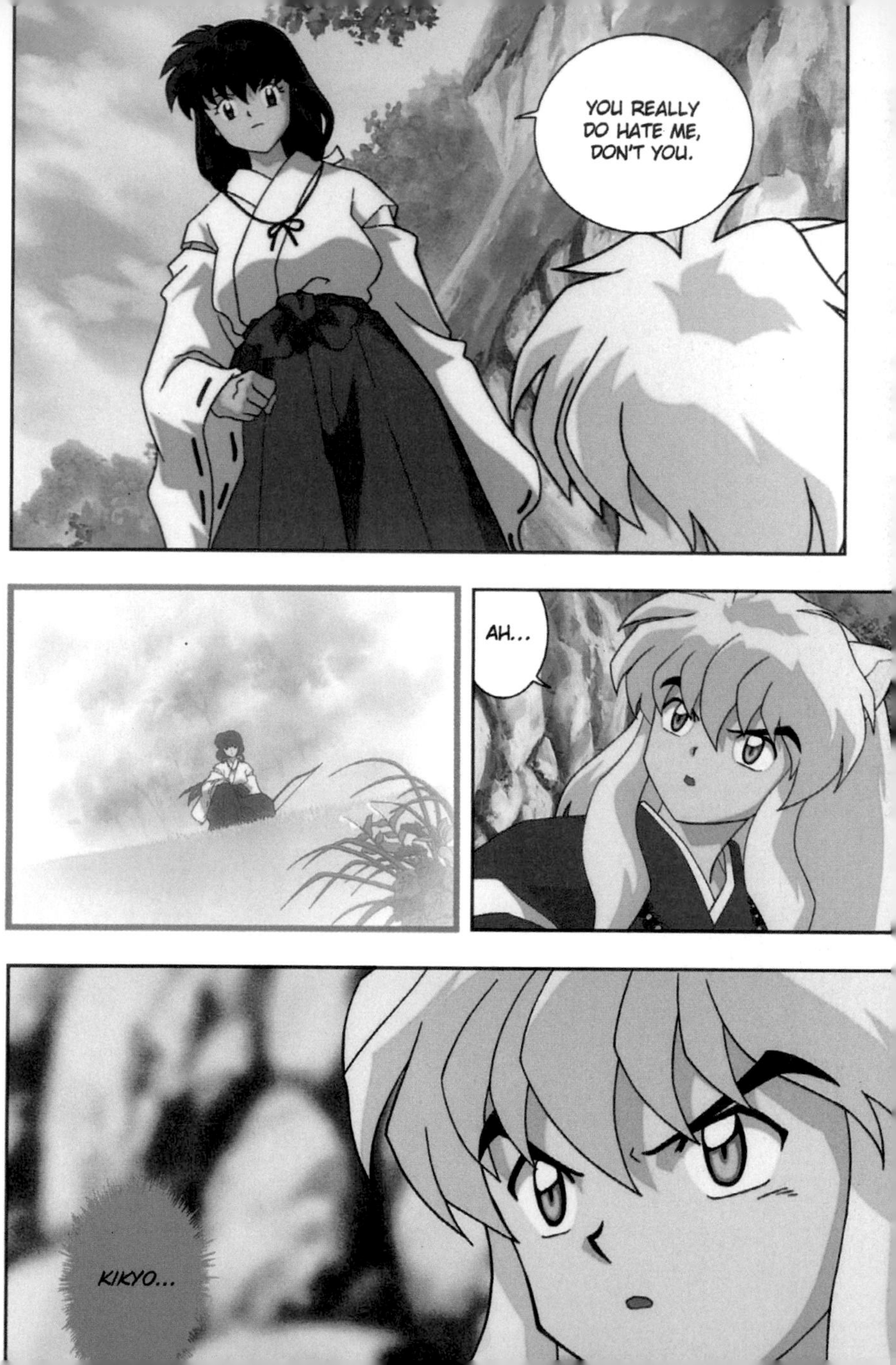
YOU REALLY DO HATE ME, DON'T YOU.
AH...
KIKYO...

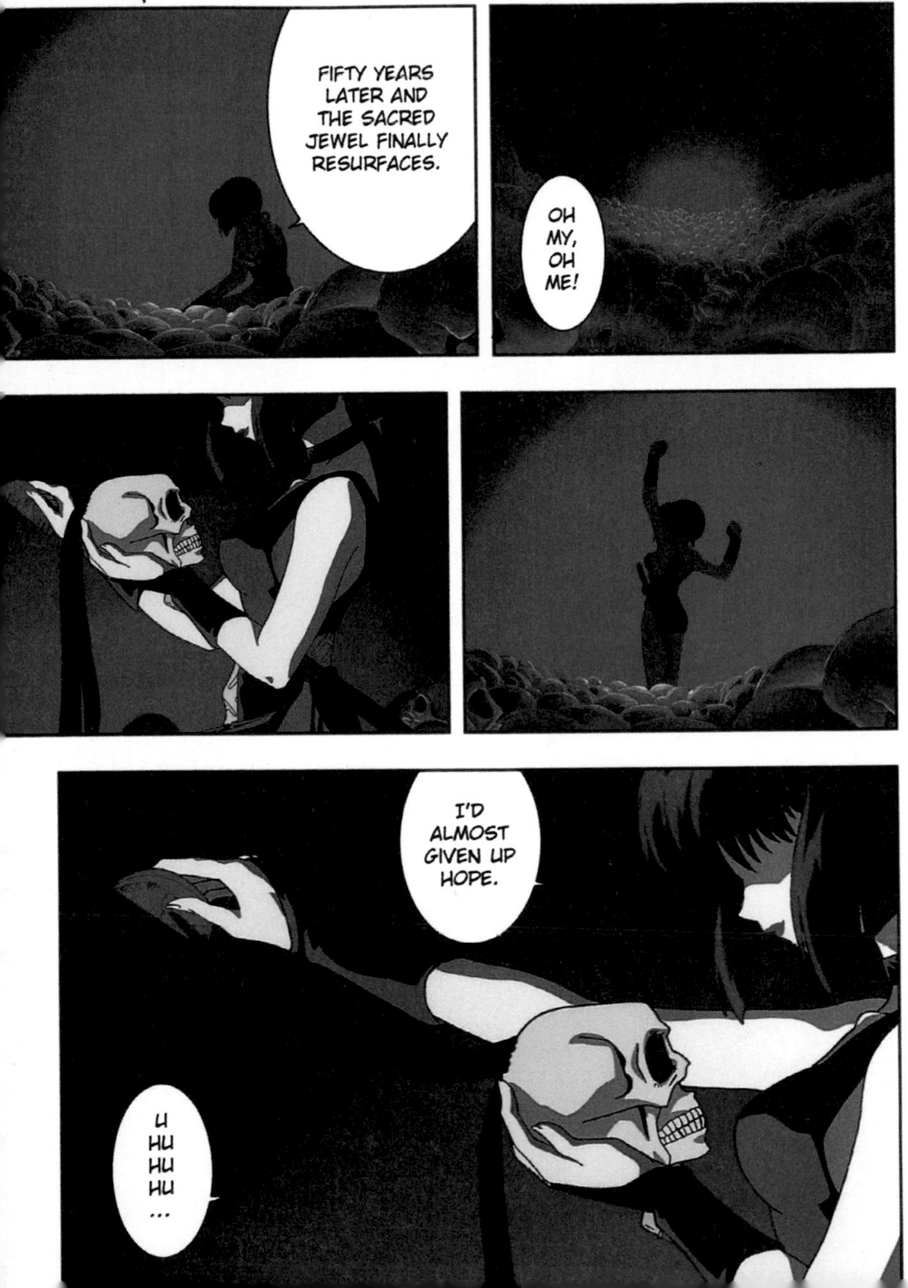
OH MY, OH ME!
FIFTY YEARS LATER AND THE SACRED JEWEL FINALLY RESURFACES.
I'D ALMOST GIVEN UP HOPE.
U HU HU HU ...

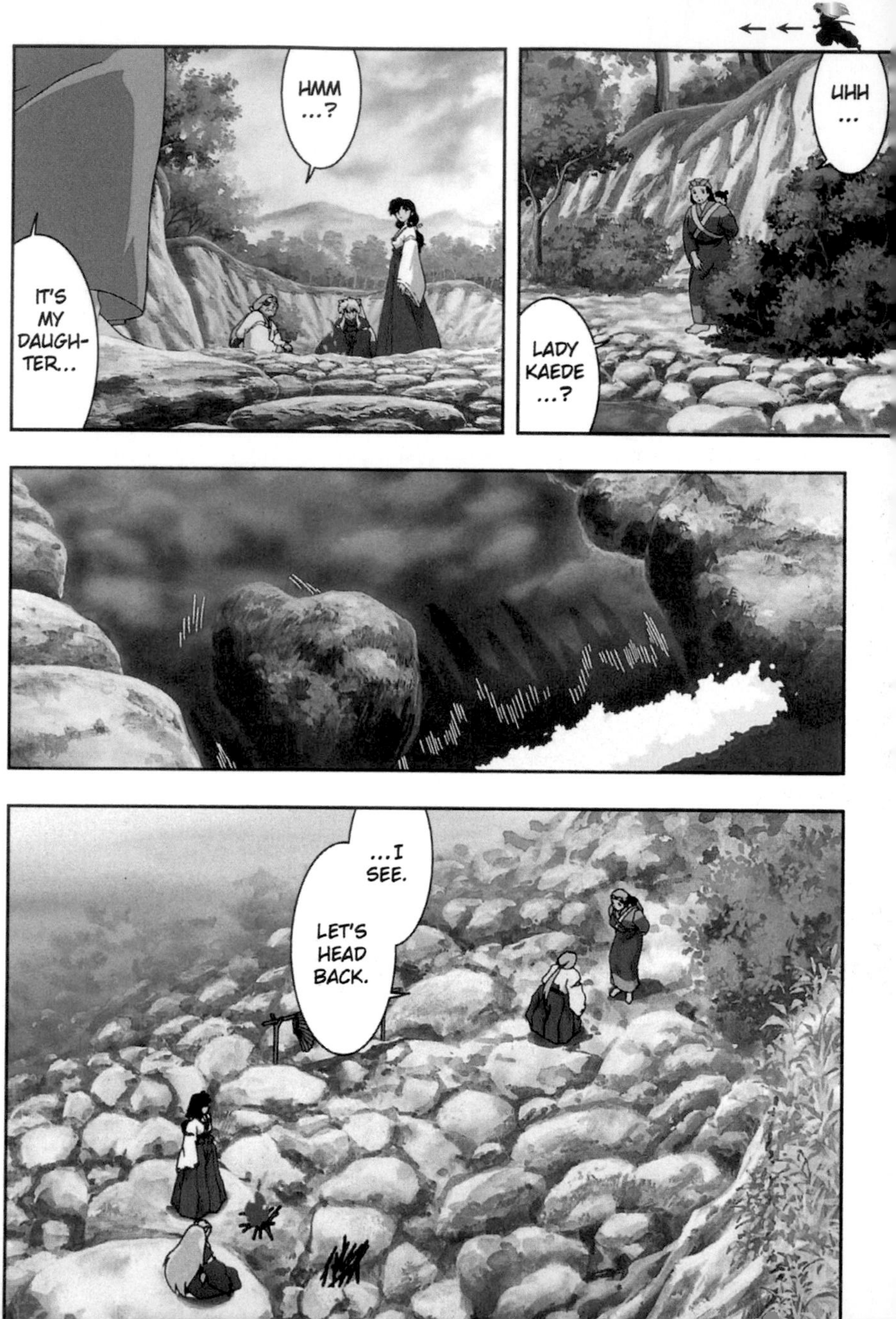
UHH ...
LADY KAEDE ...?
HMM ...?
IT'S MY DAUGHTER...
...I SEE. LET'S HEAD BACK.

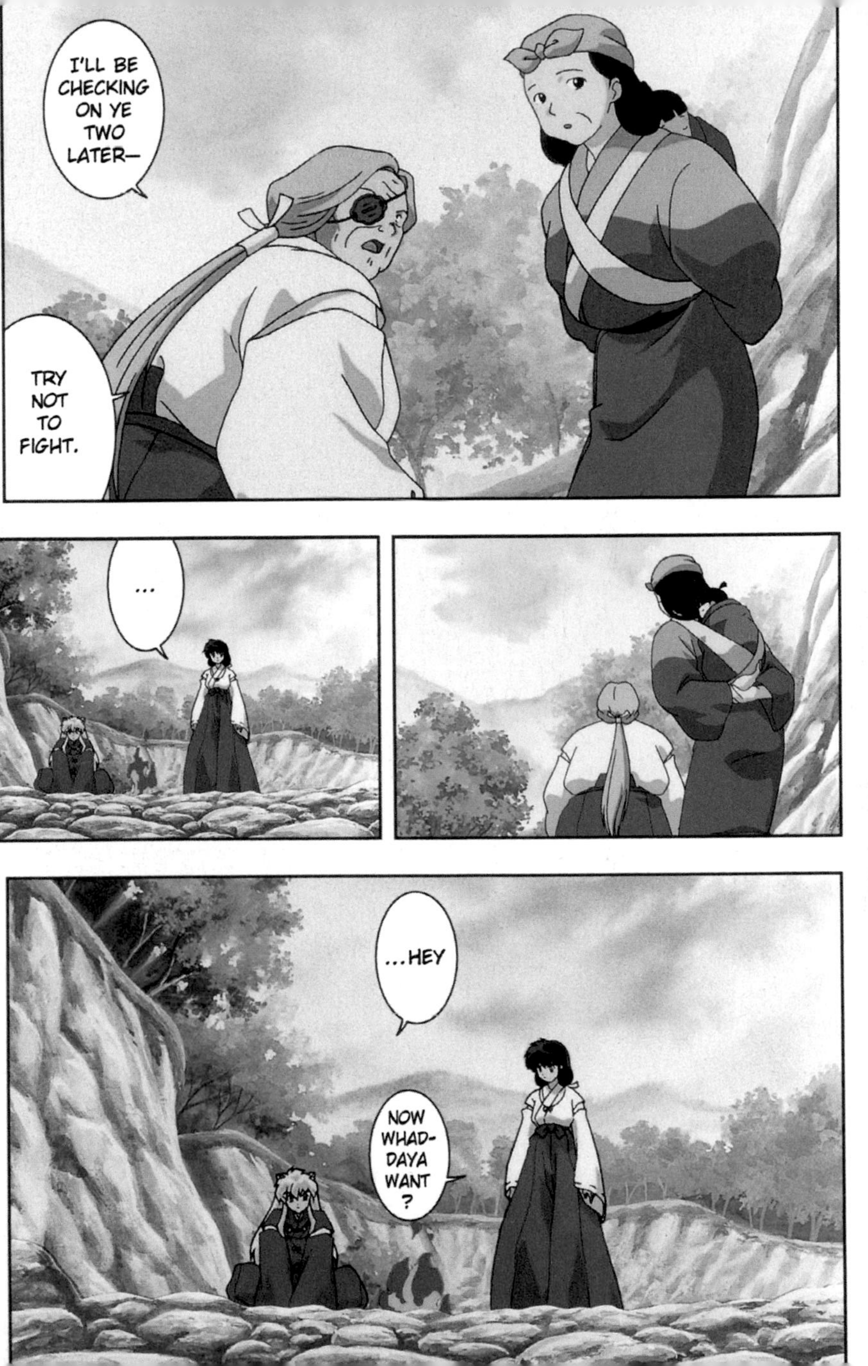
I'LL BE CHECKING ON YE TWO LATER—
TRY NOT TO FIGHT.
...
...HEY
NOW WHAD-DAYA WANT?

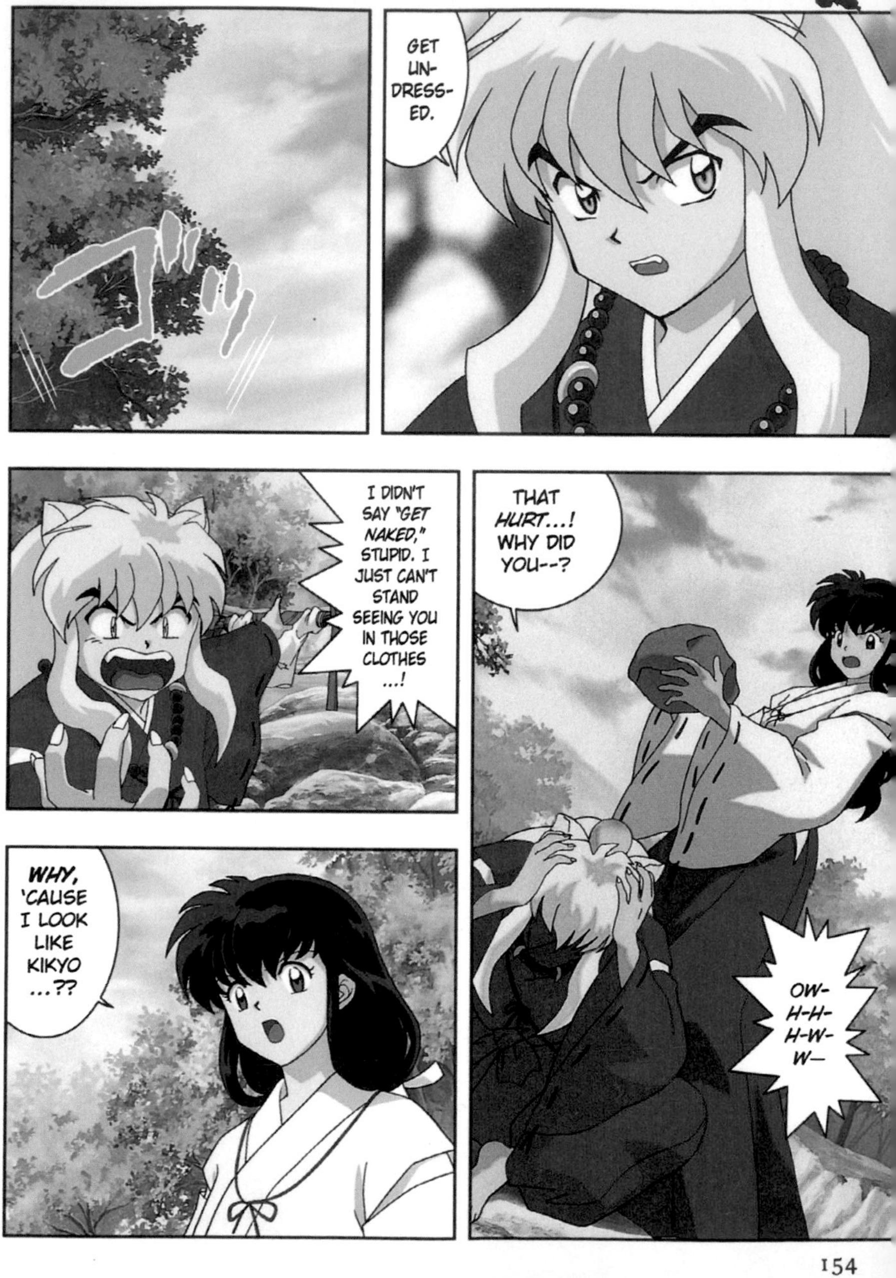

GET UN-DRESS-ED.
ゴッ
THAT *HURT*...! WHY DID YOU--?
OW-H-H-H-W-W—
I DIDN'T SAY "*GET NAKED*," STUPID. I JUST CAN'T STAND SEEING YOU IN THOSE CLOTHES ...!
WHY, 'CAUSE I LOOK LIKE KIKYO ...??

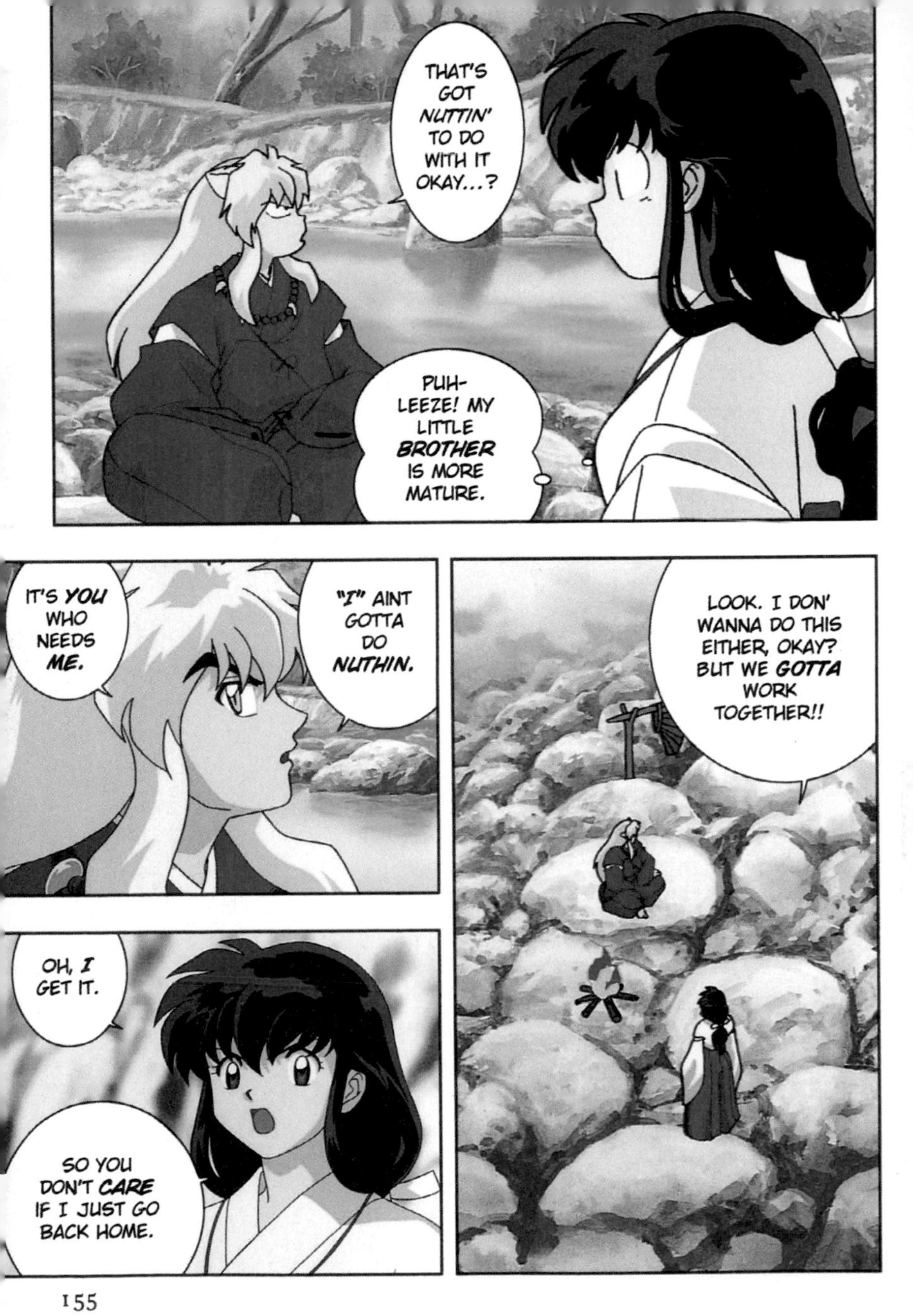
THAT'S GOT NUTTIN' TO DO WITH IT OKAY...?
PUH-LEEZE! MY LITTLE BROTHER IS MORE MATURE.
LOOK. I DON' WANNA DO THIS EITHER, OKAY? BUT WE GOTTA WORK TOGETHER!!
"I" AINT GOTTA DO NUTHIN.
IT'S YOU WHO NEEDS ME.
OH, I GET IT.
SO YOU DON'T CARE IF I JUST GO BACK HOME.

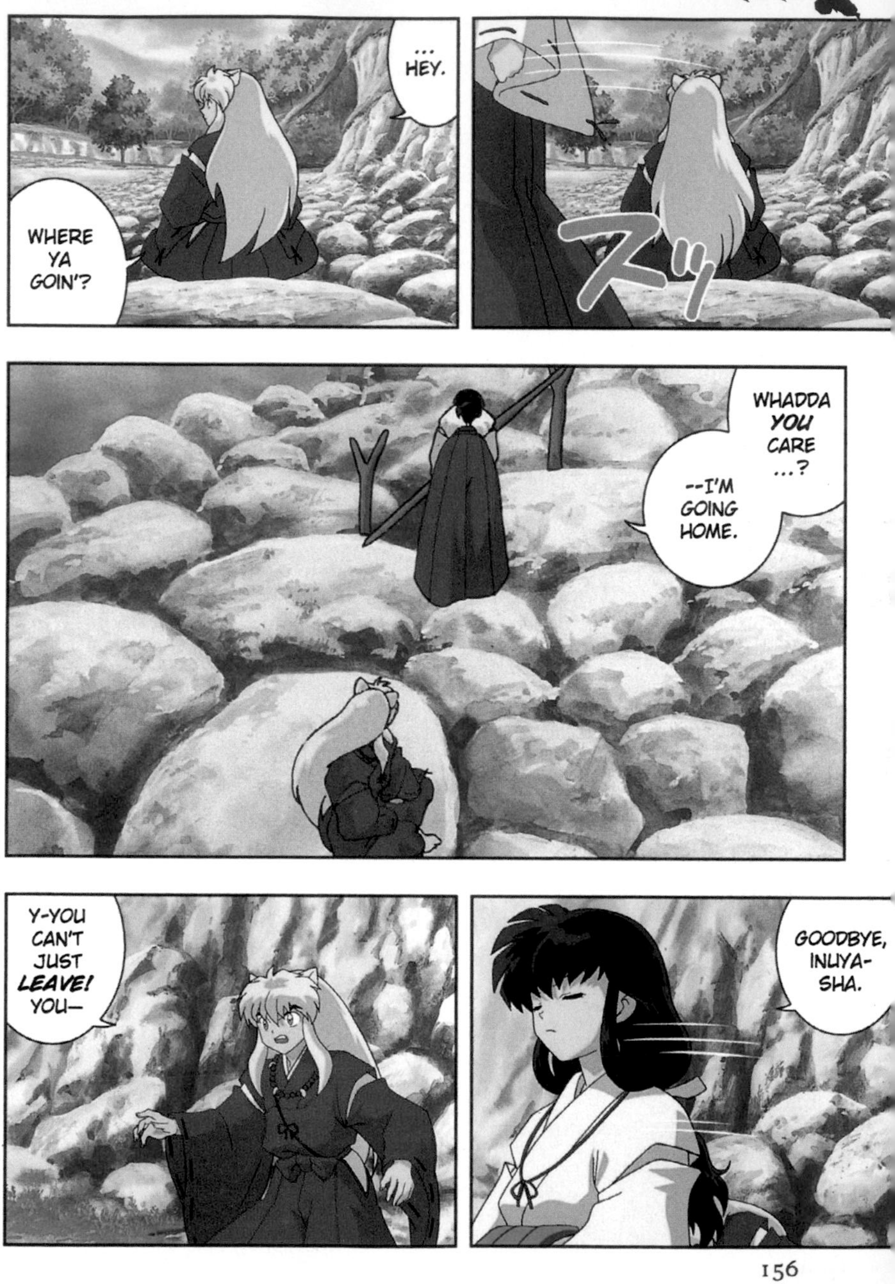
ズッ
... HEY.
WHERE YA GOIN'?
WHADDA YOU CARE ...?
--I'M GOING HOME.
GOODBYE, INUYA-SHA.
Y-YOU CAN'T JUST LEAVE! YOU—

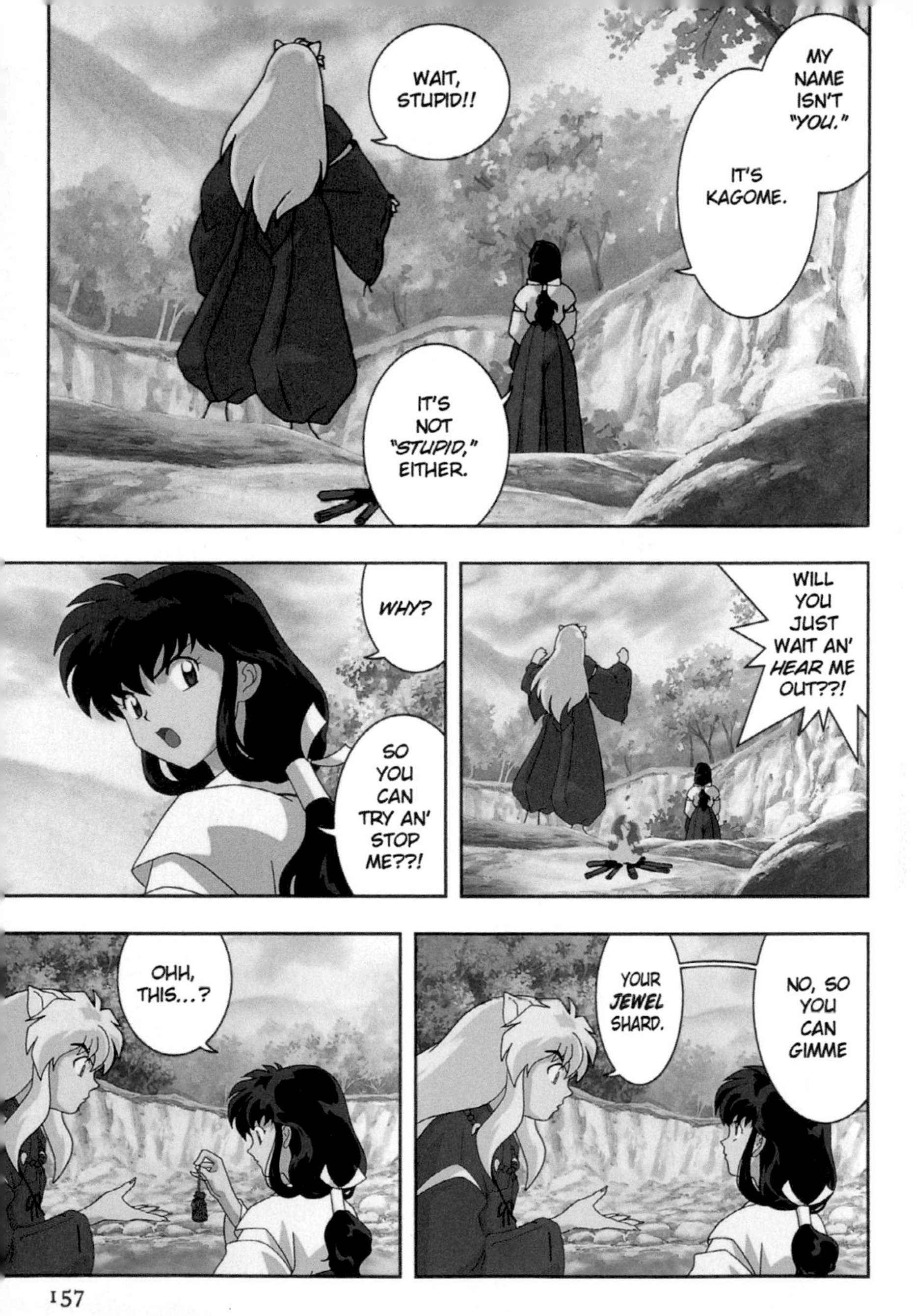
MY NAME ISN'T *"YOU."*
IT'S KAGOME.
WAIT, STUPID!!
IT'S NOT *"STUPID,"* EITHER.
WILL YOU JUST WAIT AN' *HEAR* ME OUT??!
WHY?
SO YOU CAN TRY AN' STOP ME??!
NO, SO YOU CAN GIMME
YOUR ***JEWEL*** SHARD.
OHH, THIS...?

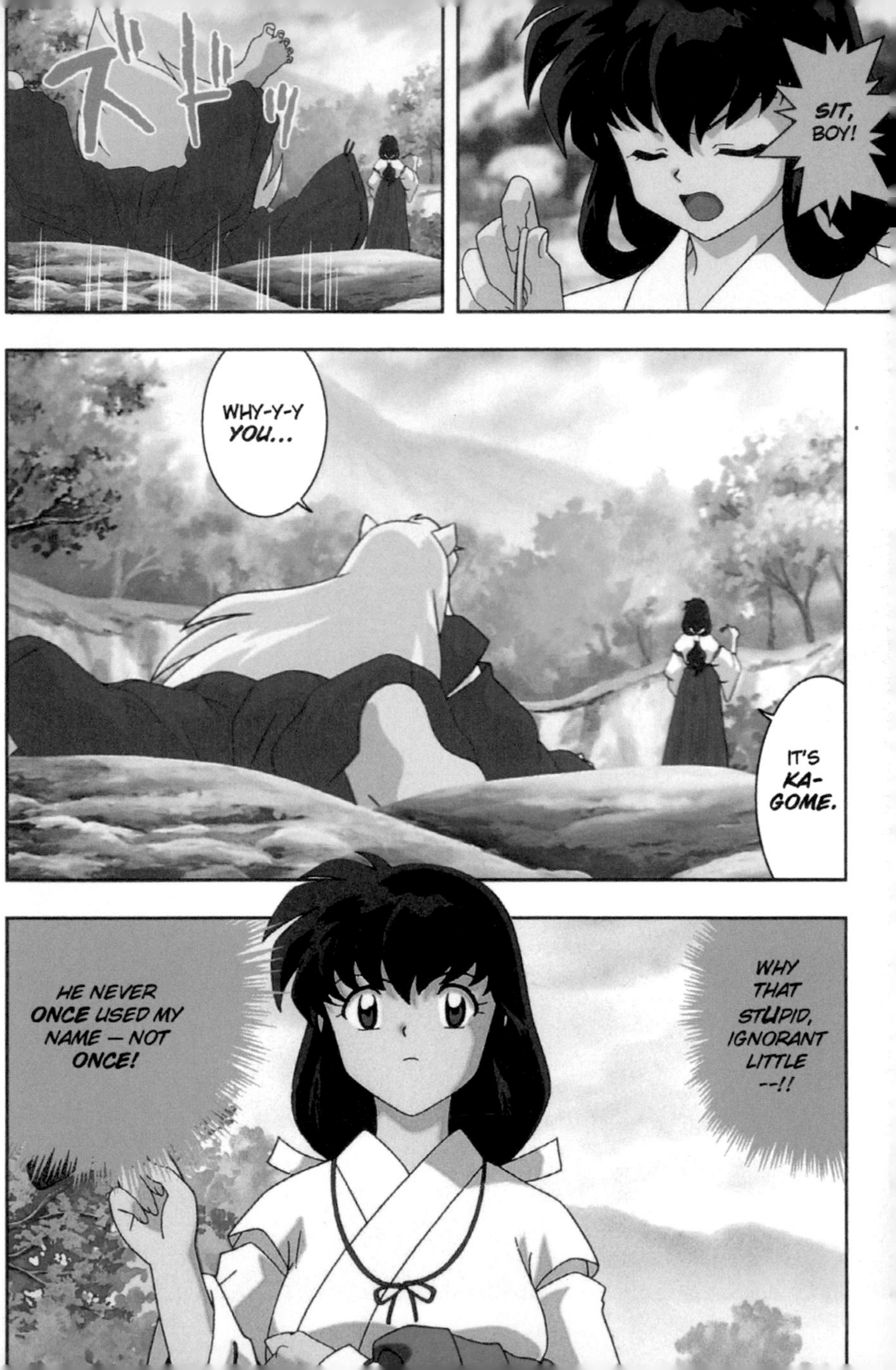
SIT, BOY!
ズドッ
WHY-Y-Y YOU...
IT'S KA-GOME.
WHY THAT STUPID, IGNORANT LITTLE --!!
HE NEVER ONCE USED MY NAME — NOT ONCE!

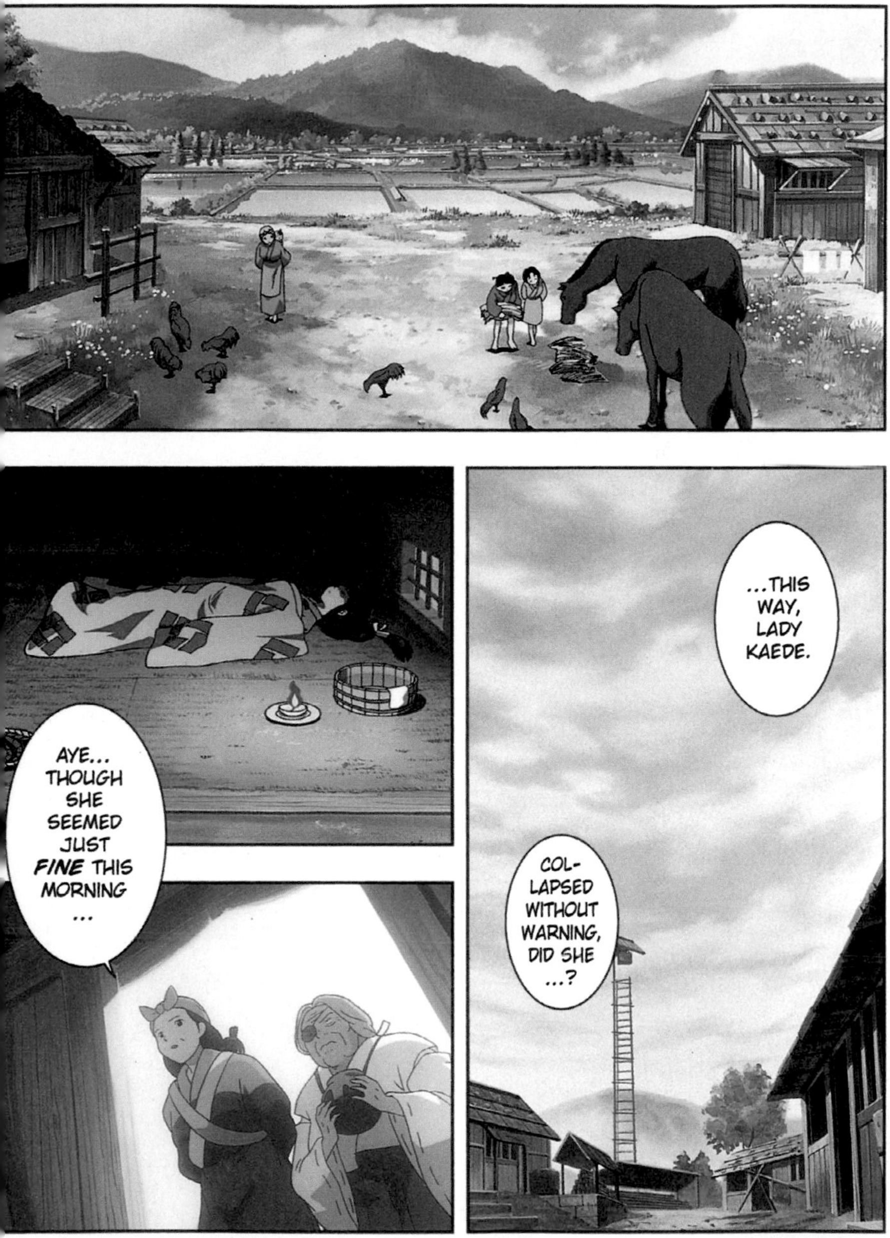
...THIS WAY, LADY KAEDE.
COL-LAPSED WITHOUT WARNING, DID SHE ...?
AYE... THOUGH SHE SEEMED JUST FINE THIS MORNING ...

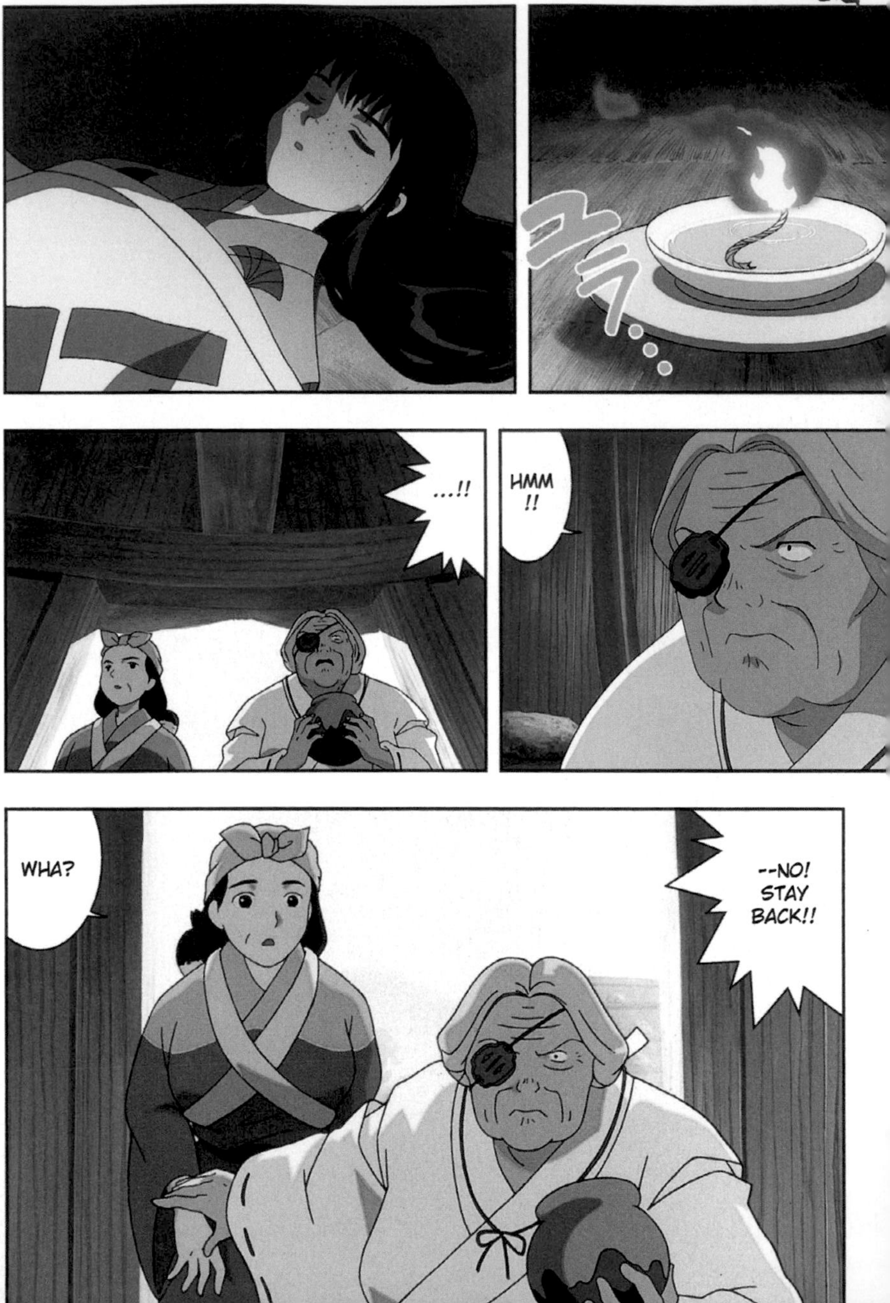

ユラ...
HMM !!
...!!
--NO! STAY BACK!!
WHA?

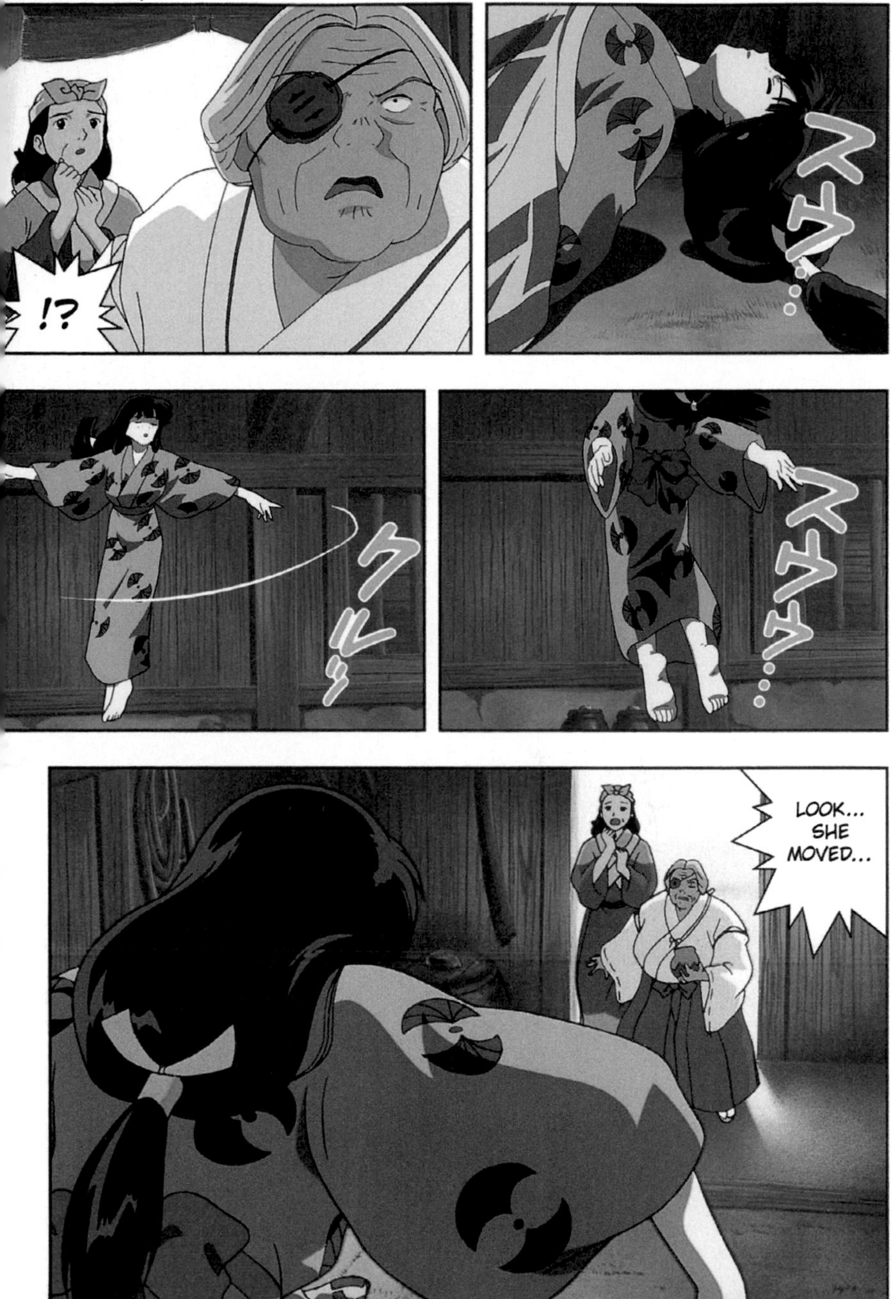
スゥ…
!?
スゥゥ…
クルッ
LOOK... SHE MOVED...

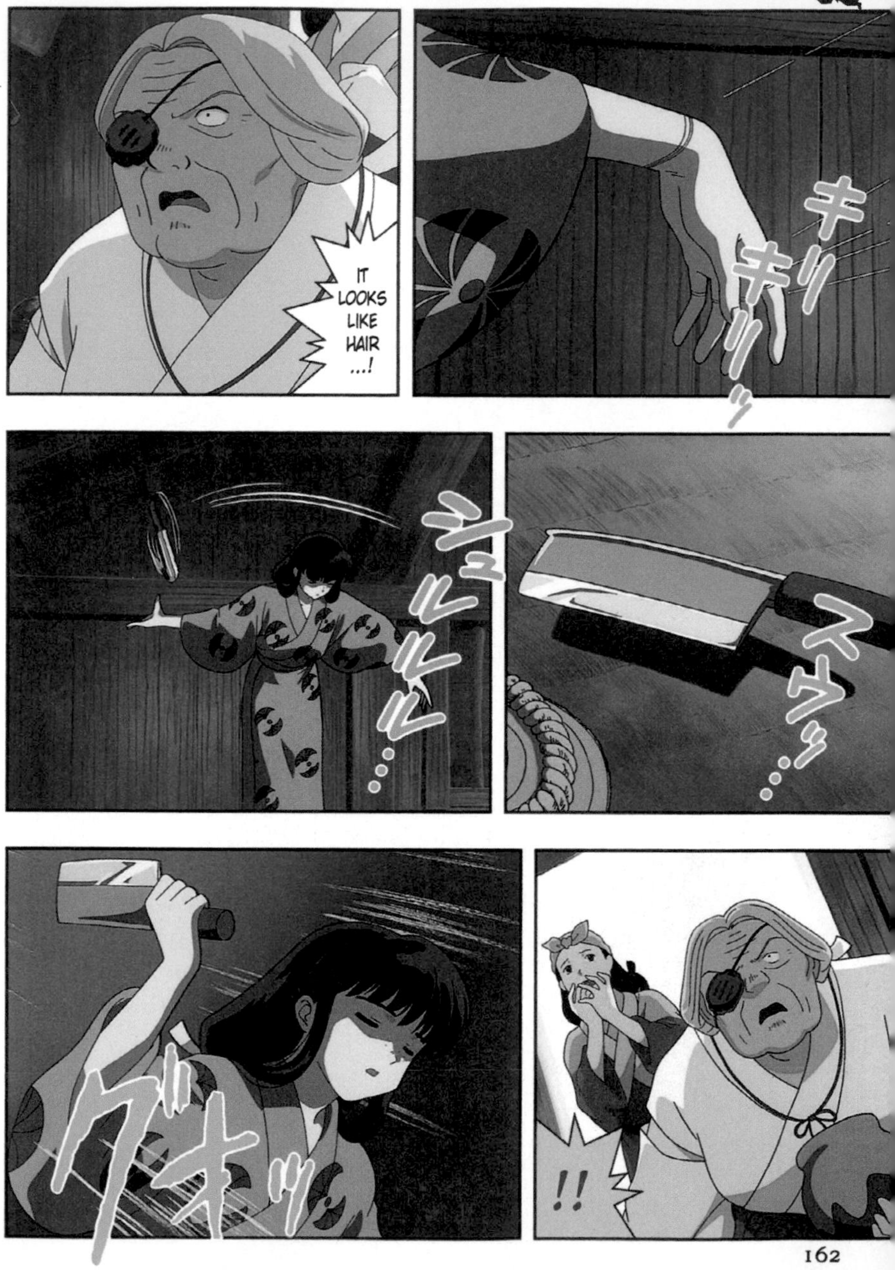
キリキリッ
IT LOOKS LIKE HAIR ...!
スゥッ...
シュルルル...
!!
グオッ

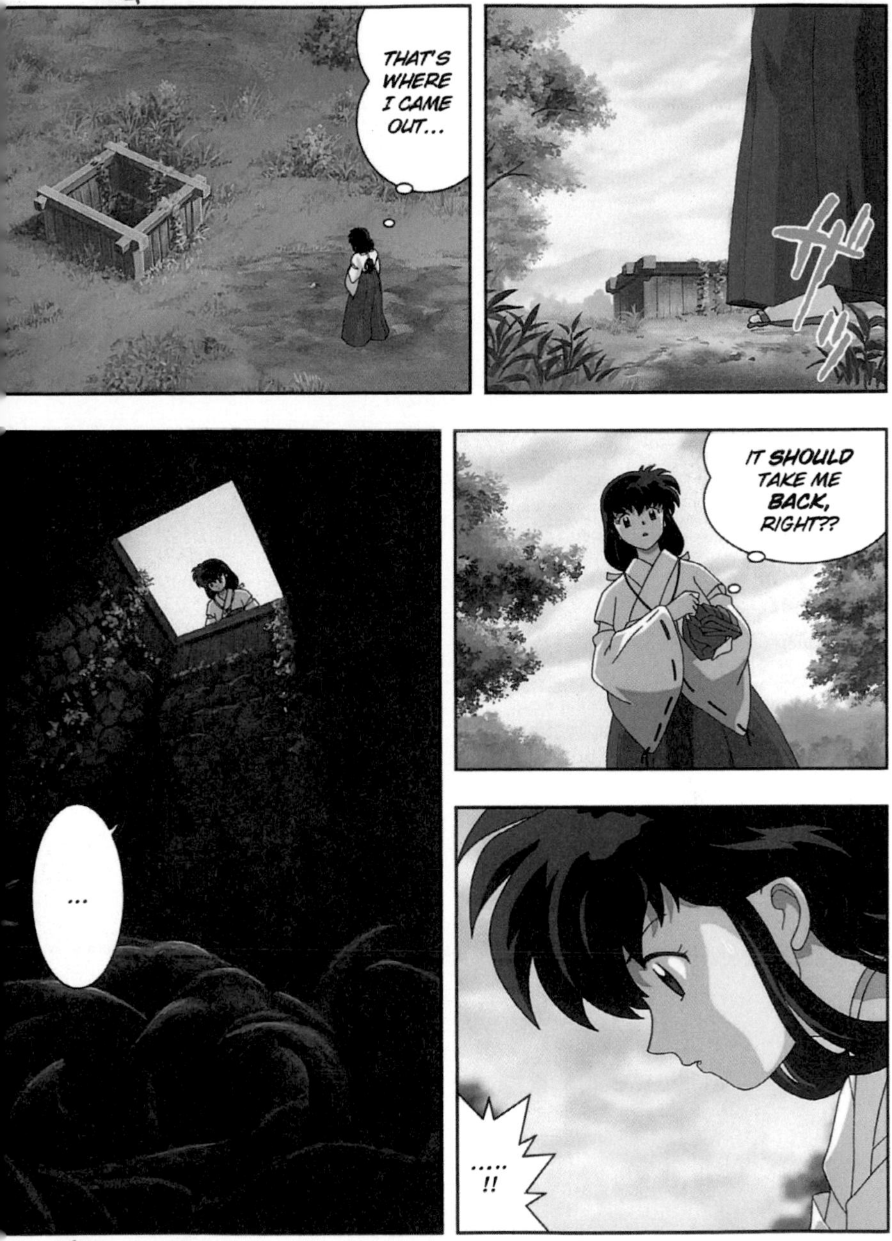
ザッ
THAT'S WHERE I CAME OUT...
IT SHOULD TAKE ME BACK, RIGHT??
.....
!!
...

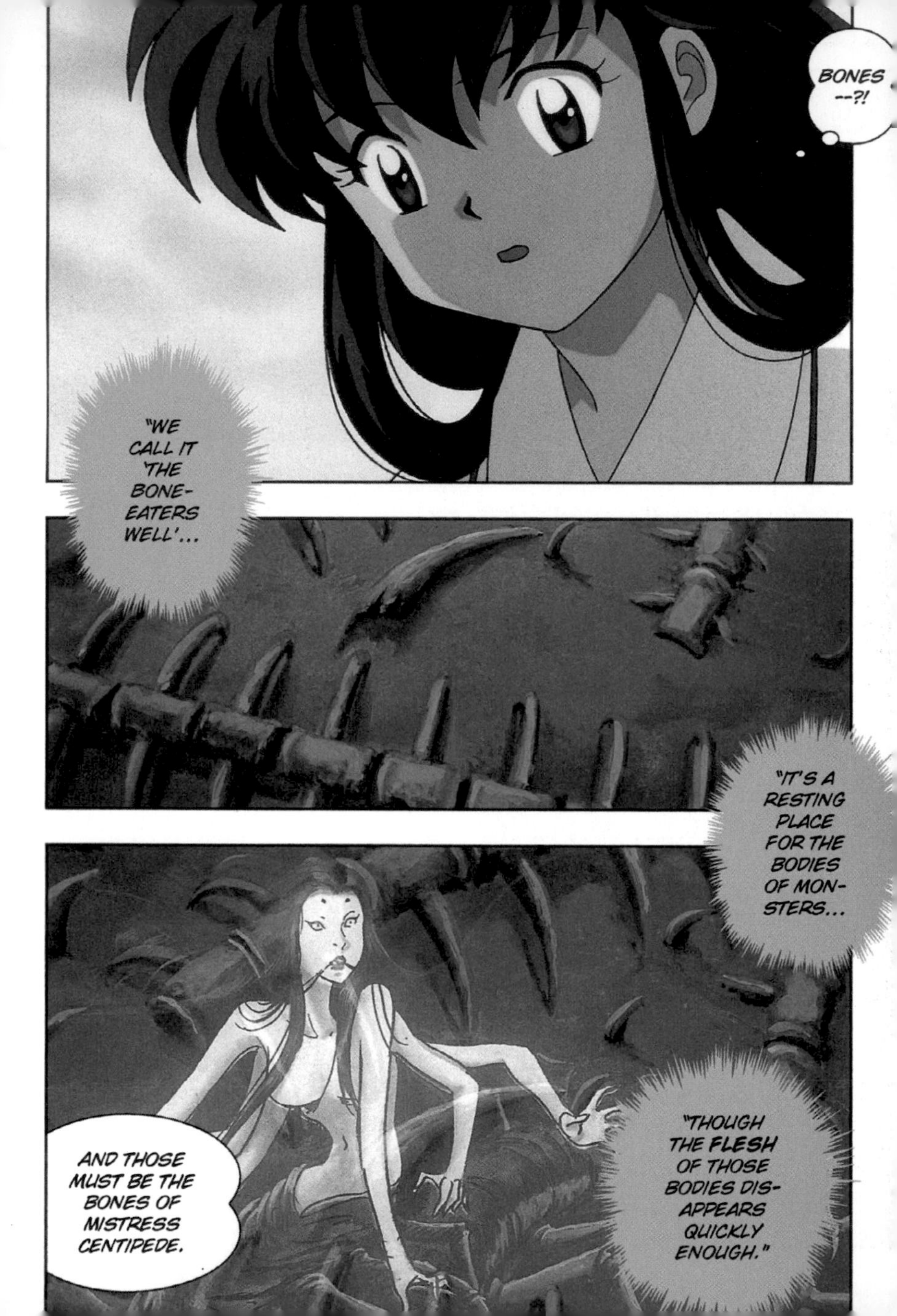
BONES --?!
"WE CALL IT 'THE BONE-EATERS WELL'...
"IT'S A RESTING PLACE FOR THE BODIES OF MON-STERS...
"THOUGH THE FLESH OF THOSE BODIES DIS-APPEARS QUICKLY ENOUGH."
AND THOSE MUST BE THE BONES OF MISTRESS CENTIPEDE.

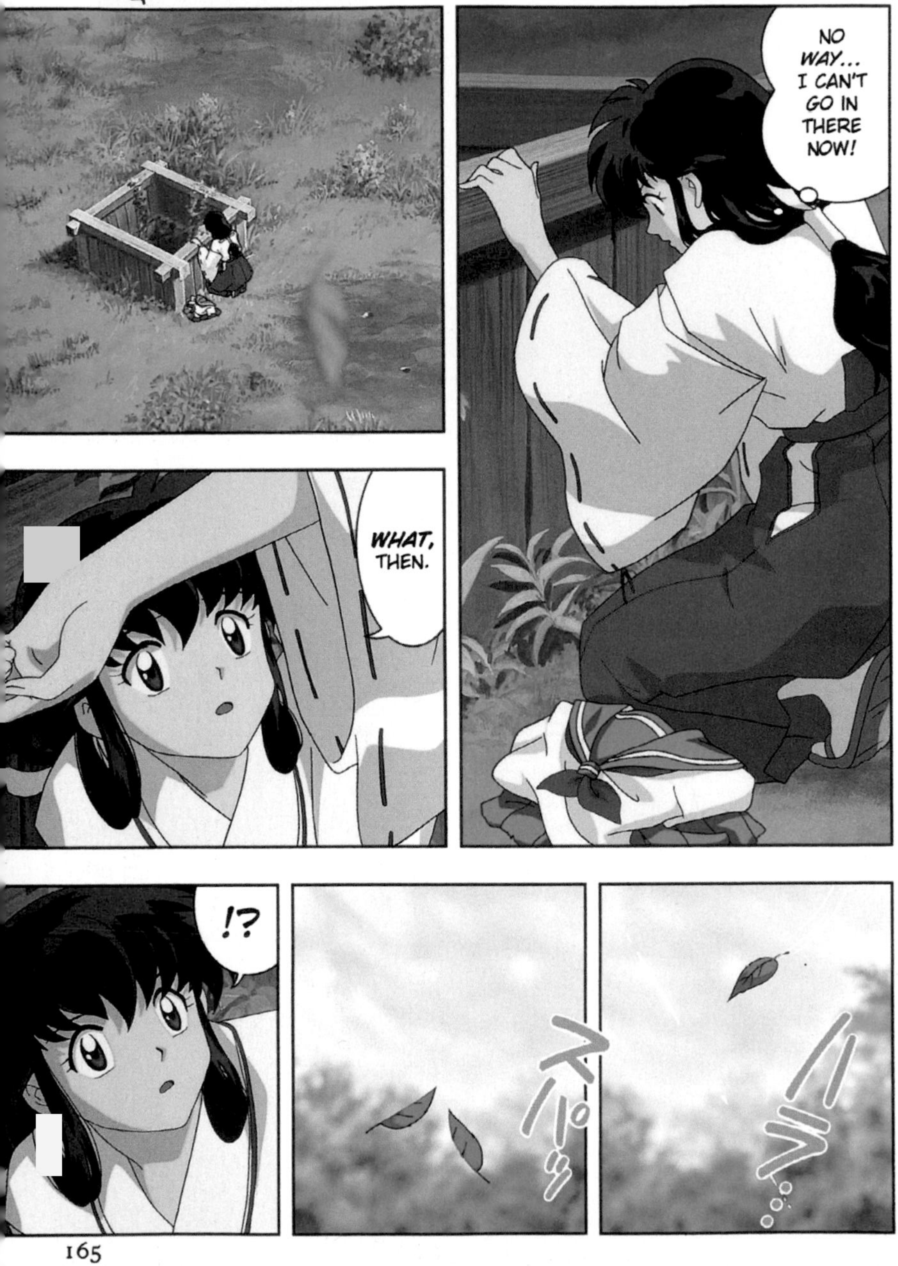
NO WAY... I CAN'T GO IN THERE NOW!
WHAT, THEN.
ハラ
スパッ
!?

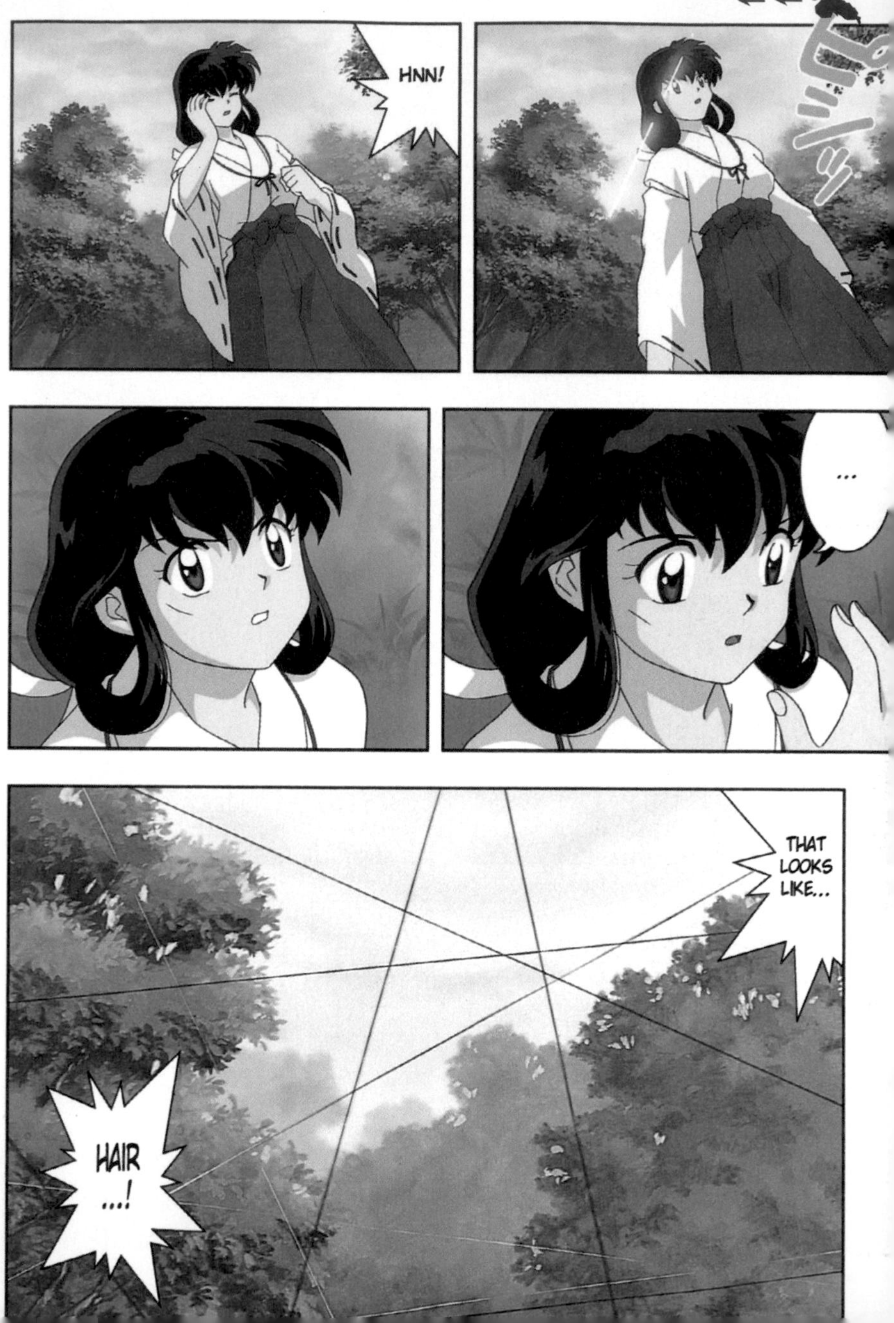
ピシッ
HNN!
...
THAT LOOKS LIKE...
HAIR ...!

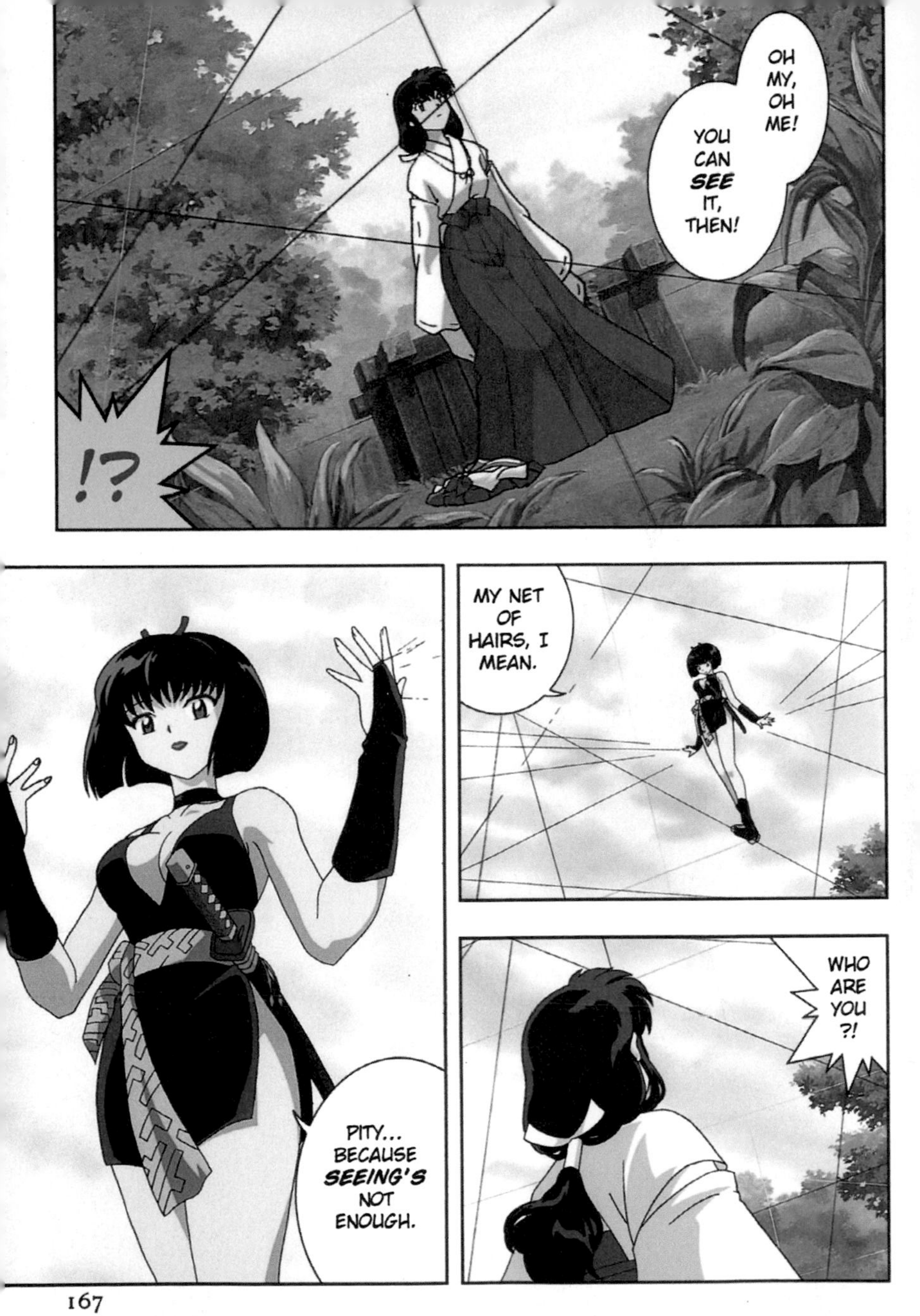
OH MY, OH ME!
YOU CAN SEE IT, THEN!
!?
MY NET OF HAIRS, I MEAN.
WHO ARE YOU ?!
PITY... BECAUSE SEEING'S NOT ENOUGH.

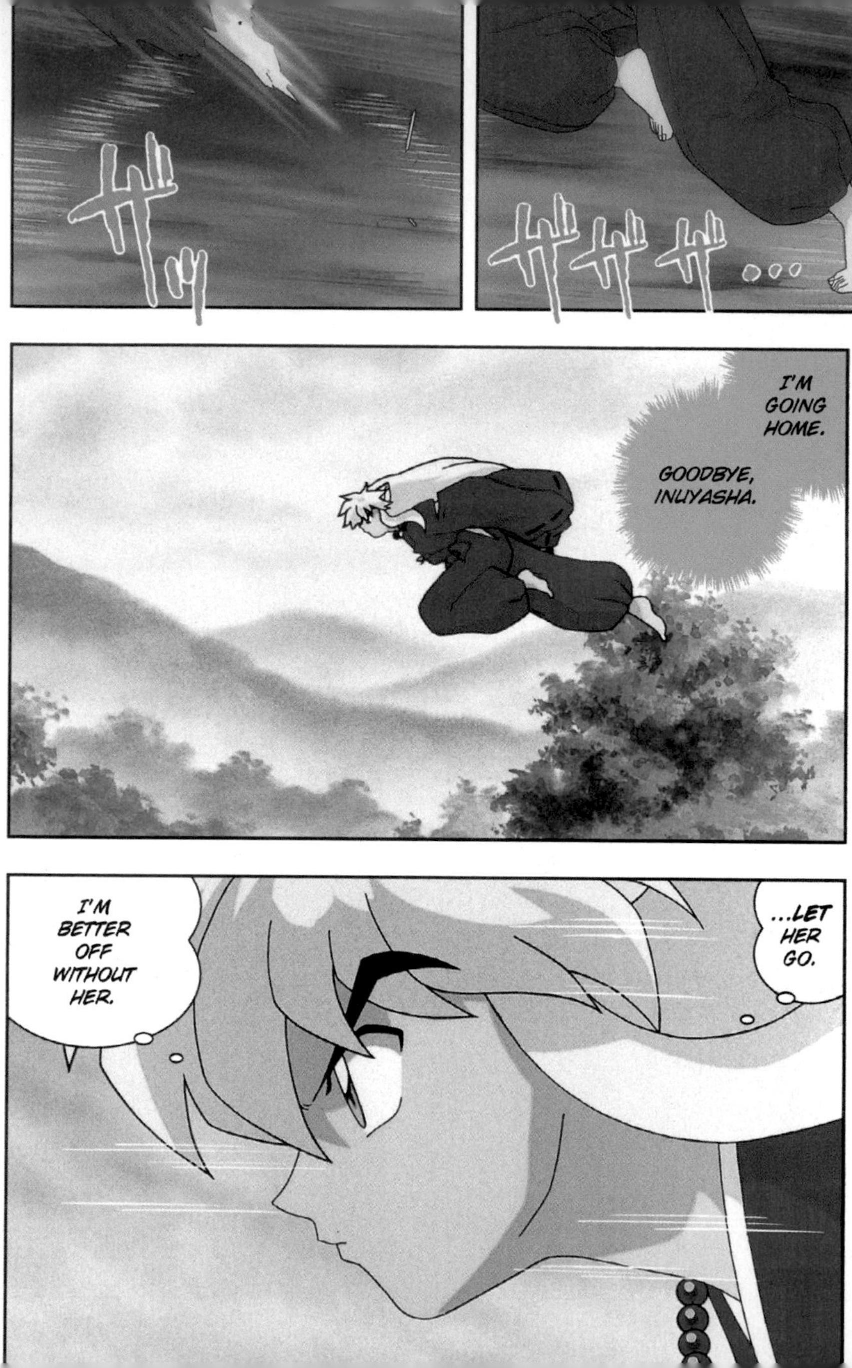
ザザザ…
ザッ
I'M GOING HOME.
GOODBYE, INUYASHA.
...LET HER GO.
I'M BETTER OFF WITHOUT HER.

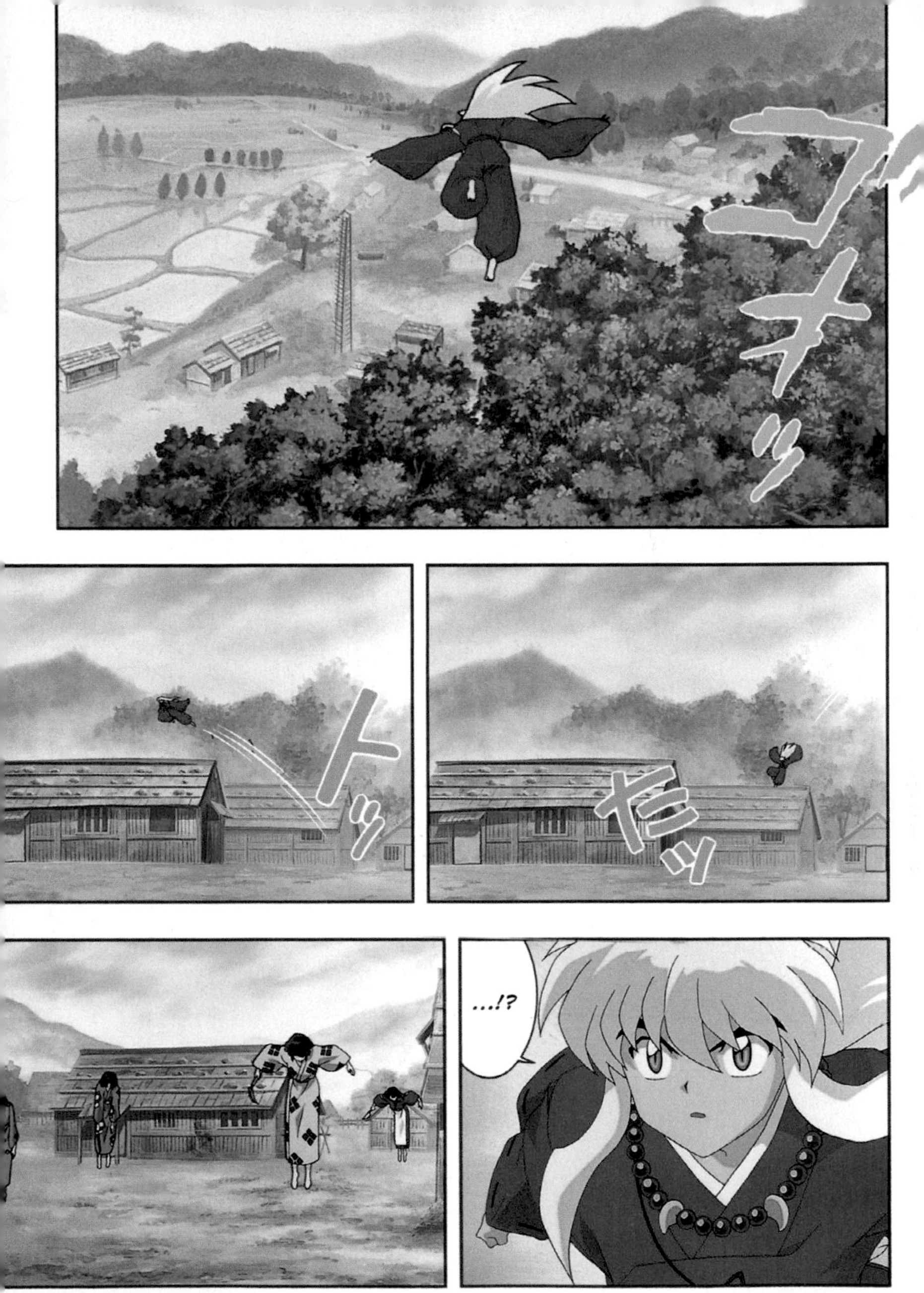
トッ
...!?

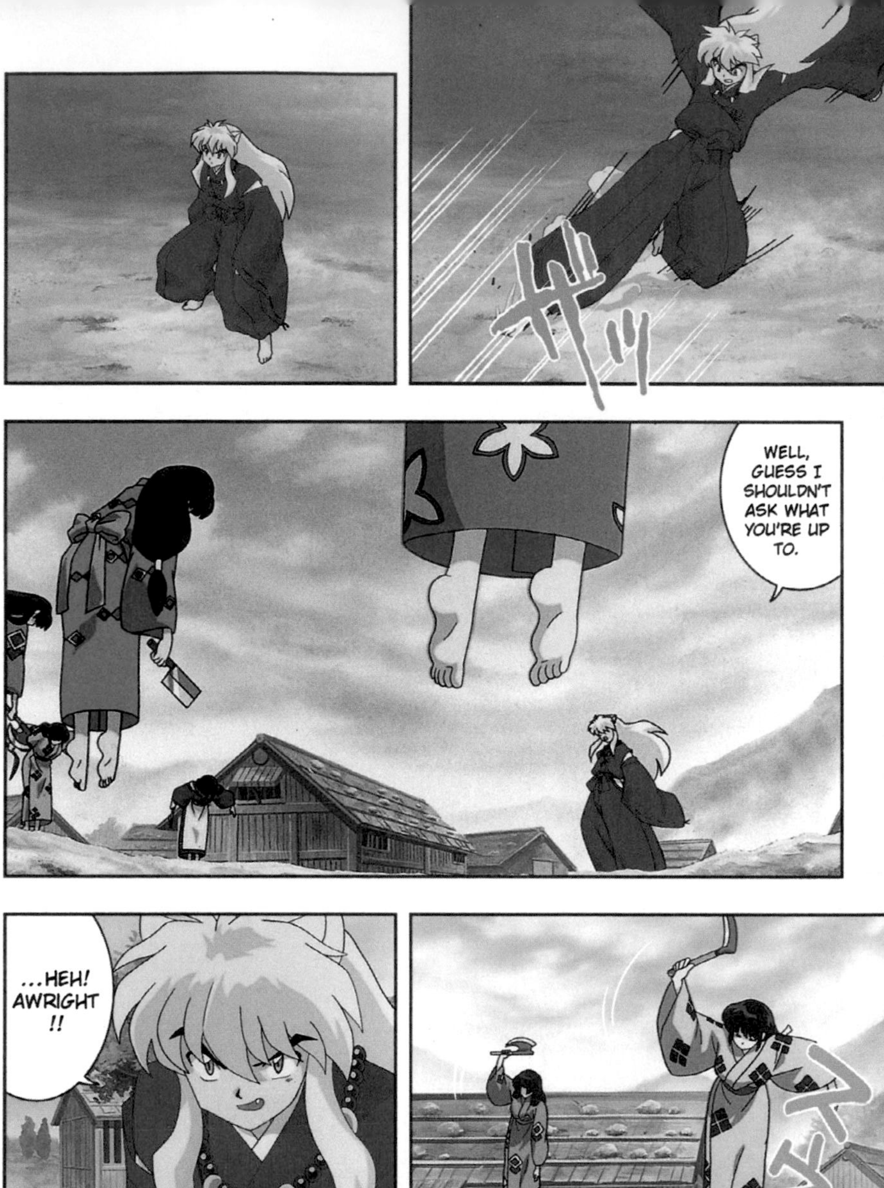

ザッ
WELL, GUESS I SHOULDN'T ASK WHAT YOU'RE UP TO.
...HEH! AWRIGHT !!

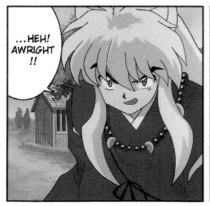

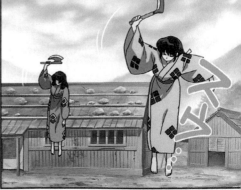

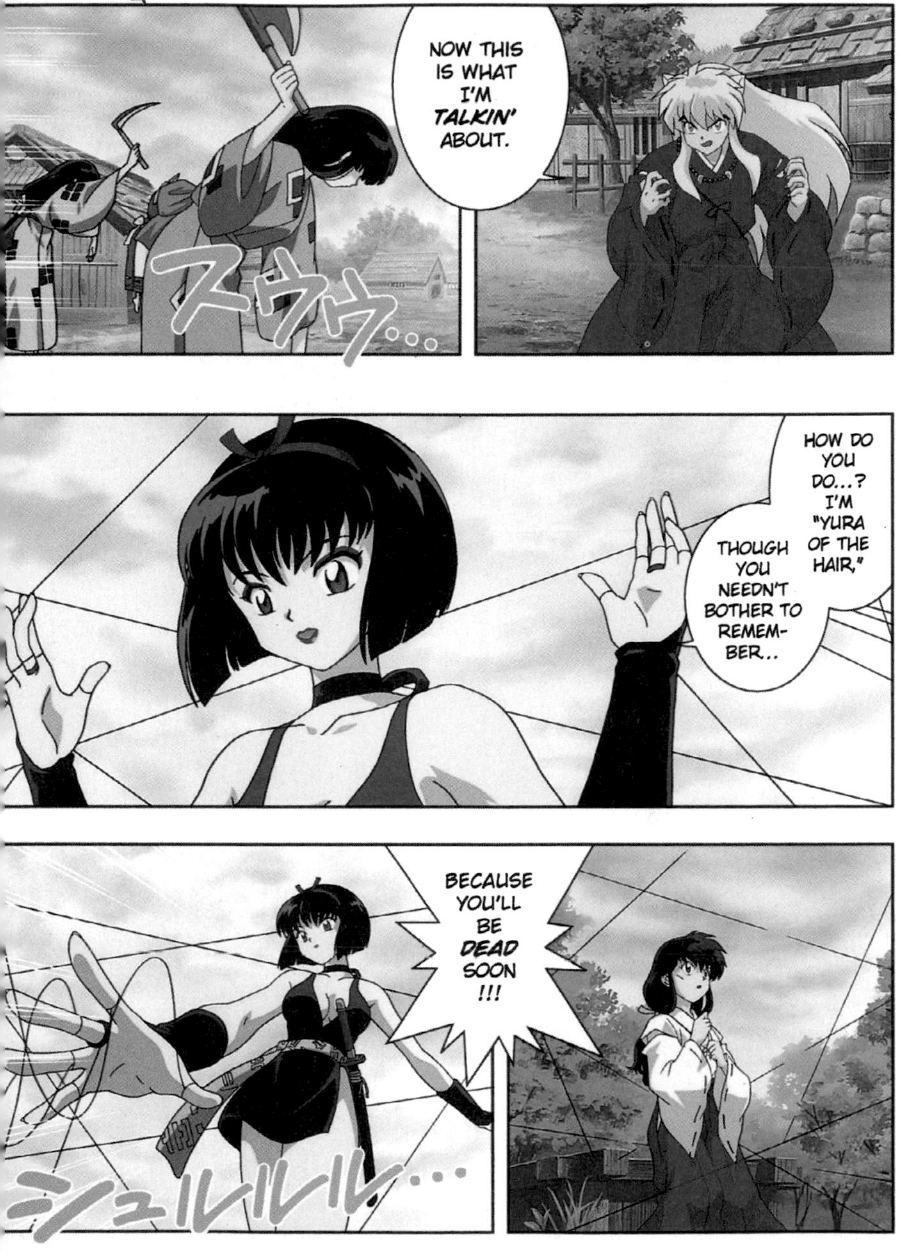
NOW THIS IS WHAT I'M TALKIN' ABOUT.
スウウ...
HOW DO YOU DO...? I'M "YURA OF THE HAIR,"
THOUGH YOU NEEDN'T BOTHER TO REMEMBER...
BECAUSE YOU'LL BE DEAD SOON!!!
シュルルルル...

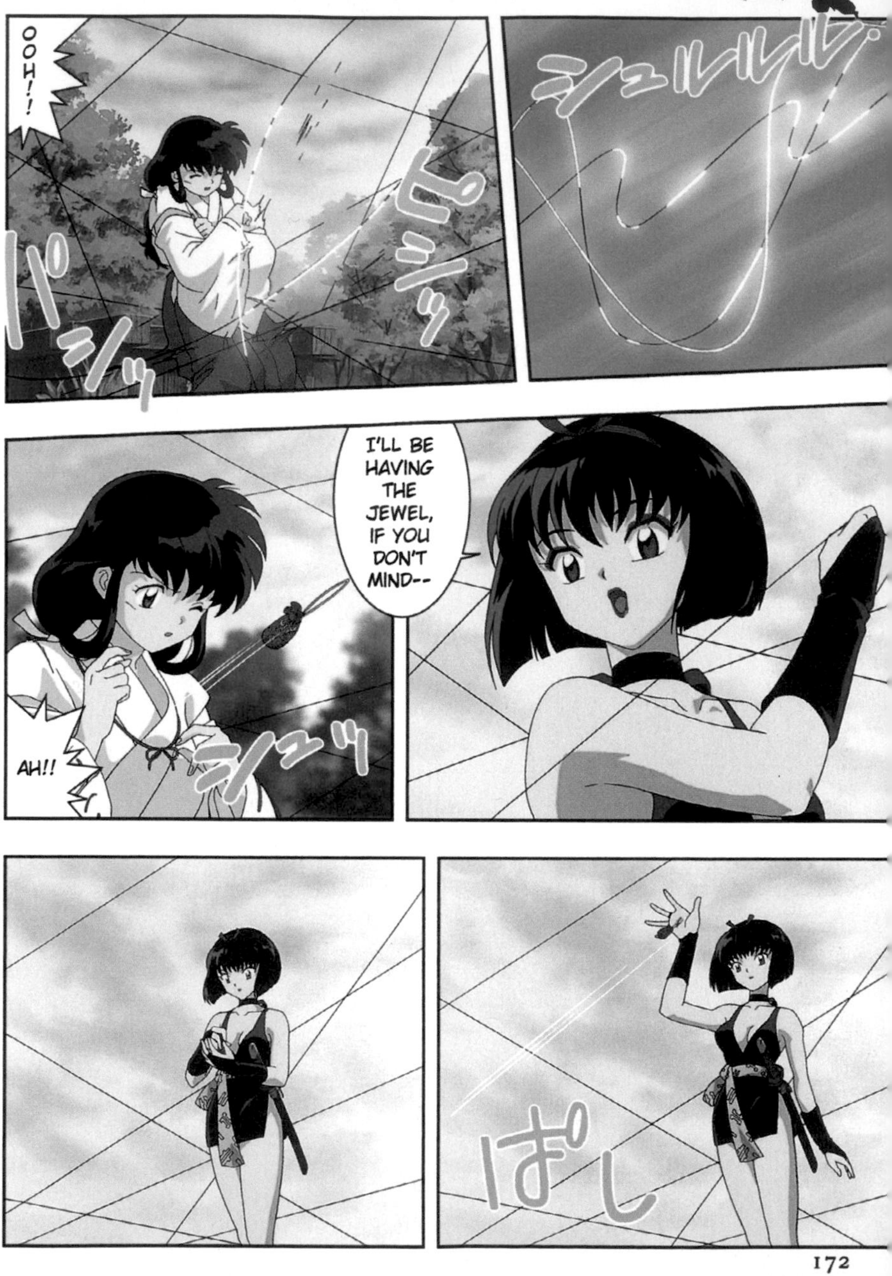
シュルルル
OOH!!
ピシッ
パシッ
I'LL BE HAVING THE JEWEL, IF YOU DON'T MIND--
AH!!
シュッ
ぱし

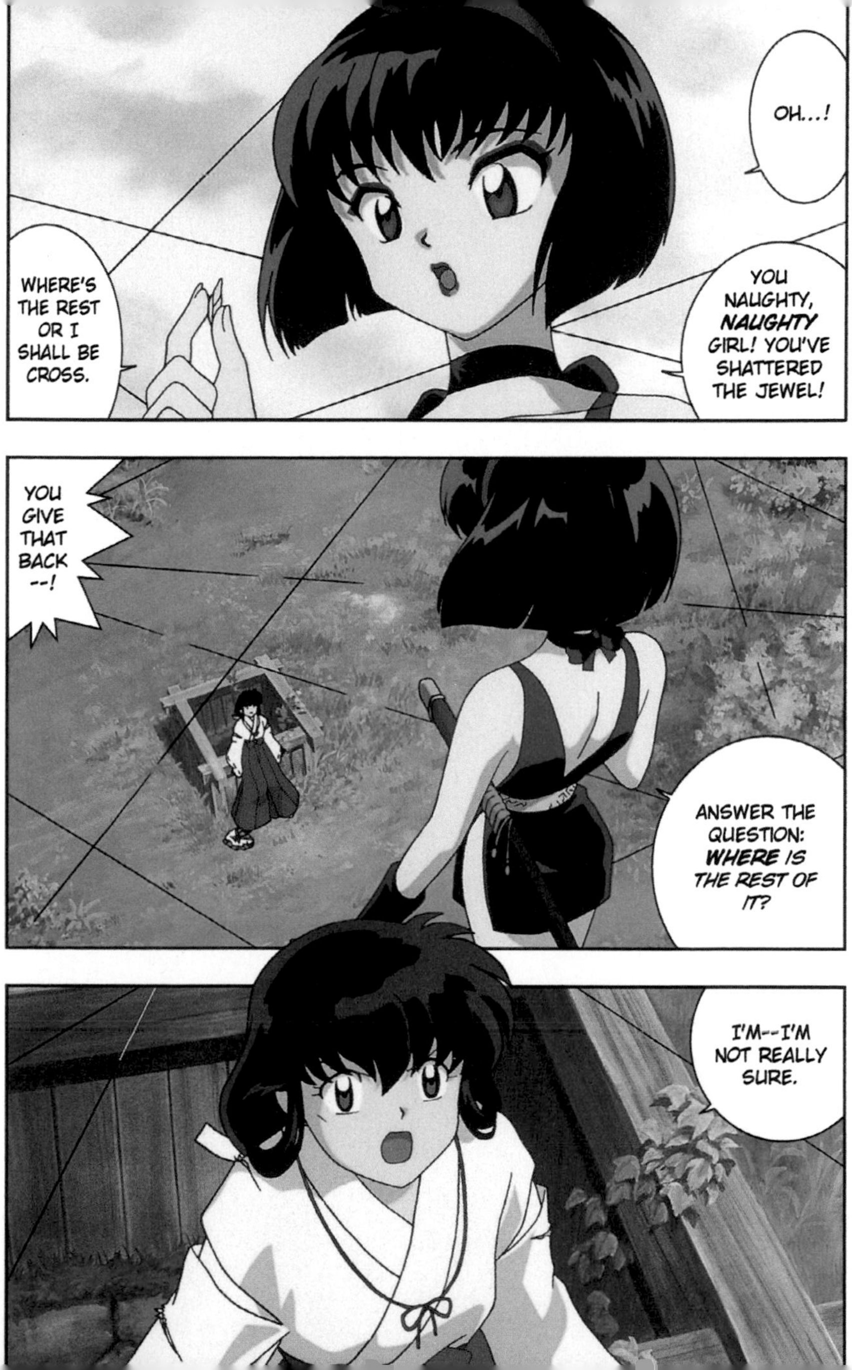
OH...!
YOU NAUGHTY, *NAUGHTY* GIRL! YOU'VE SHATTERED THE JEWEL!
WHERE'S THE REST OR I SHALL BE CROSS.
YOU GIVE THAT BACK --!
ANSWER THE QUESTION: *WHERE IS THE REST OF IT?*
I'M--I'M NOT REALLY SURE.

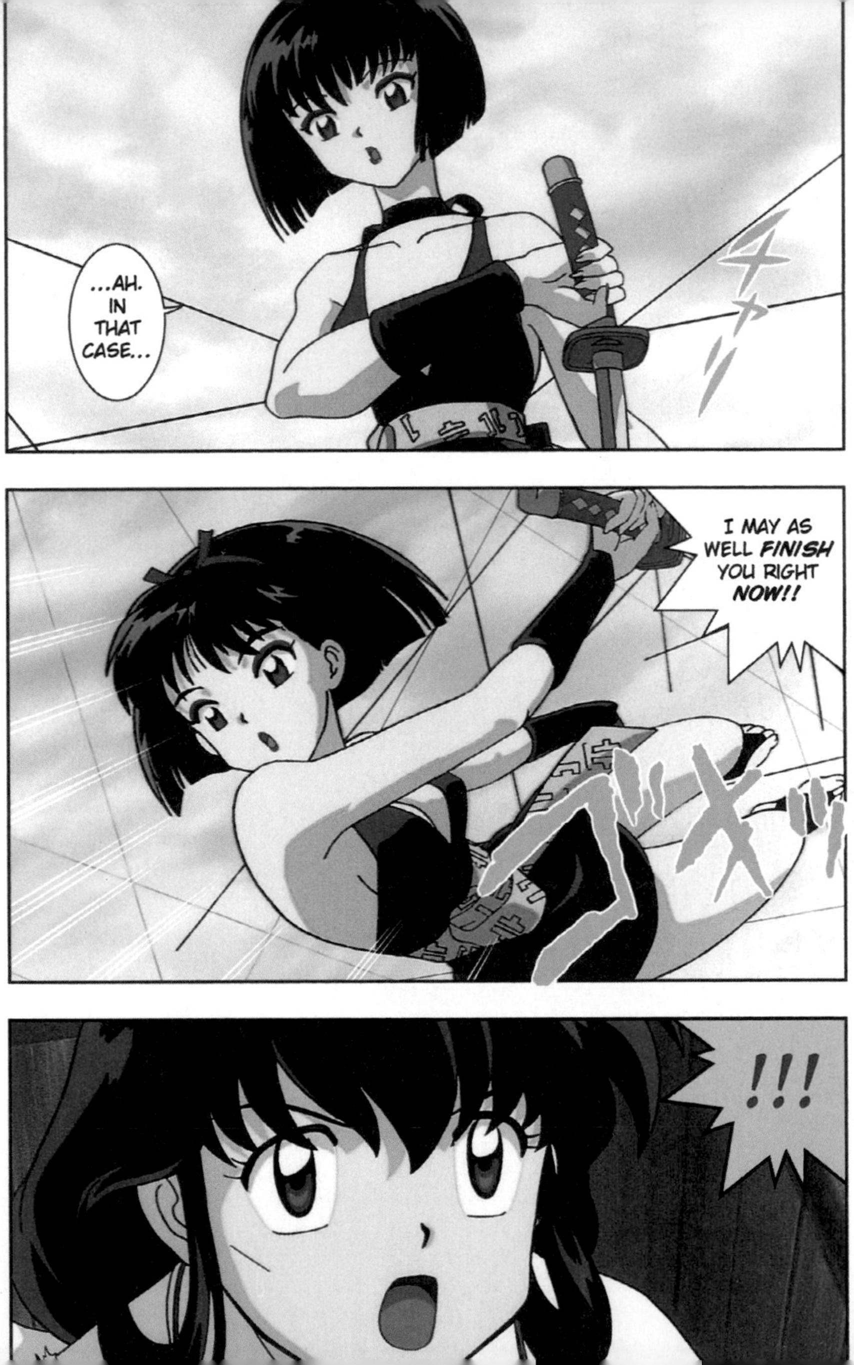
...AH. IN THAT CASE...
I MAY AS WELL FINISH YOU RIGHT NOW!!
!!!

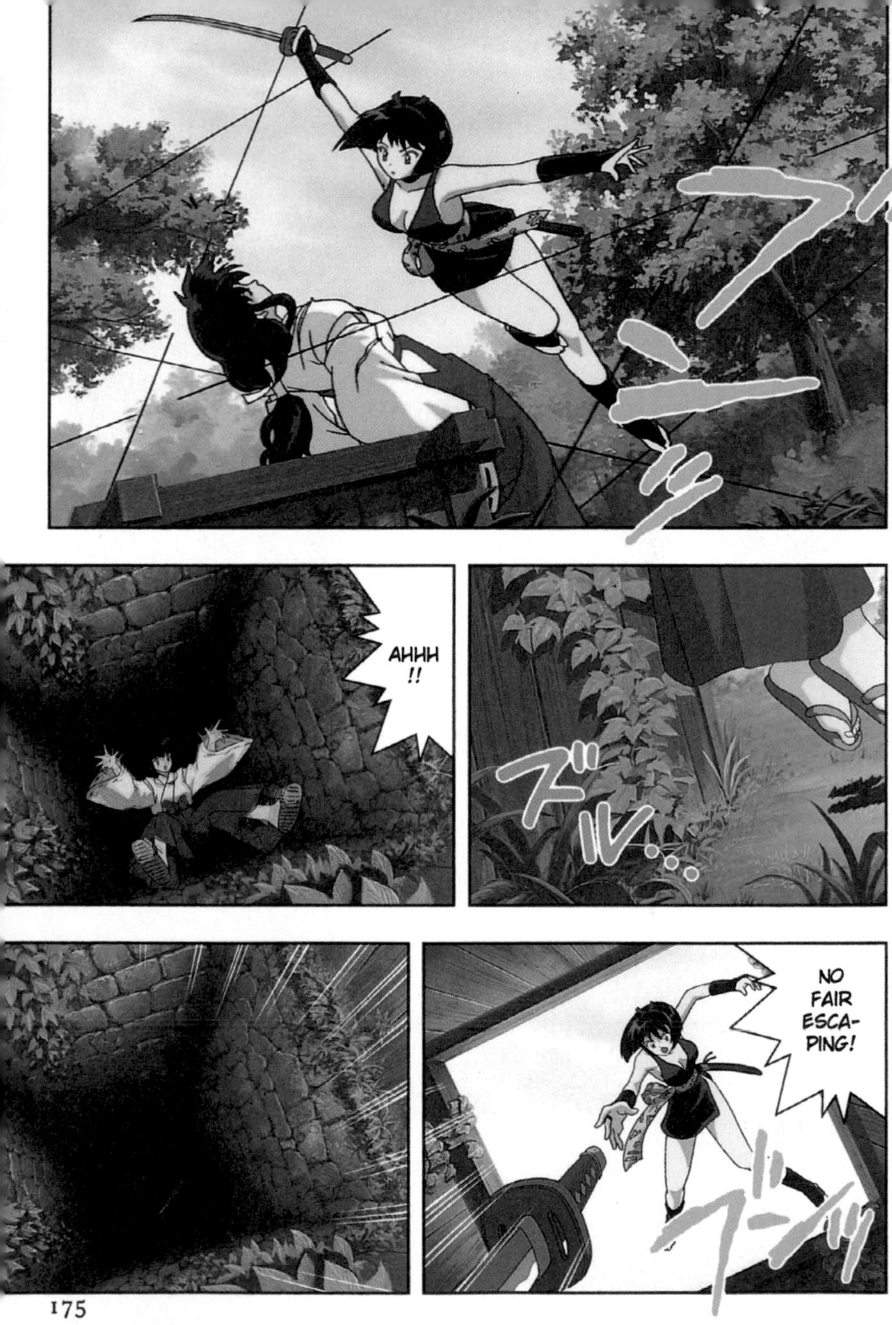
フンッ
ズル…
AHHH
!!
NO FAIR ESCA-PING!
ブーンッ

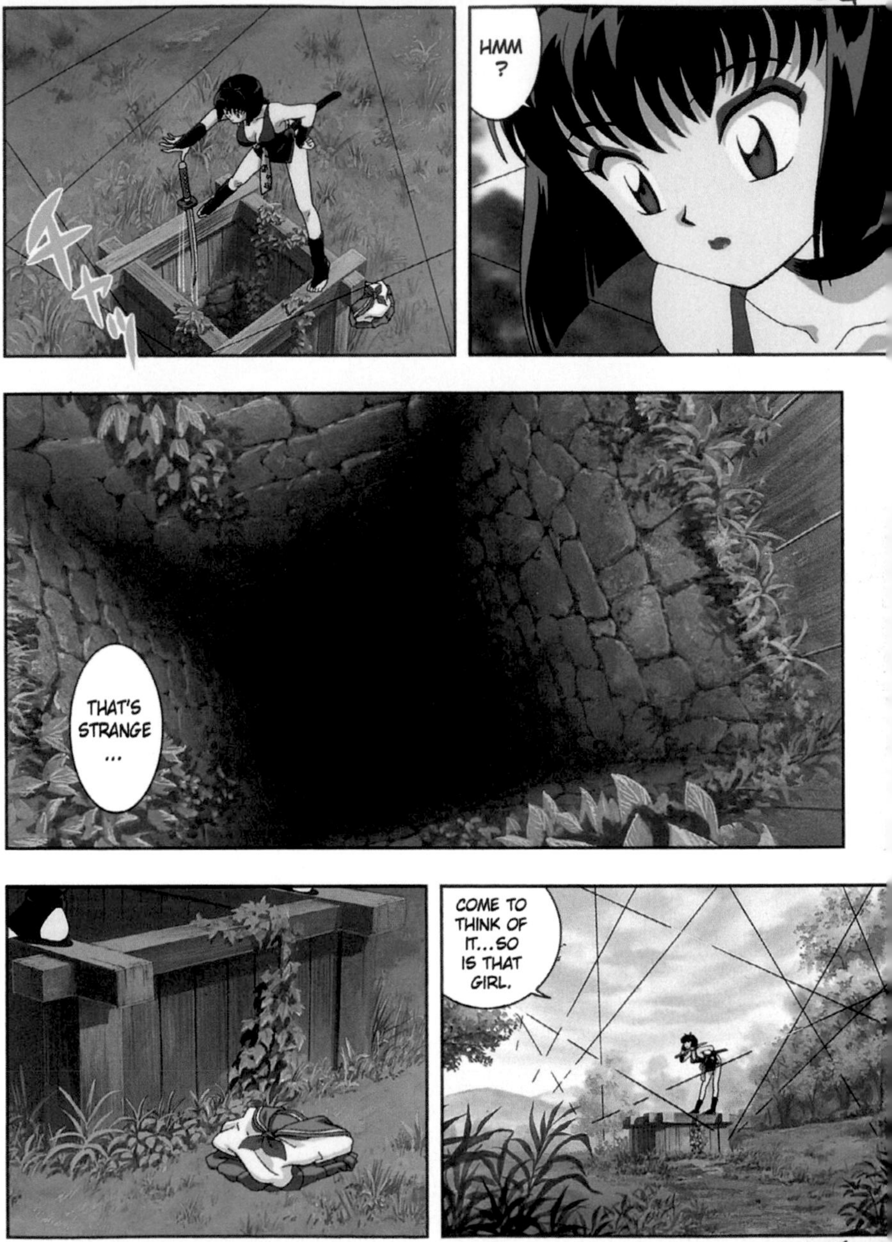
HMM ?
THAT'S STRANGE ...
COME TO THINK OF IT...SO IS THAT GIRL.

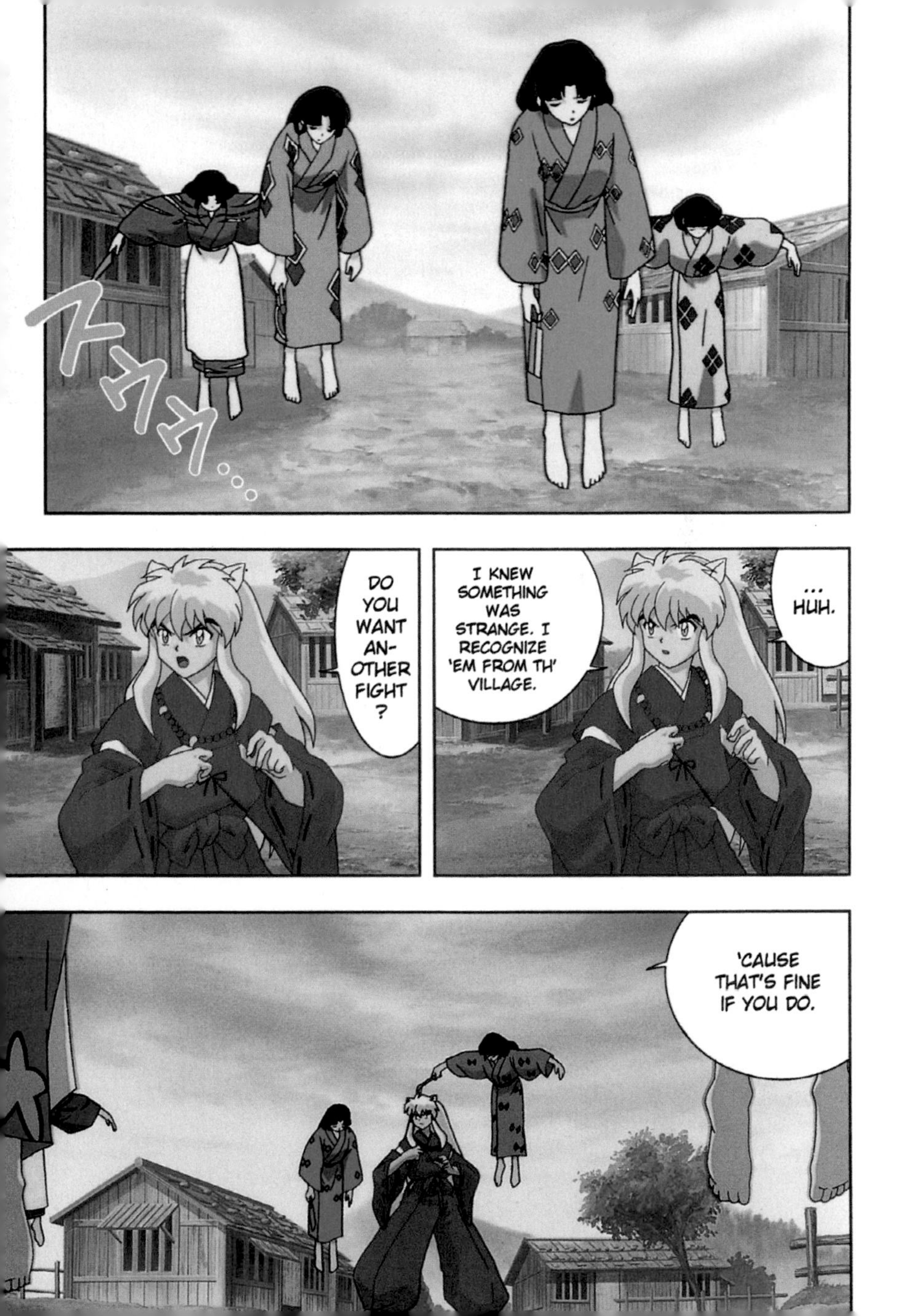

スウウ...
... HUH.
I KNEW SOMETHING WAS STRANGE. I RECOGNIZE 'EM FROM TH' VILLAGE.
DO YOU WANT AN-OTHER FIGHT?
'CAUSE THAT'S FINE IF YOU DO.

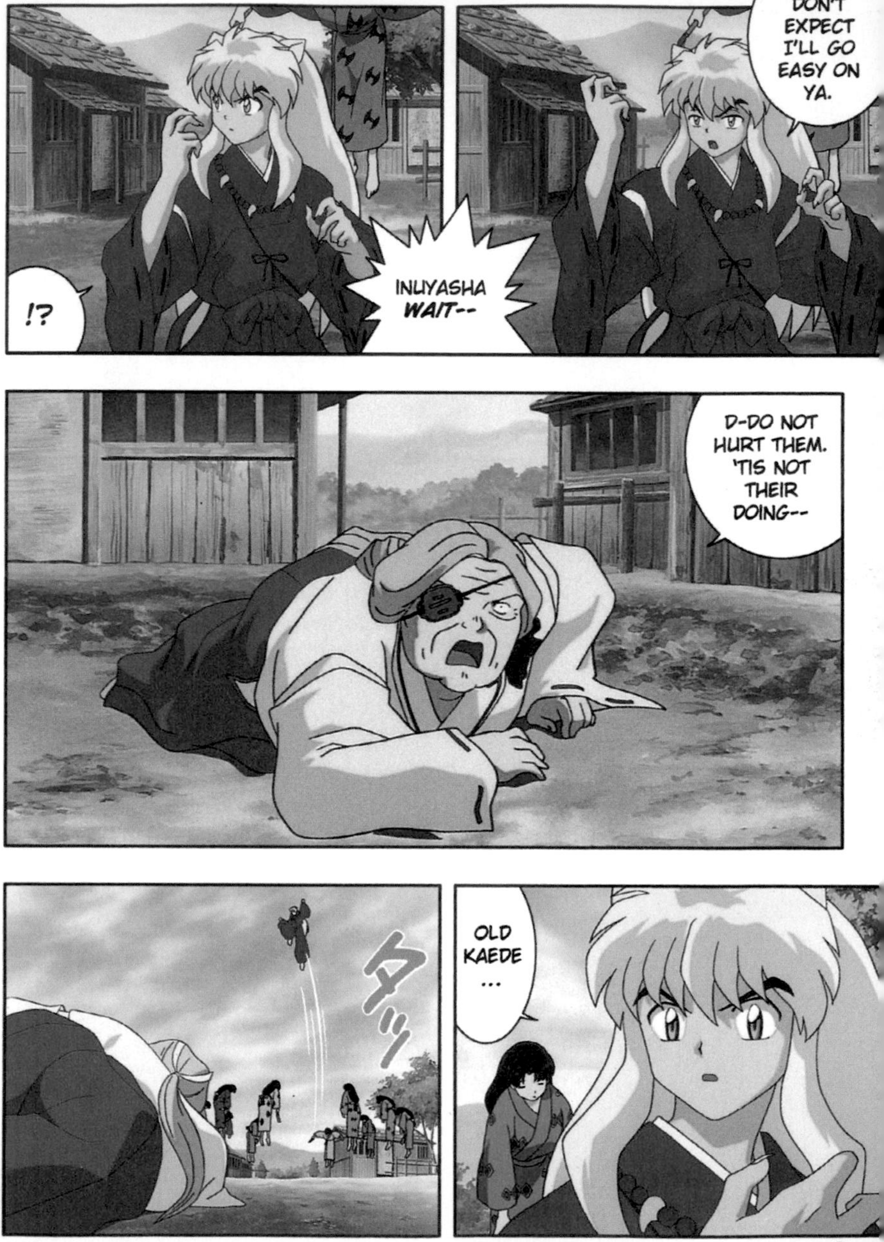
JUST DON'T EXPECT I'LL GO EASY ON YA.
INUYASHA WAIT--
!?
D-DO NOT HURT THEM. 'TIS NOT THEIR DOING--
OLD KAEDE ...
タッ

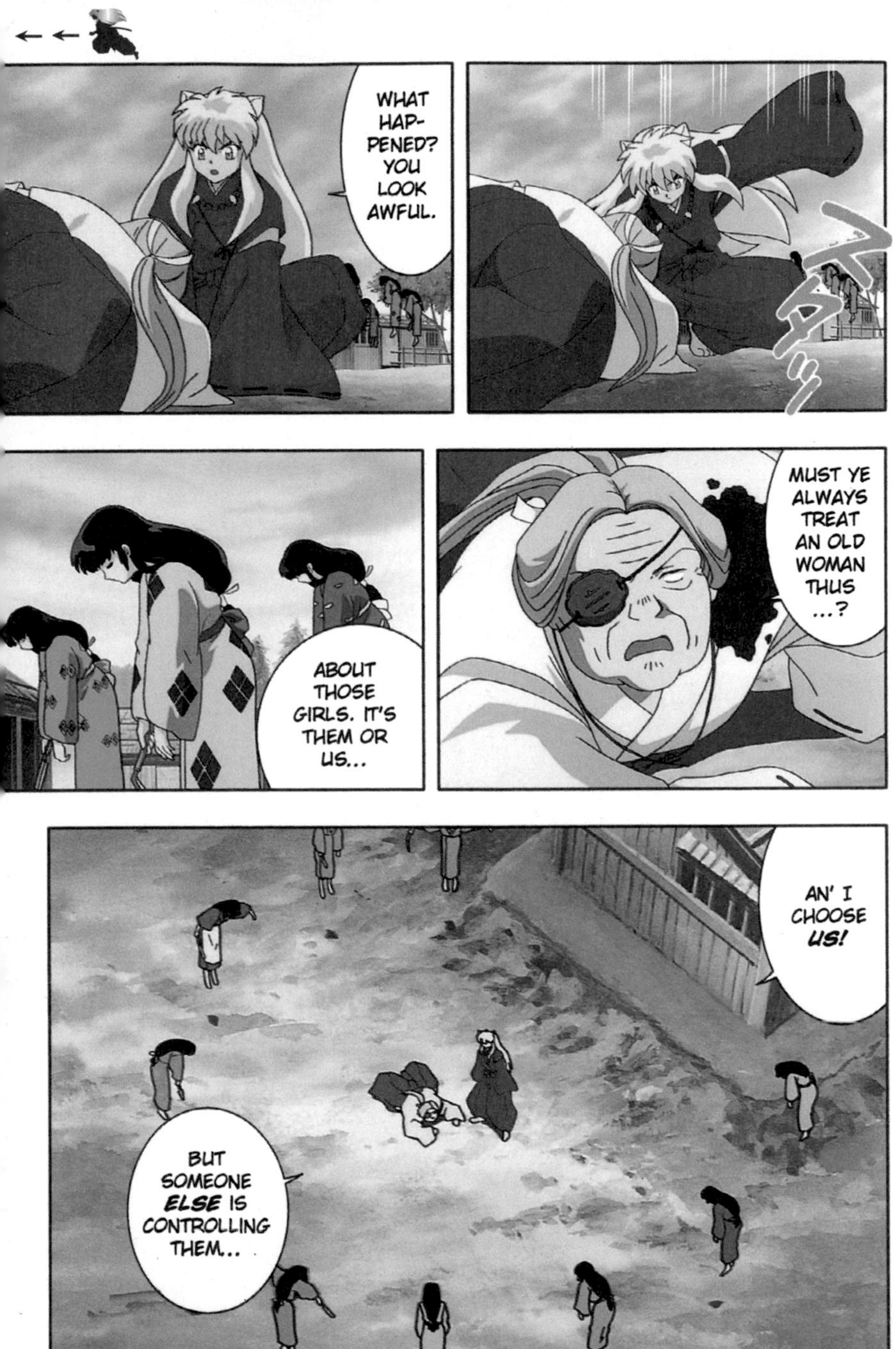
スタッ
WHAT HAP-PENED? YOU LOOK AWFUL.
MUST YE ALWAYS TREAT AN OLD WOMAN THUS ...?
ABOUT THOSE GIRLS. IT'S THEM OR US...
AN' I CHOOSE *US!*
BUT SOMEONE *ELSE* IS CONTROLLING THEM..

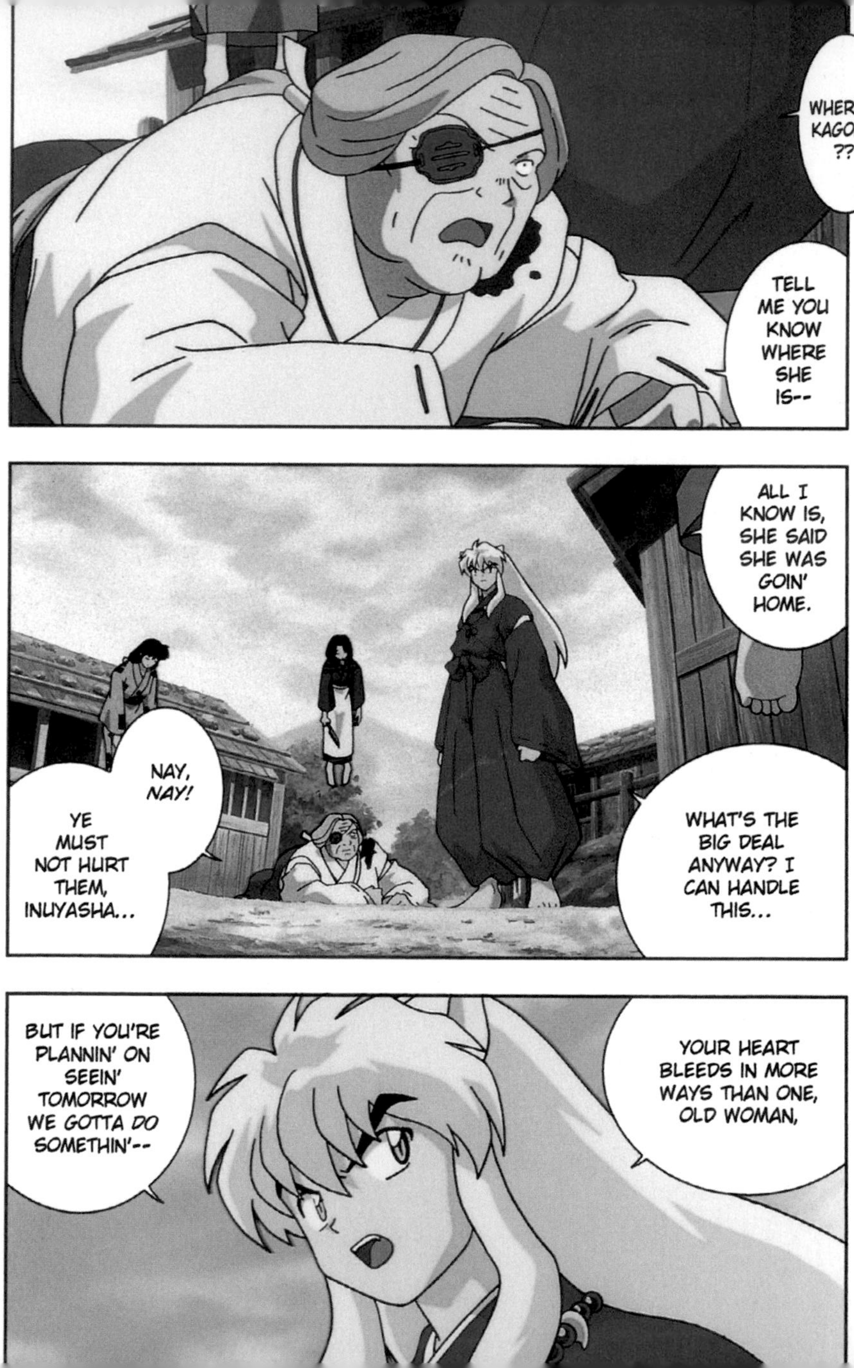
WHERE'S KAGOME ??
TELL ME YOU KNOW WHERE SHE IS--
ALL I KNOW IS, SHE SAID SHE WAS GOIN' HOME.
NAY, NAY!
YE MUST NOT HURT THEM, INUYASHA...
WHAT'S THE BIG DEAL ANYWAY? I CAN HANDLE THIS...
YOUR HEART BLEEDS IN MORE WAYS THAN ONE, OLD WOMAN,
BUT IF YOU'RE PLANNIN' ON SEEIN' TOMORROW WE GOTTA *DO* SOMETHIN'--

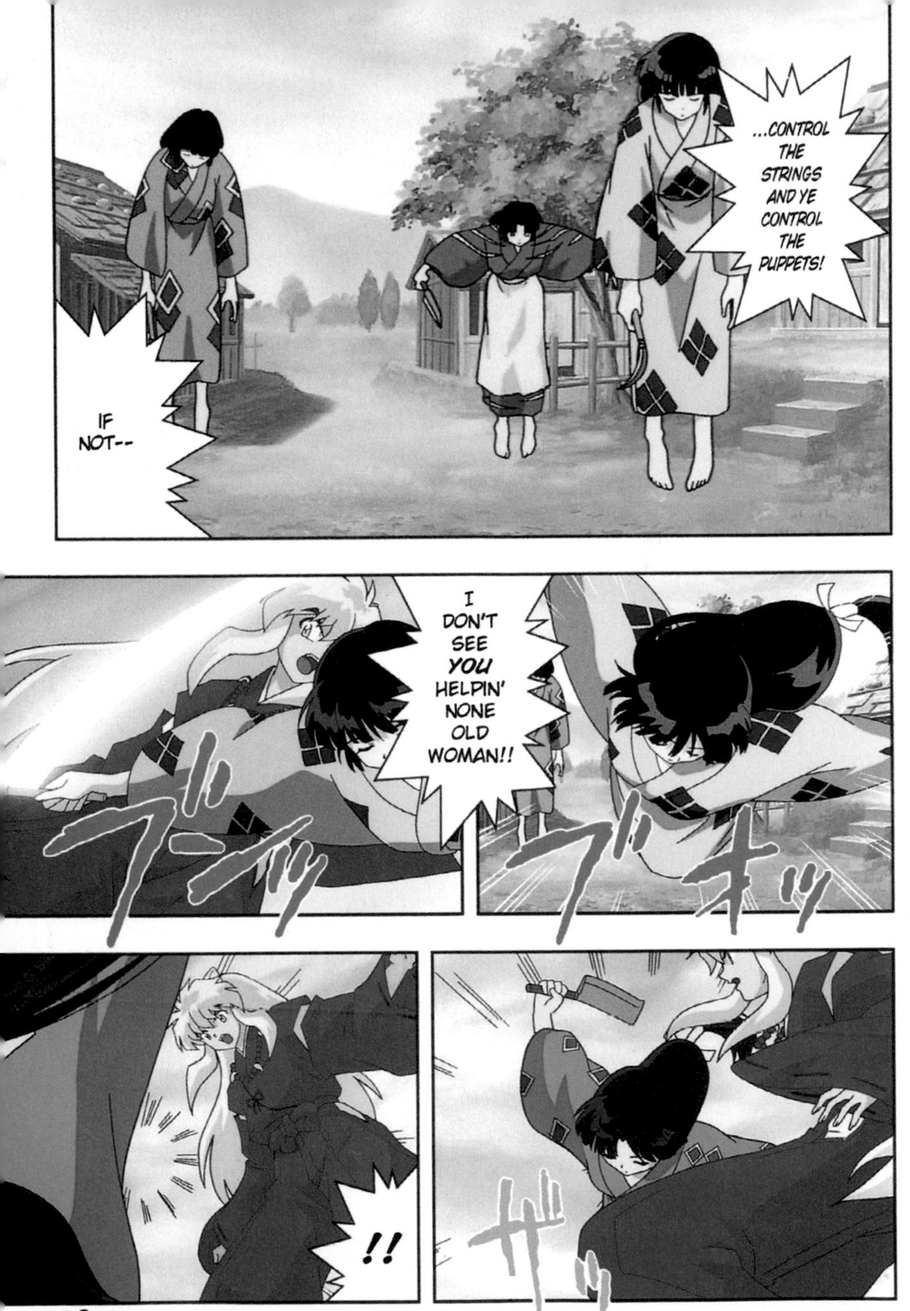
...CONTROL THE STRINGS AND YE CONTROL THE PUPPETS!
IF NOT--
ブオッ
I DON'T SEE YOU HELPIN' NONE OLD WOMAN!!
ブンッ
ザッ
!!

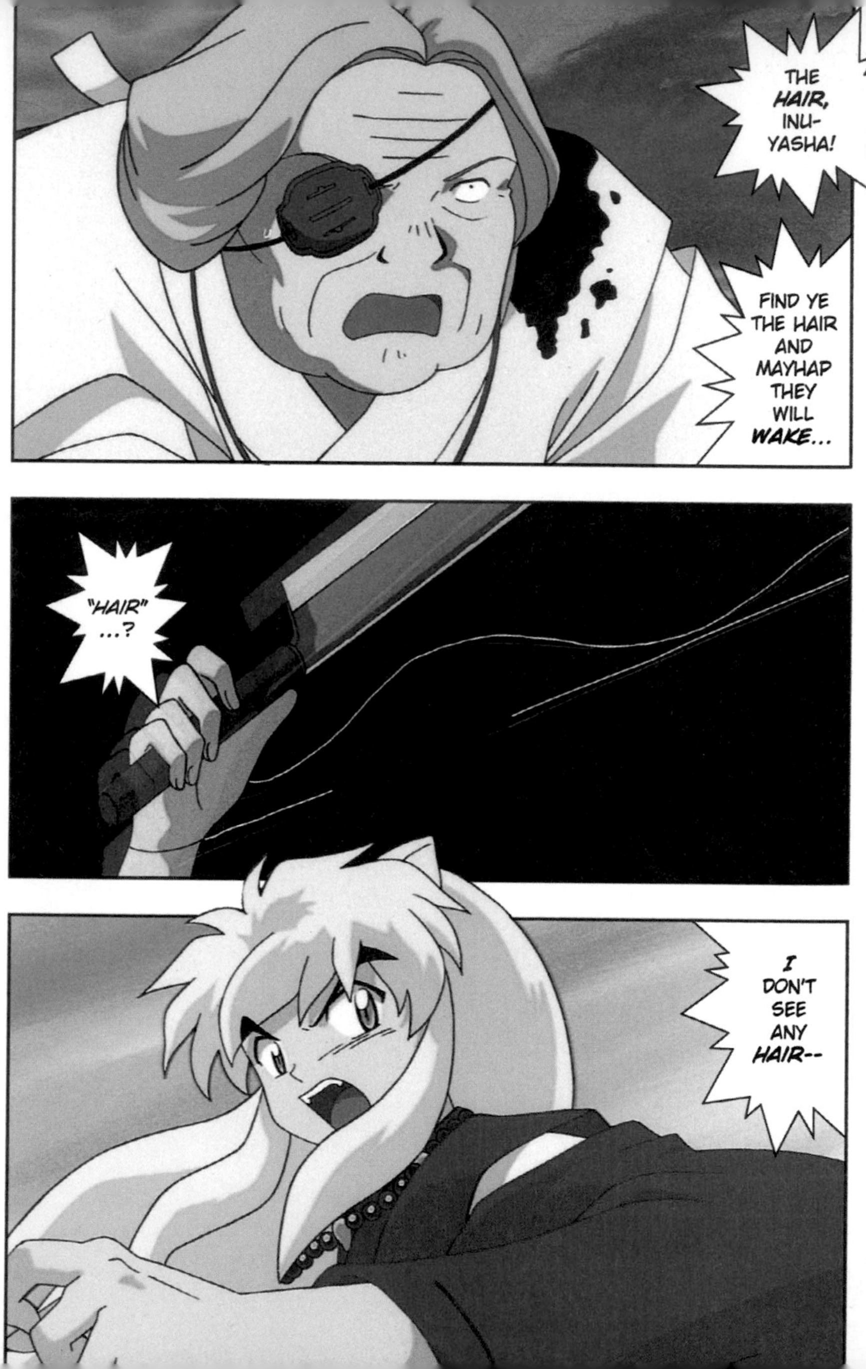
THE HAIR, INU-YASHA!
FIND YE THE HAIR AND MAYHAP THEY WILL WAKE...
"HAIR" ...?
I DON'T SEE ANY HAIR--

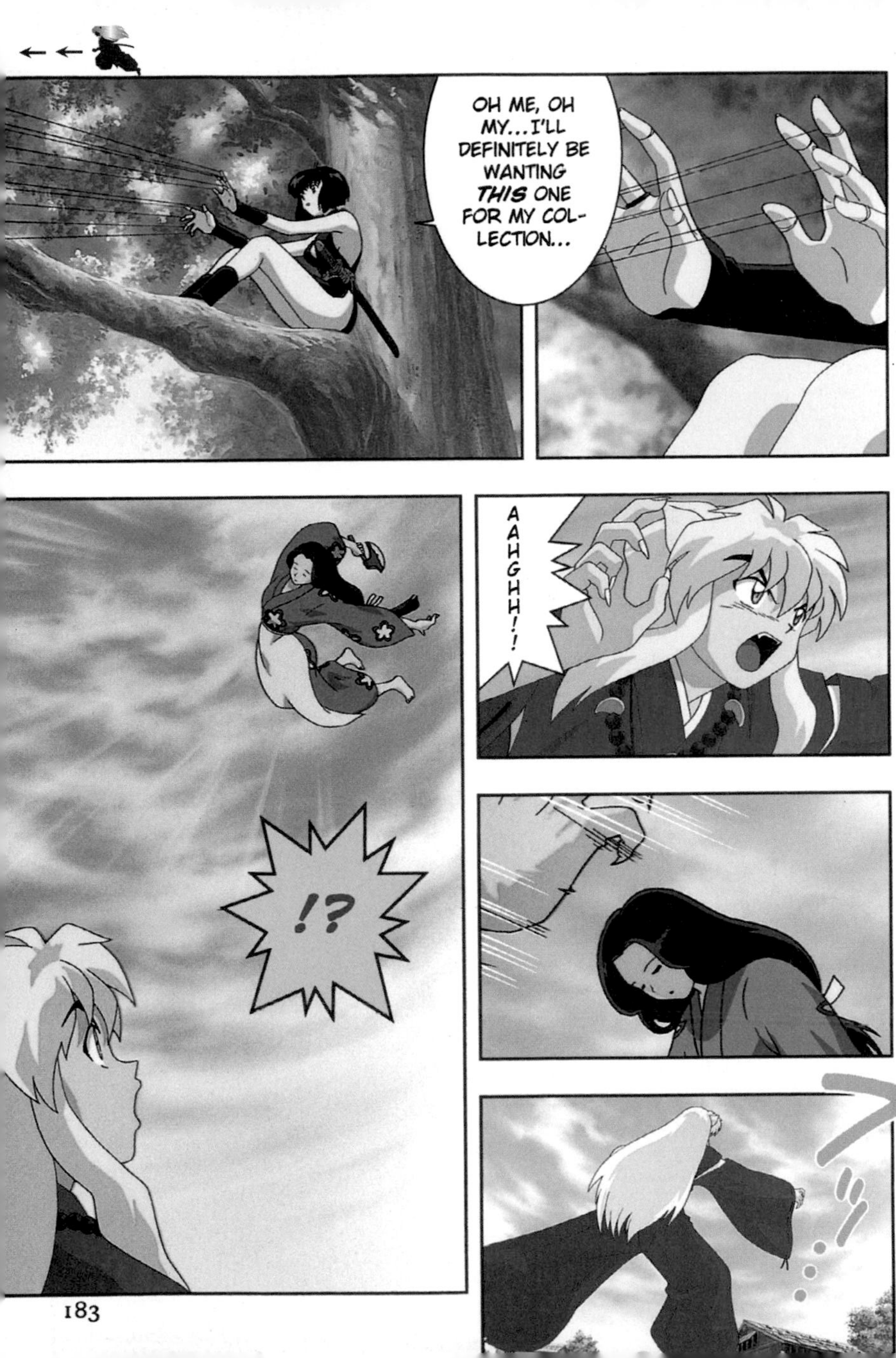
OH ME, OH MY...I'LL DEFINITELY BE WANTING THIS ONE FOR MY COL-LECTION...
AAHGHH!!
!?

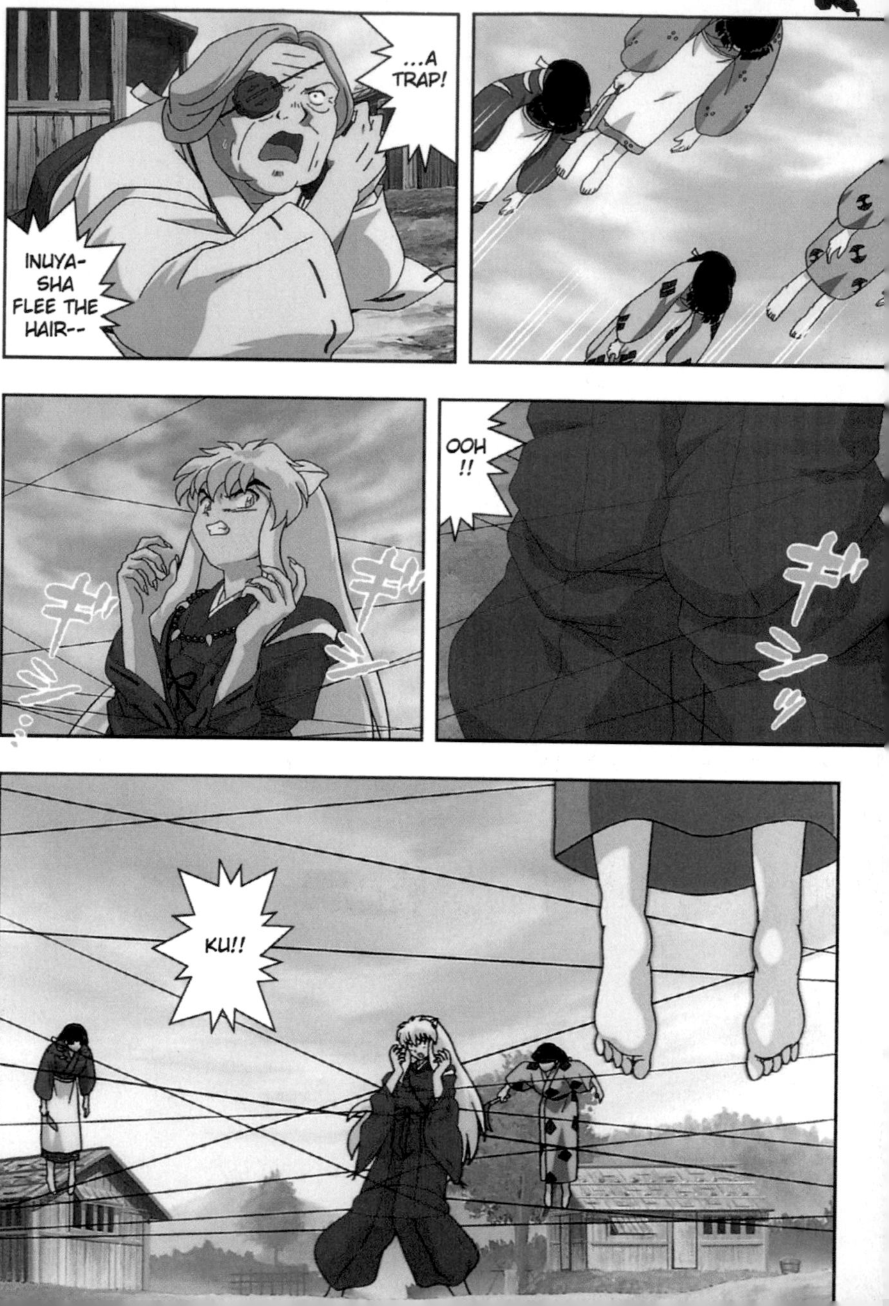
...A TRAP!
INUYA-SHA FLEE THE HAIR--
OOH !!
ギシッ
KU!!

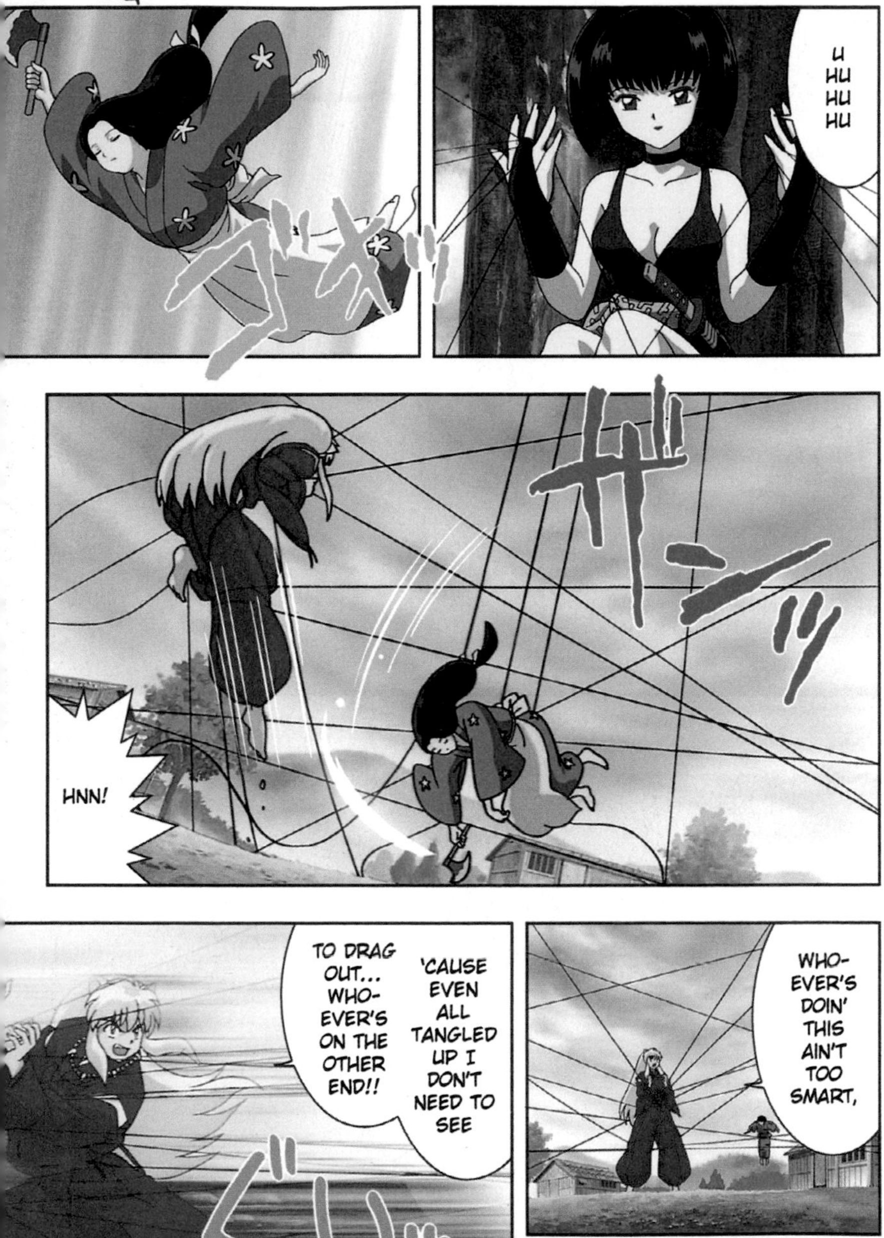
U HU HU HU
ザーンッ
HNN!
WHO-EVER'S DOIN' THIS AIN'T TOO SMART,
'CAUSE EVEN ALL TANGLED UP I DON'T NEED TO SEE
TO DRAG OUT... WHO-EVER'S ON THE OTHER END!!
ぐいっ

OOF!!

AW, SO SORRY ...

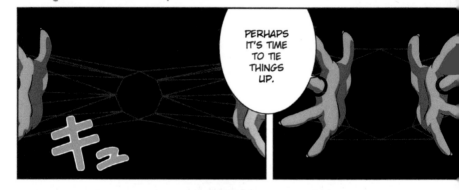

PERHAPS IT'S TIME TO TIE THINGS UP.

AAGHHH !!

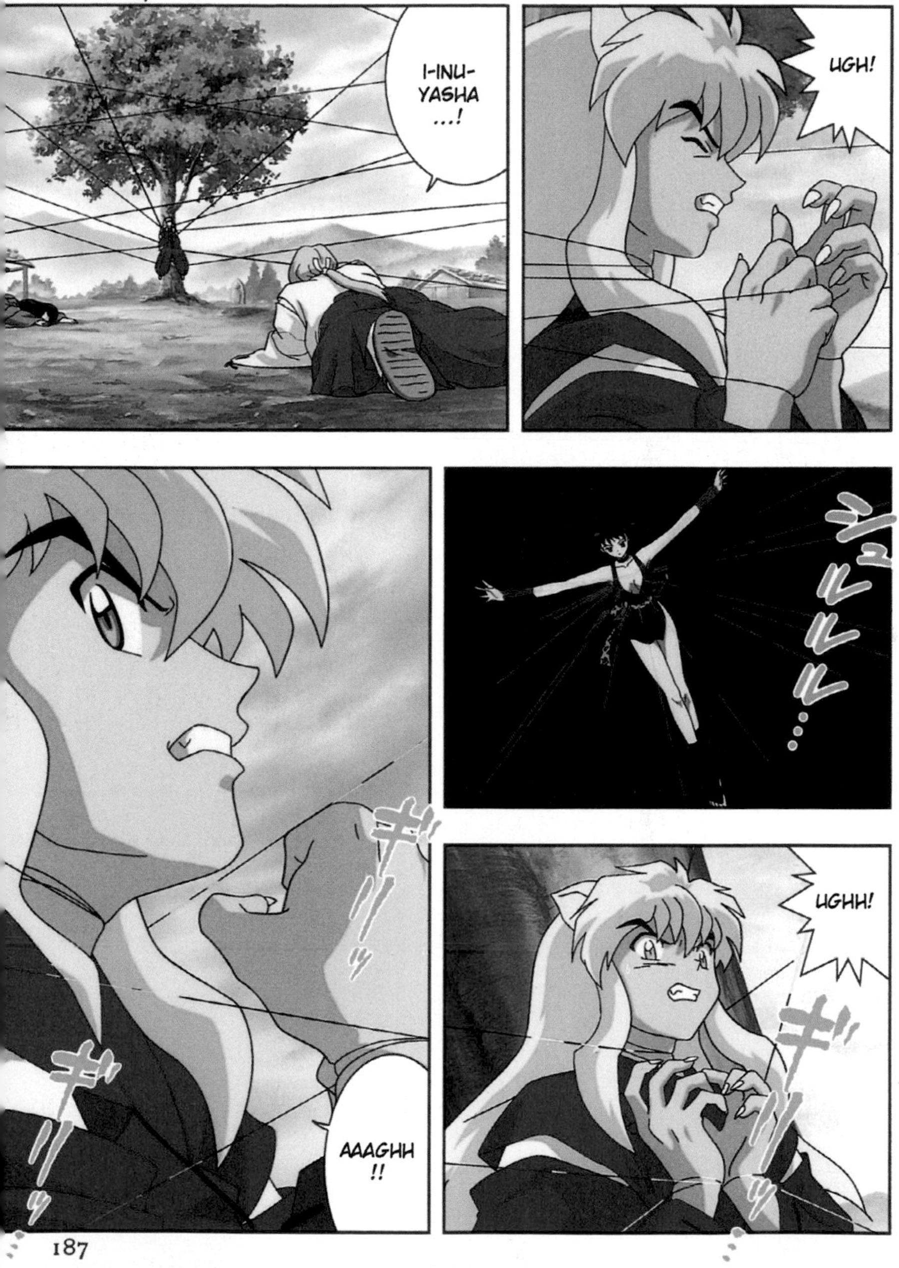
UGH!
I-INU-YASHA ...!
シュルルル…
UGHH!
ギリッ
AAAGHH !!
ギリッ
ギリッ

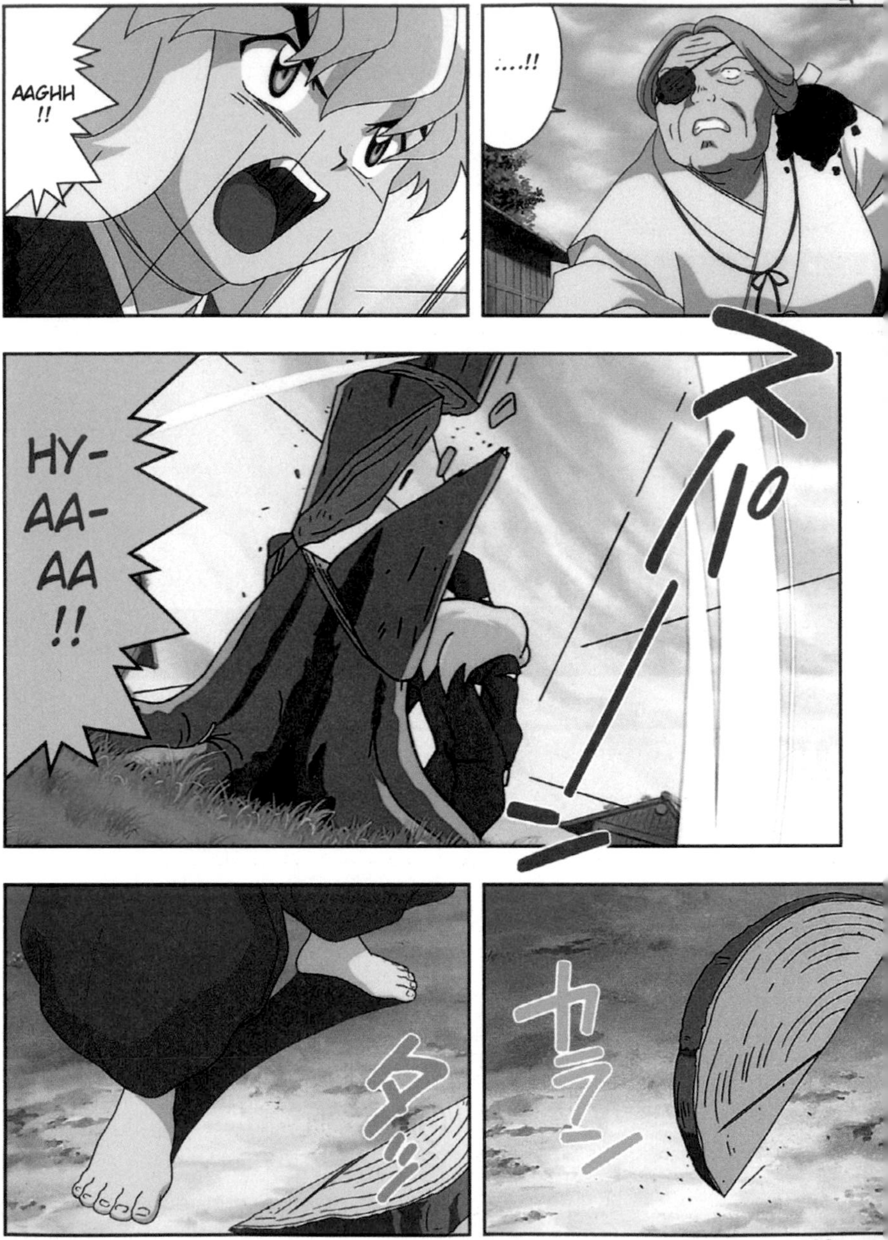
...!!
AAGHH !!
スパーン
HY-AA-AA-AA !!
タッ

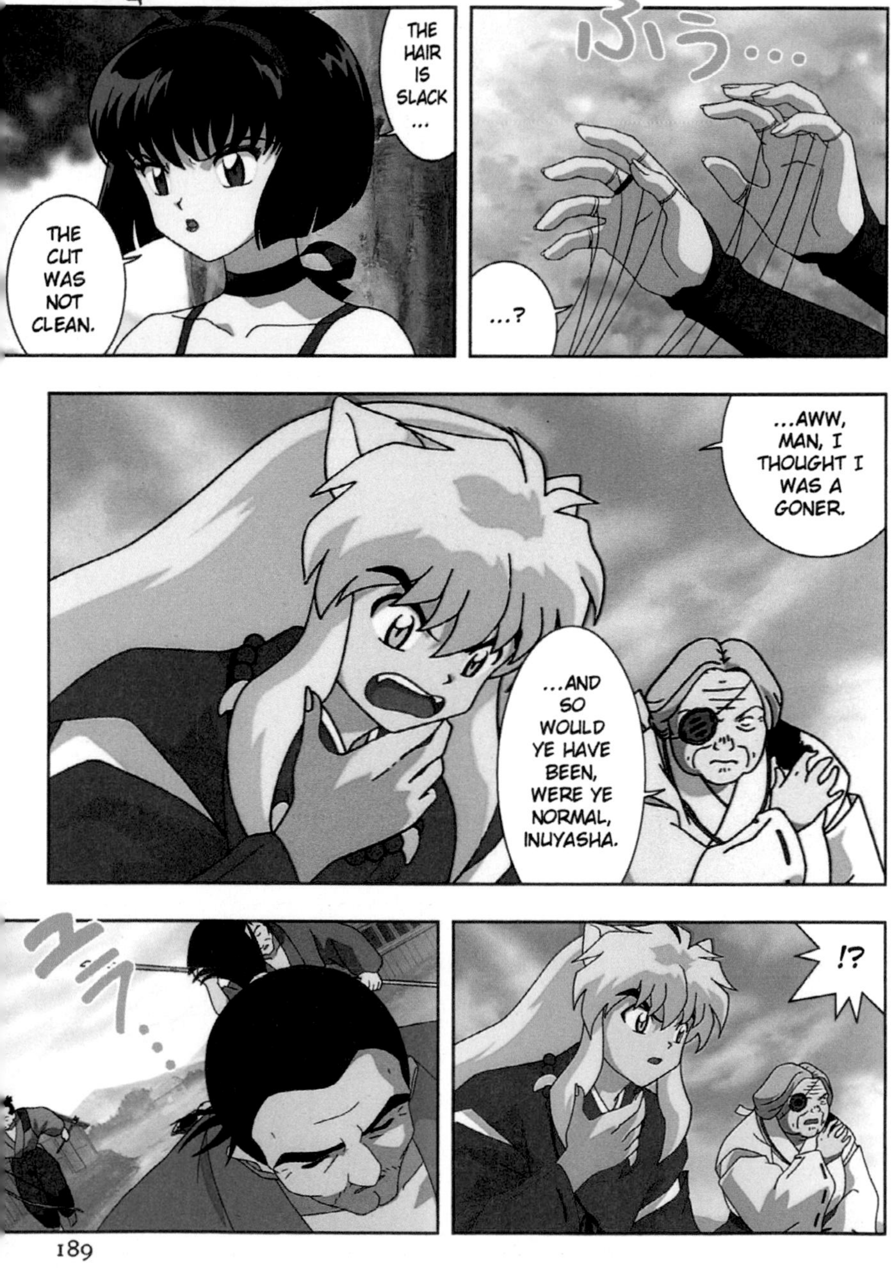
ふう…
...?
THE HAIR IS SLACK...
THE CUT WAS NOT CLEAN.
...AWW, MAN, I THOUGHT I WAS A GONER.
...AND SO WOULD YE HAVE BEEN, WERE YE NORMAL, INUYASHA.
!?

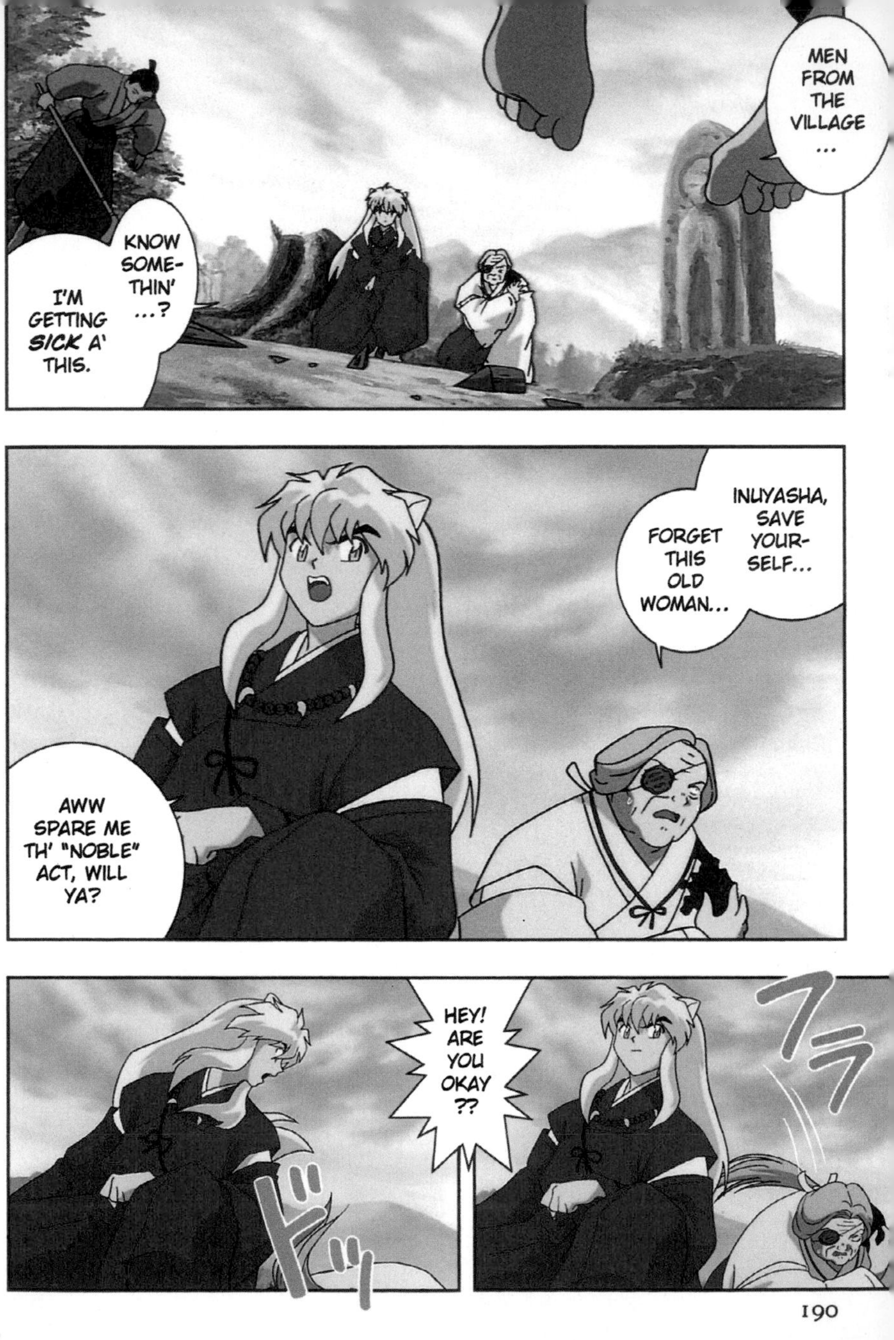
MEN FROM THE VILLAGE ...
KNOW SOMETHIN' ...?
I'M GETTING *SICK* A' THIS.
INUYASHA, SAVE YOURSELF...
FORGET THIS OLD WOMAN...
AWW SPARE ME TH' "NOBLE" ACT, WILL YA?
フラ
HEY! ARE YOU OKAY ??
ドッ

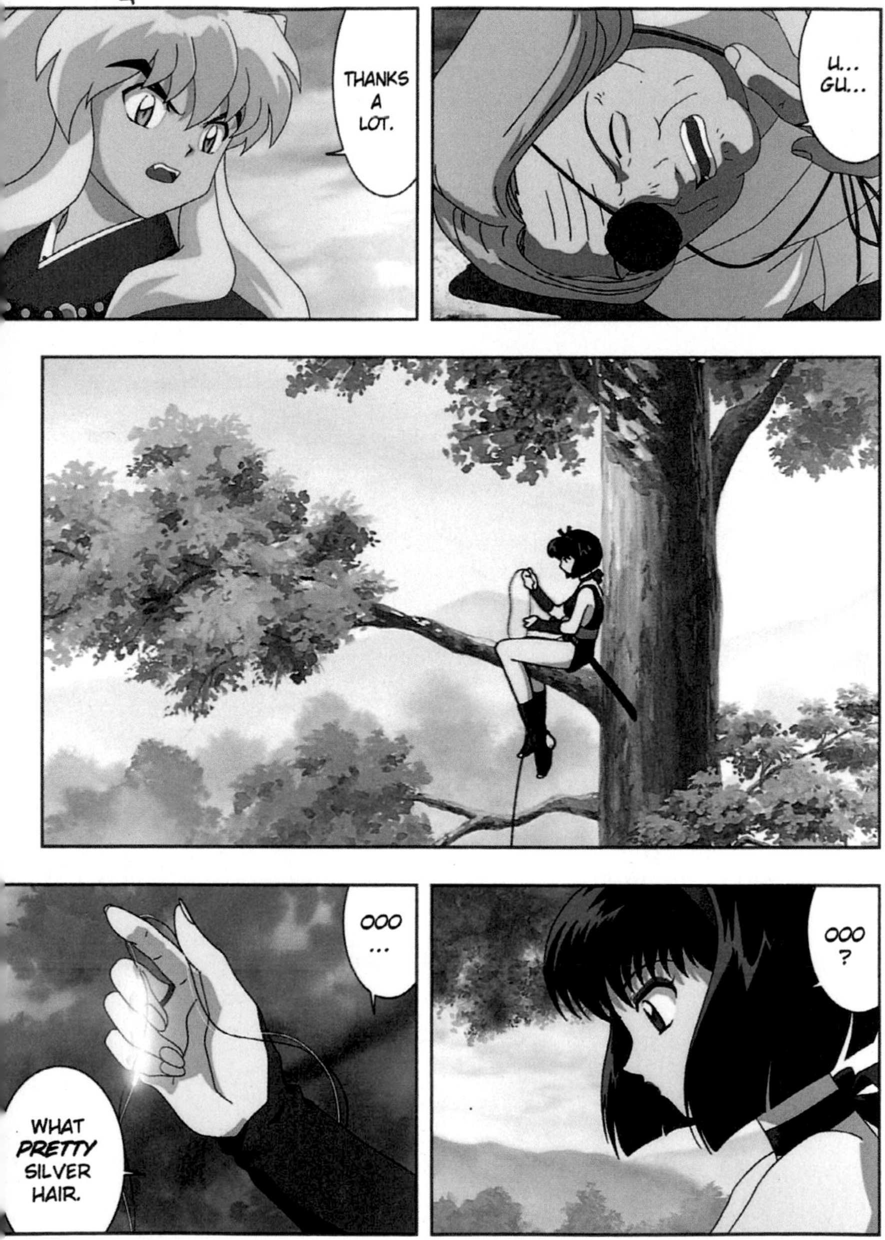
U... GU...
THANKS A LOT.
OOO ?
OOO ...
WHAT *PRETTY* SILVER HAIR.

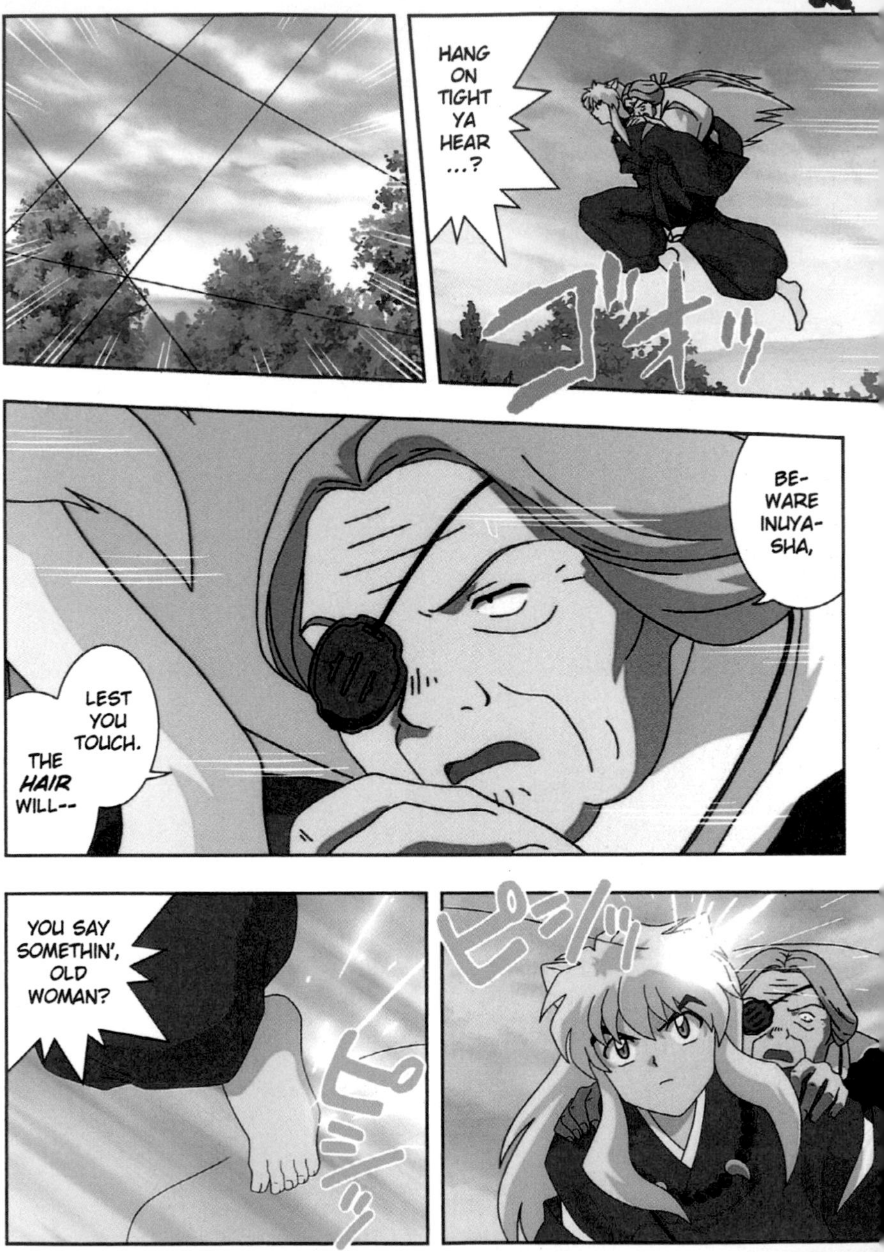
HANG ON TIGHT YA HEAR ...?
ゴオッ
BE-WARE INUYA-SHA,
LEST YOU TOUCH.
THE *HAIR* WILL--
ピシッ
YOU SAY SOMETHIN', OLD WOMAN?
ピシッ

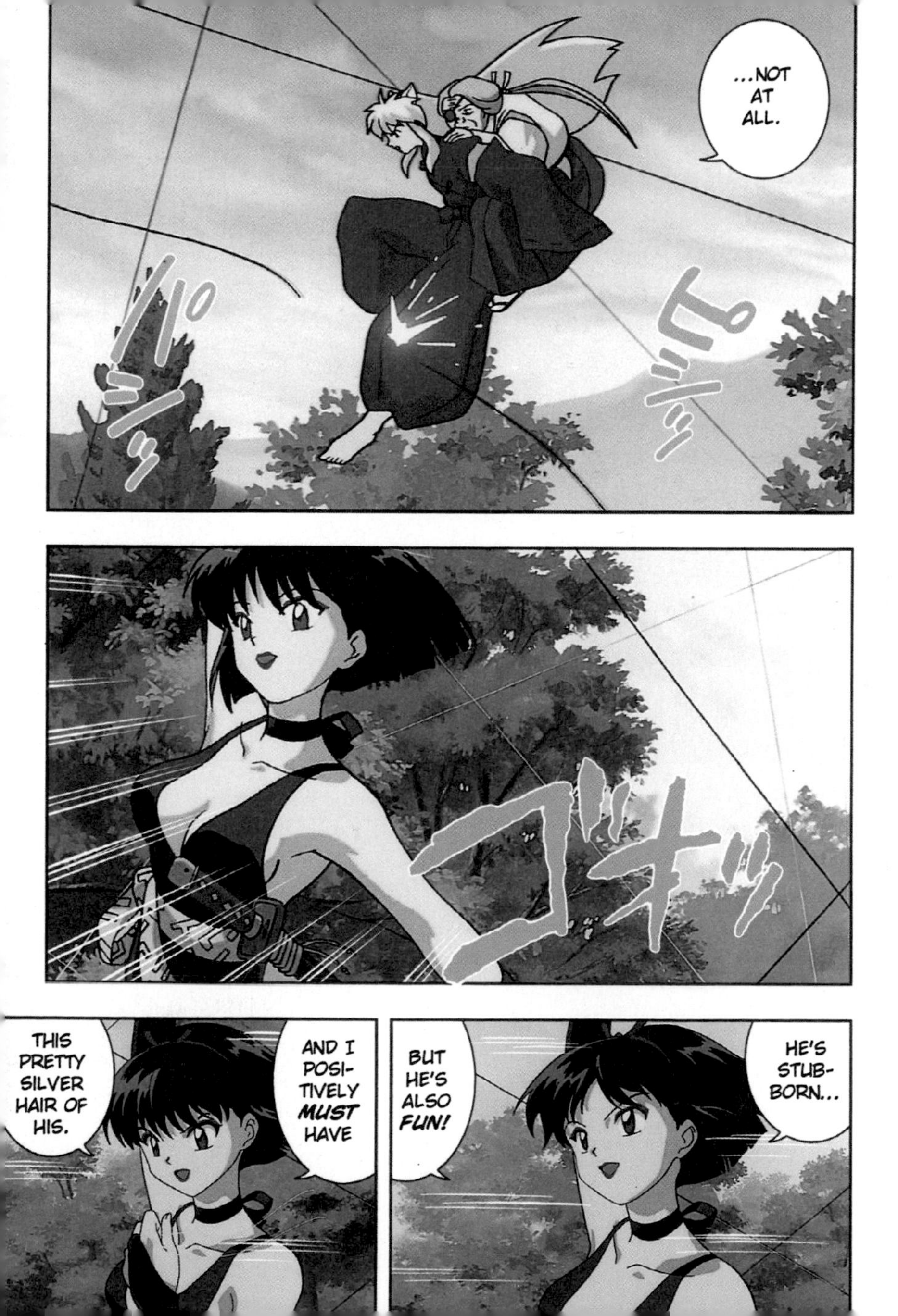
...NOT AT ALL.
ピシッ
パシッ
ゴオッ
HE'S STUB-BORN...
BUT HE'S ALSO **FUN!**
AND I POSI-TIVELY **MUST** HAVE
THIS PRETTY SILVER HAIR OF HIS.

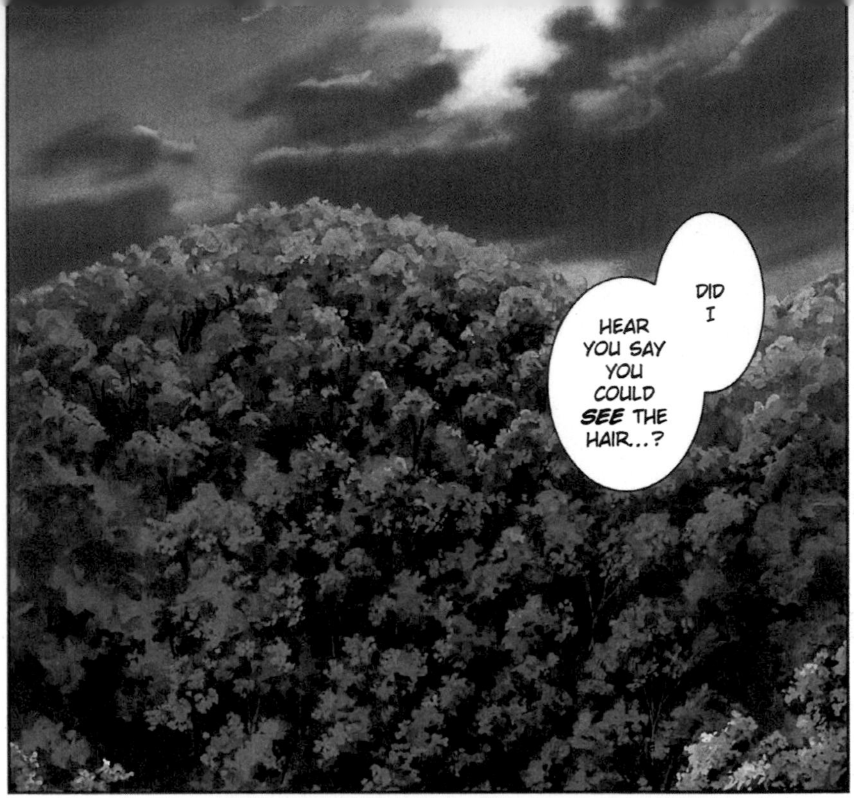
DID I HEAR YOU SAY YOU COULD ***SEE*** THE HAIR...?

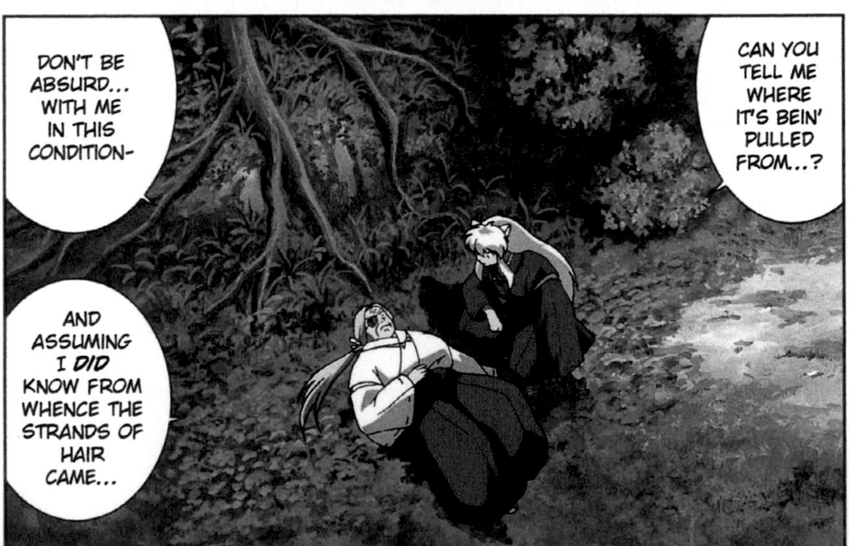
CAN YOU TELL ME WHERE IT'S BEIN' PULLED FROM...?
DON'T BE ABSURD... WITH ME IN THIS CONDITION-
AND ASSUMING I ***DID*** KNOW FROM WHENCE THE STRANDS OF HAIR CAME...

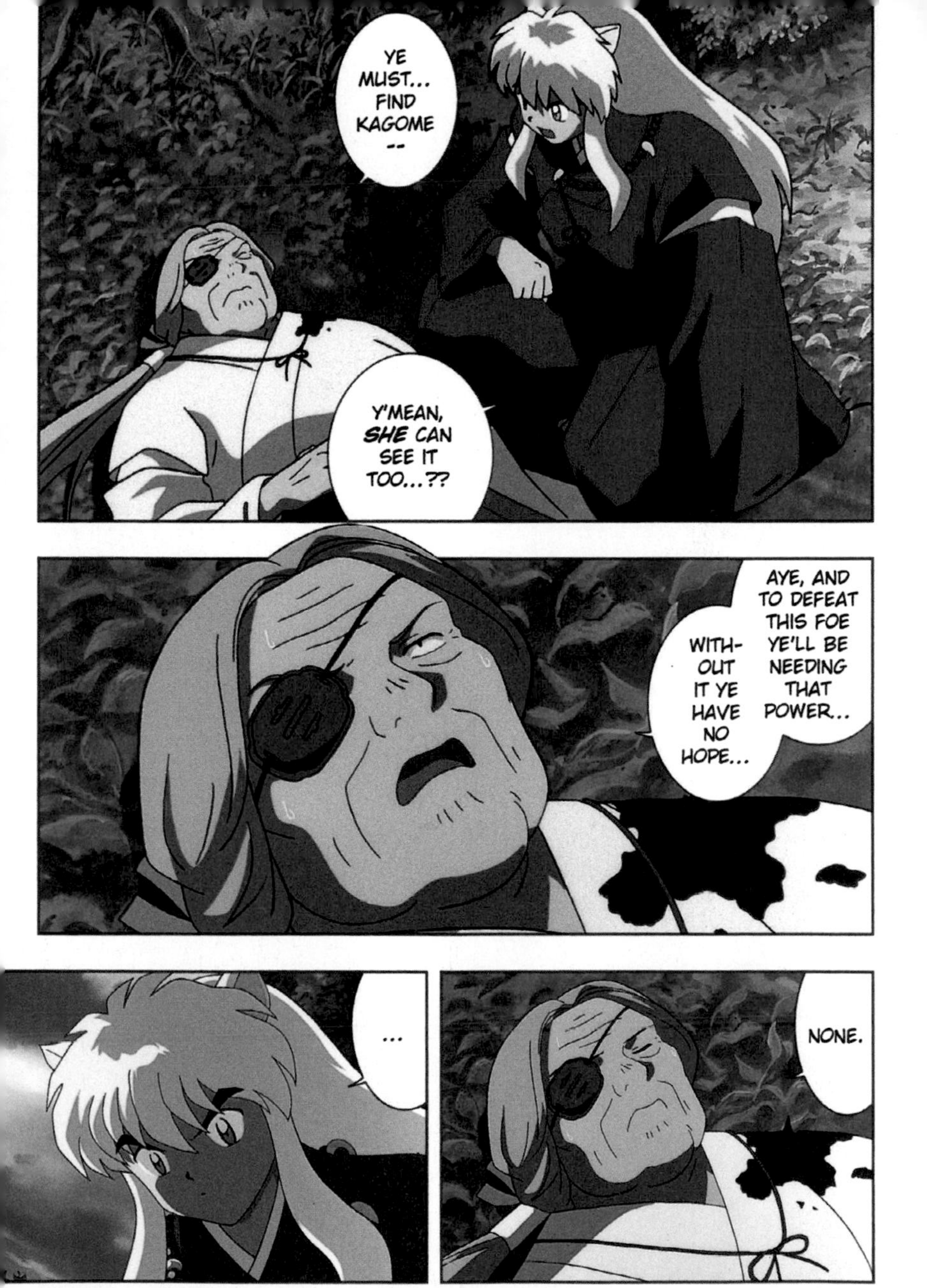
YE MUST... FIND KAGOME --
Y'MEAN, *SHE* CAN SEE IT TOO...??
AYE, AND TO DEFEAT THIS FOE YE'LL BE NEEDING THAT POWER...
WITH-OUT IT YE HAVE NO HOPE...
NONE.
...

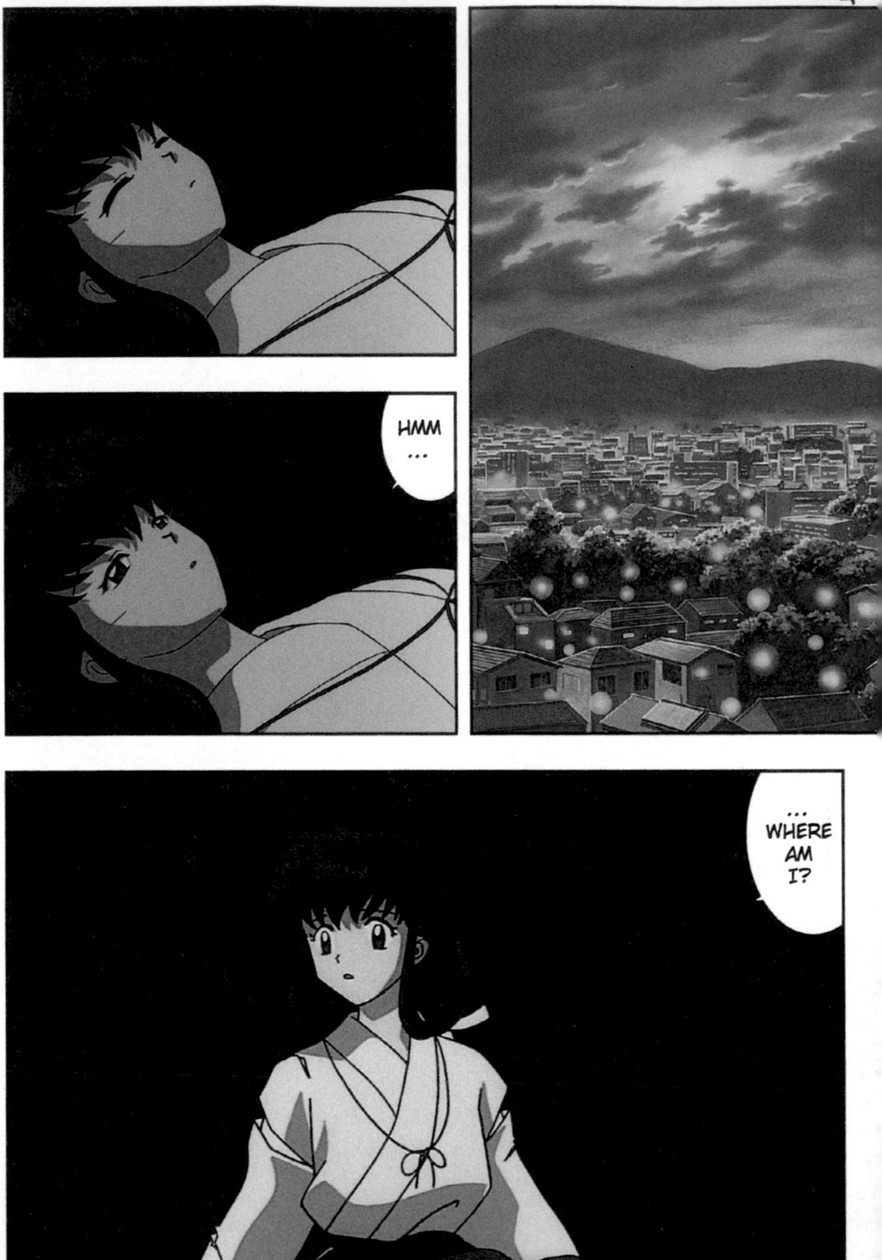
HMM ...
... WHERE AM I?

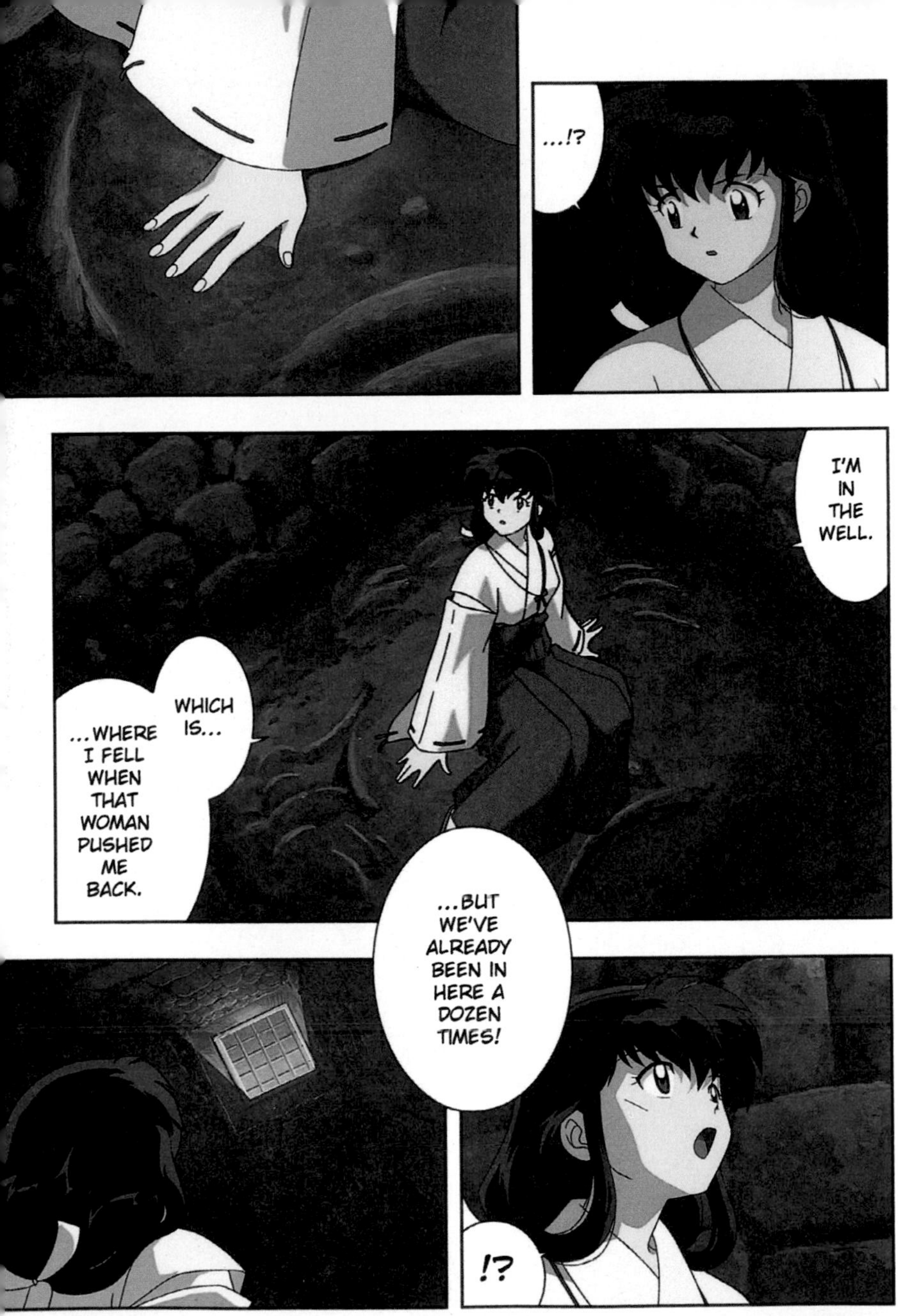
...!?
I'M IN THE WELL.
WHICH IS...
...WHERE I FELL WHEN THAT WOMAN PUSHED ME BACK.
...BUT WE'VE ALREADY BEEN IN HERE A DOZEN TIMES!
!?

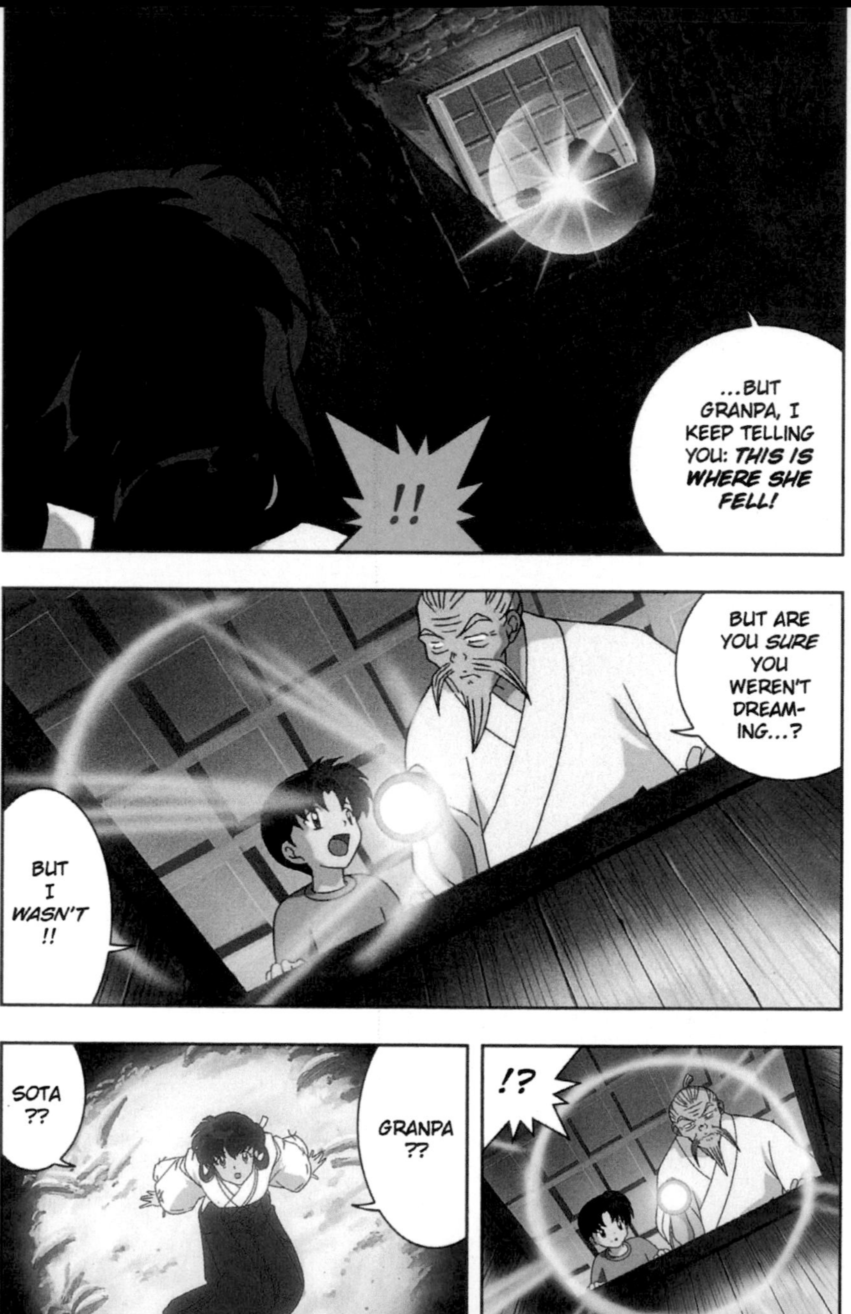
...BUT GRANPA, I KEEP TELLING YOU: THIS IS WHERE SHE FELL!
!!
BUT ARE YOU SURE YOU WEREN'T DREAMING...?
BUT I WASN'T !!
!?
GRANPA ??
SOTA ??

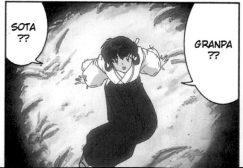

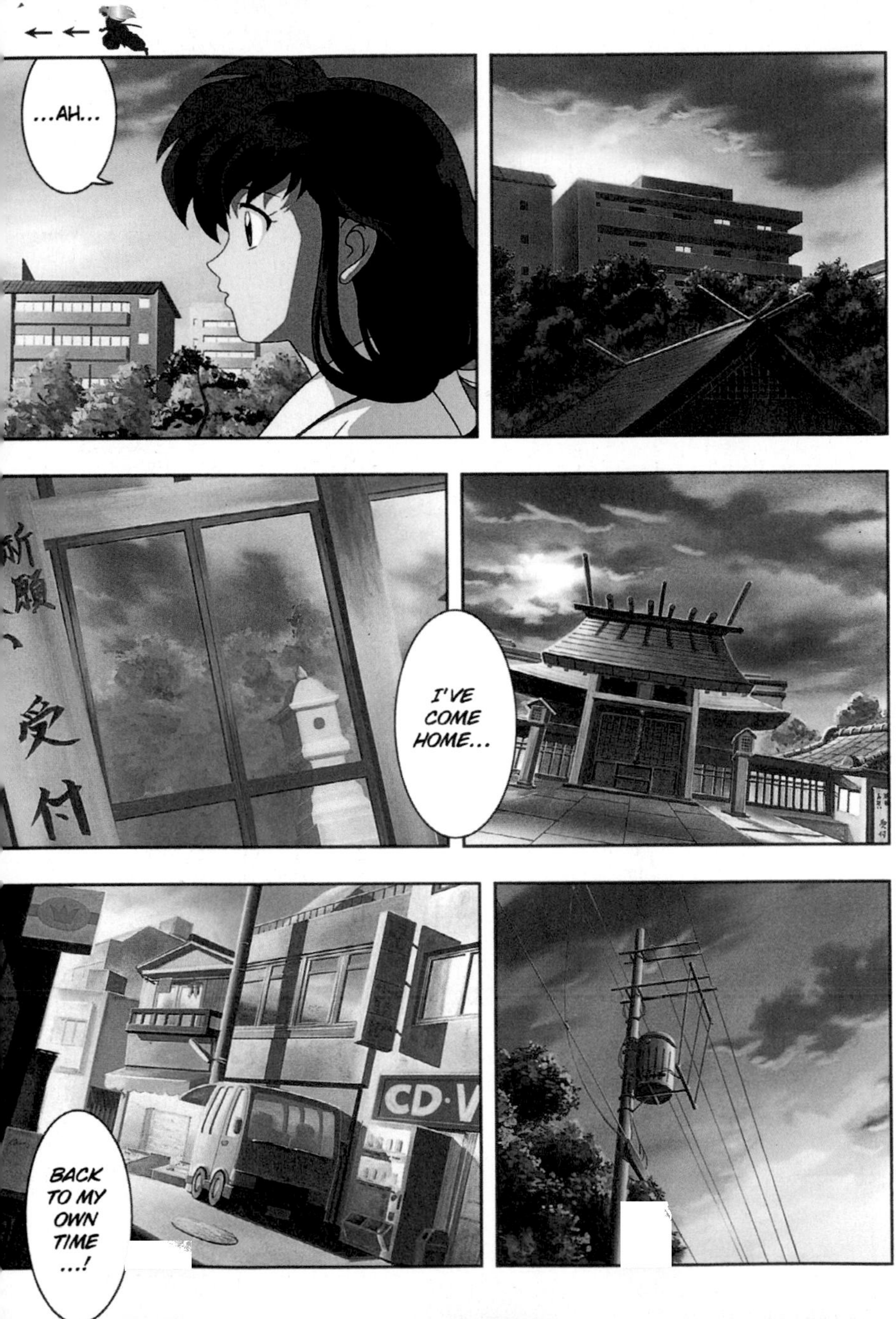
...AH...
I'VE COME HOME...
CD·V
BACK TO MY OWN TIME ...!

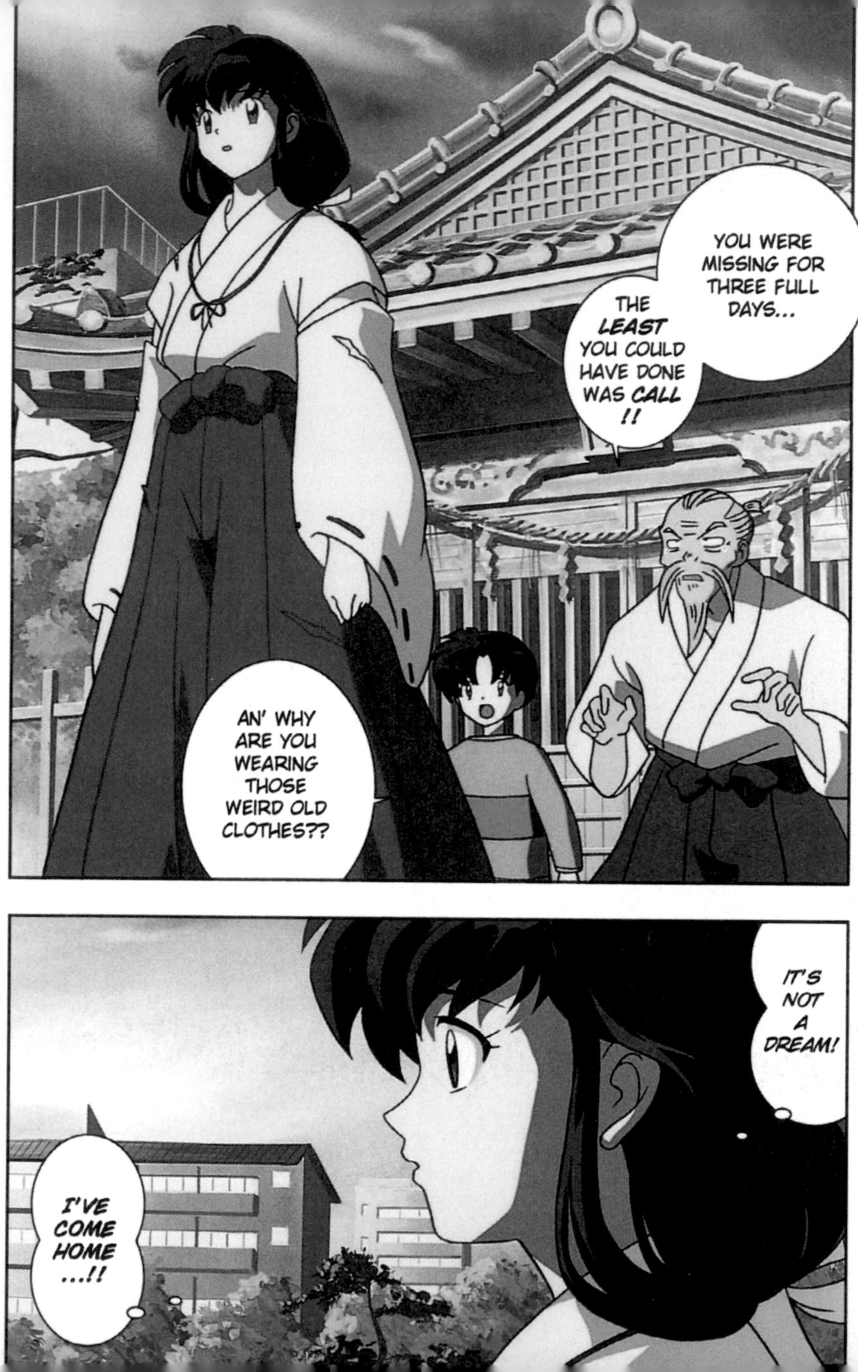
YOU WERE MISSING FOR THREE FULL DAYS...
THE LEAST YOU COULD HAVE DONE WAS CALL!!
AN' WHY ARE YOU WEARING THOSE WEIRD OLD CLOTHES??
IT'S NOT A DREAM!
I'VE COME HOME...!!

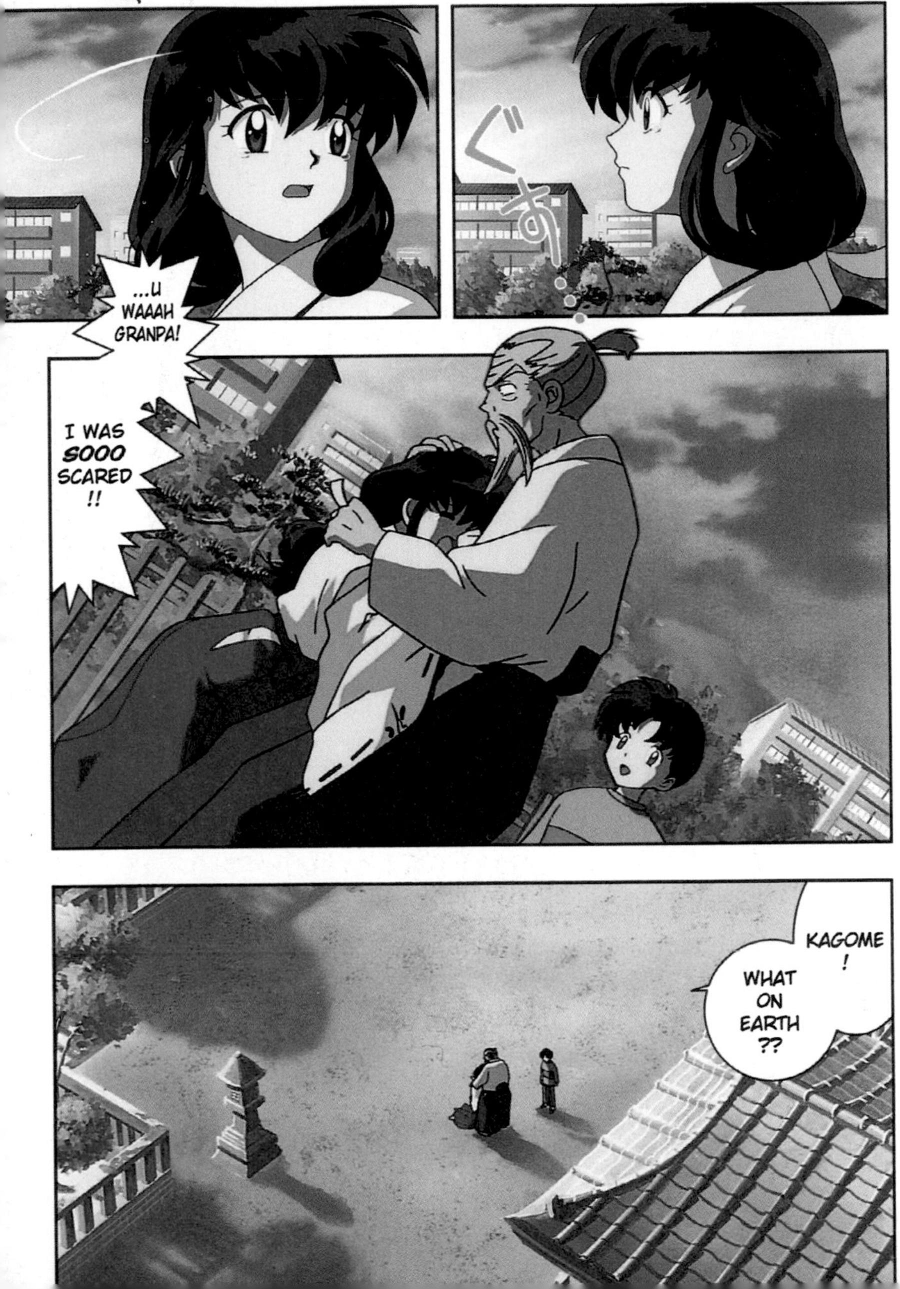

ぐお
...u WAAAH GRANPA!
I WAS SOOO SCARED!!
KAGOME! WHAT ON EARTH??

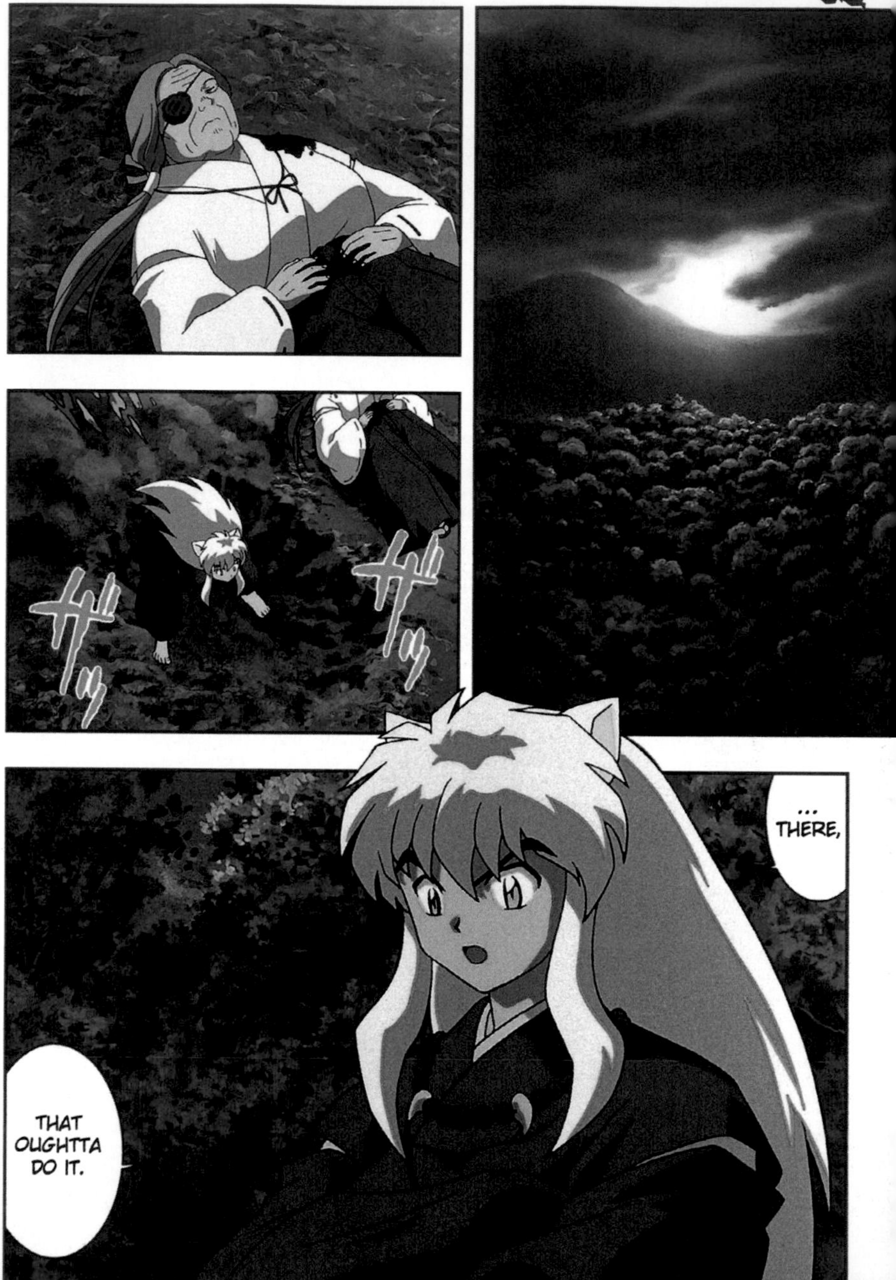
...THERE,
THAT OUGHTTA DO IT.

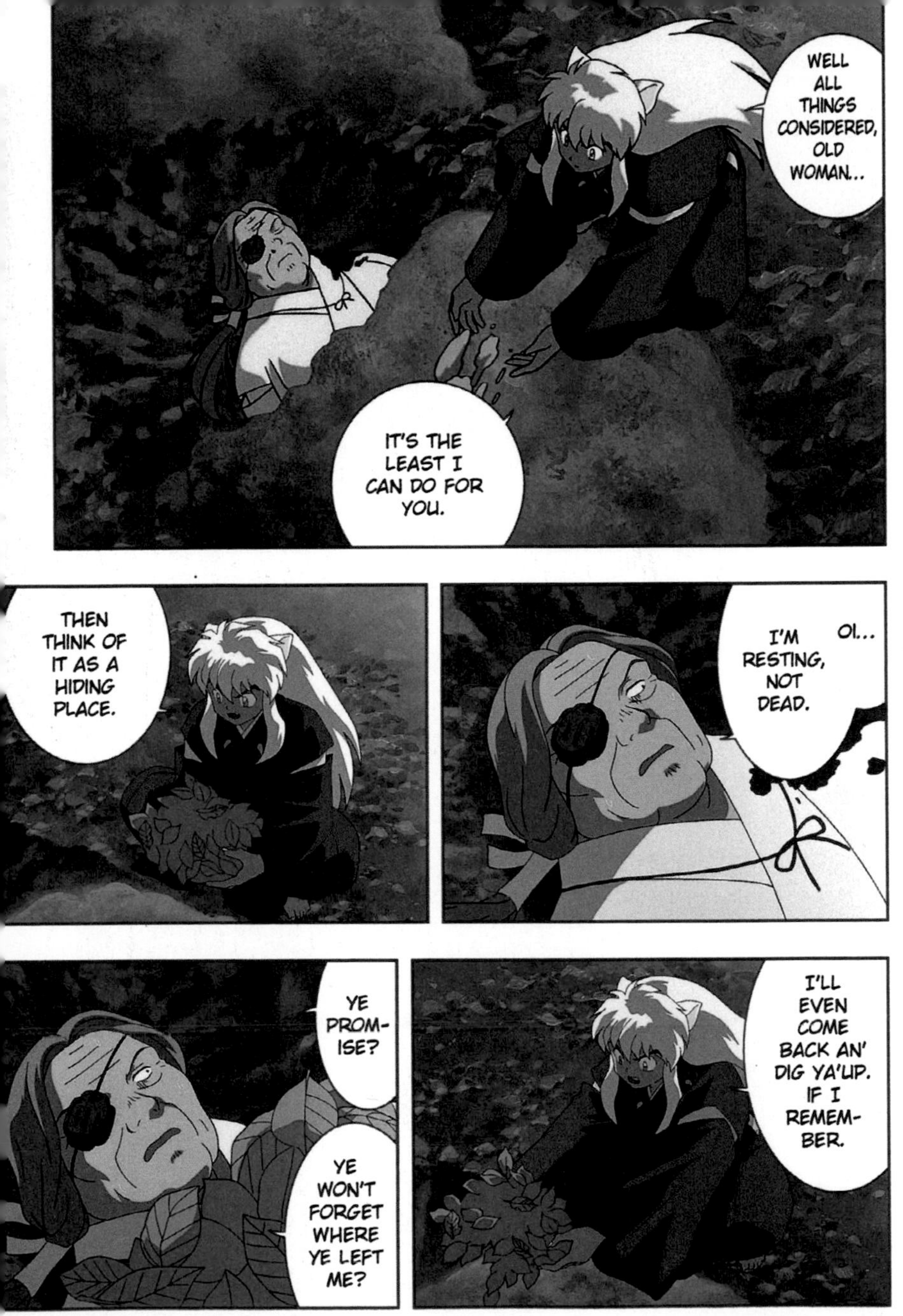
WELL ALL THINGS CONSIDERED, OLD WOMAN...
IT'S THE LEAST I CAN DO FOR YOU.
OI...
I'M RESTING, NOT DEAD.
THEN THINK OF IT AS A HIDING PLACE.
I'LL EVEN COME BACK AN' DIG YA'UP. IF I REMEMBER.
YE PROMISE?
YE WON'T FORGET WHERE YE LEFT ME?

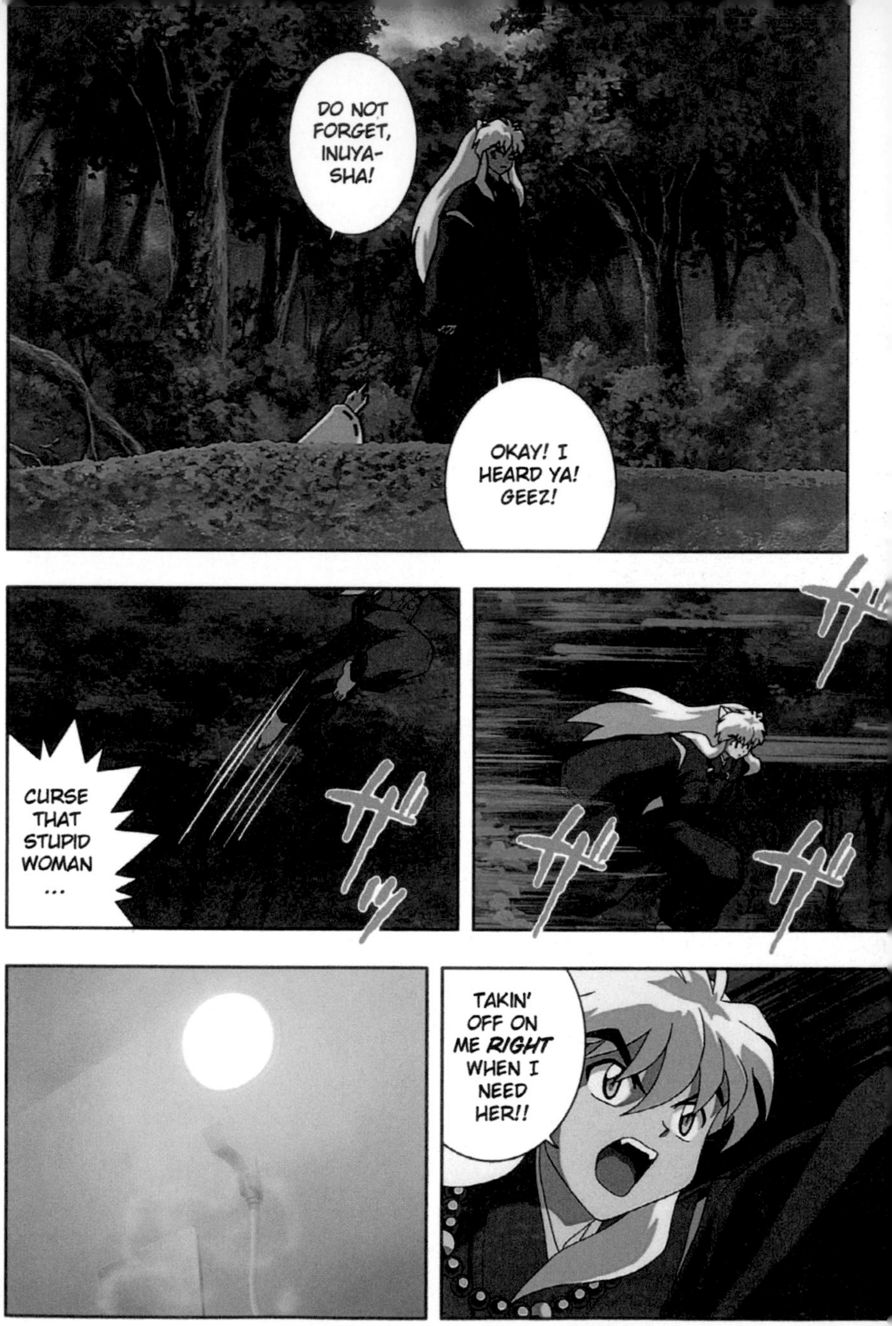
DO NOT FORGET, INUYA-SHA!
OKAY! I HEARD YA! GEEZ!
CURSE THAT STUPID WOMAN ...
TAKIN' OFF ON ME *RIGHT* WHEN I NEED HER!!

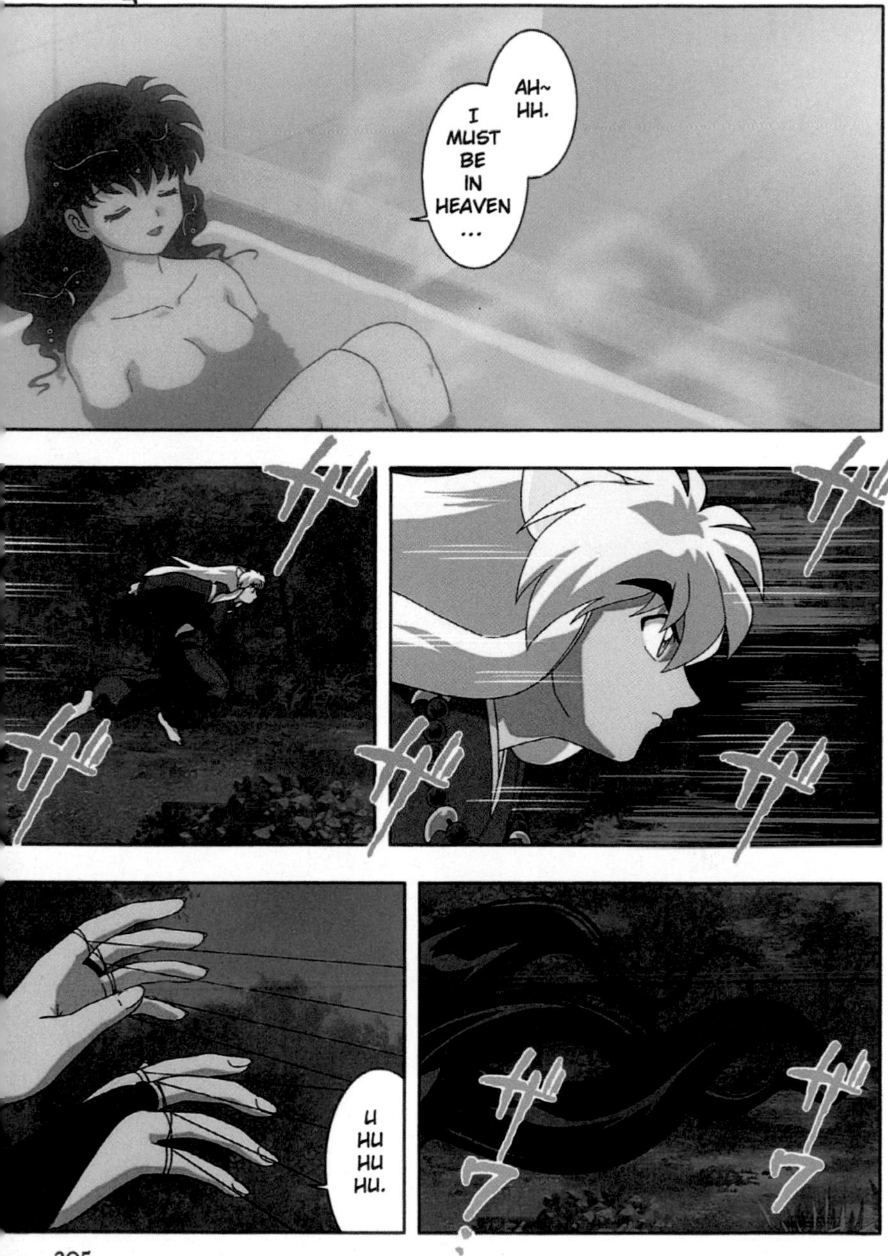
AH~ HH. I MUST BE IN HEAVEN...
U HU HU HU.

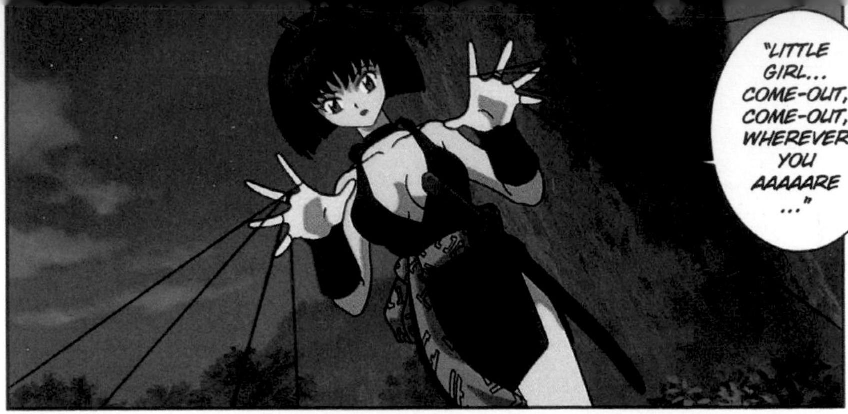
"LITTLE GIRL... COME-OUT, COME-OUT, WHEREVER YOU AAAAARE ..."

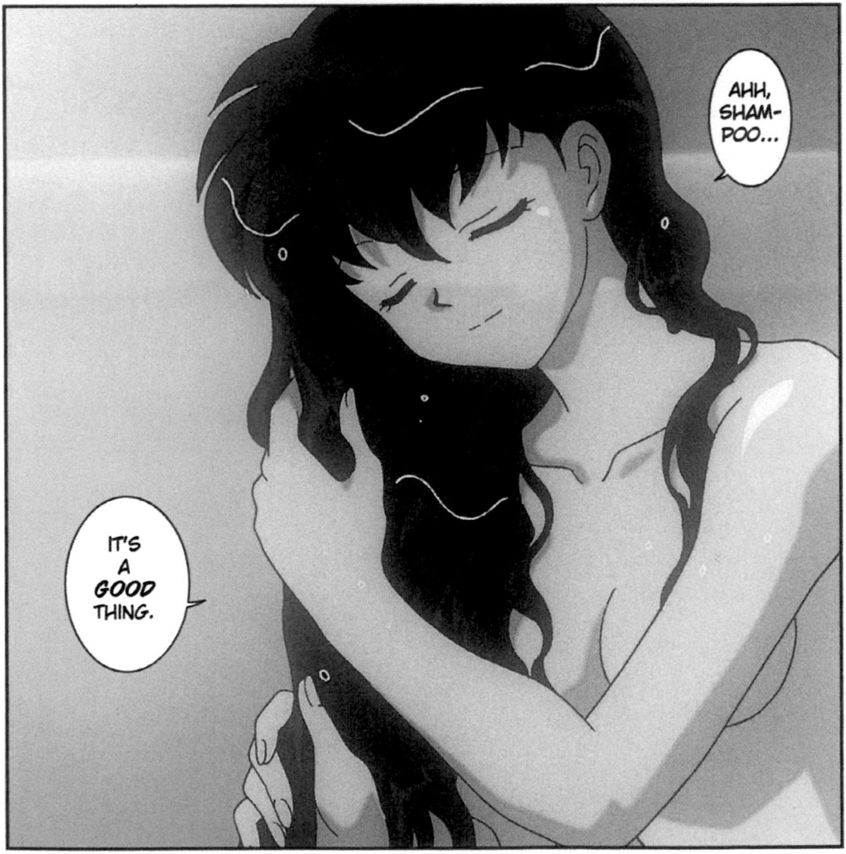
AHH, SHAM-POO...
IT'S A GOOD THING.

Glossary of Sound Effects

Each entry includes: the location, indicated by page number and panel number (so 3.1 means page 3, panel number 1); the phonetic romanization of the original Japanese; and our English "translation"—we offer as close an English equivalent as we can.

24.6	FX:Kaaaa... (light shining behind doors)
25.2	FX:Shuuuu... (power build up behind doors)
	FX:Doh kin (doors slamming open)
25.3	FX:Gui (bursts open)
26.1	FX:Gohhhhh... (roar)
27.6	FX:Kaaaaa... (repels)
28.1	FX:Ka (grab)
28.3	FX:Zu zu zu (arms lingering)
28.5	FX:Doh (falling/landing?)
33.5	FX:Doh doh doh (thunk thunk thunk)
33.6	FX:Za (running)
35.5	FX:Ba (throwing salt)
39.4	FX:Zuzu... (sluuurp)
41.1	FX:Za za za (centipede snaking through town)
41.2	FX:Za za (same)
41.3	FX:Dokin (smash)
41.4	FX:Zu zu zu (same as 1, 2)
42.1	FX:Zu zu zu (Mistress Centipede snaking around)
42.3	FX:Doga (smash)
42.4	FX:Dosa (crashe)
43.2	FX:Goh (whoosh)
45.2	FX:Ta (running)
45.3	FX:Goh (centipede going by)
45.4	FX:Ta ta ta... (running)
45.5	FX:Ta ta ta (running)

3.3	FX:Za (running)
3.4	FX:Doh (Inu appearing)
6.2	FX:Doh (jump)
6.3	FX:Dokin (crash into shrine roof)
6.4	FX:Gara gara (rattle rattle)
7.1	FX:Niya.. (sneaking around)
8.1	FX:Ba (snatch)
8.2	FX:Ban (door flung open)
8.3	FX:Do do (bang)
8.4	FX:Toh (jumps)
8.5	FX:Do ga (takes off through roof)
9.1	FX:Dokin (explosion)
9.4	FX:Toh (landing)
9.5	FX:Shuta (springing off again)
10.3	FX:Giri giri (string being stretched)
10.4	FX:Shun (arrow flying)
11.1	FX:Za (jump)
11.2	FX:Shurururu (object flying through air)
11.3	FX:Doh (impact of arrow "thunk")
11.4	FX:Karan (necklace landing)
12.1	FX:Biiii...n (twang)
15.1	FX:Huu (Kikyo collapsing)
15.2	FX:Gohhhhh.. (flames burning Kikyo's body)
21.2	FX:Ta ta ta... (Kagome's footsteps)
23.1	FX:Kari kari kari... (rattle)
23.4	FX:Kari kari kari... (rattle)
24.2	FX:Na—oh... (cat sound)

46.1 FX:Ta ta ta (running)

47.1 FX:Dokun (waking up)
47.2 FX:Piku (hand moving)
47.3 FX:dokun dokun (heart beat)

48.1 FX:Za za za (movement)
48.3 FX:Za za za (movement)
48.4 FX:Zuun (MC hits something)

49.1 FX:Zuzaza (slide)

51.1 FX:Ba (sudden appearance)
51.2 FX:Doh doh (arrows hitting)

52.2 FX:Kun kun (sniffing)

53.2 FX:Gui (reaching)

54.5 FX:Ka (hand power)

55.1 FX:Kaaaaa… (the power of the hand)
55.2 FX:Dosa (hitting ground)
55.3 FX:Boto Boto (falling apart)

56.2 FX:Goh (moving again)
56.3 FX:Doka (lunge)
56.5 FX:Bun (whoosh)
56.6 FX:Doba (jewel goes flying)

57.3 FX:Dosa (smacks into ground)
57.4 FX:Koron (jewel falls)

58.2 FX:Zu zu zu movement)
58.3 FX:Ga (sudden appear)
58.4 FX:Giri giri… (squeeze)
60.6 FX:Shuuu… (arms being cut off)

61.3 FX:Bari (transformation)
61.5 FX:Giri giri (squish)

63.2 FX:Guohh… (roars)

64.4 FX:Paan (arrow comes lose. Seal broken)

65.3 FX:Dokun dokun(heart beat)

66.3 FX:Doh (bursting)
66.5 FX:Bara bara (body pieces landing)

67.1 FX:Shururu通… (flying through air)
67.2 FX:Toh (landing)

68.1 FX:Zuba (slash)
68.2 FX:Ga ga ga (splitting)
68.3 FX:Do (roar)
68.4 FX:Do-- (roar)

69.1 FX:Bara bara (coming apart)
69.5 FX:Piku piku (twitch, twitch)

70.5 FX:Shuu…Shuu (smoking centipede pieces)
70.6 FX:Shuu shuu… (same)

71.5 FX:Baki (crunch)

74.3 FX:Zaza… za… (running)

75.2 FX:Da (running)
75.3 FX:Ta ta ta (running)
FX:Da (running)
75.4 FX:Ga (tripping)
75.5 FX:Zuba (swiping)

76.1 FX:Zuzaza… (falling down)
76.2 FX:Za (skdding to stop)
76.5 FX:Shun shun (arrows flying)
76.6 FX:Bishi (arrows finding their mark)

77.1 FX:Zuba ga (crisscrossing swipes)
77.4 FX:Zu--n… (tree falls and hits ground)
77.5 FX:Goh (jumping)
77.6 FX:Toh (landing)

78.4 FX:Jara.. (pulling out beads)

79.1 FX:Ta ta ta… (running footsteps)
79.3 FX:Guoh (being chased)
79.4 FX:Zuba (swipe)
79.6 FX:Koron (the jewel falling)
FX:Zuzaza… (fall)

80.2 FX:Toh (lands)
80.4 FX:Bachi bachi (summoning spell for beads)

102.3	FX:Gasa (sneaking)
102.4	FX:Za za (popping out of bushes)
103.1	FX:Dosa (hitting)
104.4	FX:Sura… (sword being drawn)
105.2	FX:Zuba (zombie smacking into men)
105.3	FX:Dosa (falling down)
105.6	FX:Zuga (sword killing bad guy)
106.4	FX:Bun (big thump)
107.2	FX:Za za za (jump-running through grass)
107.3	FX:Sa (springs up to tree)
107.4	FX:Kun kun (sniffs)
107.6	FX:Za (Inu springs off)
108.1	FX:Zuba (religious statues being cut)
108.2	FX:Doga (impact)
108.3	FX:Ga (Boss cuts pillar)
108.4	FX:Gara gara (stuff comes tumbling down)
110.3	FX:Bun (Boss swings sword)
110.4	FX:Dosa (boss collapses)
111.1	FX:Bun (jewel flies out of Kag's hand)
111.2	FX:Karan (jewel flies out)
	FX:Doka (people smacking wall)
112.2/3	FX:Gohh (sword whooshing)
112.5	FX:Doga (smack)
113.1	FX:Paki--n (metallic sound of blade snapping)
114.1	FX:Baki (smack)
114.2	FX:Ga (bam)
114.3	FX:Zu—n… (swoop)
	FX:Suta (fwump)
115.4	FX:Yura (flesh opening up)
115.6	FX:Guiiii… (crow opening maw.)
116.3	FX:Ba (charge)
116.4	FX:Dosu (reaches hand into boss)
116.5	FX:Basa basa (flapping wings)
117.1	FX:Basa (flapping wings)
	FX:Basa (same)
80.5	FX:Hyurururu… (beads ricocheting and finding their mark)
81.1	FX:Shurururu… (here come those beads)
81.2	FX:Pa--n (gotcha!)
81.3	FX:Ta (Inu jumps down from tree)
82.1	FX:Ta (step)
82.2	FX:Gara… (fall)
82.3	FX:Doh (landing)
82.5	FX:Koro koro (Jewel rolling)
83.1	FX:Koro koro… (more rolling)
83.3	FX:Toh lands)
83.4	FX:Koro koro (rolling)
83.5	FX:Koro… (rolling)
84.2	FX:Kaah (magic starting up)
84.3	FX:Doh (magic taking effect)
84.4	FX:Shuuuu.. (smacking into ground)
85.2	FX:Giri giri (trying to remove beads)
86.1	FX:Doga (striking bridge)
86.2	FX:Baki (smacking through bridge)
86.4	FX:Bochan (kersplash)
87.1	FX:Ton ton (hammer, hammer)
	FX:Kan kan (knock, knock)
87.3	FX:Ton ton (hammer, hammer)
90.2	FX:Baki (foot through floorboards)
91.4	FX:Piku (Ears moving)
94.6	FX:Ta! (surprise)
95.3	FX:Shurururu… (pear flying through air)
95.4	FX:Pashi (smack)
96.5	FX:Ta (Injumping)
97.4	FX:Dosa (smacks into ground)
99.3	FX:Po— (jewel glowing)
99.4	FX:Basa basa (wings flapping)
99.6	FX:Basa baas (wings flapping)

117.5 FX:Basa (same)
FX:Basa (same)

118.1 FX:Dohn (gaboom)
118.4 FX:Zan (jumping up)

119.1 FX:Za za (jumping from tree to tree)
119.3 FX:Ta ta ta… (footsteps)

120.4 FX:Giri giri (knocking arrow)
120.5 FX:Za (Inu jumps up)

121.2 FX:Shu (arrow takes off)
121.3 FX:Suu (arrow flies)
121.4 FX:Doh (lands)

122.2 FX:Gugyaaaa (Caw)
122.4 FX:Bishu (sproing)
122.5 FX:Suu… (arrow flies)

123.1 FX:Zuzaza (running)
123.2 FX:Dosa (hitting ground)
123.3 FX:Za (runs)

124.1 FX:Guge-- (caw)
124.3 FX:Gohh (crow sees new victim)
124.4 FX:Bah (crow taking boy)

125.1 FX:Za za (flying)
125.4 FX:Ta (Inu jumps)
125.5/6 FX:Zuba (Inu's magic blowing crow to hell)

126.1 FX:Doh doh doh (stuff plopping in water)
126.2 FX:Zan (splash)
126.6 FX:Ba (taking off shoes)

127.1 FX:Toh (dives)
127.2 FX:Zan (splashes in water)
127.3 FX:Gobo gobo (blub, blub)

130.1/2 FX:Zu zu zu (crow reconstituting)
130.3 FX:Zan (crow emerging from water)
130.4 FX:Basa basa (flapping wings)

131.1 FX:Gui gui (grabbing)

132.1 FX:Giri giri (knocking arrow, stretching string)

132.2 FX:Shu (arrow takes off)
132.3 FX:Shurururu…(arrow flies through air)

133.1 FX:Shurururu…(same as previous)
133.2 FX:Doh (strike)
133.3 FX:Pa—n (crow blows up)
133.4 FX:Kaaaa… (jewel falls)
133.5 FX:Pishi (jewel cracks)
133.6 FX:Pishi (more cracks)

134.1 FX:Pa—n (jewel explodes)
134.2 FX:Ka ah (shine)

135.1 FX:Kaaaaa… (shine)
135.3 FX:Pa—n (light)
135.4/5 FX:Kaaaaaaa… (shards scattering)

137.4 FX:Gukyaaa…(crow conversation)

138.1 FX:Za (running)
138.2 FX:Zuba (claws)
138.3 FX:Karan (shard landing and bounces)

141.4 FX:Zabu (dunks under water)

146.1 FX:Zaba (water sounds)

147.3 FX:Dohn (slam)

154.2 FX:Goh (rock on head)

156.1 FX:Su (turning away abruptly)

158.1 FX:Zudoh (Inu's body slams into ground)

160.1 FX:Yura… (flicker)

161.1 FX:Suu… (body rises)
161.3 FX:Suuu… (body rises higher)
161.4 FX:Kuru (body revolves)

162.1 FX:Kiri kiri (squeaky hair)
162.3 FX:Suu… (cleaver levitates)
162.4 FX:Shururu.. (cleaver flies through air)
162.6 FX:Guoh (cleaver strike)

163.1 FX:Za (footstep)

184.4 FX:Gishi gishi (hairs winding)

185.2 FX:Gohh (girl flying through air with axe)
185.3 FX:Zan (strikes and misses hitting hair instead)
185.5 FX:Gui (pulls on hair)

186.1 FX:Fu (hair noise)
186.2 FX:Zuzaza (Inu fighting hair)
186.4 FX:Kyu (pulling strings tight)
186.5 FX:Kyuru kyuru… (Inu being strung up)

187.3 FX:Shurururu… (Yura flying through air)
187.4 FX:Giri… (hair pulling tight on Inu)
187.5 FX:Giri (hair pulling tigh)
FX:Giri (hair pulling tight)

188.2 FX:Supa—n (Inu slices tree by pulling on hair)
188.4 FX:Karan (trunk falls)
188.5 FX:Ta (Inu's feet touch ground)

189.1 FX:Fuu… (sound of magic)
189.5 FX:Yura… (man in air?)

190.3 FX:Fura (Kaede collapses)
190.4 FX:Doh (Kaede hits ground)

192.1 FX:Goh (Inu flies off with Kaede)
192.4 FX:Pishi (hair comes after them)
192.5 FX:Pishi (Inu's foot breaks hair)

193.1 FX:Pishi (hair moves)
FX:Pashi (hair gets broken)
193.2 FX:Goh (whoosh)

201.1 FX:Gusu… (Kag realizes she's home)

202.3 FX:Za za (Inu digging)

204.2 FX:Za za za (Inu running hard through underbrush)
204.3 FX:Za (Inu springs)

205.2 FX:Za za za (Inu runs)
205.3 FX:Za za (same)
205.4 FX:Zawa zawa (launches hair)

165.4 FX:Hara… (leaf flutters)
165.5 FX:Supa (leaves are cut)

166.1 FX:Pishi (cheek is cut)

168.1 FX:Za za za… (running footsteps)
168.2 FX:Za (Inu's jump)

169.1 FX:Goh (Inu's flying leap)
169.2 FX:Ta (touch down)
169.3 FX:Toh (Inu springs up again)

170.1 FX:Za (Inu skids to halt)
170.40 FX:Suu… (girls chopping in air)

171.2 FX:Suu… (same)
171.5 FX:Shurururu… (Hair flying through air)

172.1 FX:Shurururu... (hair flying through air)
172.2 FX:Pishi (Hair flying towards Kag)
FX:Pashi (same)
172.4 FX:Shu (Kag's bag w/shard flying out of her clothes)
172.5 FX:Pashi (bag ending up in Yura's hand)

174.1 FX:Chari (Yura drawing sword)
174.2 FX:Gohh (sword being drawn back)

175.1 FX:Bun (Yura jumping w/sword to cut)
175.2 FX:Zuru… (overbalancing)
175.4 FX:Bun (Yura throws blade down well)

176.2 FX:Cha (blade returns)

177.1 FX:Suuuu… (girls hanging in air)

178.5 FX:Ta (dashes off)

179.1 FX:Sutah (Inu lands)

181.2 FX:Buoh (girl flying)
181.3 FX:Bun (whoosh)
181.4 FX:Za (strike)

183.5 FX:Fu… (hmph)

184.3 FX:Gishi (hairs winding around Inu)

Inuyasha Ani-Manga
Vol. #1

Created by
Rumiko Takahashi

Translation based on the VIZ anime TV series
Translation Assistance/Katy Bridges
Lettering/John Clark
Cover Design & Graphics/Hidemi Sahara
Editor/Ian Robertson

Editor in Chief, Books/Alvin Lu
Editor in Chief, Magazines/Marc Weidenbaum
VP of Publishing Licensing/Rika Inouye
VP of Sales/Gonzalo Ferreyra
Sr. VP of Marketing/Liza Coppola
Publisher/Hyoe Narita

Printed in U.S.A.

Published by VIZ Media, LLC
P.O. Box 77010
San Francisco, CA 94107

10 9 8 7 6 5 4
First printing, January 2004
Fourth printing, February 2007

www.viz.com
store.viz.com

LOVE MANGA?
LET US KNOW WHAT YOU THINK!

HELP US MAKE THE MANGA
YOU LOVE BETTER!